S0-ASN-979

DESIGNING THE PHYSICAL EDUCATION CURRICULUM

Third Edition

Vincent J. Melograno, EdD
Cleveland State University

Human Kinetics

Library of Congress Cataloging-in-Publication Data

Melograno, Vincent.
Designing the physical education curriculum / Vincent J. Melograno. -- 3rd ed.
p. cm.
Includes bibliographical references (p.) and index.
ISBN 0-87322-525-2 (case)
1. Physical education and training--United States--Curricula.
2. Curriculum planning--United States. I. Title.
GV365.M45 1996
375.6137'0973--dc20 95-20773
CIP

ISBN: 0-87322-525-2

Chapter 1, 2, 3, 7, and 8 photos courtesy Instructional Media Services, Cleveland State University, Shaker Heights City School District, Shaker Heights, OH. Chapter 4, 5, and 6 photos © Terry Wild Studio.

This book is a revised edition of *Designing the Physical Education Curriculum: A Self-Directed Approach*, published in 1979 and 1985 by Kendall Hunt.

Acquisitions Editor: Rick Frey, PhD; **Developmental Editor:** Ann Brodsky; **Assistant Editors:** Julie Marx Ohnemus, Ed Giles, Karen Bojda, and Dawn Cassady; **Copyeditor:** Lee Erwin; **Proofreader:** Jim Burns; **Typesetter and Layout Artist:** Francine Hamerski; **Text Designer:** Judy Henderson; **Photo Editor:** Boyd LaFoon; **Cover Designer:** Jack Davis; **Illustrators:** Francine Hamerski and Tom Janowski; **Cartoonist:** Bruce Morton; **Printer:** Braun-Brumfield

Printed in the United States of America 10 9 8 7 6 5 4 3 2 1

Human Kinetics
P.O. Box 5076, Champaign, IL 61825-5076
1-800-747-4457

Canada: Human Kinetics, Box 24040, Windsor, ON N8Y 4Y9
1-800-465-7301 (in Canada only)

Europe: Human Kinetics, P.O. Box IW14, Leeds LS16 6TR, United Kingdom
(44) 1132 781708

Australia: Human Kinetics, 2 Ingrid Street, Clapham 5062, South Australia
(08) 371 3755

New Zealand: Human Kinetics, P.O. Box 105-231, Auckland 1
(09) 523 3462

For Craig and Laura . . . two great kids!

Contents

Preface

Although teachers are a diverse group, they share two basic needs: to have control over their teaching environments and to have an impact on their students. Control over curriculum development is basic to these needs. The key to educational reform is the role of empowered teachers as curriculum designers instead of curriculum consumers. Traditionally, as consumers, teachers have been locked in a bureaucratic tangle in which they are forced to spend almost all of their creative energy making instantaneous decisions. "Consumer-teachers" implement someone else's philosophy, program, materials, and strategies. They neither desire nor expect to be involved in any creative process of curriculum development. On the other hand, as designers, teachers choose and plan day-to-day activities that assume accountability for student learning. "Designer-teachers" can create curricula tailored to the existing abilities and interests of their students. Many teachers, however, are not able to design curricula that are personalized and responsive to the contemporary needs of learners.

With this book, you can develop skills to design physical education curricula. Chapters are arranged systematically to advance the "teacher designer" role and to satisfy the individualized curriculum needs brought about by societal and educational forces (e.g., multicultural education, racial integration, gender integration, appropriate programming for learners with disabilities).

Designing the Physical Education Curriculum is written for various audiences. It is recommended to higher education personnel for use in undergraduate and graduate curriculum courses and in teacher in-service seminars or workshops. For teachers in training (preservice), it should be used in upper-level undergraduate courses prior to student teaching, preferably in conjunction with field experiences. This assumes that basic study has been completed in educational psychology, philosophy, and physical education. For graduate courses and in-service programming, professionals will find the book useful in designing, revising, and evaluating physical education curricula. As resource material, the book is valuable to school personnel (administrators, supervisors, and physical education teachers) in efforts to improve existing physical education programs.

The curriculum principles and concepts presented are followed by self-directed activities. You will be asked for various kinds of responses in these 43 activities. For example, you will identify what you know, apply information to practical situations, solve curriculum-related problems, and create curriculum components. Feedback is provided for each self-directed activity.

By engaging in this self-directed process, you will develop competencies that can serve several orientations—for example, structuring physical education subject matter across a K–12 continuum, writing individual education programs (IEPs) for learners with disabilities, or developing appropriate physical education programs for culturally diverse settings.

This book also demonstrates the current emphasis on outcome-based instructional systems—a comprehensive design for teaching and learning rooted in earlier mastery-learning and competency-based education movements. Each chapter contains a set of expected outcomes. This approach is congruent with the outcomes suggested by the National Association for Sport and Physical Education (NASPE). These outcomes and corresponding grade-level benchmarks provide examples "thereby allowing for local standards to be used in writing program-specific benchmark statements that are developmentally appropriate for the local schools" (Franck et al., 1992). Planning, implementation, and assessment specific to individual school programs are encouraged. Using these benchmarks as planning and assessment aids requires competent curriculum "designers." The outcomes and benchmarks of quality physical education programs are intended for use as a framework, test, or mapping tool for developing new programs or evaluating existing ones. They can be reflected in the components of curriculum, identified in this book as organizing centers, content goals, learner analysis, learning objectives, evaluation procedures, and learning experiences.

In addition, this book satisfies the underlying principles of developmentally appropriate practices as advanced by the Council on Physical Education for Children (COPEC) of NASPE. "A developmentally appropriate physical education program accommodates a variety of individual characteristics such as developmental status, previous movement experiences, fitness and skill levels, body size, and age. Instructionally appropriate physical education incorporates the best known practices, derived from both research and experiences teaching children, into a program that maximizes opportunities for learning and success for all children" (Graham, Castenada, Hopple, Manross, & Sanders, 1992). From a curricular standpoint, these appropriate practices are reflected in this book. For example, curricular scope and sequence, development of progressive movement concepts/skills, preassessment, cognitive development, and affective development represent components of appropriate practice that are presented to you.

New features have been added to this third edition. Chapter-opening scenarios establish the need for the material that follows. Each chapter ends with a special section called "Making It Work" in which reality issues and practical considerations are addressed.

Chapter 1 is a new chapter that describes the "designer" role in curriculum decision making and analyzes contexts from which the physical education curriculum is derived (i.e., contemporary education trends, curriculum issues, a philosophical orientation, and curriculum models). Together, these contexts provide the foundation for your curriculum "theory."

In chapter 2, you will discover how to create the focus for your physical education curriculum—an organizing center. Expanded material includes the characteristics and sources of organizing centers. Examples of alternative organizing centers are presented and a basis for selection is suggested. Chapter 3 guides you in transforming organizing centers into goals and selecting content to support these goals. This transition is accomplished through an intense process of goals analysis, including the identification of prerequisite knowledge, skills, and behaviors. A technique for organizing content goals and identifying their prerequisites is introduced—the learning hierarchy. To know where your students are on the learning hierarchy, you should conduct a learner analysis, including the assessment of entry-level status. In chapter 4, various assessment options are shown to you. Informal and formal techniques are outlined that emphasize a criterion-referenced approach.

In chapter 5, you will learn how to transform content goals into precise statements of intent—learning objectives. You will see how to arrange learning objectives in a learning hierarchy, like the structure used for arranging content goals. To prove the degree to which your learning objectives have been met, you will need to develop evaluation procedures. Chapter 6 provides sample evaluation instruments and helps you to develop data collection skills. A new section covers authentic assessment, including portfolios and a suggested model for physical education.

Guidelines are presented in chapter 7 for devising learning experiences to bring about desired behavioral changes. Two broad patterns of learning experiences are explored—individualization (e.g., self-directed tasks, programmed learning, contracting, computer-assisted learning) and interaction (e.g., reciprocal learning, role playing, simulation, cooperative learning). Consideration is also given to how you can accommodate "special" learners (i.e., culturally diverse, at risk, and gifted and talented).

In the final chapter, you will see how to synthesize the curriculum designing process. This new chapter's structure and nature are unlike the others. A sample physical education design is presented, using a case study approach, that illustrates each of the curriculum components and demonstrates how you can implement the competencies developed throughout the book.

In summary, think of curriculum designing as the answer to three questions. Where am I going? How will I get there? And when will I know I've arrived? Final answers are not provided in this book since they vary from one educational setting to another. Instead, a rationale and process is presented by which these questions can be answered. Clearly, this is not a "cookbook" for a physical education curriculum. There is no single "recipe" for such a design. However, when you are done with this book, you will understand the "ingredients" and you will be able to design meaningful and effective curricula.

Acknowledgments

Fortunately, my early professional development was guided by two outstanding people—Mike Sherman (University of Pittsburgh), my first mentor, and Tom Evaul (Temple University), my "curriculum" mentor.

This book could not have been written without the contributions of others. The works of many creative teachers and students, particularly those who have completed Modes and Models of Teaching at Cleveland State, are represented throughout the book. I am especially thankful to the reviewers—John Cheffers (Boston University) and Bonnie Mohnsen (Orange County Department of Education, California). In addition, gratitude is extended to Dick Hurwitz (Cleveland State University) who provided constructive feedback throughout the writing process. Many of his ideas are included in the book. As a curriculum "designer," he truly practices what this book preaches.

I would also like to thank Rick Frey, Director, HK Academic Division. His willingness to support the project from beginning to end was a source of encouragement. Special thanks and appreciation are reserved for Ann Brodsky, my developmental editor. Her suggestions for improving the book were outstanding in terms of writing style, special elements, and organization. She truly helped me rewrite the book. But, even more important to me was her personal support and commitment to this endeavor. For that, I will always be thankful!

Vincent Melograno

Foundation for Curriculum Design

Key Concept

Curriculum designers make decisions that consider contemporary education trends, curriculum issues, their own philosophical orientations, and existing curriculum models.

In a fairly large city school district, a school-community task force has been examining the topic "Curriculum for the Year 2000." During its spring meeting, the school board expects to hear a progress report from the task force. Instead, an angry exchange occurs. One member of the task force argues for a return to the "basics"—more reading, writing, math, science, and history. Another member is visibly upset. He believes that the curriculum should be more "functional"—increased emphasis on career education, consumerism, and values. Still others call for changes that will correct inequities and lead to a more "cooperative" curriculum. The school board is stunned by this exchange. Privately, they wonder why the task force is so split and whether the differences can be resolved.

Expected Outcomes

This chapter helps you establish the foundation for your curriculum design. Upon completing it, you will be able to

- accept the role of "designer" to create a contemporary physical education curriculum,
- determine the influence of education trends on the physical education curriculum,
- resolve curriculum issues that relate to physical education,
- develop a philosophical viewpoint that helps guide the design of the physical education curriculum,
- recognize that learners' needs (cognitive, affective, and psychomotor) are basic to the meaning of physical education, and
- differentiate among various physical education curriculum models.

School curriculum reflects the role of education in society. It combines public policy and professional judgment. As a separate subject, physical education is unique because it contributes to learning in all three of the cognitive, affective, and psychomotor domains. Your challenge is to fulfill this potential by creating a physical education curriculum that guides and facilitates student learning. Therefore, curriculum is defined as the planned sequence of (1) what students are to learn, (2) how students acquire that learning, and (3) how students' learning is verified. Since emphasis is placed on planning, a systematic process is needed to *design* the physical education curriculum.

The curriculum design process should not be confused with instruction, defined as the delivery system for implementing the curriculum. Instruction also involves planning followed by teacher-student interaction. During the planning phase of instruction, teachers make several decisions regarding lesson plans, instructional materials, audiovisual materials and equipment, equipment specific to physical education, time allocation, organizational schemes, management and discipline strategies, and teaching methods. The range of actual teacher and student behaviors occurs during the interactive phase of instruction. These phases of instruction are *not* treated in the book. However, you will find that by devising learning experiences for the curriculum, you have also begun the planning of instruction. Thus, the transition from curriculum planning to instructional planning is made easier.

The rationale for your physical education curriculum comes from various contexts. Consideration should be given to the cultural context, including schools and society as well as learners and their families. Philosophy serves as another context since curriculum is an extension of your values and beliefs. Finally, you will be influenced by existing curriculum models in physical education.

Together, these contexts are the foundation for curriculum designing. It is essential that you examine them before the designing process is begun. Therefore, several questions arise. What does it mean to be a curriculum *designer*? Which education trends and issues are important? Where does your philosophy fit into a curriculum design? And, how do existing models affect your curriculum design? Answers to these questions are provided in the following sections. Ultimately, you should be able to establish the foundation for your own physical education curriculum.

Role of Curriculum Designer

As explained later in this chapter, physical education means that the learner's individual needs—cognitive, affective, and psychomotor—are satisfied explicitly through all forms of physical activity. This kind of potential can be used for developing curricula. Unfortunately, many teachers use an intuitive approach. The result is a curriculum with ambiguous purposes, inappropriate content, ignored learning sequences, casual forms of evaluation, and limited kinds of learning activities. There appear to be two options for action. One option, of course, is to take the easy way and use the intuitive approach. The other option is to translate the meaning of physical education into basic principles and competencies for designing curricula. This book is provided for those who select the second option.

This section looks at the role of the curriculum designer. A brief background shows the need for "teacher-designers." Then, the competencies associated with this role are identified. They are developed in the book through the series of self-directed activities.

Background

The 1980s saw a demand for greater educational effectiveness. Since publication of *A Nation at Risk* by the National Commission on Excellence in Education (1983), there has been much legislation and numerous education projects directed toward school improvement and restructuring (Kohl, 1992; Levine & Ornstein, 1993). Attempts to create more successful schools vary. In some schools, classroom practices identified with effective schools have been introduced (e.g., high expectations, mastery learning, high rates of time-on-task, direct instruction, safe learning environments, systems for classroom management). In other low-performing schools, services and programs have been provided to create school environments more conducive to learning (e.g., technology-based approaches, mental health teams, parental involvement, reading recovery, school-based management, magnet schools, mentoring and advocacy assistance, experiential learning).

At first, the wave of school reform was guided by the belief that excellence could be imposed from the top through increased requirements for graduation, minimum proficiency testing, and improved teaching (e.g., merit pay, career ladders, and mentoring). The second phase of school reform involved restructuring. Curricula and instruction were changed as well as how schools were organized and administered, a supportive work environment was provided for teachers, partnerships and networks were built, and parent and community participation was increased (Midgley & Wood, 1993).

More recently, *America 2000: An Education Strategy* (U.S. Department of Education, 1991) emphasized the key elements to ensure widespread educational reform. This vision of American education resulted in a set of national education goals outlined in *Executive Summary: The National Education Goals Report* (1993). By the year 2000, it is expected that the following goals will be achieved: all children ready to learn; 90% graduation rate; all children competent in core subjects; U.S. students first in the world in math and science; every adult literate and able to compete in the work force; and safe, disciplined, drug-free schools.

The realities of our culturally pluralistic society require the continued reform and improvement of American education *including physical education*. Prevailing social and educational forces that maintain this need for change include

- appropriate programming, designed and conducted in the least restrictive environment, to meet the specific and unique needs of learners with disabilities;
- coeducational programming that is gender-neutral in design, gender-integrated in practice, and congruent with current legislation;
- multicultural learning experiences designed to consider and validate each person's cultural heritage and individual potential;
- racial integration that recognizes the diversity and multiplicity of values, beginning with the teacher's genuine concern and respect for each learner's worth and uniqueness; and
- basic education that should develop greater competence in academic skills by raising expectations in terms of academic performance and learner conduct.

Attempts to deal with these forces relate to the empowerment of teachers—to their feelings of efficacy. The ability to *design* a personalized curriculum that is responsive to contemporary learner needs, rather than *consuming* someone else's philosophy, program, materials, and strategies, is essential to this feeling of efficacy (Melograno, 1978).

Developing Competencies

Curriculum designing is no doubt a challenge. When carried out correctly, it can be complex and time-intensive. Physical educators, in particular, face a continuous dilemma, being bombarded with a wealth of content options. Nevertheless, you must decide *what* to teach and *why* to teach it. Making choices and establishing priorities can be perplexing (Melograno, 1984).

A curriculum design should reflect the designer's basic philosophy. It consists of many interrelated components that must function together. The following questions and answers illustrate these relationships:

Where are you going?

- Creating organizing centers
- Determining content goals
- Conducting learner analysis
- Deriving learning objectives

How will you get there?

- Devising learning experiences

When will you know you've arrived?

- Developing evaluation procedures

Each answer represents the competencies you need in order to systematically design a curriculum. By creating organizing centers, you establish a framework around which teaching and learning are centered. This leads to content goals, statements of intent that provide general direction. Once content goals are determined, an analysis of the learner can be conducted, including entry appraisal. A point of departure is established for individual student learning. Then, learning objectives are derived that provide specific direction for measuring intended outcomes. They are also useful in developing the remaining curriculum components. By devising learning experiences, the curriculum designer can help students interact with the environment and acquire the desired concepts, attitudes, values, and skills. Finally, the curriculum designer needs to develop evaluation procedures which indicate the degree of student accomplishment.

The model in Figure 1.1 depicts the relationship among the curriculum components. The focus is organizing centers, the foundation of which is also shown. Organizing centers directly influence the development of the other curriculum components. This systematic approach to designing implies a particular starting point and sequence. However, once organizing centers are created, the *initial* development of the other components may proceed in any order. For example, you should notice that evaluation is treated right after learning objectives because of its "link" to performance criteria, even though in practice it would come later. In practice, too, learning experiences usually occur immediately after curriculum planning. Therefore, this component is covered last. Learning experiences serve as the transition from the curriculum design to the planning phase of instruction.

The *final* development of each component should follow a step-by-step approach, as shown in Figure 1.2 (page 6). Several aspects should be noted. First, the number and nature of content goals and corresponding learning objectives which support a given organizing center is not set. Second, at least one evaluation procedure is needed for each learning objective. And third, several learning experiences can be devised for the same learning objective.

You shouldn't view this system of planning as a mechanical process of education. On the contrary, the rationale for what is learned, how it is learned, and how well it is learned is organized in a way that clarifies curriculum planning and enhances the sequence of learning. A wide spectrum of imaginative and creative educational experiences can be designed for a full range of learning objectives—from simple behaviors (e.g., recall, listen, jump) to complex mental tasks (e.g., create a dance routine), values development (e.g., fair play), and advanced movement patterns (e.g., hit a golf ball).

Contemporary Contexts

One of the major criticisms of school curricula is the lack of relevance. Every attempt should be made to be up-to-date or current. Therefore, this section explores some education trends that could potentially have an impact on the nature of physical education. In addition, several curriculum issues are presented that are sufficiently controversial to warrant resolution within a contemporary context. These issues are specific to the physical education curriculum.

Education Trends

Education responds constantly to forces that operate in the larger culture. Many people expect schools to solve our "social ills." We are confronted with substance abuse, changes in family patterns, poor fitness among youth, childhood obesity, sexually transmitted diseases, greater inequities between the "haves" and the "have-nots," a TV and video game generation, high crime rates, poor school performance, abused children, teenage suicide, disruptive behavior, changing ethnic and linguistic diversity, and high dropout rates, to mention a few. The increased accountability that has resulted from these expectations has changed education through curricular reform, school restructuring, and teacher empowerment for school-based management decisions. For example,

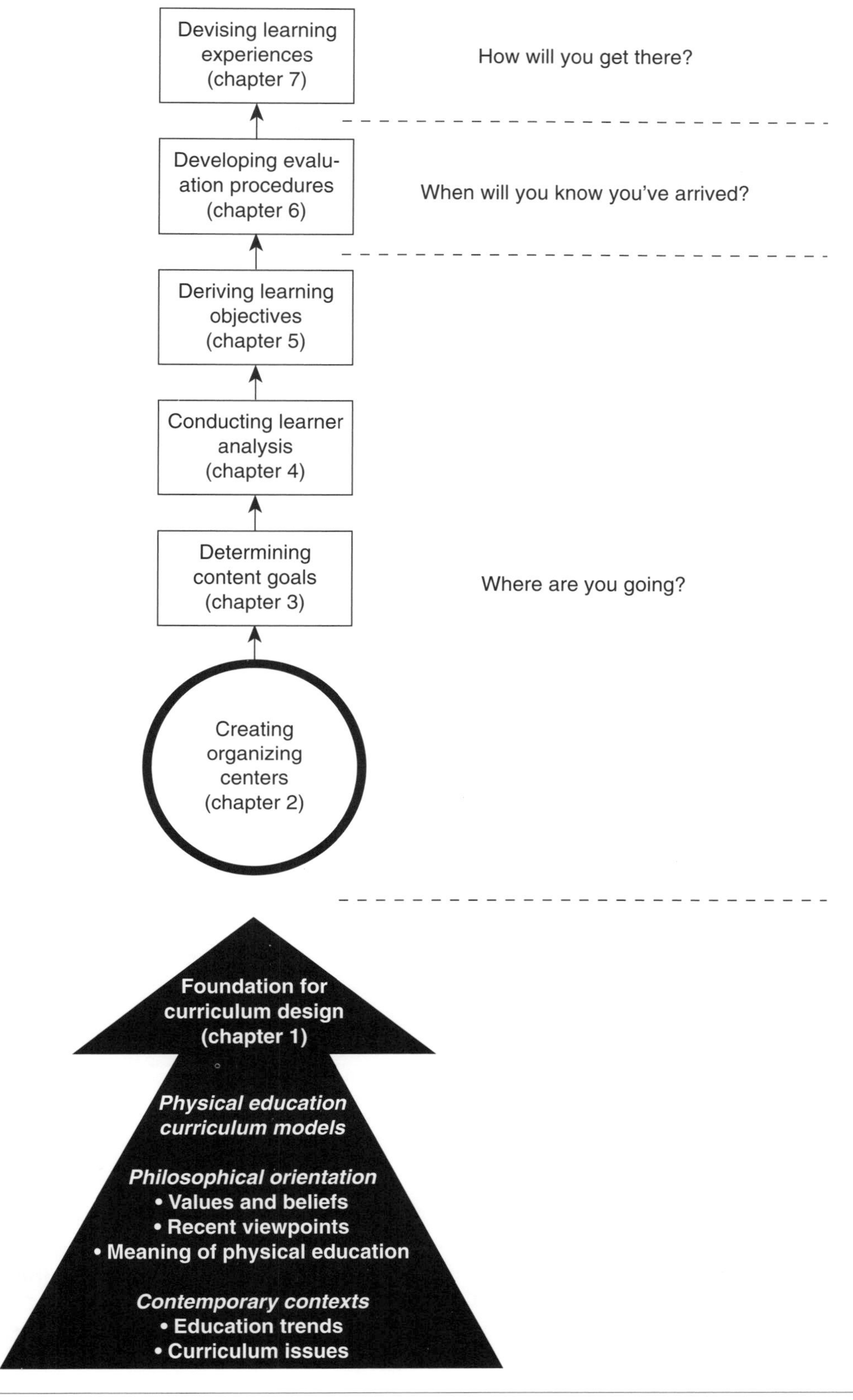

Figure 1.1 Model for designing the physical education curriculum shows the interrelationships among the curriculum components.

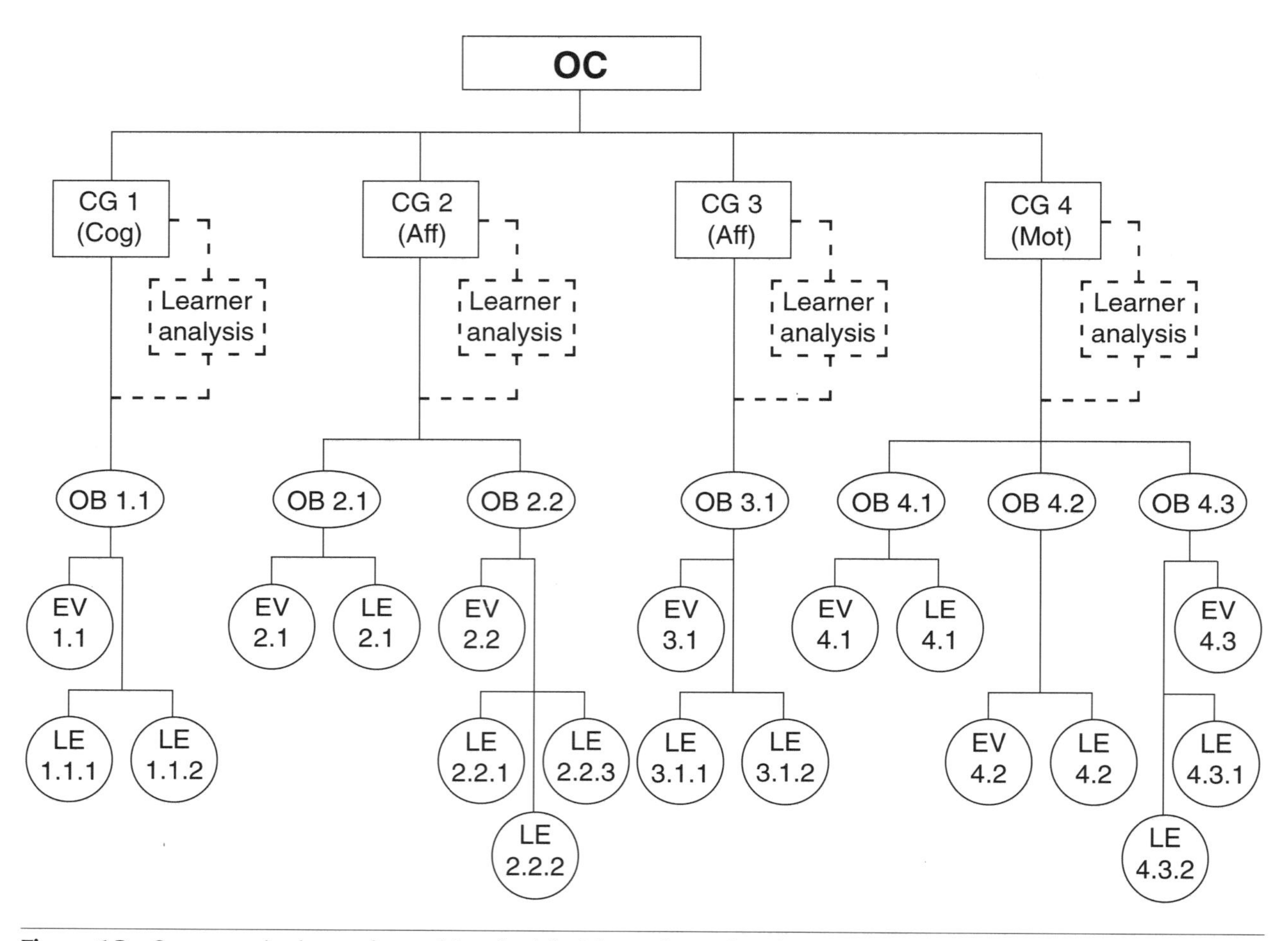

Figure 1.2 Sequence is shown for making *final* decisions about the physical education curriculum design.

along with programming for students with disabilities, special attention is being given to new categories—students from diverse ethnic groups, at-risk students, and gifted students.

Although there are many hopeful changes in education, five major trends seem important as a context for curriculum design. Your own beliefs and values should be challenged as you review these trends. Try to imagine how each might influence your physical education curriculum design.

Culturally Responsive Pedagogy

There is an emerging body of literature calling for a "culturally responsive pedagogy" (Villegas, 1991); that is, teaching that considers cultural differences. Skills are needed to accommodate the diversity found in cross-cultural school settings. For example, language differences are evident in school systems. Ethnic minorities account for over 20% of the school-age population. By the year 2000, two fifths of all school-age children will belong to minorities.

Teachers don't need to be members of students' cultural group. But they must be sensitive to the cultural characteristics of learners and accommodate these characteristics in the classroom. The implications for evaluating teachers are significant. Teachers should respect cultural differences, believe that all students are capable of learning, and see themselves as capable of making a difference in students' learning. These competencies could serve as performance criteria to ensure that teachers can instruct effectively in a multicultural society.

Current research also shows that a fast-paced curriculum is needed that actively engages students' attention. It should be stimulating rather than oversimplified, especially for students performing below expectation. This is not to reject drill, practice, and rote-learning activities, but to integrate them in realistic learning experiences. The curriculum should challenge students to develop higher order skills and knowledge. In physical education, for example, students might invent their own games or develop original sport strategies on their own or as part of a team.

Curriculum goals should enrich students' past learning, not correct deficiencies. For familiar material, several approaches should be taught so that students can monitor their own learning. Since active participation is a stimulus for learning, activities should involve *all* students. In order to accommodate cultural differences, flexible and varied teaching styles are needed. While some students learn well through direct instruction, others benefit more from self-directed activities, cooperative group projects, and reciprocal (peer) tasks.

Physical education, because of its social orientation, can play a leading role in eliminating discriminatory practices and promoting multicultural understanding. With this in mind, a series of articles edited by Chepyator-Thomson (1994) in the *Journal of Physical Education, Recreation & Dance* helps teachers develop strategies for including multiculturalism in physical education programs. This focus on culturally responsive teaching will assist you in responding to the issues of diversity raised by the wave of social and cultural change in the United States.

Inclusive Education

The concepts presented here are usually associated with special education categories. However, they are applicable to learners for whom a "regular" education is not considered appropriate, regardless of the reasons.

Integrating regular and special education has been carried out in schools in its most fundamental form—mainstreaming. Since students with disabilities are eventually mainstreamed into society, schools mainstream students to provide social and instructional integration. While mainstreaming is the appropriate setting for many students, it may be failure-laden for others (Lerner, 1993).

Currently, many students with various learning problems are not eligible for special education services. An alternative arrangement is the regular education initiative (REI). It goes beyond mainstreaming in recommending major revisions in special education, particularly in where and how students receive services (Will, 1986). This initiative assumes that students with disabilities, including those with learning and behavior problems, can be served more effectively through regular education than through special education.

Another integrated concept has become synonymous with REI. The *full inclusion* model places and instructs all students in regular settings regardless of the type or severity of disability. Teams of professionals representing different specialities (e.g., reading, math, motor development) bring their collective skills and knowledge together to provide personal programs for each student. The full inclusion model completely eliminates special education, which is viewed as an unnecessary "second system" (Villa & Thousand, 1990). It has implications for subject areas like physical education (motor development) because of the need to create individualized curricula. Inclusion focuses on everyone's abilities and possibilities, not on deficiencies and limitations. A series of articles edited by Craft (1994) in the *Journal of Physical Education, Recreation & Dance* offers ideas and strategies to help physical education teachers meet the challenge of inclusion.

Knowledge-Based Approach

Some prominent educators advocate the development of a formal knowledge base to guide program design. They argue that programs based on essential knowledge are "distinctive." To assist teachers in establishing a knowledge base, five attributes should be considered: underlying philosophy (set of beliefs), organizational theme, outcomes and evaluation processes, literature support, and program model.

Knowledge-based formats assume that subject matter cannot be left out of the designing process. Instead, they are based on the assumption that subject matter mastery is fundamental to one's ability to solve problems, think, or be creative. By contrast, process-based approaches concentrate on how information may best be learned by developing, for example, problem-solving skills, thinking strategies, and creativity. These kinds of cognitive abilities are considered prerequisite to subject matter mastery (Vickers, 1990).

The body of knowledge in physical education is relatively new. The decade of the 1970s is often called the "disciplinary years." Subdisciplines emerged which are well established today, including exercise physiology; kinesiology and biomechanics; motor learning, control, and development; sport sociology; sport psychology; sport pedagogy; and sport humanities (history, philosophy, and literature) (Siedentop, 1994a). As an extension of this development, the American Alliance for Health, Physical Education, Recreation and Dance (1987) published the *Basic Stuff* series. Disciplinary areas were used to structure the knowledge base for physical education along with corresponding concepts and learning activities.

Developmentally Appropriate Practices

The quality of educational programs is determined by many factors (e.g., cost-effectiveness, range of activities, satisfaction, achievement). But a primary determinant should be the degree to which principles of child and adolescent development are applied. In other words, is the program *developmentally appropriate?* By definition, developmental appropriateness is two-dimensional. Age appropriateness depends on universal, predictable sequences of growth and change that occur in all dimensions—physical, intellectual, emotional, and social. These typical developments provide a framework for program planning. Individual appropriateness refers to each person's pattern and timing of growth, as well as individual personality, learning style, and family background. Thus, the curriculum and instruction should be responsive to individual differences (Bredekamp, 1987).

In physical education, developmentally appropriate practices recognize each learner's changing abilities to move and they accommodate individual characteristics such as previous movement experiences, fitness and skill levels, and body size. Guidelines developed through the Council on Physical Education for Children (Graham, Castenada, Hopple, Manross, & Sanders, 1992) make a distinction between practices that are in the best interests of children (appropriate) and those that are counterproductive, or even harmful (inappropriate). For example, appropriate practice means that the physical education curriculum has an obvious scope and sequence based on goals and objectives appropriate for all children. It includes a balance of skills, concepts, games, educational gymnastics, rhythms, and dance experiences designed to enhance cognitive, motor, affective, and physical fitness development. Inappropriate practice means that the physical education curriculum lacks developed goals and objectives. It is based primarily on the teacher's interests, preferences, and background rather than the student's. Additional information is provided in a series of articles edited by Graham (1992) in the *Journal of Physical Education, Recreation & Dance*. Appropriate practices related to the design of physical education curricula are identified throughout this book.

Outcome-Based Education

Excellence in education is in the spotlight; it is a national priority. Everyone seems to know how to improve schools. One idea that is ready for widespread use is the outcome-based approach, a comprehensive design for teaching/learning and instructional management. It has its roots in the earlier mastery-learning and competency-based education movements. The premise is that student success is reflected in "goals reached" rather than in relative advantage over other students' performance or in completion of a prescribed set of courses. The system recognizes the limitations of a fixed-time,

Students learn physical education outcomes.

one-shot instructional delivery approach which assumes that students who don't do well within the time allowed for initial learning are inherently incapable of doing well at all (Murphy, 1984).

Clearly developed, publicly stated outcomes provide the focus for curriculum organization. The critical first step is to define desirable learning outcomes. Next, appropriate curriculum materials (learning units) are adopted. The third step is to "link" exit outcomes with objectives and then with assessment instruments. Establishing this kind of congruency is a complex task when carried out correctly. The last step is to devise a way of managing the curriculum. During this phase, learning units are monitored and formal procedures are developed for revising the curriculum based on student achievement and teacher experience (Burns & Squires, 1987).

The Physical Education Outcomes Project of the National Association for Sport and Physical Education is consistent with the described model. The guide created by the project includes outcome statements and grade-level "benchmarks" (competencies) that define the *physically educated person*. The five basic parts of the definition are (Franck et al., 1992):

A Physically Educated Person

- HAS learned skills necessary to perform a variety of physical activities.
- IS physically fit.
- DOES participate regularly in physical activity.
- KNOWS the implications of and the benefits from involvement in physical activities.
- VALUES physical activity and its contributions to a healthful lifestyle. (p. 7)

Specific outcomes are associated with each part of the definition. Since the outcomes and benchmarks offer a viable framework for designing curriculum, they are treated in greater detail throughout this book.

▶ ***Trends in education usually emerge in response to social forces. They serve as an important context when designing a curriculum. Ideally, having reviewed some of these trends, you will have found your own beliefs and values challenged. To see how these trends would influence your design, complete Self-Directed Activity 1.1 at the end of this chapter.***

Curriculum Issues

Whether you realize it or not, conflicts and problems are created by your beliefs about physical education. They should be resolved in advance of designing your curriculum so that what you believe and what you plan to do are the same thing. Conflicts are commonly referred to as *issues*. On the other hand, problems are situations that are perplexing or difficult. Issues, which generally appear in advance of problems, consist of two or more opposing views and they are controversial. Although problems are not controversial, their solution could give rise to other issues since there may be several solutions (Sanborn & Hartman, 1983).

This distinction can be easily illustrated. A controversial issue which has existed for a long time is, "Should physical education be required or elective?" There are at least three answers—that it should be required, that it should be elective, or some combination of the two. Regardless of the answer, however, problems are created. In a required program, the problem is, "What should be required?" In an elective program, the problem is, "How do you schedule a variety of activities?" In a combined program, the problem is, "What should the ratio of required to elective hours be?" Clearly, resolving the issue can lead to many different problems.

Another example might be helpful. Although some might disagree, the problem of gender-integrated learning isn't derived from an issue. Assuming there is no argument against gender integration, then no issue exists. Without an opposing view, there exists only a problem. In this case, problems include selecting gender-neutral activities, establishing fair performance standards, and creating equal competition.

Several issues can be raised with respect to curriculum design. Their resolution requires continuous evaluation, analysis, reflection, and justification. The issues discussed in this section represent conflicting ideas and values specific to physical education. Ultimately, your curriculum should reflect the acceptance of one of the opposing views. It will be clear that one view is supported. See if you agree. Which side of the issue do you really support?

Learner-Centered Versus Content-Centered Emphasis

Attempts have been made to meet the needs and interests of learners through changes in physical education class organization and processes. However, these changes (e.g., modular scheduling, elective programming, independent study options, team teaching, mini-courses, and differentiated staffing) have not necessarily focused on learners' needs. The issue is one of selection. Is content selected to meet cognitive, affective, and psychomotor needs? Or is it assumed that these needs are satisfied by a content-centered curriculum?

When a curriculum is centered on content (activities), the chance of "cheating" learners is increased. More likely, learners will be expected to satisfy arbitrary content standards instead of having their needs met by the content. For example, it cannot be assumed that learners' need for social adjustment and responsibility (e.g., teamwork, fair play, tolerance) will be met by team sports. In many instances, the need to isolate those of lesser ability in order to win has taken precedence over such social needs. The effects of a content-centered curriculum, then, can be poor self-image, lack of confidence, and dependence. This practice is reflected often in the way males treat females, particularly during the initial phases of a game. Males have learned to expect that females' performance will be inferior.

Individualized Versus Group Focus

If a learner-centered curriculum is supported, there is the problem of *how*. The issue becomes, "Should the curriculum focus on the individual or the group?" The distinction between cohort and individualized instruction is provided (Locke & Lambdin, 1976).

> Cohort instruction includes any pedagogical strategy which leads the teacher to teach the same thing to all students at the same time, by the same method, and requires all students to practice in the same way, at the same pace, for the same length of time, and to be subject to the same kinds of standards and the same criteria for evaluating achievement. (p. 13)

Presumably, in cohort instruction teachers can't attend to individual needs and interests that deviate significantly from those selected, usually the average of the group. Theoretically, subject matter and group characteristics are paramount in such instruction.

> Individualized instruction includes any pedagogical strategy which leads the teacher to adjust objectives (ends) or content, instruction and practice (means), or all of those elements, to produce the most appropriate match with the characteristics of individual students. The process of matching educational ends and means to student needs and interests may be controlled by the teacher [or] the student, or shared by both. In short, this process adjusts learning to the student. (p. 14)

Presumably, then, in individualized instruction teachers deal with students as individuals even though their unique needs and interests will be diverse. Theoretically, such instruction focuses on the learning characteristics of individuals. Class transactions, however, would not occur on a one-to-one basis. In a traditional physical education curriculum, individuals have been manipulated to satisfy group arrangements; organization by groups has been undisputed. Instead, physical education should represent equal opportunity for learning. When *imposed*, group values, group objectives, group arrangements, and group standards contradict the meaning of physical education.

Gender-Integrated Versus Gender-Segregated Design

This issue shouldn't exist. But there are still some teachers who believe in gender-segregated programming. Clearly, the separation of males and females belongs to the past. However, separatists will continue to perpetuate the myths and misconceptions associated with the separate domains of males and females. A conflict is created between those who will examine sexuality, gain insights into self-concepts, and promote gender-neutral curricula and those who will "hold fast to the antiquated arrangements represented by that magic, omnipotent partition separating the boys' gym from the girls' gym" (Mosston & Mueller, 1974, p. 105).

Inclusion Versus Exclusion

Although physical education has been acclaimed as providing "learning for all," this principle of inclusion is not borne out in practice. Instead, physical education has been designed for exclusion. Learners are excluded when they stand in line waiting their turn; must meet some minimum standard based on chronological age; compete against someone of superior ability and inevitably fail; engage in tasks that require prerequisites not yet learned; and attempt activities in which entry-level abilities are deficient. Mosston and Mueller (1974) offer a vivid illustration of exclusion and inclusion:

> For example, let us look at the high jump as an educational experience. We are not concerned here with the use of the high jump in athletic competition, where the exclusion principle is congruent with philosophy and practice. We are examining the design of the high jump experience in light of the stated educational objective. After several "innings" the rope or bar excludes most participants. If the raising of the bar continues, it soon excludes

> all! The design of the activity is obviously hardly congruent with the philosophy of physical education . . . Place the bar at a slant, so that it represents variable height[,] with its intrinsic quality of *inclusion*. (p. 100)

Alternative Versus Single Learning Modes

Individuals learn in a variety of ways, and some forms of learning may actually interfere with individual learning style. With this as the premise, value judgments need not be imposed about how people learn, and learning may be individually tailored. Many physical educators fail to realize that using only one style of teaching—particularly the direct style—excludes alternative learner response and fails to accommodate variability in learning and performance. In the main, physical educators still adhere to and defend the stimulus-response learning model; nonetheless, independent, alternative learner response and discovery learning are preferable. Teachers must develop alternative teaching styles if the meaning of physical education is to become a reality.

Personalized Versus Authoritarian Approach

Meeting individual needs and interests may not be new, but problems have arisen regarding the approach. The dominant authoritarian style appears to be counteractive, that is, direct teaching (highly structured, teacher-centered) and "throw-out-the-ball" programming (teacher-directed, recreational). A more personalized style is desirable. A wide variety of personalized approaches affords the opportunity to "practice what has been preached."

The change from an authoritarian style depends on a change in the assumptions underlying many programs. The actions of many physical educators reveal these basic assumptions (Albertson, 1974):

- Learners must be required or forced to engage in physical activity, implying that they are lazy.
- Learners must be extrinsically motivated by grades, awards, and points, implying that they are unconcerned about physical activity.
- Learners must have decisions made for them, implying that they are incapable of making decisions regarding physical activity.

These assumptions should be dismissed. Physical education can develop students' abilities to direct themselves, make decisions, and accept responsibility for those decisions. The curriculum would move the learner along a continuum from dependence and irresponsibility to independence and responsibility. The assumptions underlying this approach are (Albertson, 1974)

- learners are interested in physical activity experiences,
- learners are by nature self-motivated,
- learners are self-reliant and assume personal responsibility for decisions, and
- learners need a system of education to develop rational decision-making abilities.

Explicit Versus Implicit Learning

Quality learning occurs when experiences are planned and sequenced toward the attainment of desired behaviors. Some educational outcomes, particularly psychosocial outcomes, have been concomitant to skill development and knowledge acquisition. This so-called concomitant learning includes interests, attitudes, appreciations, respect for others, self-confidence, responsibility, decision-making ability, and independence. In addition, disrespect for others, circumvention of rules to win, exploitation of others' weaknesses, intimidation, intolerance, poor self-image, irresponsibility, and dependence are also examples of concomitant learning. Whether helpful or harmful, positive or negative, concomitant learning is inevitable.

These kinds of unintended learning are also referred to as the "hidden curriculum," what students learn from the school's culture—its values, norms, and practices (Glatthorn, 1993). The hidden curriculum consists of unplanned and unrecognized values that are taught and learned through the process of education. In other words, learners are repeatedly exposed to unconscious acts that are consistent in meaning, such as gender role modeling by teachers. These representative acts, which communicate implicit values to the learner, may or may not be consistent with the explicit philosophy of the teacher or school.

For example, the teacher might explicitly believe that differential treatment of learners on the basis of ability, gender, race, or social class is unjustified. In basketball, the teacher may use drills and lead-up games that don't result in differential treatment. However, during the game itself, no adjustment or modification is made that considers individual differences. The result might be that two out of five players dominate the game. Although the reason is likely to be ability, other factors such as gender and race serve to compound the problem. When such distinctions are promoted, learners may implicitly question the value of basketball as a "team" sport.

The issue here is whether educational outcomes should be learned explicitly or implicitly. For the most part, desirable psychosocial values are learned implicitly. Supposedly, they are learned as a result of participation in physical activities. However, unless the desired value is planned for and taught *explicitly*, it is impossible to predict its attainment. It can't be learned by chance. Let's say the concept of "shared responsibility" is to be learned. Content and learning experiences should be selected so learners can practice the concept. Simply playing doubles tennis won't be sufficient. Learners should be taught the responsibility of partner play, the use of individual and partner strengths and weaknesses, and the consequences of failing to recognize each other's responsibilities.

▶ ***To test your ability to resolve issues associated with the physical education curriculum, complete Self-Directed Activity 1.2 at the end of this chapter.***

Philosophical Orientation

Philosophy, the search for reality, truths, and proper conduct, is needed for consistency of behavior. It is made up of value assumptions that direct and guide decision making. These ultimate inferences and principles determine one's thinking and action. Thus, philosophy is a meaningful context for curriculum design.

Some people view philosophy as having little practical value. This raises the question, "On what basis are decisions made regarding daily tasks within the learning environment?" Frequently, educational behavior is based on "common sense" that is inconsistent, illogical, and confusing to the learner, a haphazard collection of concepts acquired unconsciously and uncritically. The resulting practices may be educationally sound, but directed toward objectives that are philosophically incompatible. Common sense is then reduced to doing that which requires the least effort or that which is demanded by current pressures for conformity.

For example, attempts to integrate physical education by gender have placed males and females in the same educational setting (conformity) with a "throw-out-the-ball" program (least effort). Then, this so-called common-sense approach is acclaimed for its contribution to self-directed learning, independence, social responsibility, and self-confidence. Obviously, any learning gains in these aspects are incidental, at best.

Educational philosophy should be action-oriented and dynamic. It's an ongoing assessment of beliefs and values for deciding what you're doing and why you're doing it. Without this framework, the "how to" process may actually be counterproductive to the attainment of educational needs. Moreover, teachers who struggle with inconsistencies between what they believe and the direction education is taking are usually unhappy, less productive, and overly critical. If "Where are you going?" is a valid question, then so is the inquiry, "On what basis (philosophy) are you making decisions about the direction of physical education?"

It is important for you to establish your own *tenets* of physical education. This section helps you do that by reviewing traditional values and beliefs, analyzing recent philosophical viewpoints, and examining the proposed meaning of physical education. Try to determine your values. Exactly what do you believe? Ultimately, your beliefs should be reflected in any curriculum you design.

Traditional Values and Beliefs

Physical educators should ask themselves, "Which philosophies merit my energy and commitment?" and "Which educational goals should I pursue?" Answers seem ever more elusive given the accelerating rate of change in society. Sound educational programs will not just evolve by themselves. Physical education—all of its parts, episodes, and individual actions—must relate to a *grand plan*, an overall purpose.

Over the years, prevailing philosophies have been applied to educational thinking. Traditional philosophies—idealism, realism, naturalism, pragmatism, and existentialism—continue to influence curriculum design. They are described in Table 1.1 in terms of underlying concepts (values and beliefs), general educational emphases, and implications for the physical education curriculum (Annarino, Cowell, & Hazelton, 1980; Bucher, 1983; Freeman, 1982).

As an outgrowth of traditional philosophies and historical events, the early twentieth century was dominated by two philosophies of physical education: education *of* the physical and education *through* the physical. Education *of* the physical focused on physical fitness and its outcome of strength, power, cardiorespiratory efficiency, and agility. This narrow theory viewed bodily development and health as ends, not means. From the Civil War to the end of the nineteenth century, various physical education programs competed for supremacy in what was called the "Battle of the Systems." Several European

Table 1.1 Traditional Philosophies

Traditional philosophy	Underlying concepts	Educational emphases	Implications for physical education curriculum
Idealism	• Mind is more real than anything else. • Thoughts and purpose are central ("idea-ism"). • Mind and spirit are keys to life; people are more important than nature. • Values exist independently and are permanent; people have free will. • Reasoning and intuition help people find truth; scientific methods may be used.	• Development of moral and spiritual values (whole, individual personality) • Development of mind (rational powers and reasoning) • Education process originates within self (student); learning is self-initiated. • Development of essential personality qualities (self-reliance, self-responsibility, self-direction) • Development of creativity is guided by teacher through various methods and learning environments.	• Must contribute to intellectual development • Strength and fitness acceptable if contribution is made to personality development (self-discipline) • Play and recreation important for well-balanced personality • Activities centered around ideals (courage, honesty, sportsmanship) • Teacher serves as a positive role model. • Teacher responsible for program effectiveness; guidance more important than equipment and facilities • Reflective thinking and analyzing problems more important than knowing rules/terms
Realism	• Physical world is real; world is made up of matter. • Physical events result from the laws of nature. • Truth is determined by using scientific method. • Mind and body have a close and harmonious relationship; they are inseparable and neither is superior. • Philosophy and religion can coexist; either can be used to determine individual beliefs.	• Development of reasoning powers • Education is basic to life; develop ability to understand and make adjustments to *real* world. • Education is objective (teaching, testing, evaluation). • Educational process proceeds in a step-by-step fashion; inductive reasoning is used. • Scientific orientation (experimentation, demonstration, observation) • Measurement techniques are standardized, including testing.	• Prepare students to adjust to the world; emphasis placed on *outcome* of activity. • Values physical fitness because of intrinsic contribution to greater productivity • Activities selected on basis of scientific evidence of their worth • Learning process emphasizes drill and orderly progression; skills separated into component parts • Desirable social behaviors can be developed through sports programs; winning is *not* stressed. • Play and recreation contribute to life's adjustments because of contact with real world.

(continued)

Table 1.1 *(continued)*

Traditional philosophy	Underlying concepts	Educational emphases	Implications for physical education curriculum
Naturalism	• Physical world is the key to life; everything we experience is part of nature. • Nature, as the source of value, is reliable and dependable; anything is of value if it is workable.	• Satisfy basic, inborn needs of the individual. • Educational process governed by each person's rate of mental and physical development; learning "readiness" • Education considers physical and moral development, not just mental; balanced learning. • Students are involved in own education; self-activity and self-expression. • Teacher guides by example and demonstration; use of informal inductive methods. • Use of rewards and reprimands as part of learning process	• Activities are a source of overall development, not just the physical. • Self-directed activities primary for an adjustment to environment • Play, resulting from children's interests, teaches desirable social behaviors. • Self-improvement rather than competition; people compete against themselves. • Development of whole person • Students develop at their own rates. • Teacher must know students' needs and rates of development.
Pragmatism	• Basic reality is change caused by human experience; experience is only way to seek truth. • Success is the only judge of the value and truth of a theory; a workable theory is a true theory.	• Learning occurs through experience (inquiring, observing, and participating). • Education is for social efficiency; prepare students to take their places in society. • Education is child-centered rather than subject-centered; individual differences are important (learning rates). • Problem-solving necessary to face world of change; learning is purposeful and creative. • Evaluation of adjustment to environment • Education is a broad process to develop *total* person (mind, body, soul).	• Varied activities result in more meaningful experiences; creative problems and challenges are encouraged. • Emphasis on social value of physical activities (interaction) • Needs and interests of students determine curriculum. • Problem-solving and self-discovery develop creativity (dance and movement education). • Teacher is a motivator while student is "learning by doing." • Standardization discouraged; individual differences stressed in spite of goal to integrate individual into society

Traditional philosophy	Underlying concepts	Educational emphases	Implications for physical education curriculum
Existentialism	• True reality is human existence; people are what they cause for themselves. • Persons determine their own systems of values; values must be self-disciplined.	• Discovery of inner selves; develop one's own beliefs • Individual process used because of different rates and ways of learning; schools provide environment only. • Curriculum is centered on individual student who selects subjects and methods. • Teacher serves as a stimulator; encourages students to discover their own truths. • Teach personal responsibility; students learn to assume responsibility for the consequences of their decisions. • Affective approach (attitudes and appreciations); difficult to measure	• Freedom to choose activities and programs • Balanced and varied activities to satisfy individual needs and interests; diversity • Play is used to develop creativity; "winning" has little value. • Self-knowledge is important (individual/dual activities, self-testing); through self-discovery, students know themselves. • Teacher serves as counselor and guide; shows students available options; students feel more responsible for education.

systems, more appropriately called gymnastics or physical training, had been introduced in the United States, in the process discarding a nationalistic goal (i.e., military training, the well-being of the state) in favor of an emphasis on physical and health benefits. This functional approach maintained its importance into the twentieth century. The contemporary education-of-the-physical philosophy is represented by the concept of physical fitness.

Many of the late nineteenth- and early twentieth-century programs were rivaled by the "new physical education." Known as the natural program or natural gymnastics, it represented the education-*through*-the-physical philosophy, a sharp contrast to education *of* the physical. Attempts to achieve the general goals of education through physical activity became the dominant theme during the first half of the twentieth century, and remains in the minds of many as the philosophical basis for action. Nineteenth-century terminology such as "physical culture," "physical training," and "gymnastics" gradually disappeared in favor of terms such as "citizenship," "social values," "character development," and "intellectual functioning."

Education-through-the-physical gained considerable acceptance as a result of Americans' individualism and competitiveness, the democratic principles of American society, and the broad goals of education. These factors transformed physical education from a one-dimensional gymnastics program to a multidimensional sport-activity program. Although this approach would seem to hold much potential, it has not produced the desired results. By trying to satisfy all the goals of education—that the student should become physically fit, skilled, emotionally stable, knowledgeable, a good citizen, and socially responsible—the meaning of physical activity has suffered. Unfortunately, attainment of these goals has been *implicit* (assumed) as a result of participation in physical activity. Education-through-the-physical is realized only when physical activity is directed *explicitly* toward the accomplishment of such goals.

▶ ***Now that you are familiar with traditional philosophies, you should be able to defend your own beliefs and values against these philosophies. To practice this skill, complete Self-Directed Activity 1.3 at the end of this chapter.***

Recent Viewpoints in Physical Education

Since 1950, a series of societal and professional developments (e.g., post-Sputnik education reform, the Civil Rights movement, the Vietnam War, the end of the cold war, the fitness renaissance, and specialization in universities) has caused philosophical diversity and turmoil. Serious questions have been raised concerning the assumptions underlying physical education, sport, and fitness. The major philosophical movements of the recent past were identified by Siedentop.* Try to compare your beliefs and values against these viewpoints.

Human Movement

Since its development in England in the late 1930s, the concept of human movement has received wide acceptance. In the United States, this occurred from the late 1950s onward. Within a short time, human movement has gained significant recognition as a basic theoretical approach to physical education. Numerous terms have been used to describe the concept, for example, movement education, movement exploration, educational dance, educational gymnastics, developmental movement.

This philosophy was the impetus for the disciplinary structuring of physical education. Subdisciplines such as sport physiology, biomechanics, sport sociology, and sport psychology developed under the human movement framework. In schools, a more open approach was advocated. Exploration and guided discovery were promoted in a noncompetitive, success-oriented climate, particularly at the elementary level. In a contemporary curriculum, the movement concepts and skills that provide the basis for understanding all movement are grouped as

- ***body awareness***—what the body can do, the shapes it can make, the way it balances, and transfer of weight;
- ***space awareness***—skills relating to moving in different directions, moving at different levels, and spatial aspects of movement;

*The description of these philosophical viewpoints is adapted from *Introduction to Physical Education, Fitness, and Sport* (pp. 77–83) by D. Siedentop, 1990, Mountain View, CA: Mayfield. Adapted by permission.

Human movement philosophy is put into practice.

• *qualities*—how the body can move and skills relating to speed, force, and flow of movement; and

• *relationships*—connection between the body and others or to objects. (Kirchner, 1992)

Humanistic Sport and Physical Education

The social turmoil of the 1960s and 1970s helped create humanistic psychology, which aimed toward the full development of individual potential. Personal growth and self-development were central to humanistic education. Affective learning, values clarification, and social development were considered as important as academic development.

For physical education, primary goals were organized around self-expression and interpersonal relations. This meant an emphasis on cooperation instead of competition, enjoyment instead of excellence, process instead of product, and expression instead of obedience.

Play Education and Sport Education

Educational psychologists regard learning that results from intrinsic motivation to be more substantial than learning brought about by external incentives. Intrinsic learning offers the best opportunity for retention, transfer, and positive self-concept. Learning that occurs naturally without the direction of others is often called play, and interference with or direction of learners' play is thought to jeopardize natural development. To many, this philosophical viewpoint epitomizes the potential of physical education, since a person at play is engaged in an inherently meaningful experience. The goal of play education, then, was skill acquisition and affection for the activity itself. However, play education was never really accepted as a prescription for the physical education curriculum.

A more recent philosophical orientation, sport education, is an extension of play education. Since sport is an institutionalized form of competitive motor play, it should be the subject matter of physical education. Sport education includes the organization of learners into teams, scheduled competition among teams, a culminating event, and record keeping.

Sport Sciences and Sport Studies

The discipline movement represents a philosophy of how to define a "body of knowledge." Some educators believe that school physical education should be organized around a more "academic" framework of sport sciences or sport studies. Subdisciplines that could serve as a focus include exercise physiology, kinesiology, motor learning and development, sport sociology, sport psychology, and sport humanities. The content and sequence of activities would be dramatically affected.

Fitness Renaissance and Wellness Movement

The popularity of fitness is probably connected to quality-of-life issues (e.g., consumer advocacy, ecological control, human rights). The philosophical foundation for this movement is the concept of wellness, a broad holistic view of health. Instead of health as the absence of illness, wellness means that sickness and disease are prevented. This philosophy stresses that physical, mental, and emotional health are interrelated. In the same way, work, play, and social life need to be approached positively with appropriate balance. Positive criteria include coping with everyday stress, feelings of accomplishment, an active lifestyle, and feelings of contentment. Fundamental to this philosophy is the notion of lifelong involvement in fitness and sports.

▶ ***You should have some opinions about the recent philosophical viewpoints in physical education. To see how they compare to your own beliefs and values, complete Self-Directed Activity 1.4 at the end of this chapter.***

The Meaning of Physical Education

Many view education as the dominant force in changing society rather than education as a reaction to society. In other words, if we want to shape the future, we must act on our own beliefs to avoid having it shape us. Through continued school reform, contemporary education can respond to the challenge of change and the demand for quality. While there is ambiguity in our society, some purposes of education remain constant regardless of changing educational definitions, changing views of students, or changing modes of education: Learners should be able to grow to their full potential, face uncertainty, and adjust to changes that threaten individual and group survival.

Despite the lack of a cohesive approach to curriculum and the failure to reconcile philosophical viewpoints, physical education has still survived because of its contributions to the overall school program. As physical educators, we are bombarded with a confusing wealth of program and philosophical options, as shown in this chapter. However, there is one recurring concept offering a focus for curriculum design—*needs of learners*.

Therefore, the meaning of physical education is represented by a viable curriculum that satisfies learners' changing needs. Various constructs have been developed to identify, categorize, and define these needs, such as learner capabilities (Gagné, Briggs, & Wager, 1990); developmental channels (Mosston & Ashworth, 1986); dimensional needs (Evaul, 1973); and educational domains (Bloom, 1956; Harrow, 1972; Krathwohl, Bloom, & Masia, 1964). *Note that the educational domains construct (i.e., cognitive, affective, and psychomotor) is used throughout this book.* It consists of the following kinds of needs:

- ***Cognitive***: Knowledge and intellectual abilities and skills ranging from simple recall tasks to synthesizing and evaluating information.
- ***Affective***: Likes and dislikes, attitudes, values, and beliefs ranging from the willingness to receive information and respond to stimuli to the development of an established value system; encompasses the process of socialization.
- ***Psychomotor***: All observable voluntary human motion ranging from reflex movements to the ability to modify and create aesthetic movement patterns.

In the design of curricula consideration should be given to the wide variety of student characteristics—capabilities, interests, experiences, learning styles, cultural backgrounds, attitudes, and personality traits. However, such characteristics are often ignored, risking failure or, at the least, wasting valuable learning time. Unfortunately, curriculum is usually developed from "normative assumptions" about students' performance. It is assumed that most students will perform around the mean, some will learn quickly, and others will not learn at all, and therefore teachers direct their efforts toward the average. The variation in student characteristics, however, *begs* for an alternative approach.

Curriculum design should take into account the student's background and previous experiences. It should expand the student's world, not replace it. For example, students who are members of minority groups bring experiences, cultural values, and expectations to schools that may differ from those of the predominant culture. Or, to take a different example, some students may have already learned how to assume responsibility, make decisions, or act independently. In physical education, it may be found that some students have not had opportunities to refine gross motor patterns, develop general coordination skills, or engage in and enjoy individual, team, and recreational activities. The fact that students have had different orientations and experiences will affect the way in which instruction is received.

In order to synthesize the information presented thus far, the philosophical meaning of physical education is identified. The basic assumptions which support this meaning serve as a context for designing the physical education curriculum.

Meaning

Physical education means that the learner's individual needs—cognitive, affective, and psychomotor—are satisfied explicitly through all forms of physical activity.

Assumptions

- ***Physical education is learner-centered.*** The well-being and role of the learner are primary, rather than the content or the teacher.
- ***Physical education focuses on unique, individual potential.*** Human variability (individual differences and similarities) is fundamental to matching goals, objectives, evaluation modes, and learning experiences with individual characteristics, rather than with those of the group as a whole.
- ***Learners need to grow and mature in all domains—cognitive, affective, and psychomotor.*** The needs approach to learning is based on the theory that human behavior is motivated by a desire to satisfy needs. Physical education can promote growth and maturation in all domains irrespective of the diversity of needs.
- ***Outcomes associated with needs are achieved explicitly.*** Cognitive, affective, and psychomotor objectives must be attained explicitly if learning is to be meaningful. Desirable outcomes, particularly those in the psychosocial area (self-control, responsibility, fair play, tolerance), cannot be simply implied in the design of physical activities.
- ***Physical activity encompasses all forms of fundamental, competitive, and expressive movement experiences.*** Any form of physical activity may be used, provided that the learner can engage in cognitive processing; express interests, attitudes, and values; practice proper social behavior; and develop physical fitness and simple-to-complex psychomotor skills.

▶ ***Needs of learners are basic to the proposed meaning of physical education. To test if you can recognize these needs in relation to physical education content, complete Self-Directed Activity 1.5 at the end of this chapter.***

Physical Education Curriculum Models

Historically, the goals of physical education have reflected the popular culture. During the early twentieth century, the primary goal was health and hygiene. The dominant goal of the 1920s emphasized social and recreational objectives. This was followed by the war years, during which physical fitness was almost the sole purpose. The goal of "total fitness" was evident during the 1950s. Throughout the 1970s, human rights, individual social freedom, equality, and independence defined the social scene. Individualized needs were reflected through the goals of "movement education" at the elementary level and "lifetime pursuits" at the secondary level. More recently, the concept of wellness focuses on disease prevention rather than treatment of sickness. Disease-prevention measures include personal health regimens and lifestyles that emphasize fitness.

Throughout this history, various models of the physical education curriculum evolved, some as a direct extension of the dominant values at the time. Entire models or elements from different models can serve as a context for your own design. The models are useful for making curriculum decisions since they represent a general set of beliefs. You will see how many of these models reflect the philosophical viewpoints described previously.

Allowing for overlap and duplication, the nine models were derived from various sources (Harrison & Blakemore, 1992; Hellison & Templin, 1991; Jewett & Bain, 1985; Lawson & Placek, 1981; Siedentop, 1994a; Siedentop, Mand, & Taggart, 1986). Each model includes a rationale, description, and framework for design. Determine what aspects you like and dislike . . . and why!

Movement Education

In the search for a structure for physical education, answers to two fundamental questions provide the content of the basic movement model: How do humans move? Why do humans move? Basic sequential units introduce fundamentals of movement, particularly at the elementary level. Emphasis is placed on exploring (through guided discovery and problem solving) various movement skills in areas such as dance, games, and gymnastics. Students create ways of using their bodies to achieve certain outcomes. The curriculum could be structured around the following questions (Gilliom, 1970):

- Where can you move? (space)
- What can you move? (body awareness)
- How do you move? (force, balance, weight transfer)
- How can you move better? (time, flow)

Fitness Education

Increasingly, children are inclined to sedentary lifestyles. Society and the environment make it difficult to remain active. Physical fitness is essential to wellness, an enhanced dimension of health. An active lifestyle can help eliminate health risk factors that cause degenerative diseases and chronic ailments such as atherosclerosis, high blood pressure, obesity, and low back problems. Fitness goals include knowledge of the effects of exercise, design of personal programs based on fitness principles, activities that develop fitness, and commitment to maintaining physical fitness. The curriculum could be designed around the following subject matter:

- Health-related components (flexibility, cardiorespiratory endurance, muscular strength and endurance, and body composition)
- Motor-related components (balance, coordination, speed, agility, and power)
- Assessment methods for diagnosis and activity prescription across all components
- Application of principles of training and conditioning
- Nutrition, diet, and weight control
- Stress management
- Lifestyle management including design and use of a personalized fitness program

Developmental Education

Educators have an obligation to create a learning environment that recognizes and fosters individual potential. Since students follow developmental stages and growth patterns, education should enhance cognitive, affective, and psychomotor learning. The contribution of physical education to these developmental patterns is the essence of "education-through-the-physical." It often means that basic skills are taught at the elementary level, followed by varied activities or theme units, including lifetime sports, at the secondary level. The assumption is that participation in a wide range of activities will result in cognitive, affective, and psychomotor development, regardless of individual variation. The curriculum could be designed around the following objectives (Annarino, 1978):

Organic development

- Strength (static, dynamic)
- Endurance (muscle, cardiovascular)
- Flexibility (extent, dynamic)

Neuromuscular development

- Perceptual motor abilities (balance, kinesthesis, visual discrimination, auditory discrimination, visual motor coordination, tactile sensitivity)
- Fundamental movement skills (body manipulation, object manipulation, sport)

Intellectual development

- Knowledge (rules, safety, etiquette, terms, body functions)
- Intellectual skills and abilities (strategies, movement judgments, solving movement problems, understanding relationships, understanding immediate/long-range effects)

Social-personal-emotional development

- Healthy response (positive reactions to success/failure, appreciation of aesthetics, tension release, fun, spectator appreciation)
- Self-actualization (awareness of capability, capacity, and potential; level of aspiration)
- Self-esteem (individual perception)

Activity-Based Education

Given the changing needs of learners, a wide variety of activities offers an opportunity to facilitate growth. Exposure to various activities enhances self-testing, exploration, and new interests. Usually, the program is organized around a series of activity units, whether required, elective, or in some combination. Typical categories of activities include team sports, individual/dual activities, outdoor/recreational pursuits, rhythms/dance, games, and popular local activities. In selecting activities, consideration is often given to teacher interest, teacher ability, student choice, facilities and equipment, seasonality, and the local culture. The curriculum could be designed around the categories and activities listed in Table 1.2.

Humanistic/Social Development

The anxiety and insecurity produced by a rapidly changing society warrants an emphasis on humanistic and social development. Many believe that children exhibit more and more disruptive behavior as uncertainty builds. While developmental education stresses total well-being, humanistic/social development emphasizes self-awareness and choice as a basis for personal growth. In the search for personal identity, physical activities are used as the medium. Focus is placed on both emotional concepts such as self-esteem, self-actualization, personal meaning, and self-understanding, and social concepts such as interpersonal relations, sharing, cooperation, and tolerance. A genuine, caring teacher is required who facilitates and counsels rather than one who prescribes and directs. As self-discipline emerges, students are allowed to develop and implement personal activity programs. They maintain a record of their goals, feelings, and behaviors. The curriculum could be designed around the following stages of social awareness and development (Hellison, 1985):

Irresponsibility

- Refuses to participate
- Blames others, makes excuses, ridicules others
- Is difficult to manage

Self-control

- Does not disrupt others
- Begins to participate and learn
- Displays fundamental self-discipline
- Begins to accept responsibility for own actions

Involvement

- Participates willingly in physical activity
- Accepts challenges when participating
- Shows enthusiasm without prompting

Self-responsibility

- Makes some decisions
- Takes responsibility for consequences of actions

Caring

- Exhibits behaviors beyond "self"
- Cooperates and expresses concern for others
- Demonstrates a willingness to help
- Provides support for others

Sport Education

Some people think that the health and vitality of our culture is determined by the role of sport. Since sport is a higher form of competitive motor play, it should be central to physical education. In sport education, learners are taught to be *players* in ways similar to athletic participation. Emphasis is placed on skills, rules, strategies, appreciation for play in our society, and ethical principles that define "good" sport.

Table 1.2 Content Areas for Activity-Based Model

Individual/Dual		
Aquatics	Fencing	Racquetball
• Diving	Golf	Self-defense
• Scuba diving	Gymnastics	Skiing
• Skin diving	Handball	• Snow
• Swimming	Low-organization games	• Water
• Synchronized swimming	Martial Arts	Table tennis
• Water polo	• Aikido	Tennis
Archery	• Judo	Track and field
Badminton	• Karate	Trampoline
Bowling	• Tae kwon do	Weight training
Conditioning	Mimetics	Wrestling
• Aerobic dance	• Sport actions	Yoga
• Calisthenics	• Story plays	
• Circuit training	Movement exploration	
• Jogging	• Expressive	
• Rope jumping	• Fundamental	
Team sports	**Rhythms/Dance**	**Outdoor/Recreational**
Baseball	Ballet	Adventure tasks
Basketball	Creative rhythms	Angling
Football	Folk	Backpacking
• Flag	Modern	Camping
• Touch	Singing games	Canoeing
Hockey	Social	Cycling
• Field	Square	New games
• Floor		Orienteering
Lacrosse		Rappelling
Soccer		Sailing
Speedball		Surfing
Team handball		
Volleyball		

Everyone has a role to play in the sport education curriculum model.

Sport education may occur within individual classes, across classes within a class period, and during time outside of class previously used for drop-in or intramurals. In order to maximize participation, adult forms of sport can be changed. Examples of modified sports are six-on-a-team soccer, three-person volleyball, "team" tennis, and three-person basketball. The curriculum could be designed around the six primary features of institutionalized sport (Siedentop, 1994b; Siedentop, Mand, & Taggart, 1986):

- *Seasons*—Sports are organized by seasons, not units; includes both practice and competition, and often ends with a culminating event.
- *Affiliation*—Students quickly become members of teams or clubs; membership is usually retained throughout the season.
- *Formal competition*—Sport seasons include formal schedules of competition interspersed with practice sessions.
- *Culminating event*—A competitive event highlights the season and provides goals for players to work toward.
- *Keeping records*—Records are publicized that provide feedback, define standards, and establish goals for players and teams.
- *Festivity*—The festive atmosphere of sport enhances its meaning and adds an important social element for participants.

Wilderness Sports and Adventure Education

Experiential learning is lacking in schools, particularly in relation to natural phenomena. Abstraction is substituted for sensory learning. Physical education offers unlimited potential when it comes to group involvement, leisure skills, personal commitment, risk, unique environments, and social relationships. Wilderness sports promote physically challenging outdoor activities such as camping, backpacking, canoeing, hiking, orienteering, cross-country skiing, snowshoeing, and cycling. Adventure education, although related to wilderness sports, is different. It involves activities in which obstacles are contrived or environments are created that challenge students to solve individual or group problems while under stress. Examples of activities include indoor and outdoor wall climbing, trust falls, cooperation games, high-ropes courses, and group initiative activities (Hammersley, 1992). Obviously, most of these activities are conducted away from school, at special times, and by special arrangements. The curriculum could be designed around the following general goals (Siedentop, Mand, & Taggart, 1986):

- Develop outdoor sports skills; enjoy satisfaction of competence.
- Live within the limits of personal ability in relation to the environment and physical activities.
- Derive pleasure in accepting the challenge and risk of stressful physical activity.
- Develop awareness of mutual dependency of self and natural world.
- Share experiences and learning in cooperation with others.

Conceptually Based Education

Students are always asking "why" and "how" kinds of questions. A curriculum based on concepts emphasizes knowledge and understanding. Typically, a problem-solving approach is used in laboratory and activity settings. It is assumed that concepts (e.g., follow-through, receiving force) transfer to new skills and situations, and that they are learned better when taught *explicitly*. Subject matter is organized around key ideas or principles, progressing from simple to more complex understanding.

For example, the concept of "zone defense" (i.e., defending an area as opposed to a player) and its underlying meaning can be learned and then applied to various sports (e.g., basketball, football, soccer, floor hockey, volleyball). The subdisciplines of physical education are useful for identifying and organizing concepts. The curriculum could be designed around the following biomechanics concepts (Lawson & Placek, 1981):

- Center of gravity
- Balance factors
- Application of force
- Action on objects
- Laws of motion
- Performance analysis and adjustment

Personally Meaningful Education

The search for meaning is central to the mission of education. Personal meaning can be derived either intrinsically or extrinsically. For example, feelings of joy, pleasure, and satisfaction may be inherent to a movement experience (e.g., gymnastics routine, kicking a ball into a goal). The movement activity could also be used to reach some extrinsic goal (e.g., cardiovascular efficiency, object manipulation). This curriculum model responds to learners' individual and collective search for meaning. Concepts such as personal involvement with sports, self-directed learning, and individual human goals are associated with finding or extending personal meaning through movement activities. In other words, what purposes are served through "moving" that bring meaning to students? The curriculum could be designed around the following purposes (Jewett & Mullan, 1977):

I. Individual development
  A. Physiological efficiency
    - Circulorespiratory efficiency
    - Mechanical efficiency
    - Neuromuscular efficiency
  B. Psychic equilibrium
    - Joy of movement
    - Self-knowledge
    - Catharsis
    - Challenge

II. Environmental coping
  A. Spatial orientation
    - Awareness
    - Relocation
    - Relationships
  B. Object manipulation
    - Maneuvering weight
    - Object projection
    - Object reception

III. Social interaction
  A. Communication
    - Expression
    - Clarification
    - Simulation
  B. Group interaction
    - Teamwork
    - Competition
    - Leadership
  C. Cultural involvement
    - Participation
    - Movement appreciation
    - Cultural understanding

▶ ***What do you think about some of the more popular curriculum models in physical education? To rank these models to reflect your own preferences, complete Self-Directed Activity 1.6 at the end of this chapter.***

MAKING IT WORK

Have you achieved the expected outcomes (page 2)? Congratulations! You are able to establish a foundation for your physical education curriculum design. Still, you may have some practical questions that need answers, such as:

■ **Do curriculum designers really exist?**

If your K–12 experiences in physical education were negative, you probably have doubts. It's true that physical education is being reduced or eliminated in many schools, in part because of weak programs and poor teaching. However, it is strongly supported in just as many schools, where teachers have assumed the role of designer. Although curriculum designing may be difficult and time-consuming *at first*, it will save you effort and time in the long run. Once students learn your "system," your task becomes primarily one of curriculum refinement and revision. Besides, the wave of social and cultural changes in the United States is so great that teachers need to develop programs for increasingly diverse groups of students. To survive as a teacher in the current atmosphere of accountability, you will need to be competent in the role of curriculum designer.

■ **Why should physical educators be concerned with general education trends?**

We need to stop thinking that we are "outside" the school curriculum. Granted, we may be somewhat physically separated, but we have allowed ourselves to become psychologically separated as well. The result is that physical education is excluded due to its label as a special subject. Theoretically, changes in education should have the same impact on physical education as on any other subject, and the implications of recent trends for physical education have been clearly established. For example, physical education teachers can be leaders in the "culturally responsive" movement by taking advantage of our strong social orientation. Students come from radically different social, ethnic, and racial backgrounds. Physical education, through its various forms of movement, offers a unique opportunity for students to develop the understanding and sensitivity needed to function in a diverse society. Another trend that has an impact on physical education is "inclusion." Since we alone represent the physical dimension of education, our contribution to an individualized, developmentally appropriate program should be distinct. And finally, student outcome standards seem to be everywhere—at national, state, and local levels. Parents, legislators, business leaders, and others are focused on the products (outcomes) of education. Physical education has responded with its own set of standards as previously identified.

■ **Is one's philosophical viewpoint really that important?**

Without a set of beliefs and values, you run the risk of teaching by intuition. Usually, the result is inconsistent and illogical behavior leading to confusion. Curriculum designing is a conscious act. Given all the available options, you should know what you believe and value and what you do not. If necessary, write down your beliefs and values as they come to mind. It might help to compare your list with known philosophies to see if there are any discrepancies within your viewpoints. Then, make sure that your curriculum decisions are a true extension of these beliefs and values. That's easier said than done! But if you subscribe to the curriculum planning process proposed here, there are enough checks and balances across the curriculum components to give you some assurance.

■ **Can students' needs actually be used as a basis for curriculum design?**

Of course, as long as these needs are satisfied explicitly. Cognitive and psychomotor needs are usually easier to satisfy than affective needs, because they are more easily observed and measured. Don't make the mistake of many physical educators, that is, establishing lofty affective goals (e.g., teamwork, sportsmanship, tolerance), but not planning for them explicitly. Instead, these qualities are learned implicitly, if at all. The claim that students have met these affective needs is oftentimes false. Careful curriculum designing can help avoid this error. Without a doubt, students' needs are probably universal to any curriculum design. They may be called learner capabilities, developmental channels, or dimensions, but all these terms are referring to the same thing. Kids *need* to develop and mature physically, intellectually, socially, and emotionally. It's difficult to argue against needs as the foundation upon which curricula are built.

■ **With so many curriculum models to choose from, which one is best?**

There is no single best model. They all may be equally valuable. Your challenge is to eventually develop your own model, however similar it might be to one or more of the known models. Whatever it is, establish a solid rationale for its structure. That is, consideration should be given to various contexts, such as student preferences, parent/guardian preferences, administrative feasibility, school district and state guidelines and standards, and developmental appropriateness. The remaining curriculum components should be developed with reference to your model.

Self-Directed Activity 1.1

Trends in education usually emerge in response to social forces. They serve as an important context when designing a curriculum. Having reviewed some of these trends, ideally, your own beliefs and values were challenged. How would these trends influence your design? In other words, what are the *general* implications for your physical education curriculum?

1. Culturally responsive pedagogy

   Implications: ______________________________

   ____

   ____

2. Inclusive education

   Implications: ______________________________

   ____

   ____

3. Knowledge-based approach

   Implications: ______________________________

   ____

   ____

4. Developmentally appropriate practices

   Implications: ______________________________

   ____

   ____

5. Outcome-based education

   Implications: ______________________________

   ____

   ____

Feedback

1. For many learners, the culture of the home and the culture of the school fail to match. Try not to think of these learners as "disadvantaged" or "culturally deprived." Instead, see them as experiencing *cultural discontinuity* (Glatthorn, 1993). The physical education curriculum should expand their horizons. A "watered-down" curriculum is counterproductive. Movement experiences should offer new ways of knowing, feeling, and moving. Accept students from diverse ethnic backgrounds in a way that will maximize their strengths, not their differences. An accurate and deep knowledge-based curriculum that emphasizes problem solving is recommended.
2. In some ways, the implications of full inclusion are staggering. Physical education would be integrated with other subjects representing a continuum of learning. A progressive, sequential curriculum would serve the full range of learner variability. Because of the

multidisciplinary nature of full inclusion, personally designed physical education programs would be needed.

3. A knowledge-based physical education curriculum would appear to emphasize intellectual rather than psychomotor skills. Content would revolve around the subdisciplines of physical education rather than actual forms of movement.
4. A developmentally appropriate curriculum in physical education means that teacher interests and preferences are *out* and developmental levels of individual learners are *in*. Thus, the curricular scope and sequence needs to balance learning opportunities that enhance physical, intellectual, emotional, and social development.
5. Curriculum articulation from grade level to grade level is essential in an outcome-based design. For physical education, enabling and final movement expectations would be critical. A systematic "spiral" curriculum is needed. That is, outcomes would build on each other as learners progress on a K–12 continuum.

Self-Directed Activity 1.2

You should be able to resolve issues associated with the physical education curriculum. Each of the following descriptions represents one of these issues. Which of the opposing views (A or B) is supported by the description?

1. The scope and sequence for an elementary school curriculum emphasizes various activity categories: movement exploration (15%), low–organization games and activities (10%), rhythmic activities (10%), individual/dual activities (5%), apparatus activities (10%), basic sports skills (30%), physical fitness testing (5%), team games (13%), and aquatics (2%).

   ____ A. Learner-centered emphasis

   ____ B. Content-centered emphasis

2. Learners direct their own daily exercise programs, a calisthenic routine based on circuit training principles. They begin at Level # 1. As the tasks of each level are completed, they record the date, have it verified, and move on to the next higher level. The partial sequence is:

   - Level #4: Perform exercise routine on own and help someone still performing at a less intense level; produce pulse rate of at least 150 BPM.
   - Level #5: Answer correctly 80% or more of the questions on quiz EX-2; continue exercising on own producing pulse rate of at least 150 BPM.
   - Level #6: Compute submaximum threshold for exercises of routine using the "2/3 method."
   - Level #7: Perform correctly exercises of routine by applying circuit training principles at a submaximum threshold; repeat routine three (3) times; produce pulse rate of at least 150 BPM.
   - Level #8: Determine fitness areas for improvement; add at least two (2) exercises to the routine, one of which must use a piece of available gym equipment; continue to produce pulse rate of at least 150 BMP.
   - Level #9: Redetermine submaximum threshold for all exercises from the routine; attain improvement in three (3) exercise areas.

   ____ A. Individualized focus

   ____ B. Group focus

3. In gymnastics, apparatus for males (high bar, side horse, and parallel bars) and apparatus for females (uneven parallel bars and balance beam) are arranged alternately (i.e., high bar next to balance beam which is also next to the side horse, etc.) so that males and females engage in activity within adjacent areas. Males and females are expected to interact and exchange ideas because of the physical setup. Feedback may be carried out by members of the opposite gender.

____ A. Gender-integrated design

____ B. Gender-segregated design

4. One of the minimum standards for an eighth-grade tennis unit is to hit 25 consecutive shots off the wall at 20 feet using alternating strokes—forehand and backhand. Basic instruction is provided for these strokes. The standard is based on the "average" expected performance for 13-year-old beginners. No pretesting is indicated.

_____ A. Inclusion

_____ B. Exclusion

5. A cognitive goal for a high school curriculum is: "Understand the reasons for maintaining a predetermined level of physical fitness." To help students reach the goal, the following learning experiences are devised:

- Observe a slide/tape presentation concerning the benefits of maintaining fitness; complete a worksheet as participation questions are asked.
- Read printed material describing the relationships among physically active individuals and forms of cardiovascular disease, physical activity and weight control, and physical activity and psychological advantages.
- Complete a physical fitness self-appraisal checklist.
- View a film concerning the design of a personalized physical fitness program.
- Participate in a discussion group; review case studies of individuals with varying physical fitness needs.

_____ A. Alternative learning modes

_____ B. Single learning mode

6. Learners "contract" (or agree) with the teacher to complete certain objectives in order to receive a certain grade. The contract is part of a comprehensive learning packet in beginning swimming. The learner assumes major responsibility for completing learning activities and conducting self-assessment. For example, the competencies for earning a "B" are:

- Perform front crawl for 50 yards with 75% rating for form.
- Perform back crawl for 50 yards with 75% rating for form.
- Perform elementary backstroke for 50 yards with 75% rating for form.
- Perform sidestroke for 50 yards with 75% rating for form.
- Perform breaststroke for 50 yards with 75% rating for form.
- Perform a standing dive with 80% rating for form.
- Demonstrate three elementary lifesaving techniques using correct procedures.
- Pass written test (60%).

_____ A. Personalized approach

_____ B. Authoritarian approach

7. Cooperation is an essential element of any society that requires a balance between personal and group needs. It includes sharing and assisting. In an attempt to develop a cooperative effort, various activities are designed that involve taking turns, sharing equipment, sharing space, sharing ideas, sharing time, and assisting others. Some sample activities are (Evaul, 1980):
   - Form groups of learners with various talents (e.g., very strong, very fast, good thinker, etc.); make up tasks, each of which emphasizes one of the talents.
   - Play games that require sharing (e.g., one-sided volleyball).
   - Participate in "double stunts" in which each partner must perform a task for success (e.g., swan balance, doubles roll).
   - Demonstrate how to take turns on a piece of apparatus; have groups determine and implement their own systems.
   - Have partners work with each other in learning a skill; explain how one spots, gives feedback, and in other ways assists the other in learning.
   - Discuss concept of teamwork; identify various roles on a sports team (e.g., star, playmaker, substitute, coach, manager, statistician, etc.).

   _____ A. Explicit learning

   _____ B. Implicit learning

Feedback

1. B

   This scope and sequence emphasizes content (activities) as the focus, although there is no implication that learners are unimportant.

2. A

   The inherent qualities of individualized instruction (i.e., self-pacing, various levels of development, self-feedback) are reflected.

3. B

   It is suggested that traditional gender-related apparatus are appropriate. However, there is no justifiable rationale for limiting activity to specific pieces of apparatus. At least initially, learners could be encouraged to develop prerequisite skills and abilities and then to improve entry-level skills by a certain amount. As the activities are described, individual needs and equal opportunity to engage in all forms of movement are not afforded.

4. B

   While the description relates to various issues, it primarily deals with inclusion vs. exclusion. Failure is built in for some learners since the standard is geared to the norm (average). A number of learners will lack prerequisite abilities. Ideally, different entry points would be established for individual learners with "improvement" standards based on beginning competencies.

5. A

   Various patterns of learning are planned that contribute to the same goal. Because of learning style preferences, alternative experiences should enhance overall learning. Thus, another set of individualized options emerges when such consideration is given.

6. A

   By definition, personalized learning means that *what* is to be learned is adjusted to learner needs and characteristics. That is, the learner product is personalized. Such is the case with contract learning as described.

7. A

Learning has been described for social (affective) outcomes by creating activities that result in the *explicit* development of cooperation. Behaviors associated with a cooperative effort are elicited directly; they do not occur in an assumed (implicit) way. In this example, cooperation is the purpose; it becomes the focus for learning.

Self-Directed Activity 1.3

Now that you are familiar with traditional philosophies, you should be able to defend your own beliefs and values against these philosophies. Indicate whether you agree or disagree with the following statements, and briefly explain why.

1. The *idealist's* program enhances the individual by developing the mind; values such as dedication and sacrifice are developed through one's experiences; play and recreation can be used to develop a well-balanced personality.

   Agree _____ Disagree _____ Why? ____

   ____

2. *Realism* advances the idea that the mind and body are inseparable; an adequate physical body permits the intellect to function; the world is accepted as it is because people are unable to change the "world of cause and effect"; greater productivity results from the development of physical fitness.

   Agree _____ Disagree _____ Why? ____

   ____

3. *Naturalism* is fairly simple, based on individual rates of development (learning readiness); individual goals are more important than social goals; self-improvement is emphasized, in which students compete against themselves.

   Agree _____ Disagree _____ Why? ____

   ____

4. The experimental approach of the *pragmatist* (learn by doing) results in the pursuit of many different goals; students have a great deal of flexibility in their learning since there are no predetermined or fixed aims and values.

   Agree _____ Disagree _____ Why? ____

   ____

5. The educational process of the *existentialist* revolves totally around each student's individual needs and interests; students create their own values and ideals without much regard for their impact on society.

   Agree _____ Disagree _____ Why? ____

   ____

6. Physiological outcomes dominate the *education-of-the-physical* philosophy; physical education that focuses on the components of physical fitness will make a significant contribution to society in the long run.

   Agree _____ Disagree _____ Why? ____

   ____

7. The multidimensional nature of *education-through-the-physical* attempts to satisfy all the goals of general education; physical education serves as the medium for developing goals such as emotional stability, intellectual functioning, worthy use of leisure time, psychomotor skills, and social responsibility.

   Agree _____ Disagree _____ Why? ____

   ____

Feedback

1. The idealist's concern for the mind could result in too little attention to the body. In terms of past experiences, there's always the chance that those experiences were inadequate in establishing the values as worthwhile. Finally, some view physical education as work. Thus, it might be difficult to accept play as the basis for programming.
2. Physical education serves a unique function for the realist because of the harmonious relationship between mind and body. This view of the world can lead to more healthful living, particularly if people are more productive in society due to a high level of physical fitness.
3. Education based on a more natural, simple world might be a welcomed change. However, students with such education may have difficulty coping with an increasingly complex world. In a highly technological, scientifically oriented society, an education based on naturalism could have its limitations.
4. In its pragmatic attempt to seek any and all broad goals, the physical education program may be spread too thin. The stability and direction needed by many students is not available because of the indefinite goals and values of the pragmatist.
5. With existentialism, individuality may become more of the focus in school than in real life. Students could develop values and ideals that counter society (e.g., uncooperative behavior) and work only outside of society.
6. Granted, the development of cardiorespiratory efficiency, muscular strength and endurance, power, and motor ability is of primary importance in the physical education curriculum, but it might be too limited. Psychosocial values could be neglected in a one-dimensional, education-of-the-physical approach.
7. Education-through-the-physical aims at the broad goals of education. This philosophical basis for action helps justify physical education in the school curriculum. However, this potential has not produced the desired results in all cases.

Self-Directed Activity 1.4

You should have some opinions about the philosophical viewpoints in physical education. To see how they compare to your own beliefs and values, indicate whether you agree or disagree with the following statements. Then briefly explain why.

1. The content of *human movement* is also its method (exploration, problem solving, challenge); concepts of movement are the core; skill patterns and behavior are developed and refined according to movement principles.

   Agree _____ Disagree _____ Why? ______________________________

   ____

2. Personal growth and self-development define the *humanistic* philosophy; values clarification and social development are considered as important as academic development.

   Agree _____ Disagree _____ Why? ______________________________

   ____

3. The *play approach* stresses intrinsic aims and objectives, since activities are inherently meaningful; intrinsic learning offers the best opportunity for retention, transfer, and positive self-concept.

   Agree _____ Disagree _____ Why? ______________________________

   ____

4. *Sport sciences* defines physical education by its subdisciplines; content is based on the body of knowledge underlying exercise physiology, kinesiology, motor learning and development, sport sociology, sport psychology, and sport humanities.

   Agree _____ Disagree _____ Why? ______________________________

   ____

5. *Fitness* and the concept of *wellness* represent a holistic view of health; work, play, and social life are approached positively; lifestyle management is needed.

   Agree _____ Disagree _____ Why? ______________________________

   ____

Feedback

1. There may be a lack of emphasis on sport and an overemphasis on cognitive aspects. Human movement does provide a basis for organizing the curriculum, however.
2. In many ways, society has become more conservative. Although there is clearly a back-to-basics emphasis that rejects more affective approaches to education, humanistic goals are still valid.
3. The play approach is intriguing and thought-provoking, and in many ways desirable. But it may not fit today's educational scene and lifestyles, in which people seem to prefer both intrinsic and extrinsic motivation. However, the prospects for sport education at the secondary level seem promising. Interest among participants may be enhanced since the play approach models itself on competitive sports.

4. As a potential program for school physical education, sport studies represent an extreme departure from activity-based approaches. The academic rigor associated with this philosophy would need to be endorsed by practitioners.
5. The health-related benefits of fitness-wellness are universally accepted. Lifestyle management begins with children and youth, not adults. It is difficult to imagine a program of physical education without some fitness component.

Self-Directed Activity 1.5

Needs of learners are basic to the proposed meaning of physical education. You should be able to recognize these needs in relation to physical education content. Indicate which need is associated with the philosophical descriptions.

C = Cognitive
A = Affective
P = Psychomotor

_____ 1. An essential purpose of physical education is an understanding of scientific principles of movement and of the relationship of physical fitness to personal well-being and long-term health.

_____ 2. The development of self-esteem (personal evaluation of basic beliefs about self) is enhanced by one's perceptions of one's own performance in a movement activity.

_____ 3. Movement education contributes to one's ability to function in harmony with others (cooperation) by pursuing common goals (teamwork), seeking individual or group goals (competition), and influencing others' achievement of goals (leadership).

_____ 4. In order to develop and maintain motor efficiency, the nervous and muscular systems function harmoniously to produce locomotor, nonlocomotor, manipulative, and sport skills.

_____ 5. Such concepts as aesthetic appreciation, fair play, and democracy can result from participation in physical activity.

_____ 6. Various forms of physical activity serve a "therapeutic" function by releasing tensions and reducing the stress brought on by the pressures of contemporary life.

_____ 7. Since communication is a fundamental human activity, movement forms such as dance, gymnastics, and synchronized swimming are important media for sharing and evaluating ideas within a group.

_____ 8. The ability to explore, discover, and solve problems through movement establishes relationships among physical activity, body function and structure, and mental judgments of distance, time, form, space, speed, and direction.

_____ 9. The development of interests and values regarding physical activity, maintenance of physical fitness, and success in movement are challenging, worthwhile goals of physical education.

_____ 10. Development of flexibility, strength, and muscular and cardiorespiratory endurance allows one to meet the activity demands placed upon each of us by the environment.

Feedback

1. C

   Knowledge and application of movement principles could include the design of a personal fitness program. An intellectual (cognitive) need is satisfied by carrying out this process. Obviously, an individual must also enjoy physical activity (affective domain) if the program is implemented.

2. A

   Positive self-image, self-confidence, and self-respect fulfill a basic emotional (affective) need as one moves to gain self-understanding and appreciation.

3. A

   People need to grow and mature socially (affective domain). The elements incorporated in this description include the feeling of belonging, having status or respect in social groups, and having a helping relationship with others.

4. P

   This integration of the nervous and muscular systems satisfies the need for neuromuscular efficiency, which is clearly psychomotor (optimal body functioning).

5. A

   The description suggests that values are realized through physical performance. As a result, affective needs are satisfied.

6. A

   Emotional (affective) response is concerned not only with the control of emotions (enthusiasm, hostility, depression) but also with outlets for pent-up emotions and self-expression that can be provided through movement.

7. A

   Physical education provides a unique setting for sharing ideas and feelings with others. This social (affective) need, to express personal ideas and feelings, can be met through other forms of nonverbal communication.

8. C

   The need to develop intellectual (cognitive) capabilities is satisfied through challenges involving exploration, discovery, and problem solving. Related intellectual abilities such as original thinking, creative thinking, reflective thinking, critical thinking, and decision making are fundamental to this philosophical orientation.

9. A

   Values assessment, development, and clarification are indicated, which meet needs associated with the affective domain.

10. P

    Although a social environment is suggested by this description, a psychomotor need (organic development) is served. Proper functioning of body systems is necessary for an active life.

Self-Directed Activity 1.6

What do you think about some of the more popular curriculum models in physical education? Rank these models to reflect your own preferences (1 = most preferred; 9 = least preferred). Then, indicate the reasons for your top two or three ranked models as well as your bottom two or three ranked models.

_____ Movement education
_____ Fitness education
_____ Developmental education
_____ Activity-based education
_____ Humanistic/Social development
_____ Sport education
_____ Wilderness sports and adventure education
_____ Conceptually-based education
_____ Personally meaningful education

Reasons for top rankings: ______________________________

____

____

____

____

Reasons for bottom rankings: ______________________________

____

____

____

____

Feedback

This was probably a difficult task. Some of the models overlap in meaning. You may also feel that some models are more suited to elementary-aged learners whereas others are more appropriate for adolescents or young adults. Furthermore, there are probably elements of some models that you like, while other aspects of those same models make them less appealing. In any case, there are no right or wrong answers. By now, maybe you have identified your own model based on your own set of beliefs or assumptions. Have you?

2

Creating Organizing Centers

Key Concept

Curriculum designers develop organizing centers representing broad learning perspectives around which physical education curricula are designed.

Tax levies have been defeated three consecutive times at a poor, rural school district. Voters claim they are disappointed with the overall quality of education. They are determined not to support any tax increase until there is improvement. School officials agree that a systematic approach is needed for curriculum revision and therefore they establish a general K–12 curriculum committee with subcommittees for each subject area. The physical education subcommittee, chaired by the district supervisor, includes two teachers each from the elementary, middle, and high school levels. Initially, each subcommittee is asked to propose a set of elements or concepts around which to organize its curriculum. Members of the physical education subcommittee realize, for the first time, that they have a difficult task ahead of them. In fact, one of the teachers says, "Where do we begin?"

Expected Outcomes

This chapter helps you create organizing centers as the focus for your curriculum design. Upon completing it, you will be able to

- define the characteristics of organizing centers;
- identify organizing centers from the following sources: society, learner needs and interests, and physical education subject matter;
- generate alternative organizing centers for the physical education curriculum; and
- select organizing centers using philosophical and psychological screens.

The most critical factor in the designing process is establishing a consistent basis for the curriculum that can be understood by all. This helps answer the question, "Where are you going?" A broad perspective is recommended as a starting point—the organizing center. It serves as the criterion by which content goals are determined, learner analysis is conducted, learning objectives are derived, evaluation procedures are developed, and learning experiences are devised. The curriculum designing model in Figure 2.1 shows this first step, *creating organizing centers*.

Because of the central role of organizing centers, some questions arise. "What are organizing centers?" "Where do they come from?" "What are some exemplary organizing centers?" "How are organizing centers chosen?" Answers to these questions are provided in the following sections. Ultimately, you should be able to create organizing centers for your own physical education curriculum.

Focus for Curriculum Design

In all probability, the most important curriculum decision you'll make is the one that establishes the central reason for your design. Organizing centers serve this purpose. Therefore, this chapter defines and illustrates them; explains their vertical and horizontal dimensions as ways to sequence and integrate a curriculum; compares traditional organizing centers to alternative ones; and applies the principle of specificity.

Organizing Centers Defined

Usually, school curricula lack focus. Organizing centers, however, help to identify elements that can serve as focal points. They become the frames of reference around which curricula are designed. Organizing centers combine those concepts, skills, attitudes, and values underlying physical education goals and content. *They are global in nature.* The resulting program is a series of organizing centers sequentially arranged over various time periods (e.g., teaching episode, single lesson, series of lessons, unit of instruction, semester, academic year, four-year high school curriculum, or comprehensive K–12 curriculum).

Organizing centers range from comprehensive themes such as "Education for a Global Community," "Worthy Citizenship," or "Meeting the Challenge of a Changing Society" to specific emphases such as "Body Awareness," "Teamwork," or "Solving a Problem." Intermediate ideas can also be used such as "Growth and Development," "Success," or "Decision Making." Regardless of their complexity, organizing centers offer a basis for the subsequent development of the other curriculum components.

Vertical and Horizontal Dimensions

The relationship between what is learned at one level and what is learned at another determines the *vertical* organization of curriculum. Organizing centers foster vertical articulation (continuous use) and sequence (progressive development). For example, if the learner is to develop a meaningful concept of "body awareness," the concept must be dealt with

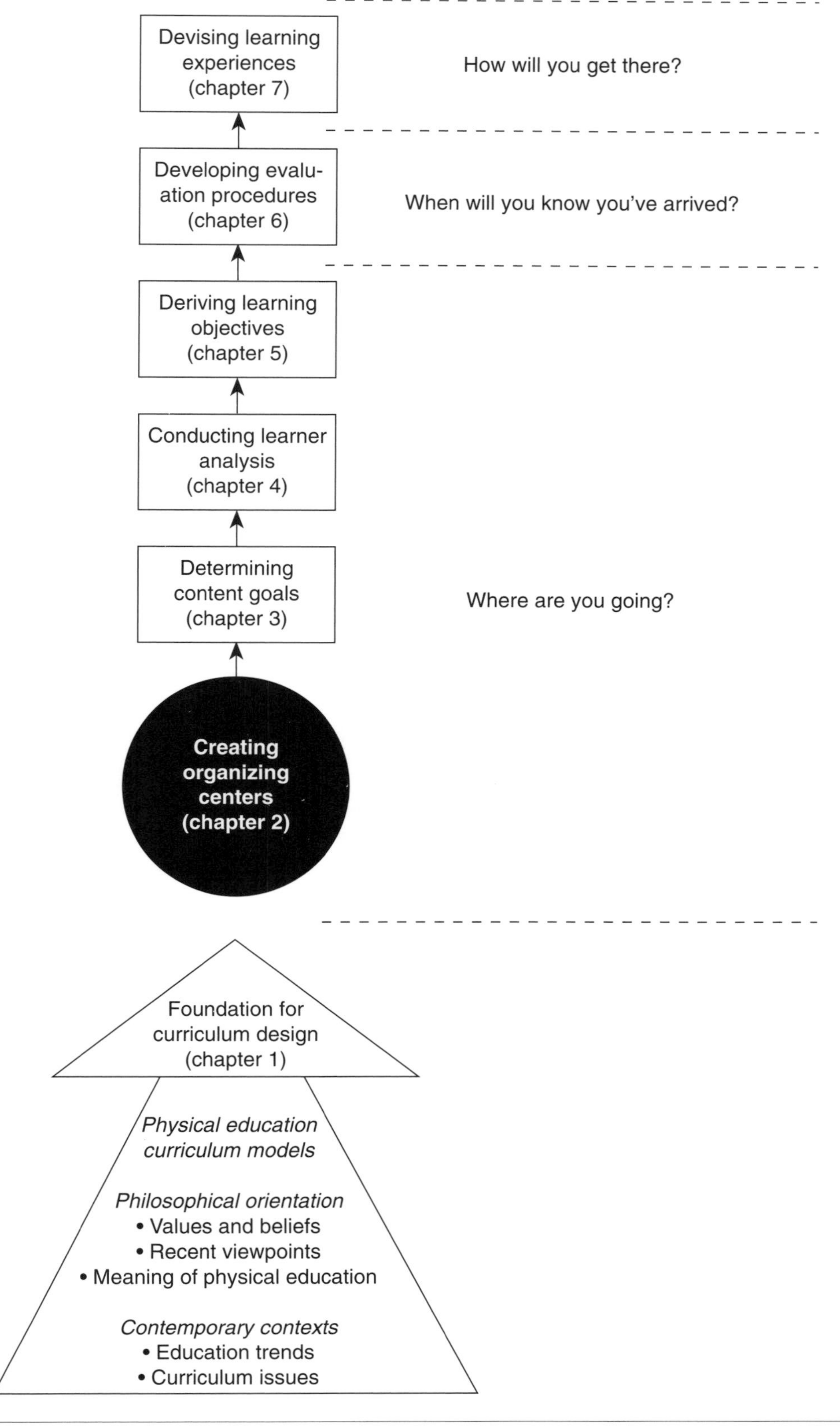

Figure 2.1 Model for designing the physical education curriculum shows the first step, *creating organizing centers.*

continually at planned intervals. The progression could begin with an awareness of self (body parts, movement potential, kinesthesia) followed by the development of fundamental motor skills (appropriate use of body parts, productive movement combinations). The next phase might include the understanding of and proficiency in various combinations of movement elements (space, time, force, quality). The appreciation for and application of specialized movement skills (bowling, volleyball set, softball pitch) would occur in later phases. In Figure 2.2, "Developmental Movement" is used as an organizing center to illustrate vertical articulation and sequence.

The relationship between physical education and other subjects, like art and science, determines the *horizontal* organization of curriculum. Organizing centers can integrate the overall curriculum. For example, the concept of "interdependence" could apply to different subjects and serve as a thread for weaving a more unified curriculum. Horizontal integration is also shown in Figure 2.2.

As a curriculum becomes more integrated and physical educators find themselves on teams with other subject specialists, units may be developed around organizing centers. In such units, forms of movement (sports, games, stunts, dual activities) function as the medium for learning rather than as

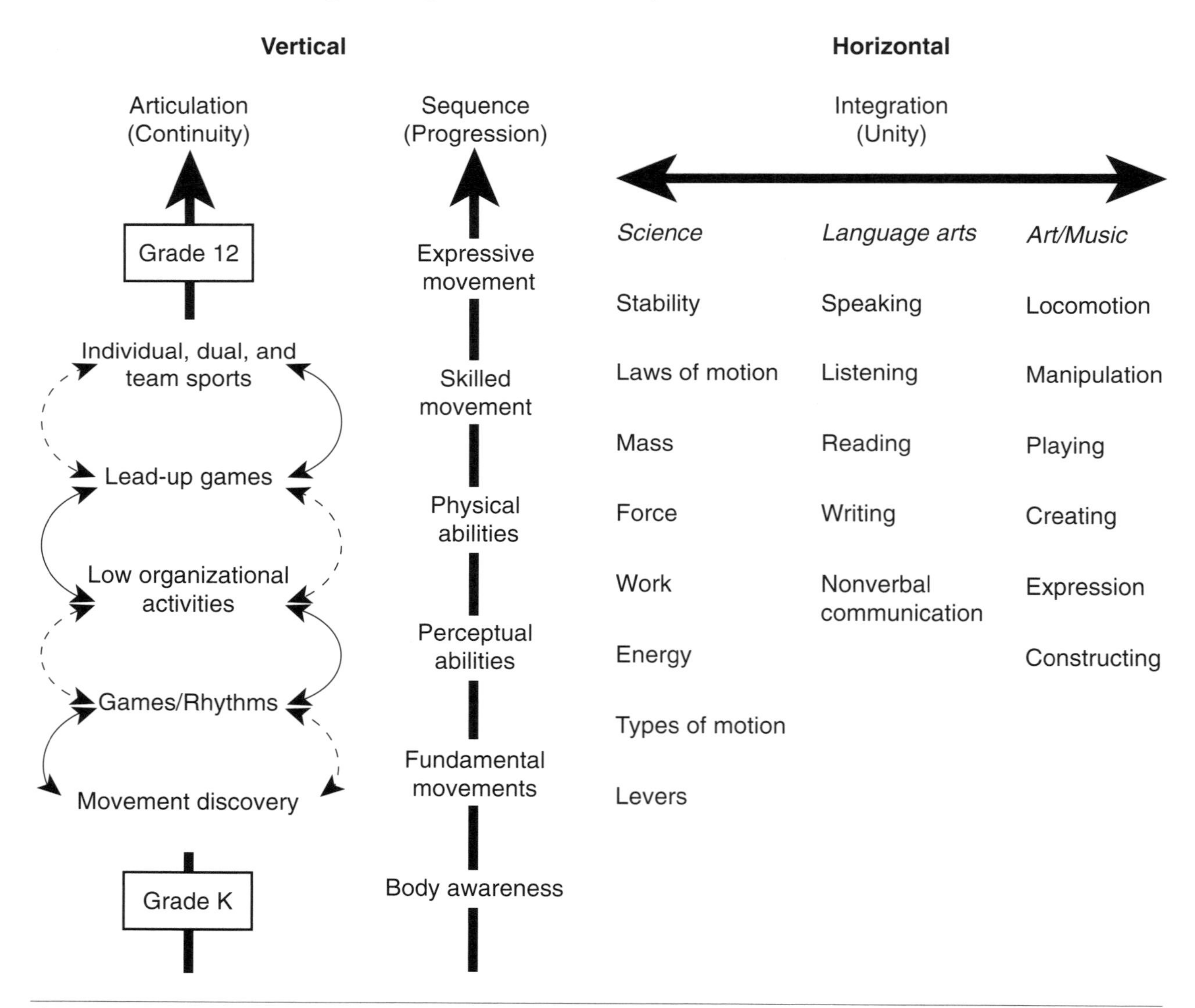

Figure 2.2 "Developmental Movement" is used as an organizing center to illustrate the vertical and horizontal relationships in a curriculum.

ends in themselves. Exemplary organizing centers are (Evaul, 1980)

- Mechanics of Movement (physics, math, physical education),
- Movement and the Arts (music, art, humanities, physical education),
- Measuring Human Performance (math, biology, physical education), and
- Communication (language arts, speech, physical education).

Traditional Organizing Centers

The idea of designing a curriculum around some frame of reference is certainly not new. However, efforts have not always produced the desired results. Many traditional organizing centers in physical education are not related directly to learning outcomes. Such traditional centers have included activities, seasonality, teachers' interests, available equipment, existing facilities, teachers' skill, available staff, teacher-student ratio, and time. Although these elements represent practical considerations, they are not sufficient as organizing criteria. It is impossible to determine which dimensions of activities should be emphasized, which details are relevant, and which relationships are significant.

Physical activities (games, sports, dance, gymnastics, and exercises) continue to be the dominant organizing theme. Units such as volleyball, tumbling, rhythms, and relay races are usually specified. However, even specific activities lack focus since each related detail seems equally important. For example, making volleyball an organizing center could emphasize anything, such as rules interpretation, offensive skills development, or competitive spirit. This view assumes that desirable outcomes such as self-expression, respect for others, and self-control are attained by participating in volleyball, through implicit learning.

While teachers use activities for organizing physical education, learners are expected to develop, for example, certain psychosocial values. However, learners tend to focus on the activity, not the psychosocial values. This problem is reduced if the values become the basis for organizing subject matter. These patterns are depicted in Figure 2.3. Both are logical. The primary goal of pattern 1 is to develop distinct activities, although the depth and breadth of learning would be limited. The primary goal of pattern 2 is to develop general concepts, skills, attitudes, and values. It is the recommended scheme, particularly since learners' needs could serve as the focus. The curriculum would then be based on *explicit* values as organizing centers.

Principle of Specificity

The principle of specificity has been documented through learning research. If concepts, skills, attitudes, and values are to be learned, they must be taught directly. These aspects become the focus for design, and they provide a basis for specifying the

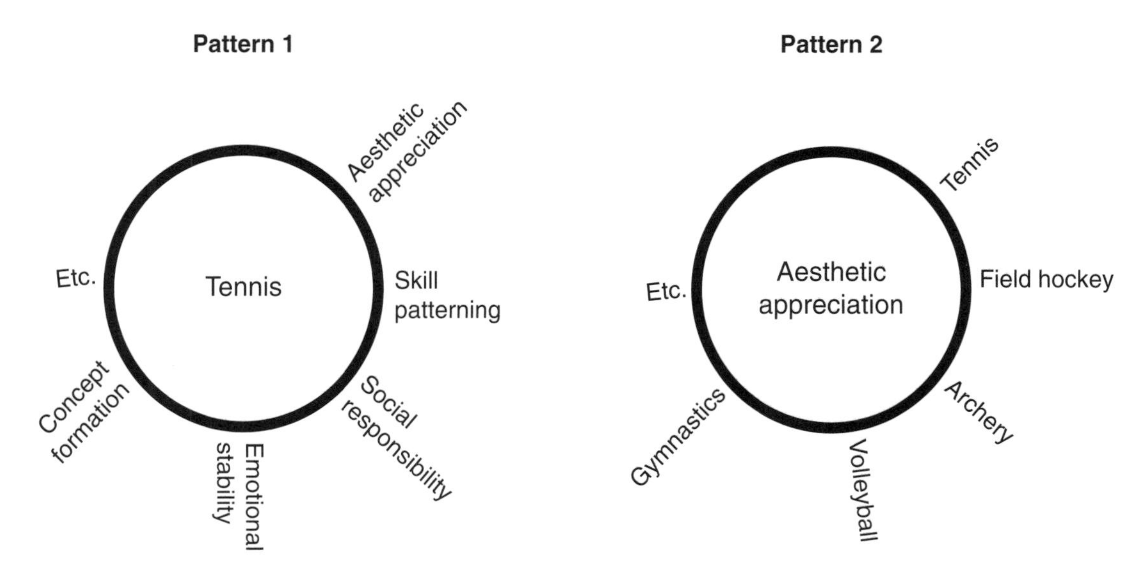

Figure 2.3 Patterns for organizing physical education subject matter are shown. Pattern 1 illustrates the use of an activity as an organizing center. Pattern 2 illustrates the use of an explicit concept, attitude, value, or skill as an organizing center.

content to be treated. For example, if the concept "interactive ethical behavior" is used as an organizing center, it is necessary to examine, plan for, and foster such things as cooperation, sharing, concern for the welfare of others, fairness, and personal reliability. Content is structured in accordance with these concepts.

This principle is illustrated in Figure 2.4. The traditional approach to organizing physical education through activities is depicted in pattern 1. It assumes that such goals as skill patterns, sportsmanship, cooperation, confidence, and progression result from learning the activity. However, history and research have not borne this out (Evaul, 1973). Therefore, the goals should be the basis for organization, rather than the activities (pattern 2). An alternative curriculum is created by simply changing the directional focus of organizing centers. First, the concepts, skills, attitudes, and values to be learned are identified, and then those activities that would contribute best to accomplishing the goals are selected.

Organizing centers also help to limit the amount of detail that must be learned. This principle supports the use of common knowledge, skills, or values as bases for organization. The relentless repetition of content can be reduced if *core* ideas are used. Suppose that skill patterns form the organizing center and that the overhand motion, follow-through, step-in-direction, and length of lever are supporting concepts. You would need to select activities that would contribute to learners' understanding and development of these skill patterns. For example, the overhand motion is used in the tennis serve, volleyball spike, and softball throw. Similarly, the effect of the length of the lever in supplying speed and power to an object is applied in the tennis forehand, volleyball serve, and softball hit. Since these concepts are common to many content areas (tennis, volleyball, softball), the amount of detail to be learned is significantly reduced and time is saved. Learning is usually more meaningful and retention is enhanced.

▶ ***To make sure you understand the concept of organizing centers, complete Self-Directed Activity 2.1 at the end of this chapter.***

Sources of Organizing Centers

You might believe that since organizing centers are consciously willed, they are simply a matter of personal preference. Not so! A systematic approach is needed to determine what organizing centers to create. In the final analysis, organizing centers are a matter of choice reflecting the collective judgments of those responsible for education. Information is usually available to help those making selections. Unfortunately, a haphazard process results since these kinds of decisions are subject to fads and pressure. Organizing centers based on standard disciplines—math, science, history, language

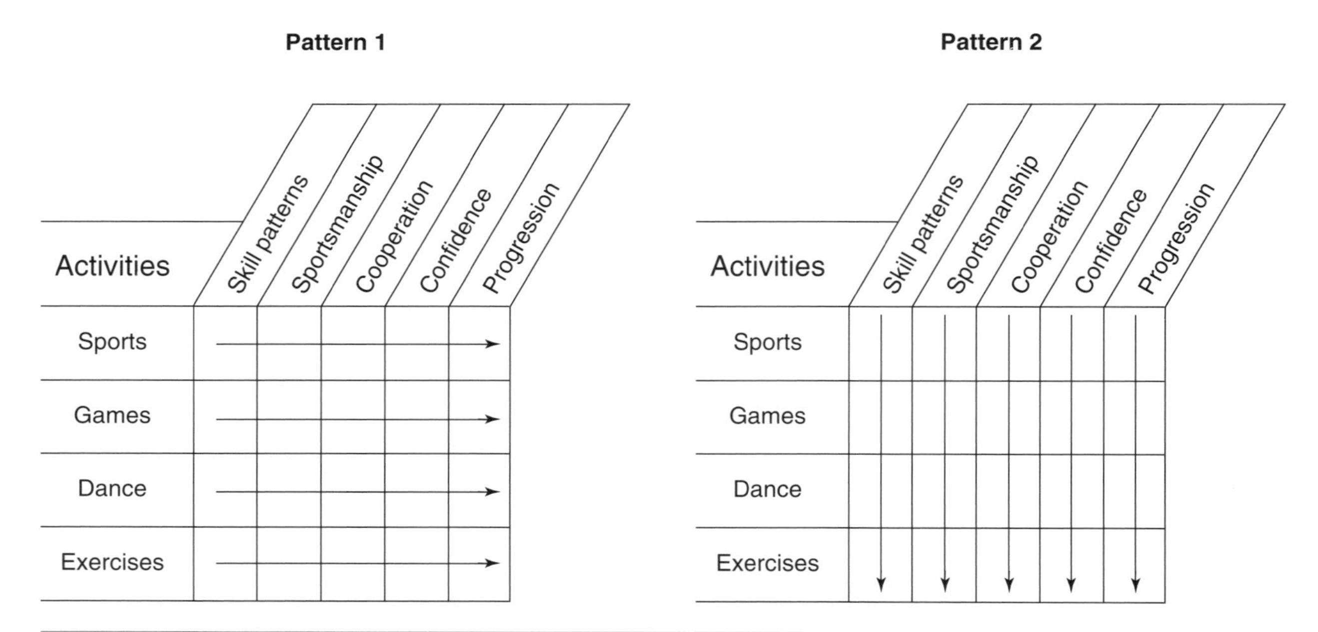

Figure 2.4 Physical education based on activities is indicated in pattern 1. Physical education based on concepts, attitudes, values, and skills is revealed in pattern 2.

arts, music, physical education—assume that learners have the same needs, which is too narrow a perspective for learners of varying abilities and characteristics. This essentialist view—that knowledge is the basis for organization—doesn't adequately consider the wide differences in maturity, physical and mental abilities, emotional state, and cultural background.

Most educators would agree that the primary goal of education is to prepare each learner for the various aspects of society to the maximum degree possible. This viewpoint recognizes that needs and interests of learners vary and that integrating learners of varying physical, intellectual, and behavioral characteristics enhances the benefits of schooling. Human diversity is valuable and relevant. If each learner's unique qualities are considered equally, then an appropriate education would include experiences tailored to the individual. In order to promote personal growth and learning, then, organizing centers should draw on a broad spectrum of sources. "Tyler's Rationale" (Tyler, 1970) is useful in identifying the primary sources of organizing centers—the needs of society, the needs and interests of learners, and subject matter mastery (physical education content). Since these sources contain a wealth of ideas, each should be considered when identifying *potential* organizing centers, knowing that some centers will overlap with more than one source. As you review each source, think of some elements around which physical education curricula could be designed.

Society

Societal trends reveal future needs. The learner's society provides a context for organizing centers. For example, the curriculum in an agricultural society would be different from one in an industrial society. You can't be expected to make firsthand observations of society, but generalizations are available. Sociologists, anthropologists, historians, journalists, and political scientists not only provide the information, but often specify its implications for education. The curriculum designer should derive organizing centers that are consistent with validated trends in society.

Historically, as described previously, needs of society have been the basis for physical education programming. These needs are an important source of organizing centers for several reasons. Since contemporary life is complex and ever-changing, education should focus on *present* complexities so that learners don't waste time on that which is no longer relevant. Areas of life that are important now or will be in the future should not be neglected. Transfer of learning is not automatic. That is, learning that takes place in an educational setting doesn't necessarily apply to life situations. Therefore, it is worth looking at contemporary society to see whether there is similarity between the situations found in life and the settings in which learning takes place. Aspects of society affecting organizing centers for physical education include

- values and attitudes of society toward males and females in sports,
- more leisure time since information is more readily available and can be compiled in less time,
- learning diversity, given our culturally pluralistic society,
- concern for the environment and the corresponding impact on outdoor education and recreation programs, and
- interest in personal health maintenance and promotion (wellness) in order to eliminate risk factors.

Other potential organizing centers from society are listed in Table 2.1.

Table 2.1 Society as the Source of Organizing Centers

Social concepts	Social themes
Acceptance	Adventure and risk
Communication	All for one and one for all
Competition	Cultural preservation
Conformity	Games in the city
Cooperation	Learning through diversity
Cultural influence	New games
Dependence	Physical coeducation
Fair play	Rituals of play
Helping relationships	Socialization through sports
Leadership	Sports as language
Respect for others	Working together
Self and others	
Sharing	
Social responsibility	
Sportsmanship	
Teamwork	
Tolerance	
Trust	

Learners

Schools should seek needed changes in learners' behavior. However, physical education—whether you think it's useful or not—may be actually forced upon learners since we expect them to participate in exercises, games, and other activities willingly and obediently. Because of the wide range of motor development within a given school or age, imposing subject matter on learners can result in significant problems. The gap between the learner—whose growth may be erratic or slow—and the expectation of the school may be so great that any hope for improvement is beyond the learner from the start. When the information presented and the skills to be learned aren't appropriate to their level of development, learners may find the experience disturbing. Therefore, organizing centers for physical education should consider the backgrounds and experiences of learners.

Although rates of growth vary, development for almost all learners follows a predictable sequence, often referred to as *developmental tasks*. Whether psychomotor, cognitive, or affective skills are involved, these tasks can serve as organizing centers. For example, manipulative skills may develop from catching balls with body and arms to throwing small objects at moving targets with accuracy. Stages of intellectual development include imitation, curiosity, and abstract thinking. Socially, learners progress from individual, self-centered concerns through a more socially mature interest in the welfare of a group, leading toward a higher level of social consciousness. From an emotional standpoint, learners need challenges that are reasonable and attainable, leading to self-control and independent behavior.

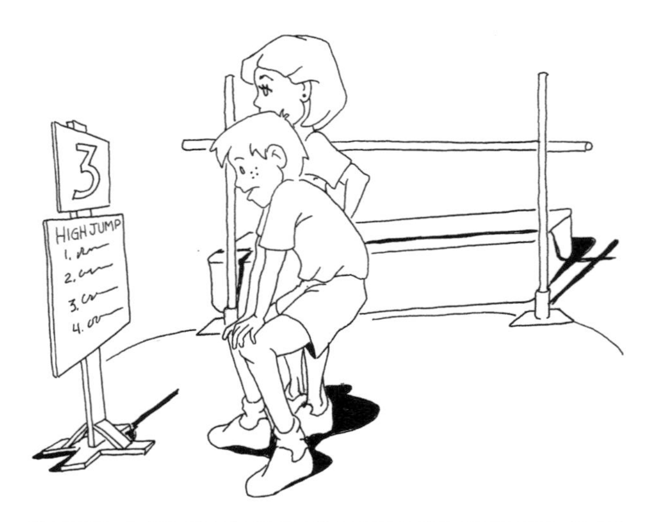

Students assume responsibility for carrying out tasks.

Learners' interests also demand attention as a source of organizing centers. At least one theory of progressive education recognizes interests as the primary basis for curricula. This is not to suggest that learners be taught only that in which they are interested; however, learners will function more actively and effectively in those learning situations that interest them. Present learner interests can serve as a point of departure. Clearly, learners are not hesitant to express preferences for games and sports. Some organizing themes in physical education that might be of interest to learners are listed in Table 2.2.

Table 2.2 Learner Interests as the Source of Organizing Centers

Themes	
Aerobics away	Improving your performance
Anything goes	Moving for fun
Creative use of leisure time	Personalized fitness
Doing my thing	Run for your life
"Hey, let me show you how I can . . ."	Taking a chance
	Wellness as a lifestyle

As a source of organizing centers, a great deal of information is available about learners. Whether information is gathered formally or informally, from other teachers and parents or from existing records, it is useful in establishing direction for the curriculum. Specific techniques for collecting information are provided in chapter 4—"Conducting Learner Analysis." In addition, the *timing* of learner analysis can vary. One of the times for conducting learner analysis is prior to selecting organizing centers (page 94).

Subject Matter

School "subjects" are the most common source of organizing centers. When content is viewed as isolated, separate subjects (e.g., mathematics, language arts, history and social studies, biology, music, physical education), there is a concern that corresponding goals are too specialized or too narrow for a large number of learners. A separate-subject approach limits the chance to generalize knowledge and skills from one situation to another. Instead, the overall curriculum should help learners deal effectively with problems of everyday living, and this can be accomplished most efficiently through an integrated approach to subject matter mastery. The product of such integration should reflect the needs of learners as well as the role of learners in society. It doesn't eliminate the usefulness of principles, concepts, and behavior patterns associated with specific subjects.

Further distinction between the separate-subject and integrated approaches is possible (Cheffers & Evaul, 1978). Traditionally, curriculum has been organized around the functions of physical education, such as movement awareness, motor skills, sports skills, physical fitness, knowledge about physical activities, expression through movement, cooperation during movement, and worthy use of leisure time. These outcomes illustrate the separate-subject approach.

Movement activities can also be used to reinforce skills in other subject areas, such as language arts (reading task cards, composing new games); mathematics (exploring geometric shapes with the body, graphing fitness scores); social studies (ethnic dances, body mimetics representing various cultures); and science (types of motion and effects on objects, use of the body as a lever). Outcomes that could integrate multiple subjects include reflective thinking, awareness of one's own and others' cultural heritage, leadership skills, the ability to function in harmony with others, values assessment, positive self-image, and decision-making abilities.

Other potential organizing centers derived from subject matter are listed in Table 2.3. The categories represent the body of knowledge of physical education (i.e., physical concepts, mechanical concepts, and psychological concepts). Subject matter defined by activities is also commonly used as organizing centers. Typical categories are team sports, individual and dual activities, outdoor and recreational pursuits, rhythms and dance, games, and popular local activities. These categories and corresponding activities were shown previously in Table 1.2 (page 21) as part of the activity-based curriculum model.

▶ ***To make sure you can recognize sources of organizing centers, complete Self-Directed Activity 2.2 at the end of this chapter.***

Table 2.3 Subject Matter as the Source of Organizing Centers

Physical concepts	Mechanical concepts	Psychological concepts
Body proportions	Angular projection	Ambition
Body rhythm	Balance	Assertiveness
Cardiorespiratory function	Buoyancy	Attitudes
Coordination	Circular motion	Body imagery
Efficiency	Dependence of body parts	Challenge
Locomotion and nonlocomotion	Flight	Commitment
Mimetics	Force	Courage
Movement awareness	Giving and receiving impetus	Creativity
Reaction and movement time	Gravity	Dedication
Spatial awareness	Laws of motion	Emotional stability
Strength	Leverage	Feedback
Use/Disuse of muscle	Momentum	Feelings and emotions
Visual imagery	Object manipulation and reception	Goal orientation
	Range of movement	Independence
	Rebound	Intelligence
	Sequential motion	Motivation
	Spin	Rivalry
	Stability	Self-expression
	Velocity	Success
		Values

Alternative Organizing Centers

The possibilities for creative and innovative organizing centers are limited only by your imagination. To further clarify their meaning and use, alternative organizing centers are presented in this section. They are not the only possibilities, nor are they derived from a single source. In some instances, all three sources are represented. For example, fitness-related organizing centers could come from society (need for healthy citizens), the learner (need for organic efficiency), and subject matter (training principles). These exemplary organizing centers are arranged according to (1) conceptual frameworks, (2) psychosocial values, and (3) learner needs.

Conceptual Frameworks

There is increasing evidence that conceptualization facilitates learning. Concepts are mental configurations, meaningful ideas, and high-level abstractions. They can't really be taught directly because they are personalized organizations of perceptions and interpretations. However, teaching can be directed toward conceptual learning. The formation of concepts requires learners' active involvement to perceive meaning and relationships. Thus, concepts provide a basis for selecting content and learning experiences that will give them meaning. A simple example of concept learning at the elementary level is (Elliot, 1990):

Topic

Object control

Concept

Angle of release (the angle at which the object is released determines the distance it will travel)

Activity sequence

Predict the landing places of objects that are projected at various angles; then, test the predictions using hoops or ropes to mark the predicted target distance and a different marker to record the actual flight.

The conceptual approach to physical education curricula has been neglected for the most part. It may be that teachers are unfamiliar with the conceptual framework, concerned that it is too complex to be workable, or satisfied with traditional organizing centers (activities). Although limited, some conceptual schemes have evolved, such as "Human Beings Function Through Movement," "Fundamentals of Movement," and "The Physically Educated Person."

Human Beings Function Through Movement

In designing a framework for the study of human movement, the concept "Human Beings Function Through Movement" was used (Evaul, 1973). Three subconcepts were identified, as shown in Table 2.4:

Table 2.4 Human Movement Framework

Human Beings Function Through Movement					
Human movement is purposeful.	The quality and quantity of human movement affects and is affected by factors within the individual and the environment.			Human movement takes many forms.	
Purposes	Physical factors	Psychological factors	Social factors	Fundamental	Complex
• Physical • Intellectual • Social • Emotional • Spiritual	• Structure • Function • Mechanics • Environment	• Learning • Motivation • Readiness • Personality	• Structure • Function • Processes • Dynamics • Culture	• Locomotion • Stability • Manipulation	• Sport • Dance • Exercise • Aquatics • Drama • Work

Note. From "Where Are You Going? What Are You Going to Do?" by T. Evaul. In *Proceedings of the Regional Conferences on Curriculum Improvement in Secondary School Physical Education* (p. 93), by W.J. Penney (Ed.), 1973, Washington, DC: AAHPER. Copyright 1973 by AAHPER. Adapted by permission.

- Human movement is purposeful.
- The quality and quantity of human movement affects and is affected by factors within the individual and the environment.
- Human movement takes many forms.

The third subconcept is commonly found in schools through forms of movement such as sports, dance, and exercise. Learners are expected to grasp the effects of these forms on themselves and their environment so that needs and purposes are fulfilled. If the principle of specificity were applied, on the other hand, the curriculum would be organized around these purposes. In this case, units were envisioned such as "Movement and Health," "Communicating Through Movement," and even "Ego Satisfaction Through Movement."

To take another example, the purposes of a unit on "fitness" would look different nowadays for several reasons: The public has become sophisticated in its approach to fitness; the concept of aerobics is the focus of numerous publications; jogging and running activities have expanded; stress testing and sports medicine are commonly understood; and various types of commercial fitness centers have emerged. The purpose of "fitness" in a conceptual curriculum can no longer be satisfied by calisthenics and running laps. The physical education curriculum must incorporate the most up-to-date scientific information about exercise and fitness if it is to remain a viable part of the total school curriculum. The types of organizing centers around which fitness content might be structured include (Evaul, 1980)

- Run for Your Life (emphasis on cardiovascular fitness),
- Improving Your Performance (focus on fitness for various types of sports), and
- Medical Aspects of Movement (features the prevention, treatment, and rehabilitation of movement injuries).

Fundamentals of Movement

In search of a structure for physical education, the question "How and why do humans move?" was answered (Gilliom, 1970). Units in basic movement can introduce the fundamentals even to young children. Organizing concepts for these sequential units and corresponding themes are:

Unit One: Where Can You Move? (space)

- Moving within one's own space and into general space (alone, with others, and in relationship to static and moving objects)
- Moving in different directions
- Moving at different levels
- Moving in different ranges and by changing shapes
- Moving in air (flight)
- Moving in different pathways

Unit Two: What Can You Move? (body awareness)

- Moving different body parts
- Changing relationships of body parts (to each other and to objects in space)

Unit Three: How Do You Move? (force, balance, weight transfer)

- Creating force
- Absorbing force
- Moving on-balance and off-balance (gravity)
- Transferring weight (rocking, rolling, and sliding on adjacent parts)
- Transferring weight (steplike movements on nonadjacent parts)
- Transferring weight when flight is involved

Unit Four: How Can You Move Better? (time, flow)

- Moving at different speeds
- Moving rhythmically (to pulse beats)
- Moving in bound or free flow
- Moving rhythmically (to phrases)
- Creating movement sequences

The Physically Educated Person

Clearly developed, publicly stated outcomes can provide the framework for curriculum organization. The question is, "What should students know and be able to do?" The answer, learner outcomes, are recommended as organizing centers.

The Physical Education Outcomes Project defined the *physically educated person*. The five parts of the definition and attendant outcomes relate to the learning domains (psychomotor, cognitive, affective). In addition, benchmark statements were offered for grades K, 2, 4, 6, 8, 10, and 12. These benchmarks allow for local standards in designing developmentally appropriate curricula. Each part of the definition and corresponding outcomes are invaluable as organizing centers (Franck et al., 1992):

*A Physically Educated Person**

HAS learned skills necessary to perform a variety of physical activities.

1. Moves using concepts of body awareness, space awareness, effort, and relationships

*Reprinted from "Outcomes of Quality Physical Education Programs" with permission of the National Association of Sport and Physical Education, 1900 Association Drive, Reston, VA 22091.

2. Demonstrates competence in a variety of manipulative, locomotor, and nonlocomotor skills
3. Demonstrates competence in combinations of manipulative, locomotor, and nonlocomotor skills performed individually and with others
4. Demonstrates competence in many different forms of physical activity
5. Demonstrates proficiency in a few forms of physical activity
6. Has learned how to learn new skills

IS physically fit.

7. Assesses, achieves, and maintains physical fitness
8. Designs safe personal fitness programs in accordance with principles of training and conditioning

DOES participate regularly in physical activity.

9. Participates in health-enhancing physical activity at least three times a week
10. Selects and regularly participates in lifetime physical activities

KNOWS the implications of and the benefits from involvement in physical activities.

11. Identifies the benefits, costs, and obligations associated with regular participation in physical activity
12. Recognizes the risk and safety factors associated with regular participation in physical activity
13. Applies concepts and principles to the development of motor skills
14. Understands that wellness involves more than being physically fit
15. Knows the rules, strategies, and appropriate behaviors for selected physical activities
16. Recognizes that participation in physical activity can lead to multicultural and international understanding
17. Understands that physical activity provides the opportunity for enjoyment, self-expression, and communication

VALUES physical activity and its contributions to a healthful lifestyle.

18. Appreciates the relationships with others that result from participation in physical activity
19. Respects the role that regular physical activity plays in the pursuit of lifelong health and well-being
20. Cherishes the feelings that result from regular participation in physical activity

Psychosocial Values

The notion of organizing centers is particularly useful in terms of affective learning (attitudes, values, social behaviors, emotional response). As shown previously, in Table 2.1 (page 41) and in Table 2.3 (page 43), the range of psychosocial values is extensive. Because of their importance, cooperation and courage are developed here as exemplary organizing centers.

Cooperation

To achieve a common goal, a cooperative effort is needed. The importance of cooperation seems even greater in today's world of increasing tensions and dwindling resources. Traditionally, team sports have been regarded as the laboratory for teaching cooperation. However, cooperation can be sought through movement forms other than competitive sports (Decker, 1990; Orlick, 1978, 1982; Sterne, 1990).

Alternative organizing centers include "Working Together" (individuals assume various roles in order to accomplish a given common task) and "All for One and One for All" (mutual support is emphasized). Activities can be used in which success depends on a group effort. See the Unit Outline for "Cooperation" as an example (Evaul, 1980). Note that the elements in the outline do not conform exactly to the recommended components in this book.

Content that supports "cooperation" as an organizing center can be illustrated in another way. Cooperative play is one of the underlying themes of "New Games" (Fluegelman, 1976, 1981). Participants assume various social roles through cooperative and competitive activities. Related qualities such as tolerance, respect for others, helpfulness, sharing, and trust are inherent to the meaning of new games. For example, cooperation is basic to the following "new volleyball" games:

- ***Rotation Ball***: Standard rules are used but players rotate, after both sides have scored, from one side to the other; game emphasizes all-out effort in order to raise the score of either side; it is possible to rotate to the losing side in time for the final point.
- ***Volley-Volley Ball***: Scoring system is changed; one to three points can be scored depending on the number of "hits" before sending ball back across the net; one point is scored if only one team member hits the ball; team gets three points if all three hits are used; game is to 35 points.

Unit Outline for "Cooperation"

▶ Organizing center: Cooperation

Philosophy (rationale)

Cooperation is the essence of a civilized society. It requires a balance in the satisfaction of personal and group needs. Sharing and assisting others are primary characteristics of cooperative effort.

Purposes (goals/objectives)

1. To assume the roles of leader and follower when appropriate.
2. To take turns when resources are limited.
3. To share possessions, space, ideas, and time.
4. To assist others in accomplishing a task.

Substance (content)

1. Leadership—Followership
   a. Leadership of different tasks requires different talents; therefore leadership may vary according to task.
   b. Leadership may be shared or absolute depending on the nature of the task and the group.
   c. Followership requires a willingness to receive instructions and carry them out.
   d. Recognizing when to assume each role requires a type of maturity that leads to cooperation.
2. Characteristics of cooperation
   a. Taking turns (when all cannot perform at once)
   b. Sharing possessions (when resources are scarce)
   c. Sharing space (when conditions are crowded)
   d. Sharing ideas (when searching for the best solution to a problem)
   e. Sharing time (when the group goal is of greater importance than one's personal goals)
   f. Assisting others (when one possesses a talent that is needed by another member of the group)

Implementation (learning experiences)

1. Present the group with problems that require cooperation to solve.
2. Form groups of students who have various talents (e.g., someone who is very strong, another very fast, another a good thinker, etc.). Make up tasks for the groups to do, each of which emphasizes one of these talents. Have them select the best person to lead the group in each task.
3. Play games that require sharing (e.g., One-Sided Volleyball).
4. Participate in "double stunts" in which two partners must perform different tasks for success (e.g., swan balance, doubles roll).
5. Explain and demonstrate how to take turns on a piece of apparatus. Have groups determine and implement the system they wish to use.
6. Have partners work with each other in learning a skill. Explain how one gives feedback, spots, and in other ways assists the other in learning.
7. Discuss the concept of teamwork. Identify various roles on a sports team (e.g., star, playmaker, substitute, coach, manager, statistician, etc.). Help students learn the importance of each role and how different talents suit different roles.

Assessment (evaluation)

1. Observe students performing various cooperative activities to determine whether they are demonstrating the characteristics of cooperation.
2. Develop an attitude scale such as the Semantic Differential to measure students' attitudes about various aspects of cooperation.

Note. This outline is reprinted with permission from the *Journal of Physical Education and Recreation*, September, 1980, p. 53. *JOPER* is a publication of the American Alliance for Health, Physical Education, Recreation and Dance, 1900 Association Drive, Reston, VA 22091.

• ***Volley-Volley-Volley Ball***: Every member of the team must hit the ball at least once before it can be sent back across the net; play to nine points.

• ***Infinity Ball***: Any number can play; standard rules apply including only three hits per side; score is the number of times the ball is hit over the net to the other side without hitting floor or ground; both teams chant score in unison; score of 50 is good; over 100 is great.

Courage

Physical education has been acclaimed for its development of personal characteristics such as self-reliance, perseverance, and courage. However, these qualities have not been the organizing focus of many curriculum designs. Instead, they develop implicitly. Dealing with them explicitly will become increasingly important if predicted shortages in resources require people to become more self-reliant.

Organizing centers have been suggested such as "Taking a Chance" (physical activities involving a certain amount of risk with appropriate safety precautions) and "Doing It Yourself" (single-handed activities challenging both thinking and physical prowess). See the Unit Outline for "Courage" as an example (Evaul, 1980). Note that the elements in the outline do not conform exactly to the recommended components in this book.

Other content can be used with "courage" as the organizing theme. For example, "Project Adventure" (Rohnke, 1977, 1989) combines risk (a willingness to move beyond previously set limits) and the satisfaction of solving problems. Learners begin to develop true self-esteem by attempting a graduated series of activities that involve physical or emotional risk. A supportive group atmosphere encourages participation and effort. Success and failure are less important. Brief descriptions of selected "courage" activities are:

• ***Trust Fall***: Learner stands upon a stump, platform, ladder rung, etc., about 5 feet off the ground and falls backward into the arms of 10 to 12 others standing on level ground; person falling should close eyes, keep arms close to side of body, and hold body rigid; the two lines of catchers stand shoulder to shoulder facing one another; arms are extended alternately with palms up.

• ***Trust Dive***: From a height of 3 or 4 feet, learner dives forward into the arms of six to eight catchers; swimming race dive is used; catchers are farther from the diving area than in the trust fall.

• ***The Wall***: Goal is for the entire group of participants to get over a 12- to 14-foot wall as quickly as possible; there may be no more than three persons on top of the wall helping other members of the group; to assist climber, someone may lean over the wall if his or her legs are on the back step and are firmly anchored by another participant; to assist climber, someone may hang from the top if his or her armpits are over the top and his or her arms are supported by two other people; activity should be carefully supervised to reduce the risk of injury.

• ***Ten-Member Pyramid***: Purpose is to build a symmetrical "4-3-2-1" pyramid with a group of 10 participants as quickly and efficiently as possible.

• ***Swing to Safety***: Learner must reach the top of an 8- to 10-foot stump, or other such obstacle, and swing with a rope over a given area to safety; group may offer help to an individual trying to get on top of the stump.

Learner Needs

The proposed meaning of physical education offers another set of organizing centers. Individual needs are satisfied explicitly through participation in physical activities. Cognitive, affective, and psychomotor needs vary in both quantity and quality on a wide range of developmental levels. Although they are analyzed separately in this section, they are continuous and interdependent in learning. Needs represent the difference between the present condition of the learner and the acceptable or desired standard. In addition, learners' behavior is primarily motivated by a desire to satisfy perceived needs. Therefore, needs offer a relevant foundation for designing curricula.

Consideration for learners' needs also represents a *developmentally appropriate practice* in physical education. These practices can be used directly as organizing centers (Graham, Castenada, Hopple, Manross, & Sanders, 1992):

• ***Cognitive development***: Learners need to question, integrate, analyze, communicate, and apply cognitive concepts, as well as gain a multicultural view of the world.

• ***Affective development***: Learners need to (1) work together for the purpose of improving their emerging social and cooperation skills, (2) develop a positive self-concept, and (3) experience and feel the satisfaction and joy which results from regular participation in physical activity.

Unit Outline for "Courage"

▶ Organizing center: Courage

Foundation (rationale)

Courage is the willingness to undertake a dangerous task. It involves taking a risk in an attempt to achieve an important goal. The development of courage involves acquiring the following concepts:

1. Evaluation of one's abilities, the task, and how it can be accomplished is a prerequisite to courageous performance.
2. All possible precautions should be taken to minimize risks.
3. Confidence is developed by successfully accomplishing progressively riskier tasks.

Purposes (goals/objectives)

1. To rationally evaluate tasks, personal potential, and values in order to decide whether the task should be undertaken.
2. To determine and take all possible precautions in order to minimize dangers.
3. To identify ways one's willingness to attempt risky tasks can be increased.
4. To attempt a variety of activities involving risks.

Substance (content)

1. Evaluation
   a. Of task
   b. Of danger
   c. Of personal potential
   d. Of safety provisions
   e. Of value of accomplishing the task
2. Safety
   a. Identify hazards
   b. Minimize dangers
      1. Help from others (e.g., spotting, instructors)
      2. Protective equipment (e.g., supporting ropes, padding)
      3. Alternative ways to accomplish goal (e.g., different routes)
3. Ways to develop courage
   a. Work with others who can teach and help.
   b. Examine and try safety equipment.
   c. Develop personal fitness and skill.
   d. Progress from small risks to greater ones.

Implementation (learning experiences)

1. Lecture and demonstration on how to evaluate a task, one's potential, and safety provisions in order to make a decision to try it.
2. Examine and test various types of safety precautions.
3. Try progressively more risky activities to gradually increase confidence (e.g., jump or climb to higher heights, walk on narrower surfaces, move at greater speeds).

Assessment (evaluation)

1. Present learners with courage tasks. Have them conduct an evaluation, develop safety precautions, and accomplish the task.

Note. This outline is reprinted with permission from the *Journal of Physical Education and Recreation*, September, 1980, p. 54. *JOPER* is a publication of the American Alliance for Health, Physical Education, Recreation and Dance, 1900 Association Drive, Reston, VA 22091.

• ***Development of movement concepts and motor skills***: Learners need to develop a functional understanding of movement concepts (body awareness, space awareness, effort, and relationships) and build competence and confidence in their ability to perform a variety of motor skills (locomotor, nonlocomotor, and manipulative).

• ***Concepts of fitness***: Learners need to understand and value the important concepts of physical fitness and the contribution they make to a healthy lifestyle.

Creating organizing centers based on needs is the first assurance that the meaning of physical education is being fulfilled. From a conceptual standpoint, "Toward Individual Needs" may be viewed as a universal organizing theme encompassing the three learning domains.

Cognitive

The need for cognitive abilities is satisfied through exploration, discovery, and problem solving. Creative thinking, critical thinking, and decision making can serve as organizing centers. These differ greatly from low-order intellectual abilities such as memorization and recall.

The cognitive domain (Bloom, 1956) consists of six categories that you can use as organizing centers. Think of it as a staircase. Simple processes like memorizing are the bottom steps while complex processes such as making judgments are the top steps. Knowledge is the most basic process followed by comprehension, application, and analysis. Synthesis and evaluation are the top two steps of this learning hierarchy. Since they build on one another, you must master a lower step before you can master a higher one. Brief definitions appear in Table 2.5. Some other organizing centers in the cognitive domain are

- recognition of body positions and relationships of body parts,
- self-knowledge (humans move to gain self-understanding and appreciation),
- movement appreciation (humans move to understand and become appreciative observers of sports and expressive movement forms),
- cultural preservation (humans move to understand and extend their cultural heritage),
- concepts and strategies,
- composition of movement, and
- solution of developmental problems through movement.

Table 2.5 Cognitive Domain Categories as Organizing Centers

Category	Definition
1. Knowledge	Ability to memorize previously learned facts, concepts, and explanations
2. Comprehension	Ability to interpret information and determine what has already been learned
3. Application	Ability to use previously learned concepts and explanations in unfamiliar situations
4. Analysis	Ability to break down information into its essential elements
5. Synthesis	Ability to combine parts into a whole
6. Evaluation	Ability to make judgments in comparison to a set of standards or criteria

Affective

The affective domain (Krathwohl, Bloom, & Masia, 1964) contains emotional responses such as feelings, interests, attitudes, appreciation, and values. Although these processes don't always follow a set, logical order, they are still arranged as a hierarchy. The five categories, from simple to complex, are receiving (awareness), responding, valuing, organization, and characterization. Learners can be helped to get in touch with their feelings and to identify and clarify their attitudes and values. Brief definitions appear in Table 2.6.

Table 2.6 Affective Domain Categories as Organizing Centers

Category	Definition
1. Receiving	Being aware of or attending to given phenomena
2. Responding	Acting in response to some belief or interest
3. Valuing	Accepting or attaching worth to some phenomenon in the form of attitudes and appreciations
4. Organization	Moving toward a system of values; recognizing conflicting values
5. Characterization	Developing a hierarchically integrated "philosophy of life"

Cooperation and helping relationships can be fostered.

Other dimensions of the affective domain should be considered as organizing centers:

- Social needs revolve around effective interactions, affection, and status or respect from the social group; learners have a need for "social responsibility."
- Control of emotions (e.g., enthusiasm, hostility, deep depression) is needed; emotional stability isn't served when learners feel anger toward physical activity, embarrassment or unhappiness in physical activity, or fear of movement; learners need to develop the "self" (i.e., self-confidence, self-image, self-respect, self-fulfillment, and self-control).
- Values assessment, development, and clarification is needed; aesthetic appreciation, a sense of fair play, and responsibility for others involve values learning; learners need to develop interests and values in physical activity.

Psychomotor

Needs associated with the psychomotor domain (Harrow, 1972) include optimal functioning of the body (organic) to meet the demands of society and the environment, and proper functioning of the neuromuscular system resulting in efficient and effective body movement. The six categories of the domain, from simple to complex, are reflex movements, basic fundamental movements, perceptual abilities, physical abilities, skilled movements, and nondiscursive communication. They can be used to guide decisions about organizing centers. Brief definitions appear in Table 2.7.

▶ ***As you can see, there's a vast array of organizing centers. Using Self-Directed Activity 2.3 at the end of this chapter, identify which organizing centers appeal to you.***

Selecting Organizing Centers

Now that potential organizing centers have been identified, they should be filtered through philosophical and psychological "screens" (Tyler, 1970). These screens are the criteria against which you select organizing centers. You need to do this because some organizing centers aren't consistent with others, the time you have available may eliminate some options, and trying to include too many may be ineffective. By using these screens, you can select a group of highly important, consistent organizing centers.

Table 2.7 Psychomotor Domain Categories as Organizing Centers

Category	Definition
1. Reflex movements	Involuntary responses to some stimuli; flexing, extending, stretching, and making postural adjustments
2. Basic fundamental movements	Include locomotor, nonlocomotor, and manipulative movements that form the basis for complex, skilled movements
3. Perceptual abilities	Judgments of one's body in relation to surrounding objects in space (kinesthetic discrimination); visual, auditory, and tactile discrimination and their coordination
4. Physical abilities	Functional characteristics of organic vigor including endurance, strength, flexibility, and agility
5. Skilled movements	Include the degree of difficulty of various movement skills and levels of skill mastery achieved by the learner
6. Nondiscursive communication	Aesthetic and creative message routines ranging from facial expressions, postures, and gestures to choreographies

Philosophical Screen

The philosophical views you developed in chapter 1 should be helpful at this point. Organizing centers should agree with your and your school's philosophical orientations. A philosophical screen allows you to accept some organizing centers, revise others, and reject still others. For example, the pragmatist is more likely than the existentialist to select organizing centers for social responsibility. Regardless of one's philosophy, it's a useful criterion or screen for selecting organizing centers, but only if that philosophy is clearly understood.

By way of illustration, suppose you believe that democratic values are important to an effective and satisfying life. One of these values recognizes the importance of every individual regardless of race, cultural background, economic status, disabling condition, or ability level. If so, then organizing centers are suggested that foster "democratic" behavior patterns and practices (e.g., fair play, equal chance, equal competition, respect for others). Goals, objectives, and learning experiences that are inconsistent with this value would be excluded.

You might also sort organizing centers based on the concept of *confluence*. This means that thinking, feeling, and moving are combined. When objectives and learning experiences are developed, you would devise activities that result in multiple outcomes. Another example is the *principle of normalization*. This means that experiences for learners with disabilities would resemble those of their nondisabled peers. When this philosophical viewpoint is used as a screen, a curriculum design is suggested that fosters interaction, instructional modifications, and integrated activities.

Philosophy and its corresponding organizing centers can also raise some controversial questions. For example, "Should education conform to society or should education seek to improve society?" Depending on the answer, organizing centers might emphasize obedience, loyalty to traditions, and skills to carry out present techniques; or they might focus on critical analysis, self-direction, and independence. Other questions include: "Should different classes of society receive different educational programs?" "Should education attempt to satisfy all of the needs of learners?" And, "Should education deal primarily with basic skills?"

▶ ***To test your ability to screen (select) organizing centers based on philosophical viewpoints, complete Self-Directed Activity 2.4 at the end of this chapter.***

Psychological Screen

Organizing centers should match a defensible psychology of learning. If learners' physical and mental capacities are known, then the possibility of attaining outcomes associated with a given organizing center can be determined. Assessing entry-level ability, as described in chapter 4 (pages 96–99), ensures that the organizing center is appropriate.

Conditions for learning are another aspect of the psychological screen. Selection of some organizing centers depends on whether or not certain skills and abilities exist. The learner may not have matured enough socially or emotionally, or may not possess necessary prerequisites (e.g., upper body strength for gymnastics; ability to catch large playground balls before catching tennis balls). Thus, the learner may not be physically, socially, or intellectually "ready" to engage in a particular learning task. A provision should be made to teach prerequisite concepts and skills that are not within the learners' existing abilities.

The time for learning will also vary according to the nature of the behavior sought. Attitudes, for example, require continuous emphasis over an extended period of time, and a difficult task may similarly involve long-term retention of many elements, whereas easy tasks (few information items to be processed) may require only short-term memory. Efficient use of time becomes important. If carefully planned, a single learning experience can lead to several outcomes. For example, a fitness development episode could involve multiple outcomes such as development of strength (psychomotor); calculation of maximum and submaximum threshold (cognitive); peer support in completing exercises (affective/social); self-directed learning tasks (affective/emotional); and selection of exercises of personal importance (affective/value).

In order to use this screen, it is suggested that you state the most relevant elements of learning psychology. Organizing centers can then be checked against your statement. Select or reject them as appropriate. It may be found that the organizing center isn't attainable, doesn't match the maturational level of the learner, or can't be achieved in the time available.

▶ ***To test your ability to screen (identify) organizing centers based on psychological aspects, complete Self-Directed Activity 2.5 at the end of this chapter.***

MAKING IT WORK

Have you achieved the expected outcomes (page 36)? Congratulations! You are able to create organizing centers for your physical education curriculum design. Still, you may have some practical questions that need answers, such as:

- **Do you really need organizing centers for a good curriculum?**

  The answer probably depends on your definition of "good." You need some kind of framework so that you can make decisions. Organizing centers help give your curriculum focus—an overall reason. Many physical education teachers actually use "seasons" as their organizing center. Because it's fall, you teach football, soccer, and volleyball. If it's spring, that means softball, track, tennis, and golf. Needless to say, this activity-based approach lacks a true *learning* focus. Do you remember the curriculum models? Their titles (e.g., movement education, developmental education, humanistic education, sport education, adventure education) are actually organizing centers. Decisions about objectives, learning activities, and evaluation would relate directly to the purpose underlying each model. Curriculum designing is supposed to be purposeful. Once your organizing centers are selected, you should try to approximate them in every way possible. They are central to your curriculum, a constant reminder of why you are doing what you are doing. They also foster explicit rather than implicit learning.

- **With so many possible organizing centers to choose from, how can you decide which ones are right?**

  At this point, you may feel mentally frustrated. Try not to think in terms of right versus wrong. But you should be able to reduce all the possible options to those that are feasible. Then, reduce the feasible ones to those that are desirable. The philosophical and psychological screens should help you do this. Also, don't try to accomplish too much all at once. Instead, start out with a few concepts or ideas and build from there. Think in terms of *mini* organizing centers for a single lesson, week, or unit. Eventually, the collection of these mini organizing centers might represent some global concept or overall theme. You could also go the other way. Start with the global concept or theme and focus on a few subconcepts or subthemes. One final thought: Organizing centers represent different levels of generality. Some are rather simple (low-order) while others are very complex (high-order). Determine at what level you want to start and go from there. Organizing centers can be refined, added, and/or dropped as you go along.

- **Can you get teachers to agree, philosophically, on a particular set of organizing centers?**

  In the real world of teaching, you probably won't be alone in selecting organizing centers. Some teachers have their own schools, particularly at the elementary level, where they can make their own decisions. Usually, at the middle and high school levels, there is more than one physical education teacher. But remember, there should be curriculum articulation from level to level, grade to grade, on a K–12 continuum. Whether you need to reach agreement within a school or on a district-wide basis, or both, other teachers will be involved who may not share your system of beliefs. In addition, don't forget the influences of the board of education, administrators, parents, and students as well as any state mandates or guidelines. Reaching agreement on organizing centers requires compromise and consensus-building, knowing that full agreement is probably unrealistic. Everyone must be willing to give and take a little. It helps if teachers accept a "no-fault" approach; that is, teachers shouldn't blame or criticize one another for their philosophical differences. A gradual process of selection could include a needs assessment in which input is solicited from students, parents, and other non-physical education teachers and staff about various organizing centers. Collectively, results could yield some powerful information about which organizing centers are most defensible and most widely accepted. A comparison to other known models would also be useful in convincing others of the strengths and weaknesses of a particular organizing center or set of organizing centers.

- **Will students be able to handle organizing centers?**

  The term itself isn't as important as the actual organizing centers. Learners at all levels are quite capable of grasping concepts or ideas if they are planned for and developed directly. Let them know what this "thing" is that you're trying to develop. Don't promote a "hidden" curriculum in which students learn implicitly. If you are trying to develop some psychosocial value (e.g., teamwork, tolerance, respect, acceptance), make sure it's actually practiced. You could demonstrate it and have the students engage in role playing. At times, students may not like it, but at least they will begin to learn the intended knowledge, skill, attitude, or value. Remember that organizing centers should be dealt with over and over again at planned intervals on a vertical, K–12 continuum.

Self-Directed Activity 2.1

Ideally, you now know what an organizing center is! Just to make sure, answer the following questions about its characteristics.

1. Briefly, how would you *define* an organizing center?

   ____

   ____

   ____

   ____

   ____

2. Why do organizing centers enhance the *vertical* and *horizontal* qualities of the curriculum design?

   ____

   ____

   ____

   ____

   ____

3. What is the difference between *implicit* and *explicit* learning, relative to organizing centers?

____

____

____

____

____

4. How is the *principle of specificity* applicable to the use of organizing centers?

____

____

____

____

____

Feedback

1. An organizing center is the emphasis, theme, concept, viewpoint, or frame of reference around which the physical education curriculum is designed. General concepts, skills, attitudes, and values are the focus.
2. Organizing centers provide a basis for what is learned from one level to another. The continuous and progressive use of organizing centers determines the vertical organization of the curriculum. Organizing centers can also be used to integrate different subject matters. Unifying the curriculum across many content areas determines the horizontal organization of the curriculum.
3. Learning outcomes based on organizing centers are sought directly (explicitly) rather than indirectly (implicitly). You can't assume that students learn, particularly in psychosocial aspects, simply by participating in activities. If you want something to be learned, then teach for it.
4. If concepts, skills, attitudes, or values are to be learned, then they become the focus for the curriculum design. It is necessary to examine, plan for, and foster the attainment of these outcomes when they are used as organizing centers.

Self-Directed Activity 2.2

You should be able to recognize sources of organizing centers. For each of the generalizations that follows, indicate the source as:

S = Needs of society
L = Needs and interests of learners
P = Physical education subject matter mastery

Then try to identify some idea or concept that could serve as an organizing center for the physical education curriculum.

_____ 1. Today's highly complex world has changed the economy and the nature of employment. Machines and computers do the work of many people more efficiently and at lower cost. Manual labor jobs are few, having been replaced by service activities and new technical occupations. There is a need to overcome the effects of sedentary lifestyles.

Organizing center: ______________________________

_____ 2. Arbitrary distinctions between men and women are being changed in spite of existing misconceptions, sex-role stereotyping, and double standards. Differential treatment of males and females needs to be eliminated in nearly every segment of life.

Organizing center: ______________________________

_____ 3. Learners experience physiological and biological changes that influence individual physical capacities and limitations.

Organizing center: ______________________________

_____ 4. A central idea of human growth and development is the concept of progression. Fundamental movement patterns (e.g., run, jump, slide) and elements (e.g., stability, force, transfer of weight) are combined to form complex movement patterns found in sports, games, recreation, and dance.

Organizing center: ______________________________

_____ 5. Perceptual abilities can be observed during purposeful movement, including kinesthetic discrimination (making body adjustments during a headstand), visual discrimination (dodging a ball), auditory discrimination (following directions from a teammate), tactile discrimination (determining object texture), and coordinated abilities (catching a frisbee).

Organizing center: ______________________________

_____ 6. Some of the values held by students from minority groups may be different from those of the dominant group in a school.

Organizing center: ______________________________

_____ 7. People have become more concerned about the environment, and this change has created a greater awareness of nature and of society's impact on the environment.

Organizing center: ______________________________

_____ 8. The change in public attitude toward persons with disabilities is designed to end discrimination in employment and education. Individuals with disabilities need to be assured that they will have access to and be integrated into all aspects of life.

Organizing center: ______________________________

_____ 9. Learners have engaged in a variety of learning opportunities (e.g., exploration, discovery, problem solving) in developing fundamental movement patterns.

Organizing center: ______________________________

_____ 10. Given our pluralistic society, schools must deal with cultural, religious, racial, ethnic, and linguistic diversity. The needs associated with these diverse elements influence the attitudes of students toward each other.

Organizing center: ______________________________

_____ 11. Intellectual functioning is developed sequentially through knowledge acquisition, application, analysis, and synthesis. Physical education concepts that deal with this ability involve rules (e.g., out-of-bounds, scoring, infractions) and strategies (e.g., two-on-one, zone defenses, formations).

Organizing center: ______________________________

_____ 12. Increased leisure time has resulted, in part, from the growth in world wealth and from advances in technology. In order to use this time wisely, people need to be stimulated through participation in lifelong learning activities.

Organizing center: ______________________________

_____ 13. Certain physical education content areas (e.g., rhythms and dance, games, dual activities) are more popular than others at the elementary level.

Organizing center: ______________________________

_____ 14. Development of a "physical" self-concept and individual self-image needs to be directed positively.

Organizing center: ______________________________

_____ 15. The family structure has been affected by economic and social changes. Traditionally, families shared many recreational and leisure activities. However, because of the transient nature of contemporary society, people depend more now on the community and its resources.

Organizing center: ______________________________

_____ 16. Through movement, learners relate to others. Physical education content areas such as low-organization games, rhythms, self-testing activities, stunts and tumbling, lead-up games, and adventure activities involve opportunities to engage in numerous social processes (e.g., accommodation, tolerance, helping relationships, sharing space, trust, and teamwork).

Organizing center: ______________________________

_____ 17. Problems in society such as extended unemployment, economic uncertainty, ecological collapse, and threats to world peace create tension and stress. As a result, people should learn how to control tension and cope with stress.

Organizing center: ______________________________

_____ 18. Learners' emotional maturity is facilitated through "self-oriented" processes. Some of these processes and corresponding physical education content include exploration (mimetics), discovery (movement in general and personal space), self-direction (tag games, obstacle course), self-pacing (jogging), and independent learning (self-testing activities, individual sports).

Organizing center: ______________________________

_____ 19. Interpersonal relations skills (e.g., cooperation, competition, tolerance, acceptance) have not emerged as a result of previous learning situations in physical education.

Organizing center: ______________________________

_____ 20. Concern for health in society is evidenced by popular concepts such as wellness, holistic health, and lifestyle changes. People are assuming greater responsibility for their own health maintenance.

Organizing center: ______________________________

Feedback

The *intended* source of each generalization is indicated. In some instances, one of the other sources may be closely related. The organizing centers offered are suggestive. Many other organizing centers may be derived from the generalization . . . including yours!

1. S Complex movement skills (leisure sports)
2. S Physical "coeducation"
3. L Optimal functioning
4. P Developmental movement
5. P Modalities and movement
6. L Personalized pursuits
7. S Recreation activities and the environment
8. S Functional life skills
9. L Learning through discovery
10. S Respecting others
11. P Challenging the intellect
12. S Worthy use of time
13. L "Doing your thing"
14. L Ego satisfaction
15. S Exploring the community
16. P Cooperative interaction
17. S Overcoming life's irritations
18. P Responsibility for decision making
19. L Interpersonal communication
20. S Healthy lifestyles

Self-Directed Activity 2.3

As you can see, there's a vast array of organizing centers. Pretend you are going to design a physical education curriculum at the elementary, middle/junior, or high school level. What organizing centers appeal to you? Using the categories that follow, identify your favorite organizing centers for the level you selected. You don't need to identify organizing centers for each category and you're not limited to the organizing centers that have been presented. In fact, you are encouraged to generate your own!

Level: ❑ Elementary school ❑ Middle/Junior high school ❑ High school

Physical concepts: ______________________________

____

Mechanical concepts: ______________________________

____

Psychological concepts: ______________________________

____

Social concepts: ______________________________

____

Themes: ______________________________

____

Outcomes: ______________________________

____

Cognitive needs: ______________________________

____

Affective needs: ______________________________

____

Psychomotor needs: ______________________________

____

Feedback

Needless to say, your organizing centers are a matter of personal preference. At this point, they are all acceptable. Refinement and final selection of organizing centers will depend on various factors to be discussed in the following section. Ultimately, the trick will be to transform your chosen organizing centers into a viable physical education curriculum.

Self-Directed Activity 2.4

You should be able to screen (select) organizing centers based on philosophical viewpoints. Write *yes* or *no* in the spaces to indicate whether or not you think the organizing center reflects its philosophical description.

Essentialism: Education is concerned with teaching essentials—the three Rs, government, geography, the sciences. For physical education, emphasis is placed on basic movement, skill development, physical fitness, and functional motor skills.

__________ 1. Functioning in the outdoors

__________ 2. Creative movement

__________ 3. Controlling the body

Cognitivism: The focus of education is on higher intellectual skills and abilities. Through discovery and problem solving, processes such as applying, analyzing, synthesizing, and evaluating are learned and transferred.

__________ 4. Mechanical principles and motor control

__________ 5. Personal accomplishment

__________ 6. Linking goals and performance

Social reconstructionism: Needs of society are more important than individual needs. Social reform and responsibility to society's future are given priority. Education deals with social issues and serves as an agent of change.

_________ 7. Cross-racial and -cultural relationships

_________ 8. Controlling the body

_________ 9. Cooperative participation

Individualism: Personal fulfillment and self-discovery are highly valued. Education fosters individual integration and personal growth. Emphasis is placed on emotional response and values formation. Less concern is shown for subject matter.

_________ 10. Creative movement

_________ 11. Mechanical principles and motor control

_________ 12. Personal accomplishment

Feedback

1. Yes—Functioning in the environment fits the essentialist view.
2. No—Organizing center doesn't relate to *basics*.
3. Yes—"Controlling the body" is considered essential to human movement (e.g., bilaterality, laterality, sidedness, balance).
4. Yes—Principles would be applied to forms of movement.
5. No—There's no direct focus on cognitive functioning.
6. Yes—The process of goal setting and evaluation requires the use of more complex intellectual processes.
7. Yes—Social behavior is clearly a product of "cross-racial and -cultural relationships."
8. No—Organizing center doesn't relate to social aspects.
9. Yes—"Cooperative participation" is absolutely necessary to the social reconstructionist.
10. Yes—Creative movement is vital because of its expressive potential.
11. No—There's no reference to the development of *self*.
12. Yes—No doubt, "personal accomplishment" is fundamental to individual self-actualization.

Self-Directed Activity 2.5

The following statements relate to some aspect of developmental psychology. Identify a physical education organizing center for each.

1. Motor ability is a function of maturation. Skills are acquired progressively from simple gross movements to more complex movement patterns. The gross movement and manipulative skills of primary-aged learners are unrefined.

   Organizing center: ______________________________

2. During late childhood (7–12 years), cognitive ability develops sufficiently so that learners can plan and carry out *concrete* operations. They can combine, separate, and consider two aspects of a situation at once and see their systematic relations. Most learners are not able to apply operations to hypothetical situations; that is, they can't apply logic to arrive at an answer.

   Organizing center: ______________________________

3. Characteristically, adolescents display feelings of insecurity, particularly in a group. There is a need for acceptance by and conformity with others of the same age. There's a great desire to be part of the group. Adolescents seek both dependence and independence and opportunities to make decisions.

   Organizing center: ______________________________

4. Between the ages of 12 and 18, learners achieve patterns of motor development (sporting roles). Coordination is very highly developed, although flexibility may be decreasing. Motor ability consists of specialized skills. Muscular strength and endurance are also reaching high levels of development.

   Organizing center: ______________________________

5. Motor skill and body development are important factors in social acceptance among intermediate-school-aged learners. Therefore, learners are interested in how their bodies develop and how fitness and skill can be increased. There is greater concern for peer group acceptance than for adult approval. Learners at this age are adventurous.

   Organizing center: ______________________________

6. Movement is sensorily satisfying to learners 6 to 8 years old. Learners develop feelings about their bodies and an essential awareness of their physical being. They use their bodies as expressive outlets for both positive and negative feelings. Learners of this age seek socially acceptable emotional outlets.

   Organizing center: ______________________________

Feedback

The following organizing centers are suggestive. A rationale is offered in support of each. Obviously, your organizing centers are equally acceptable.

1. "Learning to Move"

   Basic movement skills are appropriate for learners of this age level. Locomotor skills consist of those with even rhythm (walking, running, jumping, hopping, leaping) and those with uneven rhythm (skipping, sliding, galloping). These skills involve movement through space. Nonlocomotor skills, which are executed without moving the base of support, include bending, stretching, twisting, turning, pushing, pulling, swinging, swaying, falling, and rising. All of these skills are fundamental to the development of more complex movement patterns.

2. "Using Strategies"

   While learners can't engage in formal logic at this age, they can use abstractions in concrete situations. This organizing center might include the application of offensive and defensive strategies in selected individual and dual sports.

3. "Moving Together"

   The statement deals with a social need. Learners could share in and influence group members in the achievement of common movement goals.

4. "Fitness for Life"

   This organizing center could combine fitness parameters with movement patterns necessary for sporting roles such as those found in lifetime pursuit activities. It matches the age level for which it was intended.

5. "New Games"

   The statement refers to movement and social acceptance. Learners could recognize and use mechanical principles of movement in "new game" activities, for example, novel ways of moving in which common group goals are sought (see Fluegelman, 1976, 1981).

6. "Self-Expression"

   This organizing center clearly matches the statement about primary-school-aged learners. Movement activities play a role in helping learners find socially acceptable emotional outlets and recognize the source of their feelings. Learners of this age need the chance to be creative, expressive, and unrestrained in movement experiences.

3

Determining Content Goals

Key Concept

Curriculum designers transform organizing centers into goals and analyze these goals relative to physical education content.

Every October, parents are invited to an open house at the high school. They follow their child's schedule, and hear individual teachers presenting brief overviews of their classes, followed by questions. For physical education, however, the department head makes the presentation. He says that the goal of the program is to offer a wide variety of individual and team sports. During the third-period session, a parent is critical of the program. Her daughter doesn't like "gym" because she's not good at sports. Furthermore, she says, "It's a waste of money!" The department head offers a vague response and basically says that that's the way it's always been. Afterward, one of the physical education teachers admits to a colleague that she was embarrassed. She knows that there are more valid goals for physical education.

Expected Outcomes

This chapter helps you determine content goals that provide general direction for your curriculum design. Upon completing it, you will be able to

- convert organizing centers into goals that reflect general learning outcomes;
- select physical education content that supports identified goals;
- analyze content goals according to level of generality;
- use the content outline, structure of content, and task analysis approaches to identify goal prerequisites; and
- construct a learning hierarchy based on content goals.

Since organizing centers are global in nature (e.g., intellectual functioning, healthful living, social responsibility, movement awareness), you need to transform them into operational terms. Statements of purpose that establish *general* direction are called content goals. The task of converting organizing centers into content goals can be challenging. The curriculum design model in Figure 3.1 shows this next step, *determining content goals.*

Content goals communicate intended learning. Therefore, several questions arise. "What are content goals?" "How are content goals derived from organizing centers?" "How are content goals supported by physical education subject matter?" "What processes should be used to analyze content goals?" Answers to these questions are provided in the following sections. Ultimately, you should be able to determine content goals for your own physical education curriculum.

Establishing Direction

Content goals are important to the curriculum-designing process. They bridge the gap between abstract ideas (organizing centers) and specific outcomes (learning objectives). To determine content goals, a five-step approach is recommended. Each step is highlighted and numbered within the chapter. Completing them results in a learning hierarchy that combines content goals and prerequisites. The steps are also summarized in Table 3.6 (page 79).

To start, content goals are defined and illustrated in terms of educational domains and levels of generality. Guidelines for stating content goals are suggested. Then, the task of deriving content goals from organizing centers is described, and examples are provided. Finally, content (subject matter) is selected in support of goals.

Content Goals Defined

Content goals are statements of intent that describe large blocks of subject matter found in a unit or course of study. They are *not* stated in precise, measurable language—that is the purpose of learning objectives (chapter 5). Rather, they are stated as general outcomes or patterns of behavior representing the educational domains, such as:

Cognitive

- Develop critical thinking
- Analyze mechanical principles of movement

Affective

- Appreciate individual, lifetime sports
- Exhibit favorable social attitudes

Psychomotor

- Demonstrate perceptual abilities
- Perform complex adaptive skills

Content goals vary in level of generality based on the intended time period. Some are to be acquired over a long time such as a yearlong curriculum (e.g., develop ability to participate in lifetime

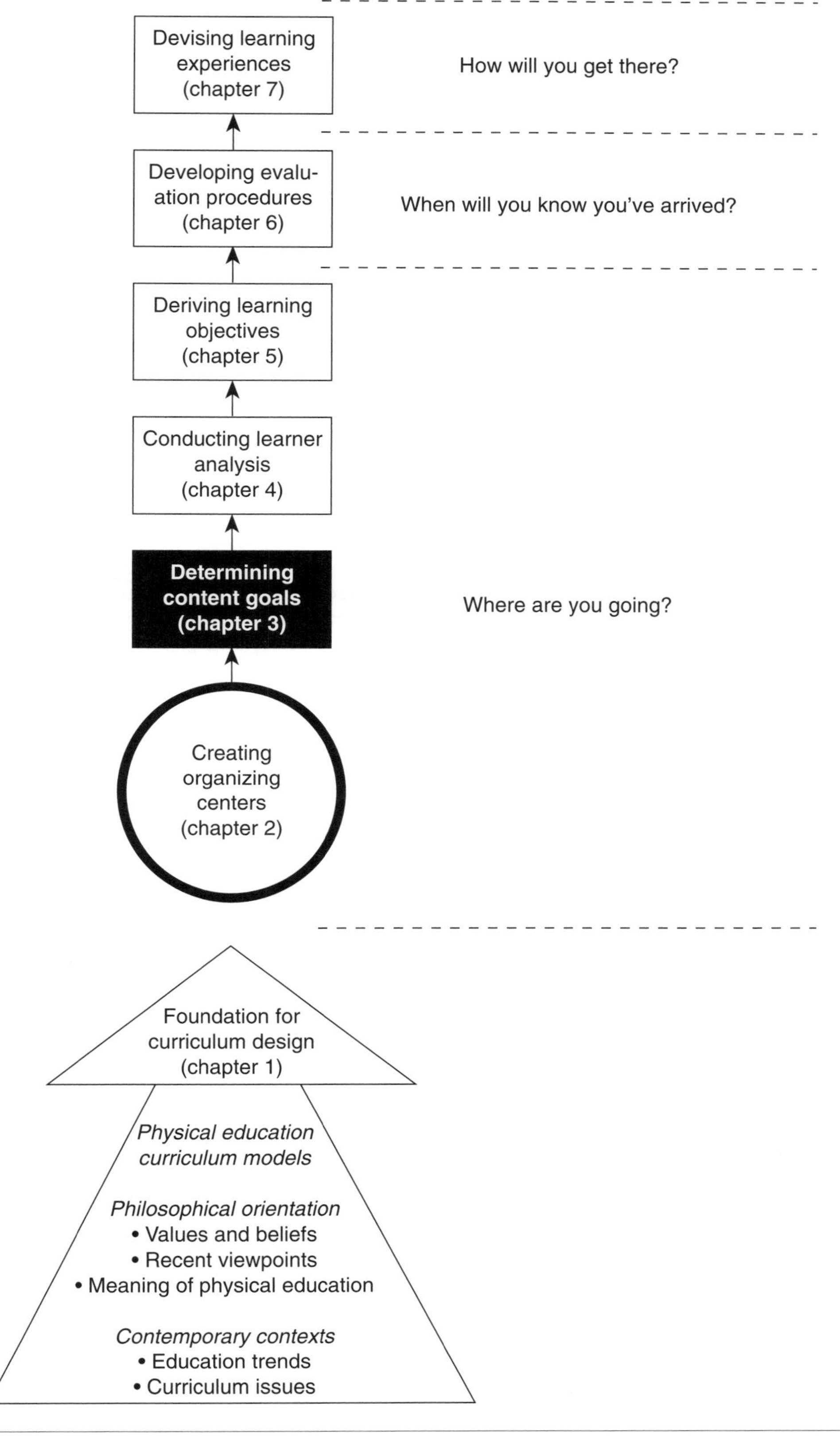

Figure 3.1 Model for designing the physical education curriculum shows the next step, *determining content goals.*

sport activities). Others represent intended learning over a series of lessons (e.g., know the rules of tennis). Like organizing centers, the time period for a given goal could be a teaching episode, single lesson, series of lessons, unit of instruction, academic school year, 4-year high school curriculum, or comprehensive K–12 curriculum.

You must decide the appropriate degree of generality according to your organizing centers and intended time periods. For illustrative purposes, three of the previous content goals have been selected, with examples ranging from most to least general.

Analyze mechanical principles of movement

- Understand the basis for stability
- Determine the variety of postural deviations
- Know the principles of giving and receiving force

Exhibit favorable social attitudes

- Interact with others cooperatively
- Demonstrate tolerance
- Accept responsibility for self and others

Demonstrate perceptual abilities

- Show kinesthetic awareness
- Demonstrate visual discrimination abilities
- Develop eye-hand coordination

The categories of the cognitive, affective, and psychomotor domains are a primary source of content goals. They were defined previously in Tables 2.5 (page 50), 2.6 (page 50), and 2.7 (page 52), respectively. In addition, the following guidelines are suggested for stating content goals:

- State each content goal in terms of *learner* behavior (e.g., understand, appreciate, demonstrate) rather than teacher behavior (e.g., present, introduce, teach) or subject matter (e.g., history of tennis, techniques of putting, progressive overload).
- State each content goal as a learning *product* (e.g., know, value, perform) rather than some learning process (e.g., participate, learn, engage in).
- State each content goal at the degree of generality that matches the intended time period (e.g., lesson, unit, course, yearly curriculum).
- Begin each content goal with a verb denoting a general learning outcome, such as:

Analyze	Develop	Prefer
Apply	Elicit	Respond
Appreciate	Evaluate	Synthesize
Comprehend	Exhibit	Understand
Create	Know	Use
Demonstrate	Perform	Value

Deriving Content Goals From Organizing Centers

Once content goals are determined, the designing process is more directed. If *personalized physical fitness* is the organizing center, then content goals might concentrate on the understanding of, appreciation for, and ability to maintain an individualized level of fitness. Activities (games, sports, exercises, dance) would be used to attain these goals. For example, aspects of modern dance would be chosen that rely on cardiorespiratory endurance, muscular strength and endurance, and flexibility. Different aspects of modern dance would be used for an organizing center such as *self-expression*. Content goals would be more cognitive in nature, including development of flow of motion, movement exploration, and motor ability components (balance, coordination, speed).

In deriving goals from organizing centers, these examples show that the cognitive, affective, and psychomotor domains are represented. While some organizing centers are primarily associated with one domain, related goals are usually recommended from the other domains. The interdependence of the domains is clear when it comes to human learning—the premise is that motivation (affective) is the foundation upon which cognitive and psychomotor learning occurs. Although the domains are virtually inseparable, distinctions are made for practical reasons. This brings us to the first step in the five-step approach for determining content goals.

Step 1: *Decide what general outcomes in each domain support a given organizing center, and their level of generality.* General outcomes, stated in the form of goals, are *immediately* derived from an organizing center. As explained later, various "tiers" of content goals are needed to support these general outcomes. In the following examples, an organizing center is presented for each domain. General outcomes have been derived for all three domains as well. Note their different levels of generality.

Cognitive organizing center: Creative Thinking

Cognitive content goals

- Formulate new routines
- Evaluate offensive and defensive strategies

Affective content goals

- Assume responsibility for divergent thinking
- Value alternative solutions to solving problems

Psychomotor content goals

- Develop a variety of movement sequences
- Demonstrate expressive forms of movement

Affective organizing center: Responsible Living

Cognitive content goals

- Understand the meaning of wellness
- Analyze alternative patterns of nutrition

Affective content goals

- Appreciate the role of exercise in healthful living
- Value the need for emotional control

Psychomotor content goals

- Improve cardiorespiratory endurance
- Develop upper body strength

Psychomotor organizing center: Efficient Functioning

Cognitive content goals

- Know characteristics of physical abilities
- Apply principles of training and conditioning

Affective content goals

- Show interest in motor-related fitness
- Respond favorably to personalized fitness

Psychomotor content goals

- Demonstrate motor ability
- Develop overall body flexibility

The overall number of general outcomes and goals that support an organizing center is not fixed, nor is the specific number of cognitive, affective, and psychomotor goals. In fact, depending on the nature of the organizing center, content goals from one of the domains may not be warranted. The number of goals depends on the time period for the curriculum.

▶ ***Ideally, you can see the importance of transforming organizing centers first into general outcomes. Using Self-Directed Activity 3.1 at the end of this chapter, test your ability to identify general outcomes representing the cognitive, affective, and psychomotor domains.***

Selection of Content

The term *content goals,* rather than simply *goals,* is used as a curriculum component, because of the relationship between subject matter and educational purpose. There needs to be some reference to *what* is learned—content. In other words, goals are supported by physical education subject matter.

Goals are only as meaningful as the content selected to achieve them. Because of the wealth of content options, focusing on organizing centers and corresponding goals

- assures more accurate and complete content development,
- provides a perspective on the content to be treated, and
- facilitates the selection of details.

Goals are set for physical fitness content.

Selecting content without a goal means that anything and everything is potentially acceptable, including that which is irrelevant and insignificant. By determining content goals, you identify the depth and breadth of a particular subject. You should understand the nature of physical education—the logical groupings and relationships that organize its content. This will assist learners in retaining and transferring learning, relating new content to previously learned content, and learning additional content within the same subject (Pasch, Sparks-Langer, Gardner, Starko, & Moody, 1991). Since you have studied physical education (e.g., motor development, physiology, individual and team sports, dance), it is assumed that you are knowledgeable about its content. This brings us to the second step in determining content goals.

Step 2: *Select content such as games, sports, exercises, dance, and gymnastics based on its contribution to the general outcomes.* The relationship between these general outcomes and potential content is depicted in Figure 3.2. The number of content areas depends on

- the number of general outcomes,
- the nature of the general outcomes,
- learner interests and previous experiences with the content,
- relationships among the content areas, and
- the length of time for which the curriculum is designed.

▶ ***Content should be selected in support of general outcomes. To demonstrate your ability to do this, complete Self-Directed Activity 3.2 at the end of this chapter.***

Content Goals Analysis

The analysis of goals can be a difficult task, particularly for teachers who won't take the time to engage in such a thoughtful process. Unfortunately, inadequate analysis is reflected in one's teaching. For example, students are taught misinformation, innovative instructional ideas are ignored, and students are confronted with poorly sequenced learning tasks.

Analysis implies an understanding of subject matter together with the relationships that organize it. A distinction can be made between the way subject matter is organized and the way it is actually learned. What is logical to you may not be intellectually meaningful to the student. For example, in the study of history, students may be expected to develop concepts such as economic growth, social customs, resources, and types of people. However, teachers have used *chronology* to organize history. Thus, students conceptualize the development of events over time, rather than the development of the concepts themselves. With reference to physical education, this relationship was described and illustrated in Figures 2.3 (page 39) and 2.4 (page 40).

When analyzing goals, you should consider both the logical organization of content and sequential learning processes. You can do this by developing what is called the *learning hierarchy*. This technique combines two parts—organization of goals and identification of prerequisites—each of which is treated separately. Then, the learning hierarchy is described and illustrated.

	Potential content																		
General outcomes	Softball	Track	Swimming	Basketball	Gymnastics	Dance	Soccer	Tennis	Golf	Wrestling	Judo	Football	Field hockey	Jogging	Volleyball	Skiing	Archery	Badminton	Ice skating
Exhibit cooperative social skills					?	?													
Appreciate aesthetic forms of movement										?						?			
Develop a program of personalized fitness						?					?								
Demonstrate sports skill patterns			?		?				?					?			?		
Value lifelong learning																			

Figure 3.2 Relationship between general outcomes and content is shown. Content is selected on the basis of its contribution to an outcome, which in turn reflects a particular organizing center.

Organization of Goals

As you know, categories of the cognitive, affective, and psychomotor domains are arranged as a hierarchy from the simplest behavioral outcomes to the most complex. Mastery at higher levels implies mastery at lower levels. However, you shouldn't assume that the higher, complex levels are more valuable. For example, you need to *know* the rules of a game before you can *apply* them. Although knowledge is lower than application, it is just as valuable. In the same manner, goals can be arranged from simple to complex with several benefits:

- The outcome intended by the goal can be presented in a progression from less to more difficult.
- A step-by-step procedure is implied that provides the increments to the learning process out of which assessment can occur (i.e., the learning process can be systematically monitored).
- Students can "learn from success" by beginning at a level of success, reviewing what has been learned, and then building toward a higher achievement level.
- The content being used can be more directly linked to the level of the goal.

The organization of content goals *within* each domain is illustrated in Table 3.1 (cognitive), Table 3.2 (affective), and Table 3.3 (psychomotor). A general outcome is identified at the top. Content goals are presented at each level of the domain. They are considered potential first-tier, second-tier, and even third-tier goals.

The domains are elaborate schemes for identifying and organizing specific learning outcomes. Therefore, it's useful to simplify them as shown in Figure 3.3 (page 71). The range of outcomes is divided into only two categories—simple, low-order behaviors and complex, high-order behaviors. This brings us to the next two steps in determining content goals.

Step 3: *Analyze the general outcomes to develop a first tier of content goals that relates more specifically to the selected content areas, focuses on the next supporting level, and covers those behaviors necessary for achievement of the general outcomes.* The number of first-tier goals depends on the generality level of the outcomes and the number of selected content areas.

Step 4: *Develop additional tiers of content goals, as necessary, following a process similar to that described to develop the first tier.* This depends on the level of the preceding tier and the intended time period (e.g., series of lessons, monthly unit,

Table 3.1 Organization of Content Goals in the Cognitive Domain

General outcome: Develop an understanding of the principles and concepts basic to a variety of sports and games.

Cognitive domain categories	Goal/Content (volleyball)
1. Evaluation	*Compare*: advantages and disadvantages of multiple-player blocks; positive and negative features of receiving formations ("W" and crescent); various techniques of bump passing, spiking, and serving
2. Synthesis	*Determine*: interchange of positions according to players' strengths; playing territories for different formations; ball-handling techniques based on space, force, time, and flow
3. Analysis	*Recognize*: offensive and defensive matchups; spike variations resulting from space and force elements; concepts of creating space, interchange of position, and spatial arrangements
4. Application	*Use*: rules, formations, and types of passes and blocks in appropriate situations
5. Comprehension	*Distinguish*: positions and their functions; on-hand and off-hand side; spike and free ball defenses
6. Knowledge	*Know*: positions in volleyball; rules of volleyball; order of rotation

Table 3.2 Organization of Content Goals in the Affective Domain

General outcome: Develop a value for the maintenance of various physical fitness practices.

Affective domain categories	Goal/Content (muscular strength and endurance)
1. Characterization	*Continue*: personal weight training routine over an extended period of time
2. Organization	*Adhere to and adjust*: weight training routines in accordance with gains in muscular strength and endurance
3. Valuing	*Determine and practice*: preferred weight training exercises
4. Responding	*Try out and experiment with:* weight training equipment
5. Receiving	*Observe*: demonstrations of weight training equipment

Table 3.3 Organization of Content Goals in the Psychomotor Domain

General outcome: Develop abilities in rhythmic creative movement and free response activities.

Psychomotor domain categories	Goal/Content (gymnastics)
1. Nondiscursive communication	*Perform*: choreographed free exercise and balance beam routines based on transition, momentum, and flow of movement
2. Skilled movements	*Exhibit*: complex adaptive skills for free exercise (e.g., roundoff, back handspring, back somersault); vaulting (e.g., squat-on, straddle-on, stoop-on); uneven bars (e.g., forward roll dismount, hip circle mount, half knee circle, backward hip circle)
3. Physical abilities	*Develop*: arm and shoulder strength and endurance (e.g., uneven bars, horizontal bar, rings, side horse); trunk-hip flexibility (e.g., vaulting, uneven bars, free exercise); agility (e.g., balance beam, uneven bars, free exercise)
4. Perceptual abilities	*Demonstrate*: inverted balances (e.g., tripod, headstand, tip-up, hand-stand); static balances on beam (e.g., front scale, knee scale, V-seat)
5. Basic fundamental movements	*Execute*: skills basic to complex gymnastics movements (e.g., walking, running, leaping, swinging, bending, twisting, handling, gripping)
6. Reflex movements	Since reflex movements are not voluntary, content is not analyzed; these movements are prerequisites to the above classification levels.

school year). You would normally stop when second- or third-tier goals begin to focus on the lower levels of the domains (e.g., fundamental movements, perceptual abilities, knowledge of facts, responding behaviors). In Figure 3.4, content goals are organized to illustrate the development of these tiers. In this example, it was determined that goals from each domain were justified.

▶ ***In goals analysis, organizing content goals by level of complexity is an important step. To demonstrate your ability, complete Self-Directed Activity 3.3 at the end of this chapter.***

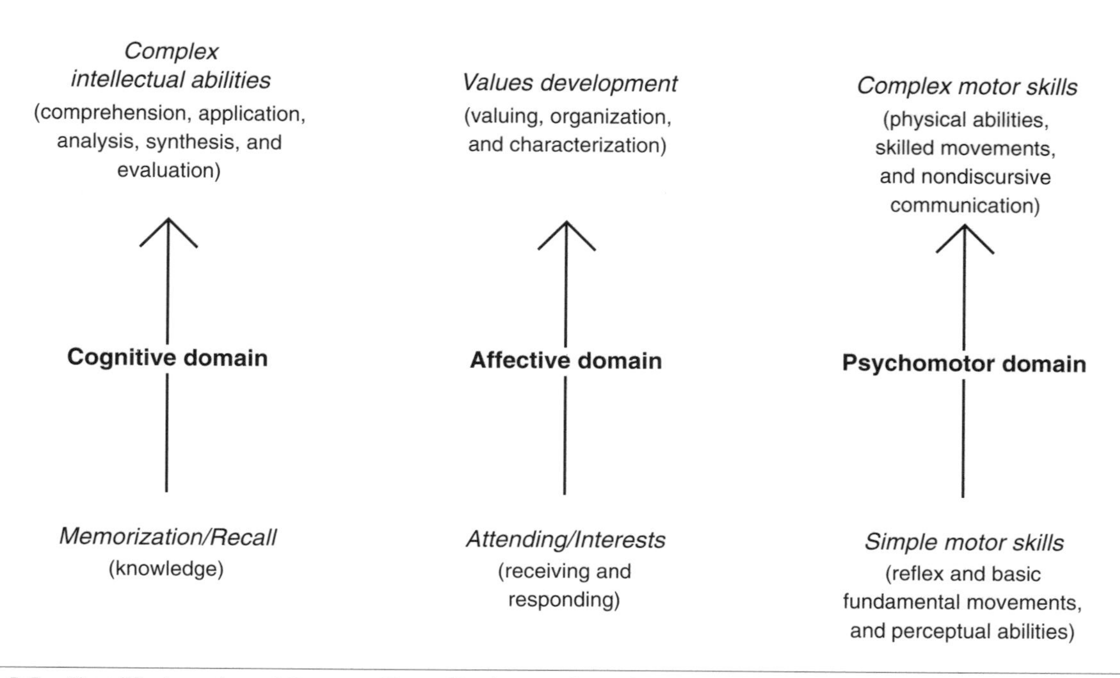

Figure 3.3 Simplified version of the cognitive, affective, and psychomotor domains shows two levels of the hierarchy.

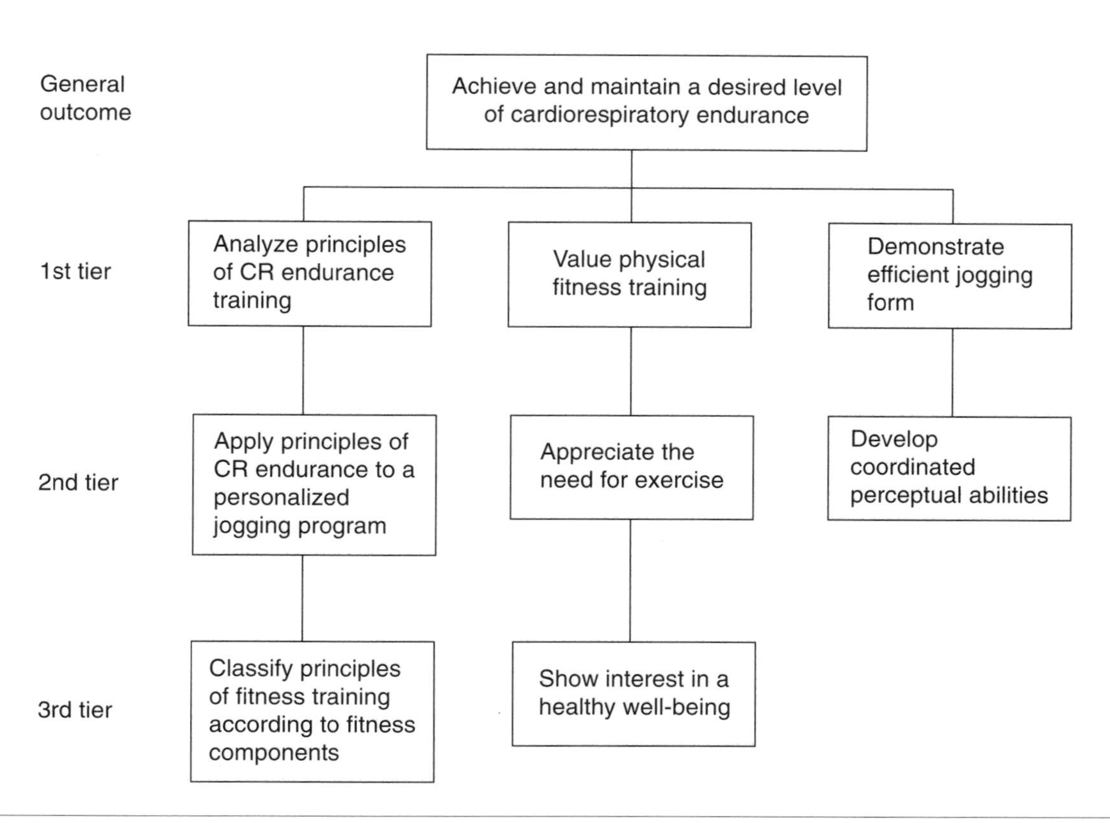

Figure 3.4 Organization of content goals is shown representing a general outcome and three tiers of goals according to level of generality (complexity).

Identification of Prerequisites

Once content goals are organized into tiers, the lower level behaviors (facts, responses, motor abilities) that support these higher level goals should be determined. These prerequisites are needed by the student in order to achieve the outcome expressed by the goal. This brings us to the final step in the five-step process for determining content goals.

Step 5: *Identify the prerequisites for each content goal in the last tier of goals*. The suggested procedure for identifying prerequisites is (Hurwitz, 1993f):

Step A: Think through or actually do the behavior (action) specified by the goal as a novice who has just learned it would, or carefully observe someone else doing it.

Step B: Take some notes as to the decisions, skills, concepts, information, processes, emotions, and attitudes needed to do the task.

Step C: Note the domain of the goal and refer to Table 3.4, which lists possible prerequisites for various kinds of learning in each domain.

Step D: See which possibilities your notes fall under; decide if there are other possibilities related to the goal.

Step E: See if there are possibilities you don't have notes for; perhaps, identify prerequisites relating to these possibilities; analyze the content to identify additional prerequisites by outlining content, structuring content, and/or conducting a task analysis. Descriptions of these approaches follow this list.

Step F: You *may* want to identify prerequisites to these prerequisites, but it is probably not necessary to go that far.

Step G: Sort your prerequisites into three groups: those that all of your students should and probably already do possess (group 1); those that some or many of your students might not already possess (group 2); and those that most or all of your students probably do not possess (group 3).

By identifying prerequisites, you account for all that needs to be learned. For example, Figure 3.5 (page 75) shows the prerequisites for the last tier of goals from Figure 3.4. To further assist you, the three approaches suggested in step E are described.

Complex sport skills represent a content goal.

Table 3.4 Possible Prerequisites for Various Kinds of Learning

Cognitive domain	Possible prerequisites
***Complex intellectual abilities* (application, analysis, synthesis, and evaluation)**	• Knows definitions of concepts involved • Has grasp of concepts and/or subconcepts which are part of or related to the task • Knows other related facts and principles • Can perform skill needed to demonstrate result of application of concept (e.g., draw circle, point) • Has necessary physical capabilities • Can demonstrate subordinate processes, rules, or procedures that are steps in demonstrating the original process, rule, or procedure • Can perform necessary motor skills • Can solve subordinate problems • Knows steps of problem-solving process
***Memorization, recall, and interpretation of information* (knowledge and comprehension)**	• Knows the larger meaningful context to which the information is related • Can perform procedures needed to convey what is learned (e.g., speak, write, label) • Can memorize, study • Has sensory capabilities • Has grasp of concepts related to the task • Knows definitions of terms, concepts involved in the task

Affective domain	Possible prerequisites
***Values development* (valuing, organization, and characterization)**	• Has a point of view • Has the capacity for voluntary activity • Is committed to underlying values • Knows the consequences of having the "attitude" and not having the "attitude" • Knows how one acts when showing evidence of having the "attitude" • Has skills necessary to show evidence • Can show preference • Can differentiate among various value perspectives • Is capable of behaving consistently • Has a favorable attitude toward a philosophy of life
***Attending behaviors and interest* (receiving and responding)**	• Is aware of the learning situation • Is willing to comply • Knows how to be actively involved • Has physical capabilities to respond • Can differentiate between favored stimulus and competing/distracting stimuli

(continued)

Table 3.4 *(continued)*

Psychomotor domain	Possible prerequisites
Complex motor skills **(physical abilities, skilled movements, and nondiscursive communication)**	• Is capable of showing satisfaction • Can analyze the motor skill • Can analyze the performance of the motor skill by self or others • Has physical capabilities (e.g., strength, flexibility, balance, sight, hearing) • Can perform component motor skills • Is capable of simple adaptive skills (e.g., sawing a piece of wood) • Is capable of compound adaptive skills (e.g., racket games, hockey, golf) • Is capable of complex adaptive skills (e.g., gymnastic stunts, twisting dive) • Can create expressive movement
Simple motor skills **(reflex and basic fundamental movements, and perceptual abilities)**	• Is capable of involuntary reflex movements • Can change from stationary to ambulatory (e.g., crawl, creep, slide, walk, run) • Is able to coordinate movements of the extremities (e.g., piano playing, typing) • Knows the procedure or criteria for performing the skill • Knows when, or under what circumstances, the skill is to be done • Has sensory capabilities

Note. Adapted from "A Suggested Process for Identifying Prerequisites: Doing a Task Analysis," by R. Hurwitz, 1993, unpublished manuscript, Cleveland State University. Adapted by permission of the author.

Outlining Content

Curriculum designers frequently break down subject matter by simply *outlining* selected content. The prerequisites needed to achieve the last tier of goals could be outlined. The two-dimensional chart in Table 3.5 (page 76) shows this relationship. Column and row intersections are marked if the content element applies to the general outcome.

▶ ***You should be able to identify prerequisites that support higher level goals. To practice this skill, complete Self-Directed Activity 3.4 at the end of this chapter.***

Structuring Content

This approach is similar to outlining content, except that the subject matter of the goal is *structured* in terms of its various generalizations, concepts, and basic knowledge and skills. A generalization states how and why content elements are related (e.g., a successful soccer instep kick depends on foot placement in relation to the ball and leg swing). It combines two or more concepts. A concept is a mental category of "things" or ideas that share a common set of characteristics—objects, people, strategies, skill patterns. They are usually expressed in one or two words. For instance, the concept *follow-through* is encountered when throwing an object, kicking an object, and striking an object with or without an implement. Specific facts, knowledge, and skills provide the foundation for the more complex concepts and generalizations.

This approach is represented by the pyramid in Figure 3.6 (page 77). Prerequisites are structured for the golf swing. Concepts are identified that support the stated generalization, and the most elementary material to be learned is shown at the base of the pyramid.

A flowchart is another way to display these relationships, as in Figure 3.7 (page 78). It expands the pyramid analysis in Figure 3.6. Whether the pyramid or flowchart is used, each represents the identification of prerequisites. Concepts, knowledge,

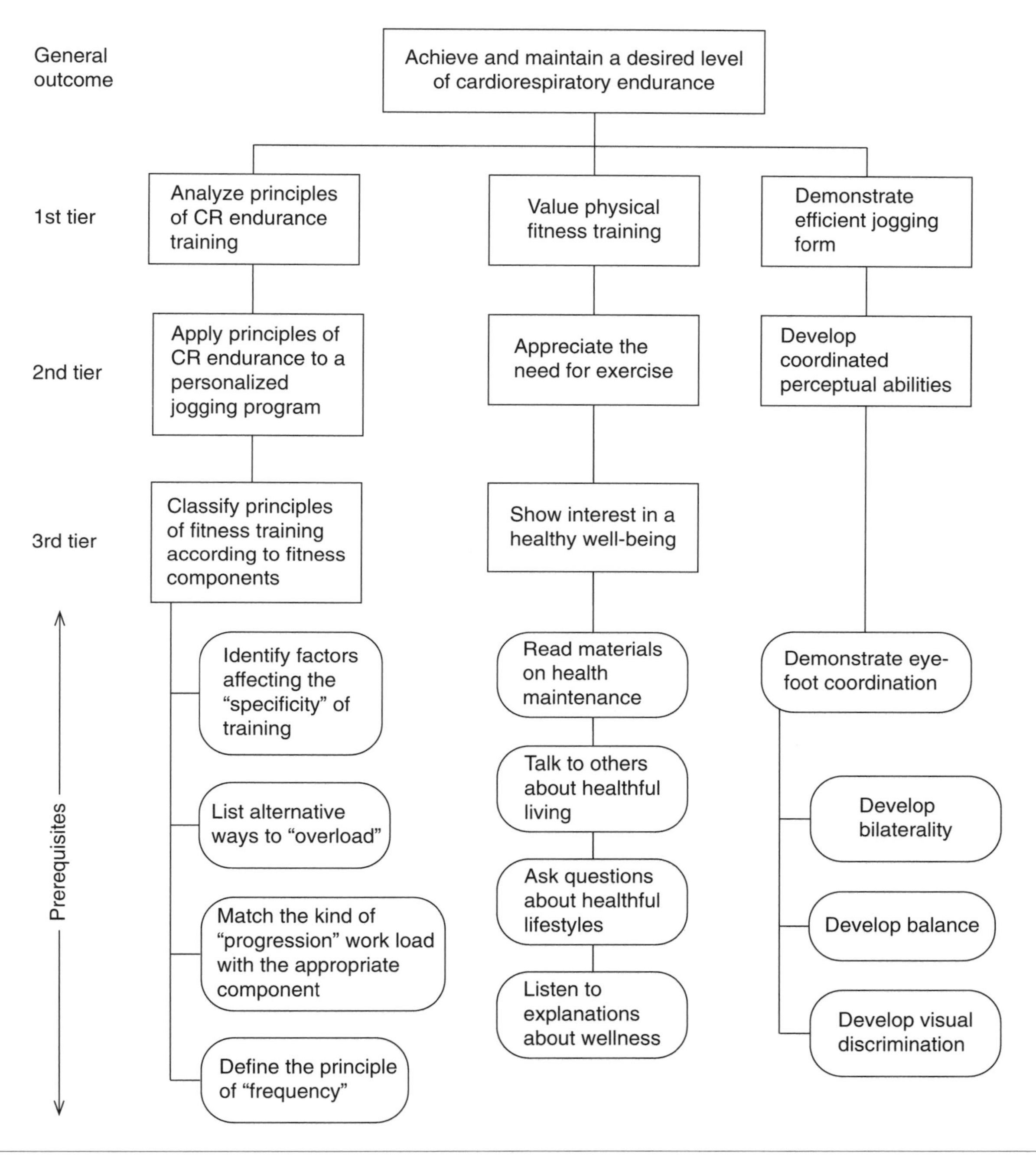

Figure 3.5 Prerequisites are identified for the last tier of goals from Figure 3.4.

Table 3.5 General Outcomes and Content Outline

Content outline of tennis	General outcomes						
	Understand facts and basic information	Apply concepts and principles	Analyze movement form	Demonstrate skill proficiency	Display social attitudes	Show interest	Exhibit values learning
A. Essential skills of tennis							
1. Forehand drive	x	x	x	x		x	
2. Backhand drive	x	x	x	x		x	
3. Footwork	x	x	x	x		x	
4. Serve	x	x	x	x		x	
5. Volley	x	x	x	x		x	
B. Auxiliary tennis strokes							
1. Ball spin	x	x	x	x		x	
2. Advanced serves	x	x	x	x		x	
3. Lob	x	x	x	x		x	
4. Overhead smash	x	x	x	x		x	
5. Dropshots	x	x	x	x		x	
6. Half-volley	x	x	x	x		x	
C. Patterns of tennis play							
1. Service	x	x	x	x		x	
2. Return of serve	x	x	x	x		x	
3. Backcourt play	x	x	x	x		x	
4. Net play	x	x	x	x		x	
D. Rules of tennis							
1. Delivering the serve	x					x	x
2. Receiving the serve	x					x	x
3. After the serve	x					x	x
4. Scoring	x					x	x
5. Changing sides	x					x	x
6. Tiebreaker procedures	x					x	x
E. Strategies of tennis							
1. Singles	x	x		x	x	x	x
2. Doubles	x	x		x	x	x	x
F. Playing courtesies							
1. Warm-up	x				x	x	x
2. Concentration	x				x	x	x
3. Ready position	x				x	x	x
4. Keeping score	x				x	x	x
5. Officiating	x				x	x	x

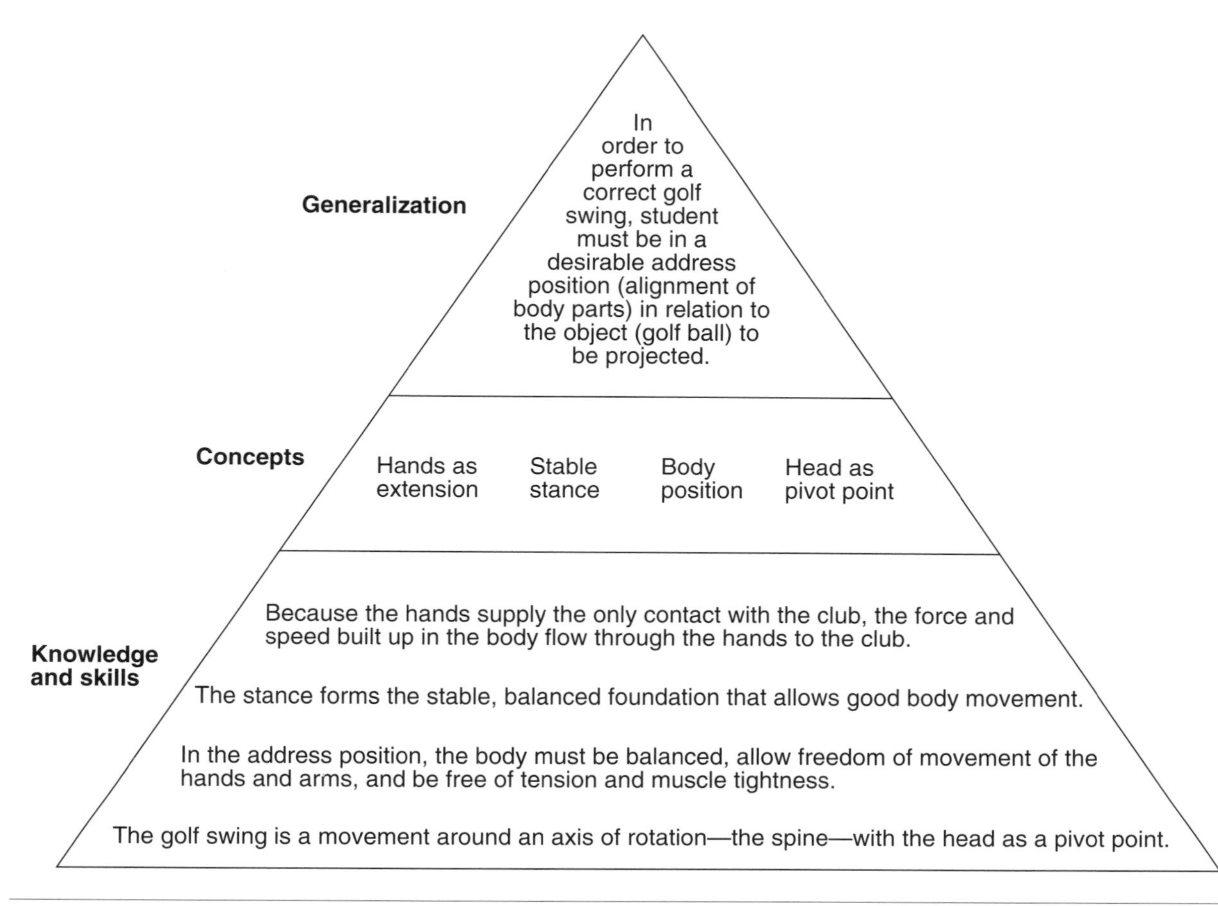

Figure 3.6 Structure of content approach is shown for identifying prerequisites to the golf swing.

and skills are identified for the generalization. Structuring content has implications for not only *what* is taught, but *how* generalizations, concepts, and facts and skills are taught. A learning sequence is suggested by the relationships among the "bits" of content.

▶ ***To practice supporting generalizations with concepts and basic knowledge and skills, complete Self-Directed Activity 3.5 at the end of this chapter.***

Conducting a Task Analysis

Structuring content involved the conceptual breakdown of that content. Task analysis is more concerned with the level of complexity or difficulty of the content. It focuses on *how* the learner acquires knowledge, skills, attitudes, social behaviors, and values. Learning sequences can be used to identify prerequisites. In other words, the tasks associated with the content are described in a step-by-step progression that identifies the elements of those tasks.

Task analysis is the process of breaking down a task into its component subtasks and arranging them from simple to complex. *Those who cannot break down, subdivide, and analyze content appropriately run the risk of teaching misinformation or confounding students with irrelevancies.* You should answer the question, "What must the student do in order to perform the task?" If this question is answered accurately, superficial or meaningless tasks will be eliminated.

A partial task analysis is shown in Figure 3.8 (page 79). It's an extension of the pyramid (Figure 3.6) and flowchart (Figure 3.7) approaches to structuring content. This single task—the golf swing—is one of many tasks that is part of the overall content. Since task analysis provides a visible reminder of the pathway for instruction, detailing all prerequisite tasks, it is used again in chapter 4, "Conducting Learner Analysis" (pages 99 and 105).

▶ ***Sequencing tasks is useful for identifying prerequisites. To practice task analysis, complete Self-Directed Activity 3.6 at the end of this chapter.***

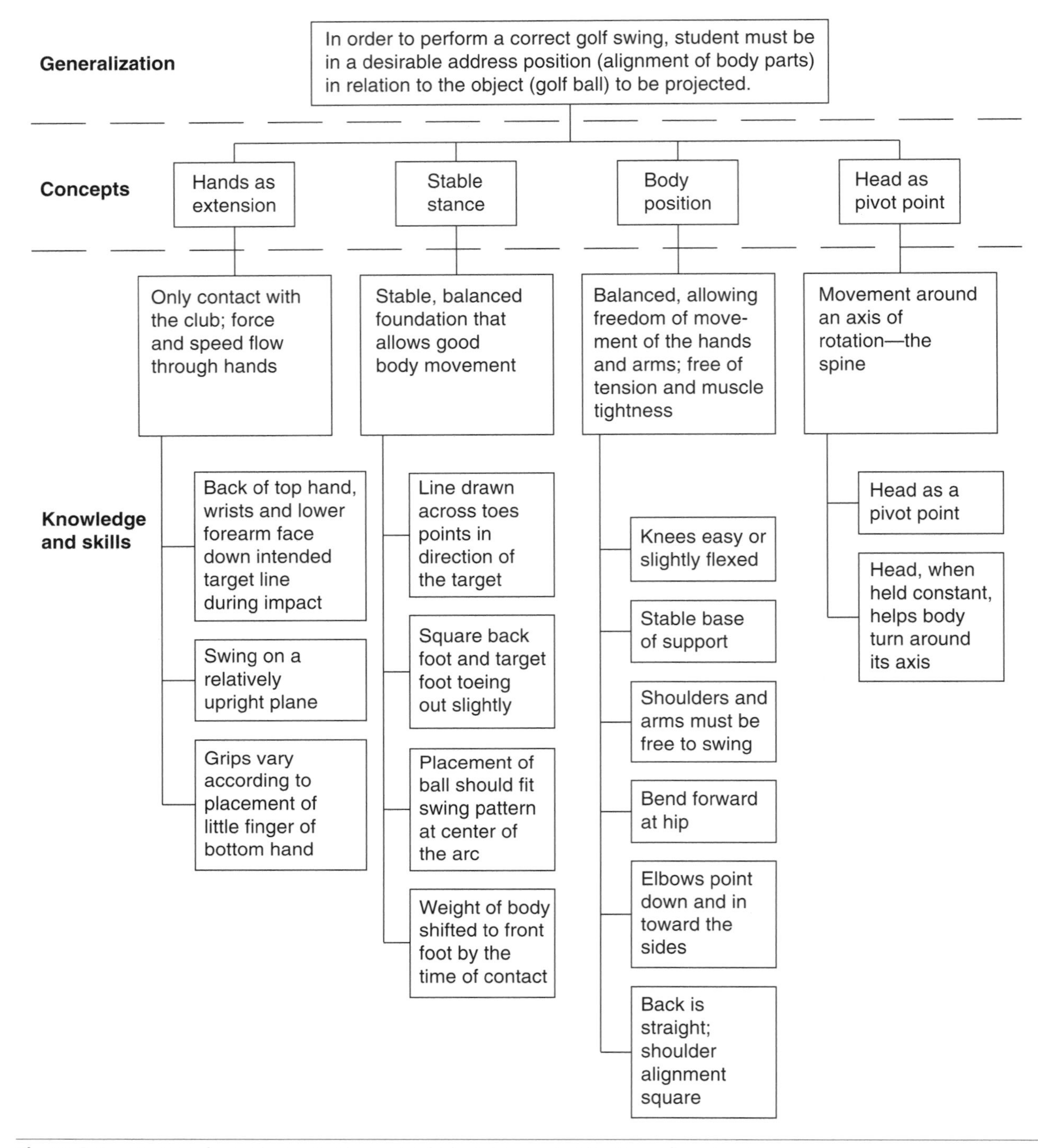

Figure 3.7 Content from Figure 3.6 is expanded and organized using a flowchart.

Learning Hierarchy

The process for establishing and analyzing content goals ends with the learning hierarchy, a practical technique that integrates the steps of this process. These steps are summarized in Table 3.6.

The learning hierarchy provides an overall view of the curriculum. It displays the relationships across all kinds and levels of content goals, usually in a flowchart. The learning hierarchy in Figure 3.9 (page 80) illustrates this synthesis of an organizing center, general outcomes, content goals, and prerequisites.

▶ ***To practice constructing a learning hierarchy, complete Self-Directed Activity 3.7 at the end of this chapter.***

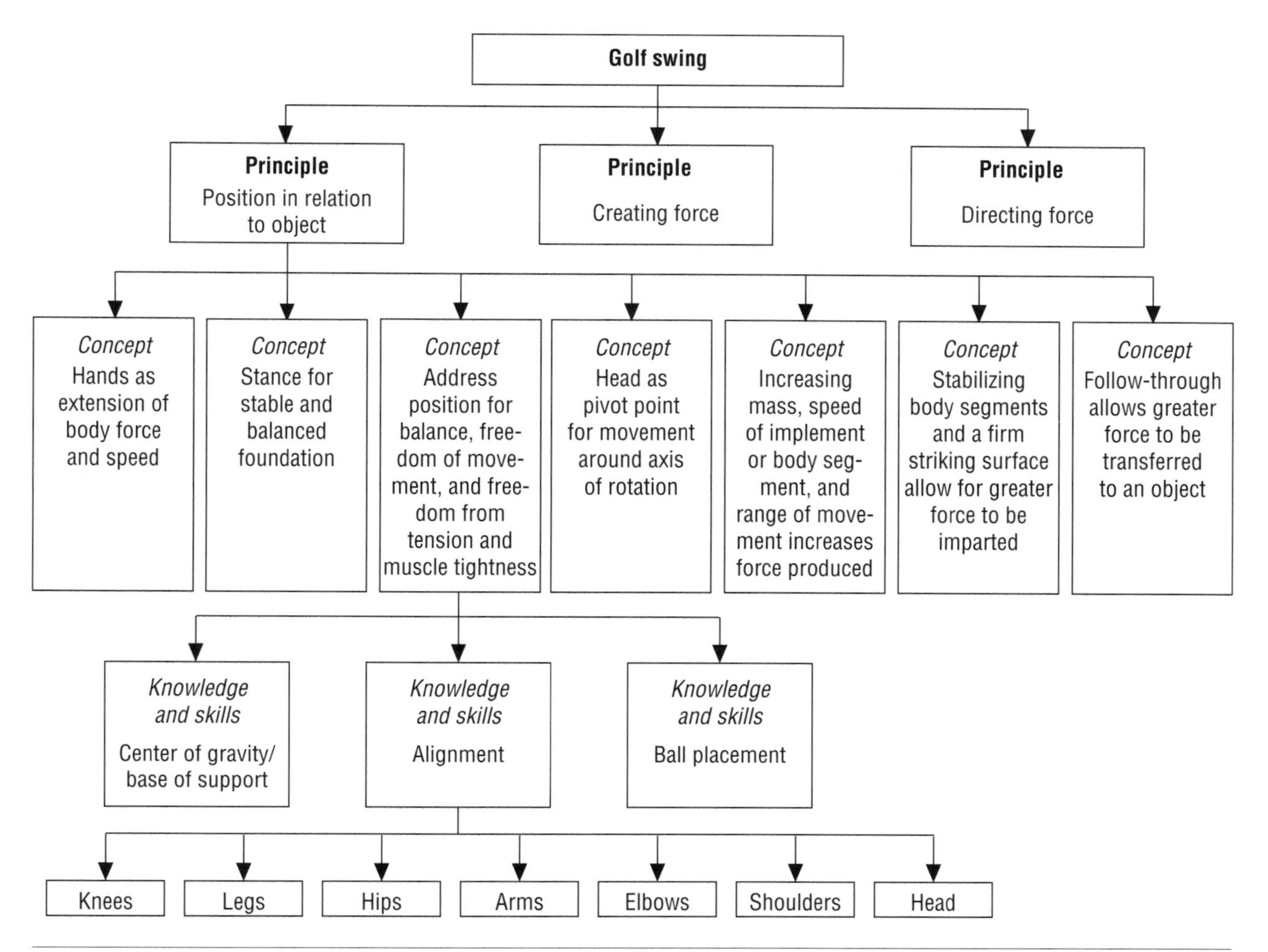

Figure 3.8 Task analysis (partial) is shown for the golf swing. The sequence of learning is suggested by the prerequisites that make up the task.

Table 3.6 Steps for Determining Content Goals

Step number	Description
1	Decide what general outcomes in each domain support a given organizing center, and their level of generality.
2	Select content such as games, sports, exercises, dance, and gymnastics based on its contribution to the general outcomes.
3	Analyze the general outcomes to develop a first tier of content goals that relates more specifically to the selected content areas, focuses on the next supporting level, and covers those behaviors necessary for achievement of the general outcomes.
4	Develop additional tiers of content goals, as necessary, following a process similar to that described to develop the first tier.
5	Identify the prerequisites (lower level facts, responses, motor abilities) for each content goal in the last tier of goals.

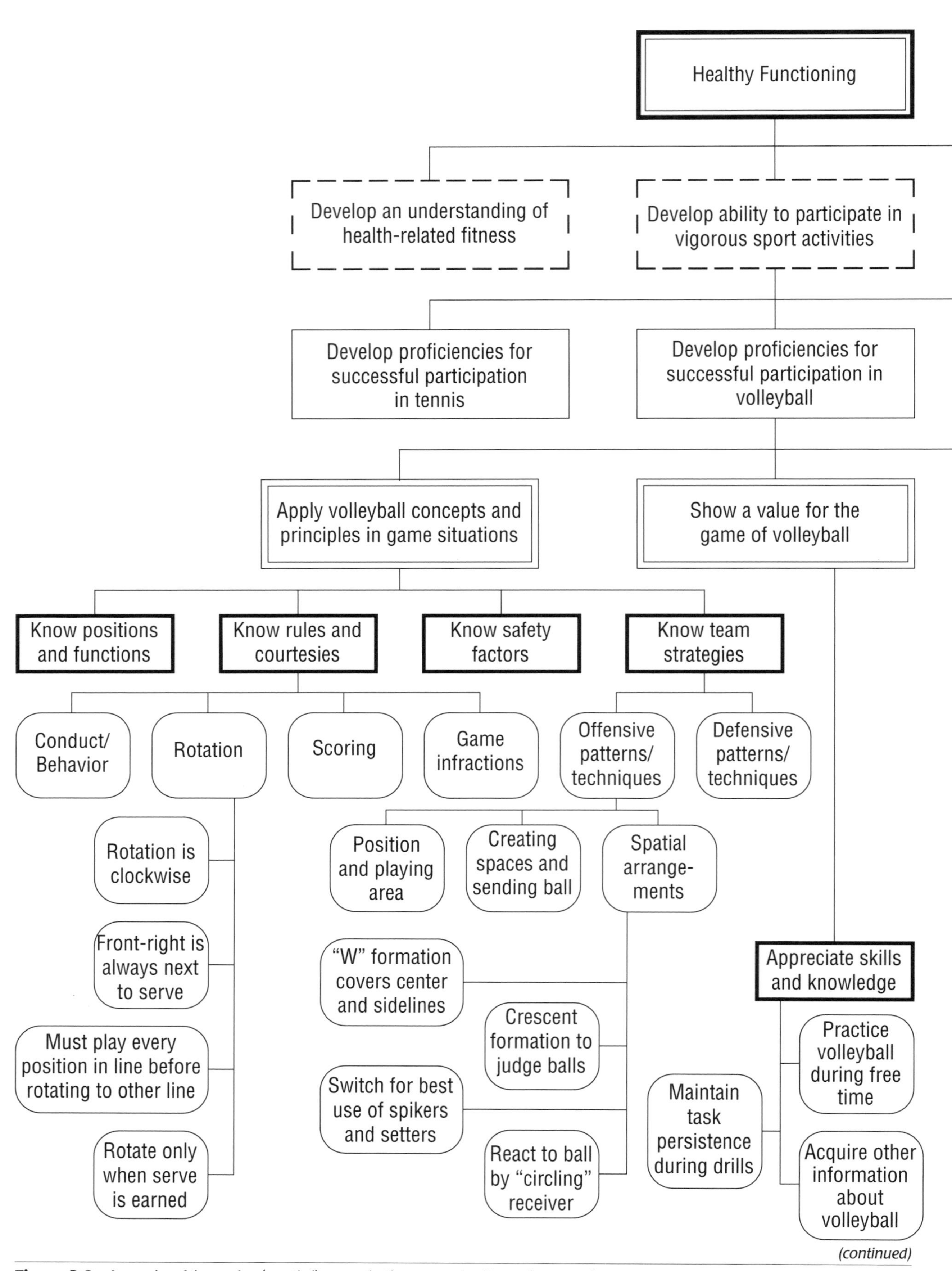

(continued)

Figure 3.9 Learning hierarchy (partial) reveals the organization of general outcomes, content goals, and the identification of prerequisites for the organizing center "Healthy Functioning."

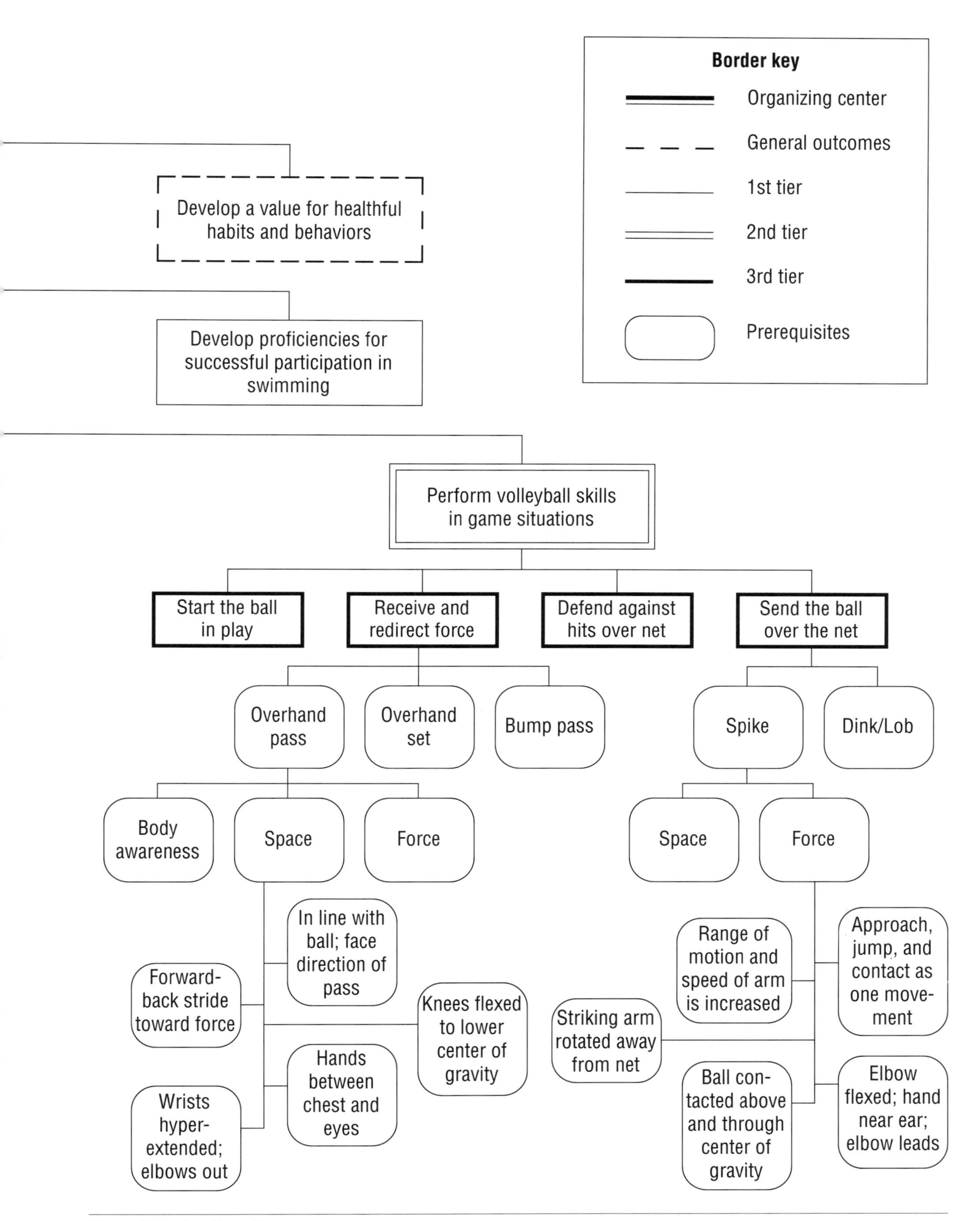

Border key
Organizing center
General outcomes
1st tier
2nd tier
3rd tier
Prerequisites
Develop a value for healthful habits and behaviors
Develop proficiencies for successful participation in swimming
Perform volleyball skills in game situations
Start the ball in play
Receive and redirect force
Defend against hits over net
Send the ball over the net
Overhand pass
Overhand set
Bump pass
Spike
Dink/Lob
Body awareness
Space
Force
Space
Force
In line with ball; face direction of pass
Forward-back stride toward force
Knees flexed to lower center of gravity
Hands between chest and eyes
Wrists hyper-extended; elbows out
Range of motion and speed of arm is increased
Approach, jump, and contact as one move-ment
Striking arm rotated away from net
Ball con-tacted above and through center of gravity
Elbow flexed; hand near ear; elbow leads

Figure 3.9 *(continued)*

Making It Work

Have you achieved the expected outcomes (page 64)? Congratulations! You are able to determine content goals for your physical education curriculum design. Still, you may have some practical questions that need answers, such as:

- **How can you think of all the general goals that might be associated with an organizing center?**

  Theoretically, you probably can't. However, you should try to generate as many goals as you think are possible given time constraints for achieving them and the level of generality you intend. That's what the domains are for. If you use their categories as a guide, you will likely come close to exhausting all the goals you want. For example, in the cognitive domain, you can decide what you want students to know, whether you want them to apply information, and whether you want them to make judgments. These goals that are immediately derived from organizing centers have been called general outcomes. Remember that other tiers of goals will follow depending on what content you choose. That's the most difficult part—trying to figure out how many supporting goals are desirable and what their level of generality is. Subject matter knowledge on your part will help in this process, as will a thorough understanding of the learning hierarchies in the cognitive, affective, and psychomotor domains.

- **Why do you select content (sports, games, exercises, dance) after you determine your general outcomes instead of before?**

  Unfortunately, many people don't anyway. It's impossible not to have certain content in the back of your mind while you're determining goals—even while you're creating organizing centers, for that matter. If you start with content (e.g., volleyball, rhythms, dual activities, weight training routines), the subject matter itself will dictate the goals. It's not wrong to do it this way, but you end up with just a series of activities. If you start with general outcomes—as an extension of organizing centers—then you should be selecting only those content areas that contribute to these outcomes. Your response to this might be that you aren't free to select all potential content because of limited equipment, supplies, facilities, etc. That may be true to some degree, but don't let these reasons become excuses. You can always modify activities or use resources outside the school if necessary. Eventually, you will find it easier to attach "bits" of content to your supporting content goals.

- **Do content goals really need to be arranged in "tiers"?**

  Yes, if you agree that learning occurs sequentially. The process may seem impractical and a waste of time, but it's really not if you're serious about maximizing learning. In practice, you don't need to draw diagrams or flowcharts as long as you have organized your content goals according to level of generality (i.e., tiers). It may not seem that significant to you now, but students will experience learning difficulties if goals are too complex or poorly sequenced. It would also help if you communicated your intent to students. Show them how mastery of one goal can lead to mastery of higher level goals.

- **Is it necessary to write out all the prerequisites to a behavior or task?**

  Oftentimes, when you ask a physical education teacher to identify all the components of a particular task (e.g., tennis backhand), the answer is, "I just know what they are. I tell my students to watch what I do." That's not good enough. The reluctance to actually jot down the basic abilities, concepts, and/or emotions needed to do a task could mean that the teacher does not truly understand the task. That's why task analysis is so important. Granted, you don't need fancy pyramids or flowcharts, but you do need some way of making sure that all prerequisites are covered. Otherwise, you will end up teaching misinformation, leaving out required subtasks, or confusing students with meaningless subtasks.

- **Isn't a learning hierarchy just busywork?**

  Remember that a learning hierarchy is used to organize your general outcomes and content goals in a scheme that communicates what it is you're trying to do. Here again, you don't need a carefully drawn flowchart or diagram to construct a learning hierarchy. But you do need some format to synthesize your content goals. Start small, with two or three general outcomes, and develop supporting goals leading to prerequisites. Add goals as appropriate, and, little by little, you will have a fully developed learning hierarchy. Then all you need to do is refine it. That's easy!

Self-Directed Activity 3.1

Ideally, you can see the importance of transforming organizing centers first into general outcomes. For each of the following organizing centers, identify a general outcome representing the cognitive, the affective, and the psychomotor domain.

1. *Organizing center*: Decision Making

   Cognitive: ____________________

   Affective: ____________________

   Psychomotor: ____________________

2. *Organizing center*: Valuing Movement Patterns

   Cognitive: ____________________

   Affective: ____________________

   Psychomotor: ____________________

3. *Organizing center*: Basic Movement

   Cognitive: ____________________

   Affective: ____________________

   Psychomotor: ____________________

Feedback

There are many possible outcomes, all equally acceptable. The following ones are provided for illustrative purposes.

1. *Decision Making*

   Apply principles of self-pacing (cognitive)

   Appreciate independent learning (affective)

   Demonstrate prescriptive weight training exercises (psychomotor)

2. *Valuing Movement Patterns*

   Understand laterality and directionality (cognitive)

   Show lifetime sports preferences (affective)

   Demonstrate body awareness (psychomotor)

3. *Basic Movement*

   Know locomotor movements (cognitive)

   Value manipulative skills (affective)

   Perform nonlocomotor movements (psychomotor)

Self-Directed Activity 3.2

Content should be selected in support of general outcomes. To demonstrate this ability, use the outcomes you generated in Self-Directed Activity 3.1. The numbered organizing centers are repeated here for easy reference. Try to identify some content areas that support your general outcomes.

1. *Organizing center*: Decision Making

   Physical education content: ______________________________

   ____

   ____

   ____

2. *Organizing center*: Valuing Movement Patterns

   Physical education content: ______________________________

   ____

   ____

   ____

3. *Organizing center*: Basic Movement

   Physical education content: ______________________________

   ____

   ____

   ____

Feedback

Some possible answers are provided. Many other content areas are equally acceptable.

1. *Decision Making*

   Mimetics; movement exploration; low-organization games; rhythms; self-testing activities; stunts and tumbling; individual sports.

2. *Valuing Movement Patterns*

   Movement exploration; self-testing activities; stunts and tumbling; rhythms and dance; folk dancing; individual/dual activities.

3. *Basic Movement*

   Walking, running, jumping, hopping, leaping (even rhythm); skipping, sliding, galloping (uneven rhythm); bending and stretching, twisting and turning, pushing and pulling, swinging and swaying, falling and rising; handling, controlling, and projecting movable objects.

Self-Directed Activity 3.3

In goals analysis, organizing content goals by level of complexity is an important step. To demonstrate this ability, identify a general outcome. Then select some content and generate at least two goals at the next supporting level (first tier). Finally, generate one more goal at the next supporting level for one of these goals (second tier).

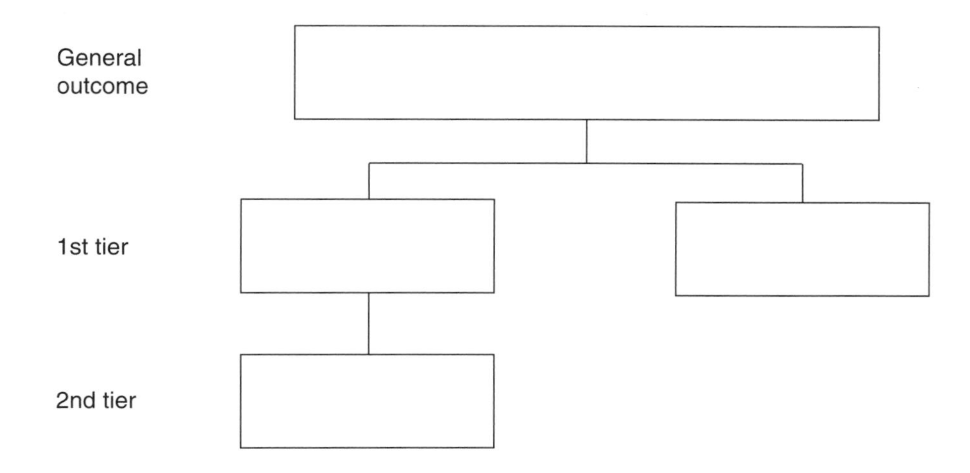

Feedback

Your goals should be arranged in order of complexity representing the cognitive, affective, or psychomotor domains. They should be similar to the ones shown in Figure 3.4 (page 71).

Self-Directed Activity 3.4

You should be able to identify prerequisites that support higher level goals. For this activity, use your goal from the second tier in Self-Directed Activity 3.3. Restate it in the box. Then, in the space provided, *outline* the prerequisites for this goal.

Feedback

Your prerequisites, presented in outline form, should have identified the facts, responses, and motor abilities needed by students to achieve your goal. They should be similar in format to the ones shown in Table 3.5 (page 76).

Self-Directed Activity 3.5

State a physical education goal that's of interest to you. Then, structure the content that makes up the goal by stating a generalization, at least two concepts that support the generalization, and the basic knowledge and skills that provide the foundation for one of the concepts.

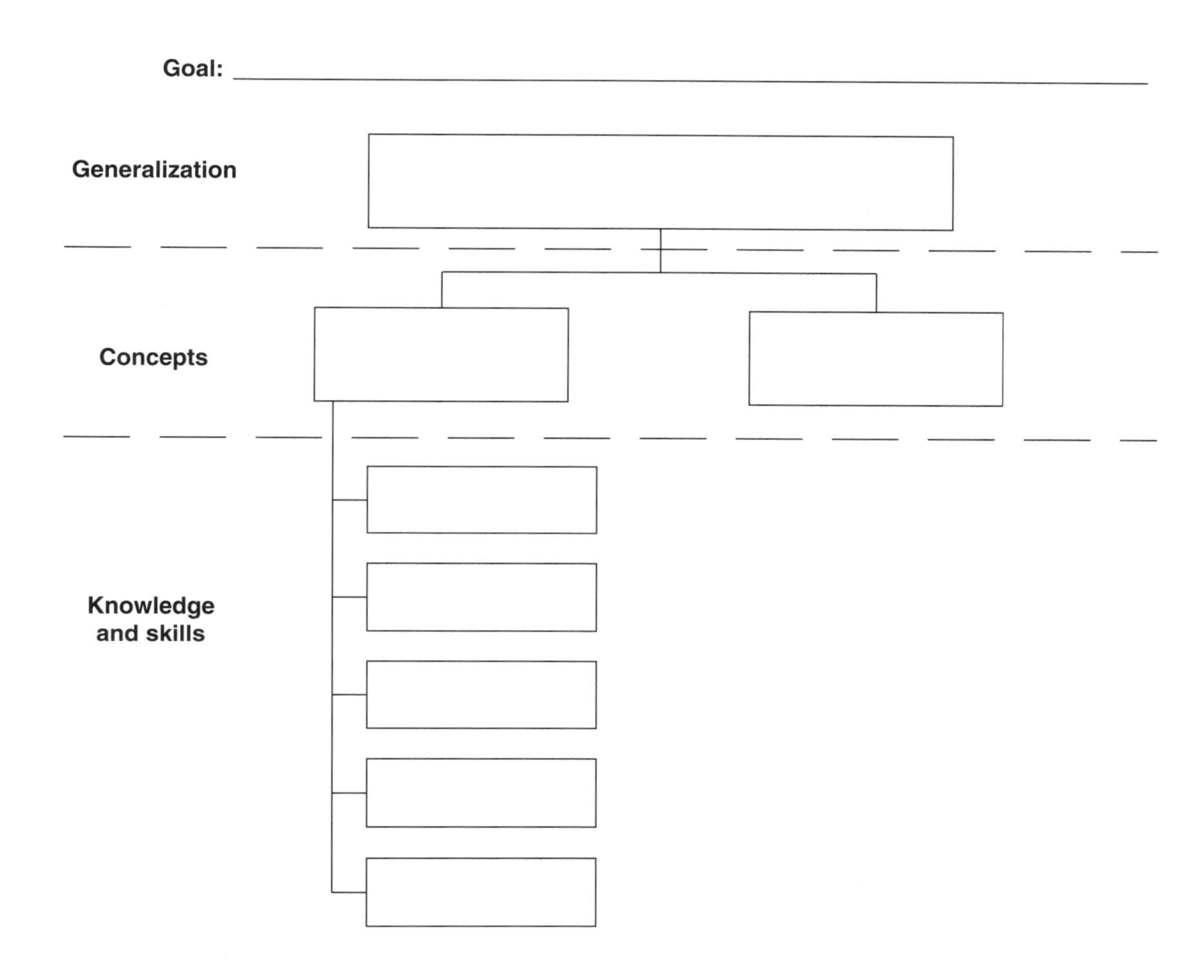

Feedback

Your generalization, concepts, and knowledge and skills should define the relationships among the goal content. For illustrative purposes, prerequisites are identified for basketball content.

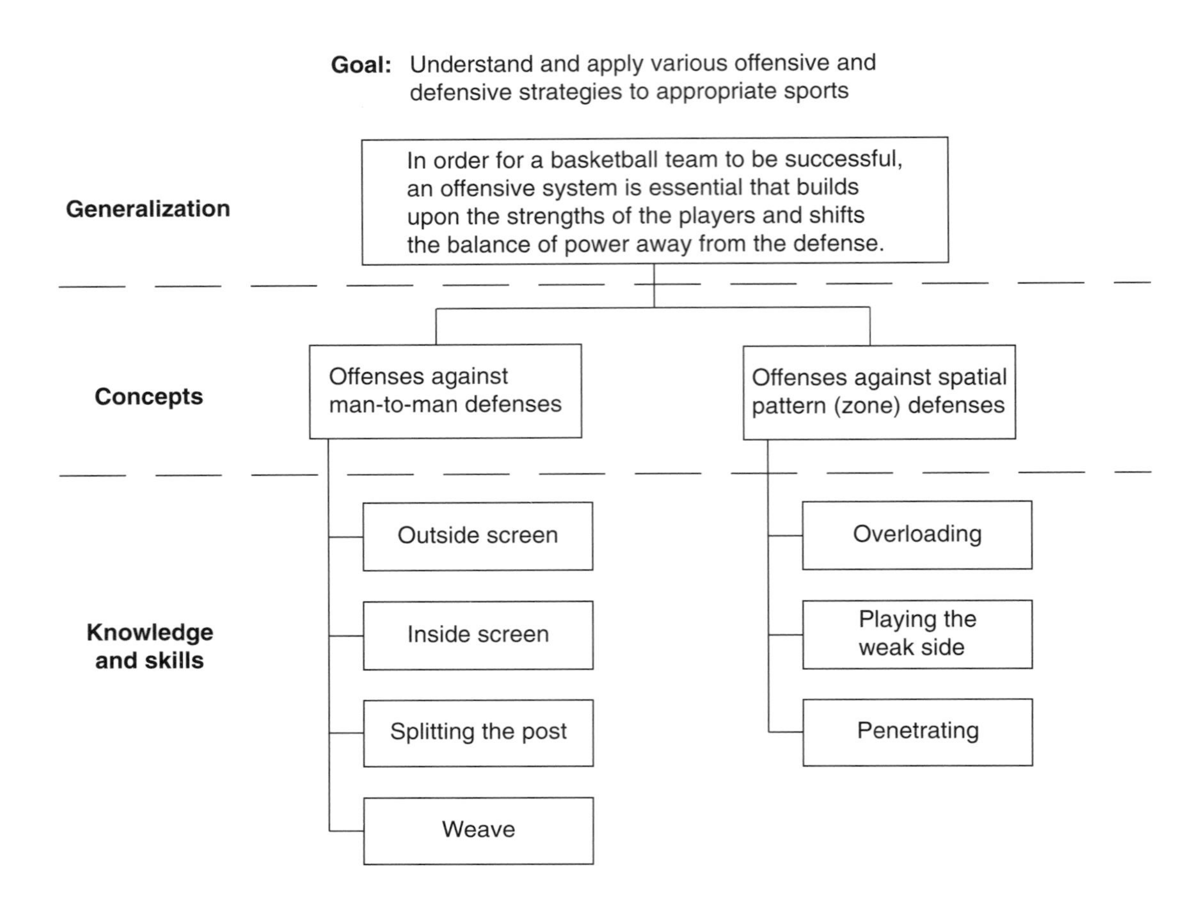

Self-Directed Activity 3.6

Sequencing tasks is useful for identifying prerequisites. This activity enables you to break down goal content through task analysis. For each of the goals, a task is identified, followed by a set of task elements that need to be arranged.

A. *Goal*: Comprehend concepts of moving the body and an object through space.

Task: Soccer dribble

Task elements: Arrange these in order of complexity from 1 (simplest cognitive content) through 5 (most complex cognitive content).

_____ The backswing and follow-through are almost nonexistent since the desired force is light.

_____ The greater the range of movement of the body segment imparting a force, the greater the distance through which speed can be developed, as well as the greater the force imparted to the object.

_____ The soccer dribble is used for moving the ball on the ground while maintaining control and possession of the ball.

_____ Eyes should be kept on the ball during contact; the supporting foot is placed next to the ball as the kicking foot makes contact.

_____ Force is produced and transferred in relation to the mass, speed, and striking surface used.

B. *Goal*: Accept responsibility for the welfare of others.

Task: Spotting in gymnastics

Task elements: The content of this kind of task is described more easily in terms of "behavioral processes." Arrange these in order of complexity from 1 (lowest affective process level) through 5 (highest affective process level).

_____ Makes spotting adjustments voluntarily to prevent injury and to facilitate partner's performance.

_____ Understands safety factors and rules for preventing injuries.

_____ Consistently assumes spotting role without direction.

_____ Understands spotting techniques in gymnastics.

_____ Carries out spotting techniques during all phases of partner's performance.

C. *Goal*: Develop perceptual motor abilities.

Task: Headstand

Task elements: Arrange these in sequence from 1 (first motor task) through 7 (last motor task).

_____ Shift weight back so that head and two hands support weight equally.

_____ Raise knees; walk toward head; place one knee at a time on each elbow.

_____ Stretch toes toward ceiling.

_____ Remove knees from elbows; extend legs toward ceiling.

_____ Shift body weight toward head until body is positioned; extend trunk and legs toward ceiling.

_____ Assume hand-knee position on mat; place head forward of hands on mat.

_____ Align body segments in an upright, reverse standing posture to complete headstand.

Feedback

A. 2, 4, 3, 1, 5

The cognitive aspects of the soccer dribble range in level of difficulty from basic knowledge to movement generalizations. In this breakdown, the movement generalization involves force (5) and the supporting concepts of range of movement (4) and control (3). The specific facts and knowledge that provide the foundation for learning include backswing and follow-through (2) and eye contact and supporting foot placement (1).

B. 4, 1, 5, 2, 3

Since the goal corresponds to the *value* level of the affective domain, content (processes) should include a full range of behaviors. The process begins with being aware of the aspects of safety (1) and spotting (2). By carrying out spotting techniques (3), the student demonstrates an appreciation for spotting. At the value level, responsibility for others is accepted when the learner makes voluntary spotting adjustments (4) and consistently assumes a spotting role without direction (5).

C. 5, 2, 6, 3, 4, 1, 7

The headstand is one kind of inverted balance that helps develop perceptual abilities (kinesthetic, visual, auditory, tactile discrimination). The task elements represent the actual breakdown of content into progressive steps. This form of sequencing focuses on how the learner acquires the given task.

Self-Directed Activity 3.7

You should be able to construct a learning hierarchy. The elements of a learning hierarchy representing the breakdown of content goals are randomly lettered. Your task is to organize them into a learning hierarchy by placing the letter of the element in the appropriate box.

A = Placing body weight on forward foot with slight forward lean

B = Demonstrating fundamental skills involving movement through space and movements executed without moving one's base of support

C = Exhibiting skills using a rope

D = Bouncing

E = Striking

F = Pushing ball, as it rebounds from ground, down toward the ground with fingertips

G = Developing basic skills necessary for specialized, complex movement forms

H = Exhibiting ball-handling skills

I = Tossing
J = Rolling and catching
K = Placing feet in a narrow stride position, one foot slightly forward
L = Pushing ball to ground with one or both hands and following through in that direction
M = Exhibiting skills using a wand/hoop
N = Demonstrating manipulative skills essential for handling, controlling, and projecting movable objects of various sizes, shapes, and compositions
O = Holding ball at waist height
P = Kicking

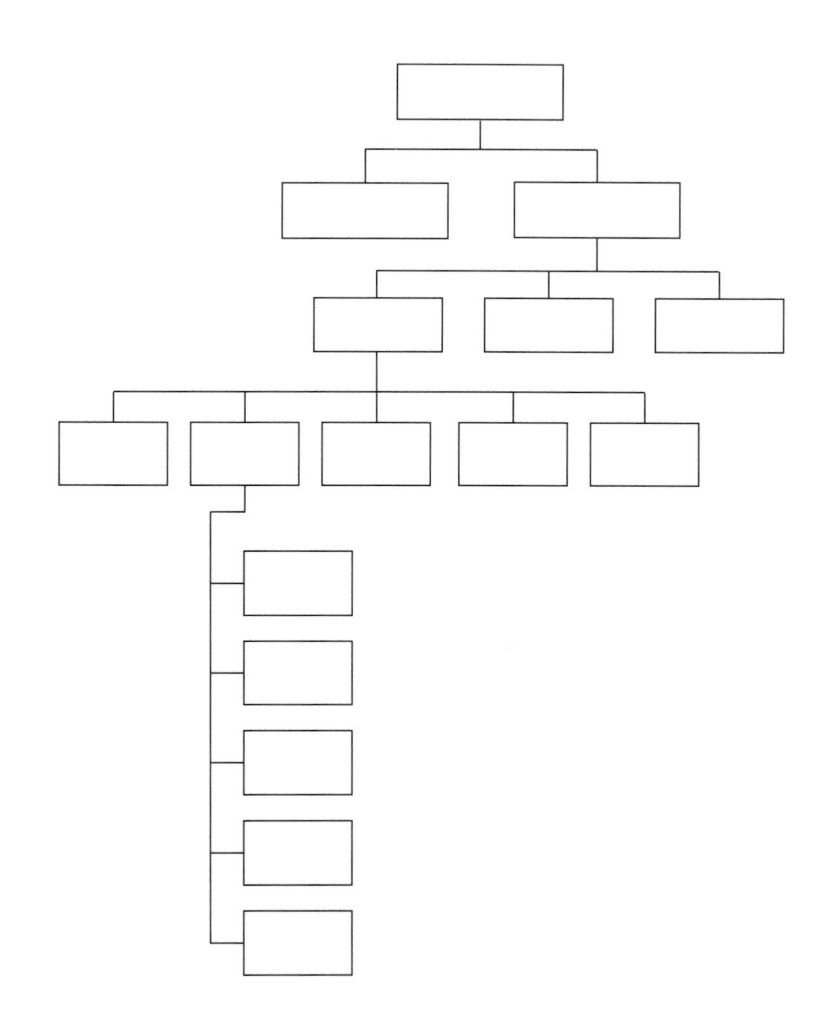

Feedback

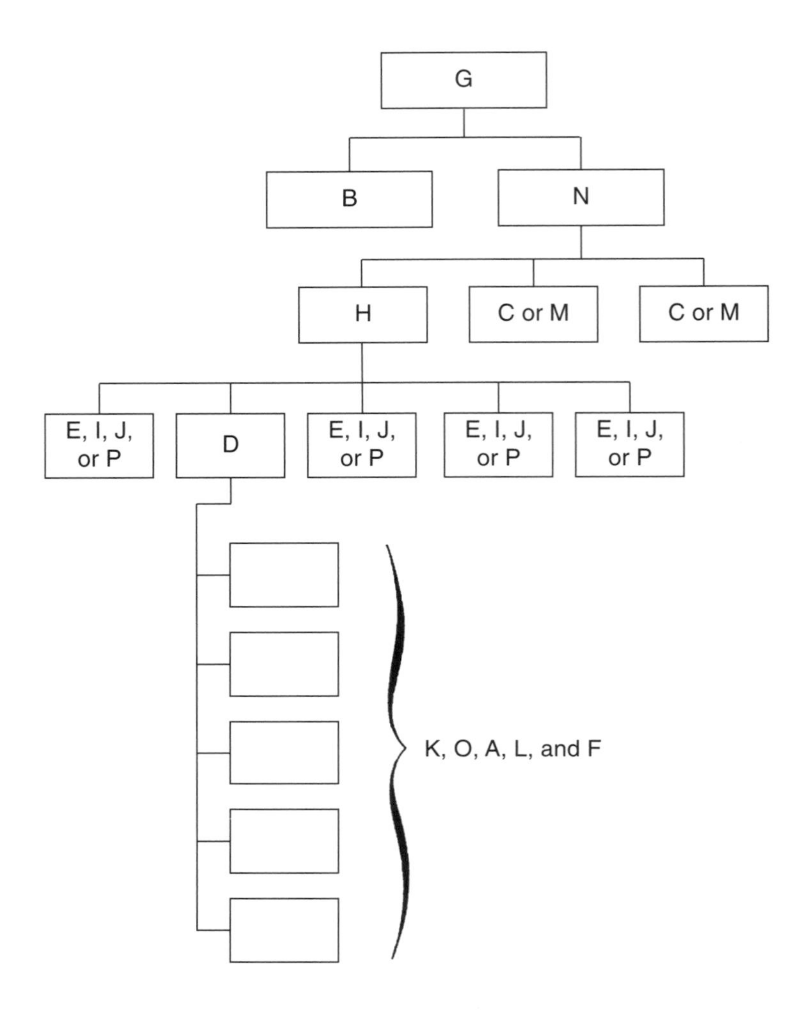

Fundamental movement skills (B) and manipulative skills (N) are the next highest goals underlying the goal of "developing basic skills necessary for specialized, complex movement forms" (G). The manipulative skills goal is supported by the goals associated with skills using a rope (C), handling a ball (H), and using a wand/hoop (M). Prerequisites to basic ballhandling skills include bouncing (D), striking (E), tossing (I), rolling and catching (J), and kicking (P). The task of bouncing is broken down further into more elementary tasks. The proper sequence for these elements is K, O, A, L, and F. It should be clear that this hierarchy incorporates complex, higher level goals and necessary prerequisites. It also reveals the sequence of learning from simple to complex.

Conducting Learner Analysis

KEY CONCEPT

Curriculum designers conduct an analysis of learners that reveals individual characteristics, learning status, and discrepancies between present and intended learning.

Although the first-year physical education teacher likes her new job at the middle school, it's been frustrating. Her kids are extremely varied, not only in terms of physical development and social maturity, but also in their abilities and attitudes. And this doesn't even consider gender and race differences or the diverse cultural and socioeconomic backgrounds of her students. Some kids can't throw, catch, or kick a ball. One group really tries to stay in shape while others couldn't care less. She can also tell who the real sports enthusiasts are because they know so much about a sport before it's taught. As it turns out, her assumptions about where sixth, seventh, and eighth graders should be are correct for only about half of her students. She begins to realize that it would help to know a lot more about her students *before* she teaches.

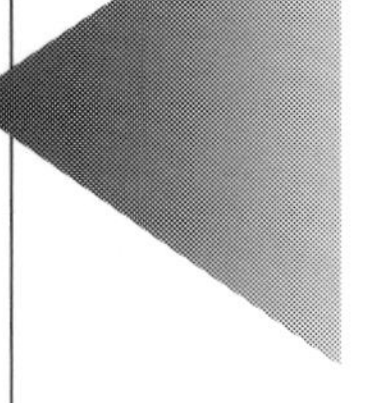

Expected Outcomes

This chapter helps you conduct an analysis of the learner for your curriculum design. Upon completing it, you will be able to

- match students' entry status with a suitable placement alternative,
- justify programming and intervention options according to assessment data,
- relate informal assessment techniques and measures with content goals,
- indicate the formal assessment technique used in situations involving entry appraisal, and
- suggest assessment data that are usable from various sources of information.

Although content goals have been determined, the question "Where are you going?" is still not completely answered. Before you make final decisions about where learners ought to be, you need to know where learners are. This is consistent with developmentally appropriate practice; that is, teacher decisions are based primarily on ongoing individual assessments of learners as they participate in physical education programming. Also, assessment of learners' progress and achievement is used to individualize instruction and identify learners with special needs (Graham, Castenada, Hopple, Manross, & Sanders, 1992). The curriculum designing model in Figure 4.1 shows this next step, *conducting learner analysis*.

Curriculum focuses on *planning*, not implementation. However, this curriculum component—conducting learner analysis—is the only exception. The other curriculum components involve planning processes. For example, organizing centers are *created*, learning objectives are *derived*, and learning experiences are *devised*, but it is not the purpose of curriculum design to carry them out. In contrast, in the case of learner analysis, you need to actually collect entry-level data. Otherwise, it would be difficult, if not impossible, to plan the remaining components, particularly deriving learning objectives. There would be little basis for projecting learning outcome standards without some information about current status.

In the curriculum designing model, analyzing learners comes after determining content goals and before deriving learning objectives. In reality, the timing of this analysis will vary. While much of the potentially relevant information about learners can and should be collected now, learner analysis occurs at points both before and after this one, including:

- ***Prior to selecting organizing centers***: Learner needs and interests were identified as a source of organizing centers (page 42). Useful information is available from behavior sampling (e.g., performance pretests, inventories, surveys), past records, and what was previously taught. These sources are described later (pages 101–106).
- ***Prior to a unit of instruction***: Learner analysis may be carried out immediately before a period of instruction, commonly called a teaching unit. For example, information from a preinstruction inventory might be collected. The Sample Items for Preinstruction Inventory on page 102 illustrates this form of learner analysis.
- ***During the interactive phase of instruction***: Other learner information may not be available until the interactive phase of instruction (e.g., performance on a task sequence). These sources are also described later (pages 105–107).

For the purpose of this discussion, learner analysis is conducted before specific learning objectives are derived from content goals. By assessing entry levels, you discover individual learner variations. Therefore, several questions arise. "What are the purposes and kinds of entry appraisal?" "How are

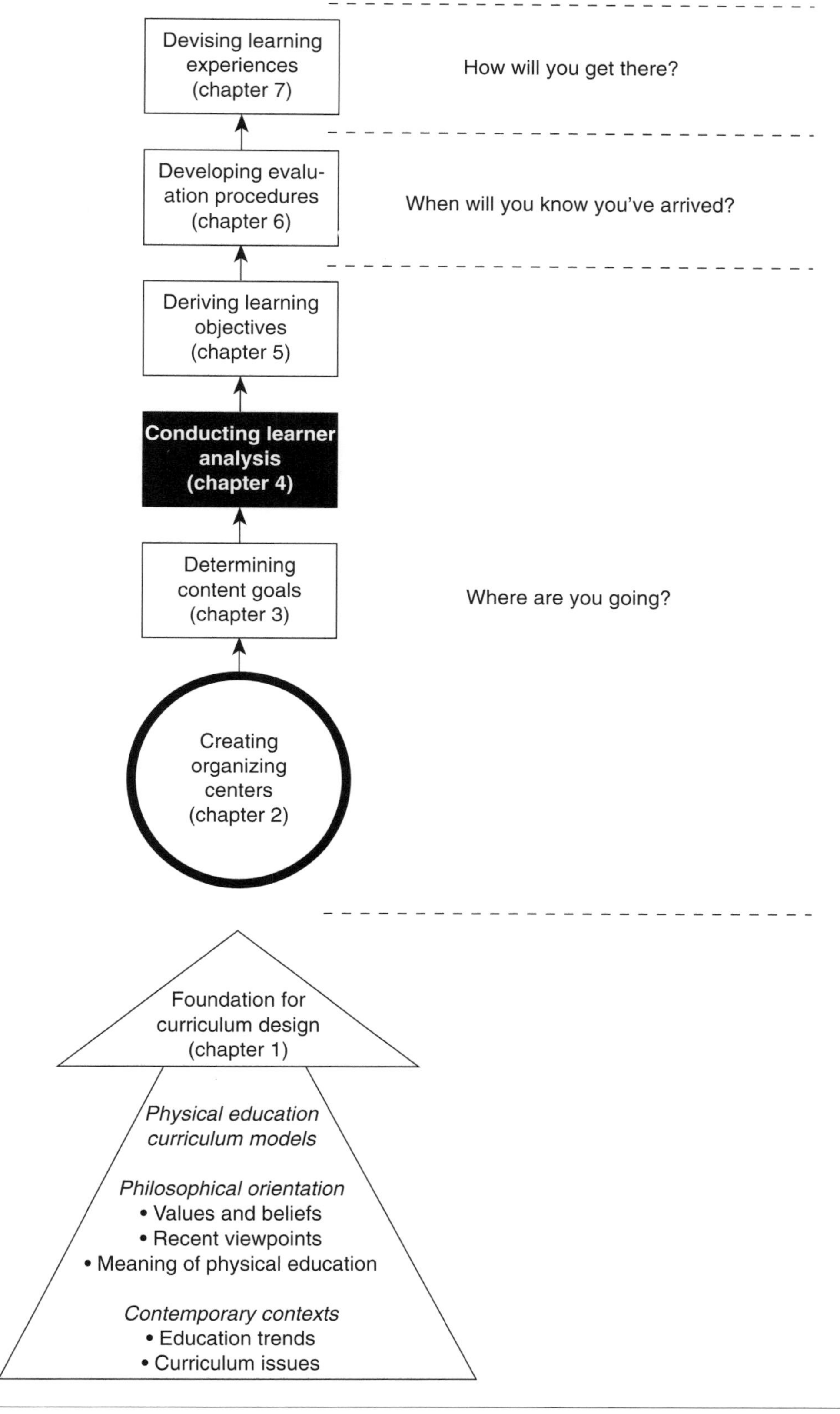

Figure 4.1 Model for designing the physical education curriculum shows the next step, *conducting learner analysis*.

the results used?" "What are the sources of information?" "How can entry assessment information be collected?" Answers to these questions are provided in the following sections. Ultimately, you should be able to conduct a learner analysis for your own physical education curriculum.

Rationale for Entry Assessment

People learn at different rates, use different learning styles, and respond differently to instructional methods. Learners of the same age, height, weight, mental capacity, and motor ability may learn in totally different ways. Even when differing characteristics are considered, the desired results are not always achieved. For example, most attempts at grouping learners homogeneously result in groups of learners with heterogeneous learning characteristics.

Individual *differences* have been a concern in physical education. However, the real concern may be individual *similarities*, because programming often focuses on single learning modes, predetermined learning rates, fixed evaluation criteria, and mass teaching. If each learner's education is to be maximized, systematic assessment is needed.

In the first section, the purposes of entry appraisal and the kinds of information that make up a learner analysis are discussed. Then, two primary outcomes of entry appraisal are examined. Identification and placement alternatives are outlined, followed by programming and intervention options.

General Purposes

Assessment involves the appraisal of students' behavior at the beginning and at the end of an instructional sequence to determine the degree of change—*learning*. This chapter deals with entry status only. Chapter 6, "Developing Evaluation Procedures," contains more specific information about exit status. Entry appraisal reveals the relationships among students' personal characteristics, students' present ability, intended learning outcomes, and the extent to which prerequisites have been satisfied. The following questions illustrate these relationships:

- Does the student have enough strength to perform activities in gymnastics?
- Can the student perform water survival skills that are needed for more complex swimming strokes?
- Is the student interested in the activity?
- How well can the student with a learning disability (e.g., perceptual motor) catch a ball?
- Does the student have enough experience in group activities to engage in partner tasks requiring peer interaction and feedback?
- Can the student be responsible for self-directed learning tasks?
- Does the student know the rules of volleyball when it is expected that games will be officiated?

While entry appraisal may be of no value in group-oriented physical education, it's important to individualization that students' readiness and learning baseline be determined. Don't try to include all desired behaviors. *A sampling of abilities is satisfactory*. Select key behaviors that are representative of other abilities or predictors of overall ability.

Entry assessment can ensure that time and energy aren't wasted where learning has already occurred, and help determine an appropriate starting point. There are also times when students need to be arranged into homogeneous or heterogeneous groups. This classification might be based on maturation (physical and mental readiness), medical condition, functional ability (motor skill), or interests. Its aim is to enhance learning potential, *not* to label, separate, and dehumanize students.

Entry appraisal is useful in identifying gifted students as well as those who may need special attention for physical, social, or emotional reasons. In this way, learner strengths and weaknesses are continually *diagnosed*. Ideally, students' interest may be aroused by entry appraisal and they will be motivated to improve. If students are convinced that entry appraisal is *not* graded, they are more motivated. Finally, the results of entry appraisal could make it necessary to eliminate, modify, or add content goals. You should ask yourself, "What is the student able to do and not do?" Learner analysis consists of the kinds of information found in Table 4.1 (Hurwitz, 1993d). The sources of this information are provided in Table 4.4 (page 107).

Entry appraisal is reflected in the Individuals with Disabilities Education Act (IDEA), which requires an individualized education plan (IEP) for every learner receiving special services. A statement of the learner's present levels of educational performance is required. Other components of the IEP (i.e., goals, objectives, services, evaluation procedures) depend on the results of this preassessment. The principles underlying preassessment for the IEP are applicable to all learners.

Table 4.1 Learner Analysis

Personal characteristics	General abilities	Learning style preferences	Social factors
Age	IQ level	Heat/Light/Sound levels	Maturation
Fitness level	Reading level	Group versus individual	Emotional status
Medical problems	Aptitude levels	Learning partners	Socioeconomic status
Disabling conditions	Motor development	Receiving information	Response to authority
Interest in content	Performance in relation to goals	Expressing information	Respect for authority
Previous experience with content		Instructional strategies	Motivation/Persistence levels
			Responsibility

Note. Adapted from "Learner Analysis," by R. Hurwitz, 1993, unpublished manuscript, Cleveland State University. Adapted by permission of the author.

Identification and Placement

You should approach the identification and placement of learners with caution. The trend is toward heterogeneous, not homogeneous, grouping. The alternatives described here *do not represent traditional "grouping by labels."* There's risk in labeling because the corresponding stigmas are difficult to overcome, even when the problem no longer exists. Any classification scheme is relative; that is, learners may be placed in a certain category for one situation, but not for another. You are the key variable. Identification and placement of learners through entry assessment will be accepted favorably as long as you use the results to maximize learning.

Approaches to Identification

Preassessment, when conducted carefully, is useful for categorizing students on the basis of similarities (e.g., characteristics, abilities, needs, previous experiences). Unfortunately, many classification systems in physical education don't facilitate learning. Instead, students are conveniently placed into categories without regard for overlapping characteristics and the development of abilities along a learning continuum. The typical reasons for classification are to

- create an effective atmosphere for students of similar ability,
- equalize competition,
- motivate student participation and performance,
- enhance program continuity,
- meet health and safety needs, and
- provide a basis for comparison with others.

In theory, these reasons seem positive. In practice, however, classification often leads to loss of prestige, poor self-image, rejection, isolation, and labeling (e.g., "retarded," "slow," "disabled," "handicapped").

Selecting an identification approach depends on factors such as the nature of the physical education program; the purpose for classification; the characteristics and size of the group; the available equipment and facilities; and the time for implementation. Some approaches are:

- ***Interests***: Students with common interests are identified by choosing activities in physical education.
- ***Age or grade level***: Although grouping by age or grade level is convenient, it reveals limited information about students' abilities.
- ***General ability***: This includes qualities such as fitness, strength, and motor ability. These factors are also referred to as physical maturity.
- ***Specific abilities***: Functional abilities such as sport skills can be used to differentiate learners. Skill tests are commonly developed for this purpose.
- ***Social/Emotional development***: The degree to which learners are able to interact with others and express emotions is sometimes a basis for grouping. Development of certain social/emotional qualities (e.g., tolerance, teamwork, confidence, independence) may influence activity selection.
- ***Medical status***: Based on a medical exam, participation in physical activities may be unlimited, modified, or restricted.

Some of these approaches may be more appealing to you than others. Nevertheless, the reference point for preassessment should always be learner needs—cognitive, affective, and psychomotor. For example, if motor ability is assessed, then the program should fit the needs of those identified as gifted, average, and low-skilled. Since experience may be a factor, planning can be targeted toward advanced, intermediate, and beginner levels. *Identified needs and abilities are specific and do not transfer to other needs or abilities.* This means that preassessment is an ongoing process and that learners are constantly reclassified.

Placement Alternatives

Once students are identified as belonging to a certain category, you need to make placement decisions. Again, the term placement should not be taken negatively. It does *not* mean that students are segregated, isolated, or somehow made to feel inferior. In physical education, students are "placed" on teams of similar or mixed abilities, assigned to a particular station, or given a task card based on identified needs. For students with special needs, alternatives should be examined for placement in the least restrictive setting. In this discussion, however, special needs are *not* limited to students with disabilities. Instead, "special needs" refers to any student for whom a regular education is not considered appropriate, regardless of the reason.

Placement should reflect the student's present level of performance. Preassessment data help you determine what's most appropriate. For students with special needs, consideration should be given to the alternatives described in Table 4.2. The middle two alternatives are transitional placements between regular and adapted physical education programming.

▶ ***To practice selecting the best placement alternative for learners with different behaviors, aptitudes, and skills, complete Self-Directed Activity 4.1 at the end of this chapter.***

Programming and Intervention

Entry appraisal is also carried out to determine appropriate programming and intervention. For the assessment results to be relevant, the data-gathering process should be based on content goals. This means that students' needs are understood *before* learning objectives are derived, evaluation procedures are developed, and learning experiences are devised, thereby enhancing the probability of individual success. Two related concepts that describe this approach are presented. The first one explains what happens to students; the second one defines the role of the teacher. Then, five programming and intervention options are identified.

Mastery Learning

Students achieve mastery at a specified level before going on to the next. Time for learning is manipulated according to individual pace. Entry assessment identifies current performance levels for each task; what remains to be learned becomes the mastery target.

Usually, to determine proficiency, a test of mastery is developed. Measurement is directed toward individual achievement and the task to be learned, not toward comparisons to other students. For example, in swimming, skill tests for mastery could determine beginner, intermediate, and advanced categories for each stroke. This doesn't mean labels and categories, but it does mean the practical use

Table 4.2 Placement Alternatives

Placement alternative	Description
1. Regular class	For students who can take part in regular physical education activities safely, successfully, and with personal satisfaction
2. Regular class with adapted physical education when necessary	For students who need supplementary programming when modifications in the activities, equipment, facilities, and student's role are impractical in the regular program
3. Adapted physical education with regular class when possible	For students who need to build confidence, gain experience, and develop skills; in this case, modification of activities, equipment, facilities, and student's role are possible in the regular program
4. Adapted physical education	For students with disabling conditions who require special attention in specifically designed activities

Appropriate placement of students is not limited by the nature of the activity.

of groups. Students then receive programming and intervention (e.g., instruction, practice, feedback) until each skill is mastered at a certain level of proficiency. At that point the student moves on to the next level of difficulty.

Diagnostic-Prescriptive Teaching

Entry appraisal is viewed as a diagnostic tool for assessing individual needs. Results are useful as a *baseline* to determine areas of needed improvement and areas of lesser need. Strengths and weaknesses are continuously examined and learning tasks are prescribed accordingly (intervention).

You need to transfer diagnostic data into precise learning objectives and relevant learning experiences that result in desired behavioral changes. By its very nature, the role of "teacher as diagnostician" places an emphasis on individual progress, improvement, and success. Using swimming again as an example, it might be found that a student rates high in the front crawl but low in the sidestroke.

Programming and Intervention Options

Where difficulty or the need for improvement is indicated, several programming and intervention options are available. They are curricular in nature even though they're actually used during instruction. Since programming and intervention are primary reasons for entry appraisal, they're introduced at this time, as follows:

- ***Conducting a task analysis***: The task to be mastered is analyzed in relation to the specific area of difficulty or needed improvement. Programming is focused on the subtasks leading to the primary task. The process of task analysis appeared in chapter 3 (page 77).
- ***Revising instruction***: This intervention matches curriculum materials, teaching style, and learning experiences with learning style preferences. A change in the teaching-learning mode might result in student improvement and success. Various teaching-learning approaches are presented in chapter 7, "Devising Learning Experiences."
- ***Repeating a portion or the entirety of the instructional sequence***: A student who has experienced difficulty often succeeds when a learning sequence is repeated. This form of "overlearning" may lead to achievement, particularly if additional feedback and encouragement are provided.
- ***Providing remediation or enrichment***: The remedial loop consists of a series of small tasks leading to mastery of a task in the regular learning sequence. This scheme for accommodating individual learning is illustrated in Figure 4.2.

▶ ***For practice using entry-level data for the purpose of programming and intervention, complete Self-Directed Activity 4.2 at the end of this chapter.***

Learning objective

To develop complex adaptive skills in tennis, the student will demonstrate the ability to perform the forehand drive by returning 75% of all return volley shots that are less than three steps away.

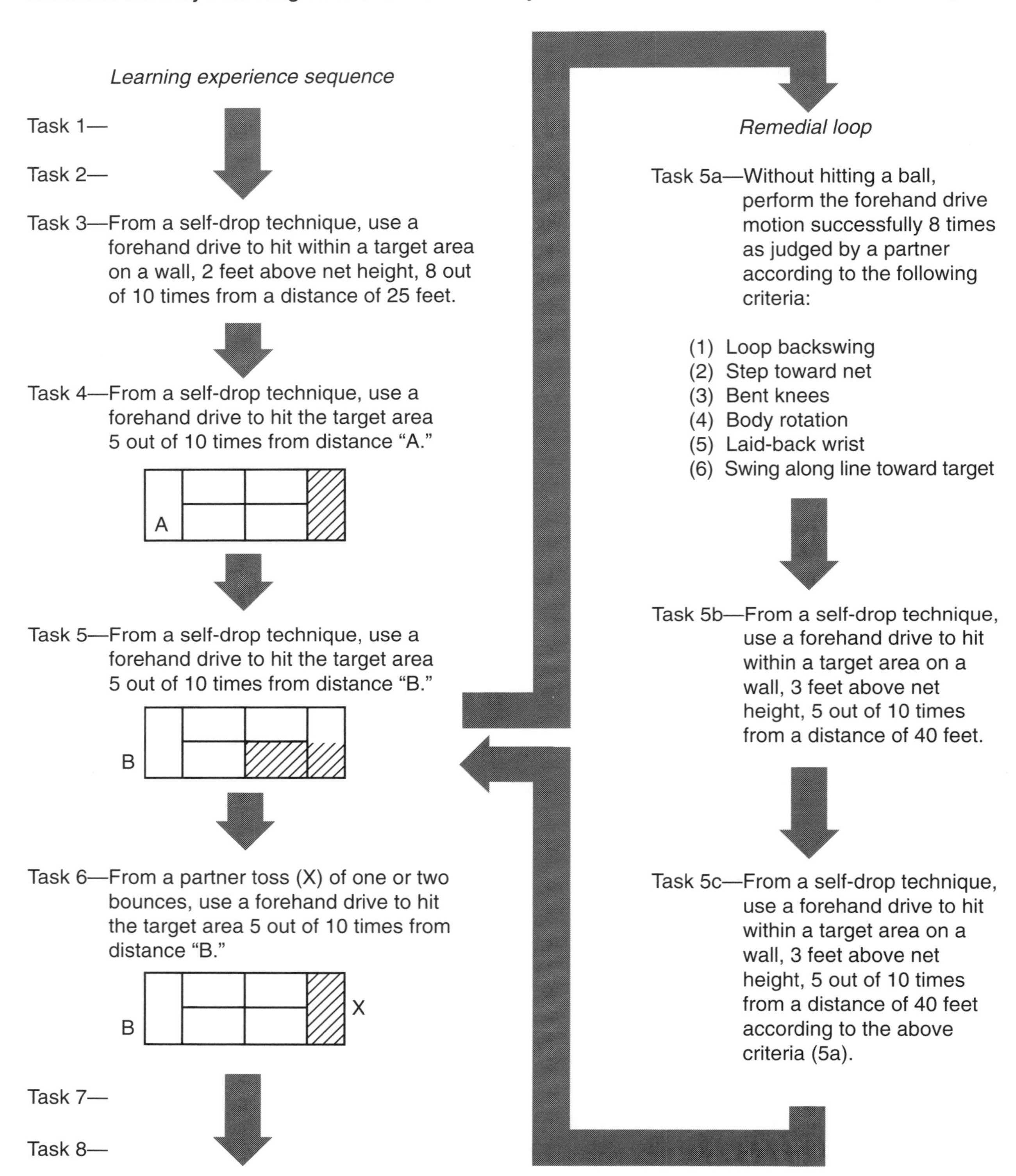

Figure 4.2 "Remedial loop" is illustrated for use when difficulty is encountered in the regular learning sequence.

Collecting Entry Assessment Information

An *individualized* physical education design requires preassessment to determine a point of departure and readiness to learn. These data are referred to as a *baseline* against which learning increases are compared. The magnitude of change indicates student improvement.

Entry appraisal should be multifactored, including the identification of ability levels in the cognitive, affective, and psychomotor domains; learning style; and any other factors affecting individual learning patterns. Measures must be reliable (consistent) and valid (accurate) indicators of student behavior, and a variety of instruments should be used. These aspects are covered in this section.

Information about learners is available from existing records, observations, formal and informal tests, parents, and other professionals (e.g., teachers, counselor, nurse). These sources are useful for *authentic assessment*, a process of documenting students' genuine accomplishments. An entire section is devoted to this process in chapter 6 (pages 169, 172–177).

Evaluation techniques are usually developed to determine exit-level status. Many of the same evaluation items can be used or modified during entry assessment. Such an appraisal, referred to as behavior sampling, is probably the most common source. Descriptions of informal and formal assessment techniques follow. Then, other sources of entry assessment information are reviewed.

Behavior Sampling

Previously, goal prerequisites were sorted into three groups (page 72). Behavior sampling should focus on those that some or many of your students might not already possess (group 2). It would be impractical to include all desired behaviors. Key behaviors can be selected that represent a set of skills or predict overall ability.

Behavior sampling may be conducted informally (observations and self-report) or formally (written and performance tests). At this point, it might help to illustrate the combined use of these techniques before they are fully described. For example, prior to a unit in tennis, a pretest inventory could determine abilities, experience, and feelings of students regarding tennis. Sample items representing informal and formal measures appear in Sample Items for Preinstruction Inventory (page 102).

Informal Assessment Techniques

In some cases, greater value is placed on information from informal assessment than on data from formal assessment such as a standardized test. The various kinds of informal techniques are categorized as observations and self-reports.

Observations. Information from observations allows you to draw inferences about students' attitudes, feelings, and preferences. Observations can be spontaneous (e.g., watching a student play, perform a task, interact with others, solve a problem, express an emotion) and they can be used to identify behavior in selected situations. Observations of this nature are either *descriptive* or *quantitative*.

Anecdotal records contain descriptive observations. Although they may seem tedious and time-consuming, they can be very useful in planning. Record keeping should focus only on significant occurrences and reflect your nonprejudicial recording of behavior. It might include an entry such as: "In games of tag and dodging, Laura has difficulty in moving her entire body rapidly in different directions and in response to unexpected situations. She needs to improve her ability to change direction and make sudden stops and starts."

Quantitative observations involve the frequency or number of behaviors exhibited. Teacher-made rating scales and checklists are commonly used. To be of any value in determining entry status, recordings must be systematic and accurate. For example, the checklist on page 103 shows quantitative criteria for the forward roll. The task could be repeated three times; criteria observed are checked accordingly.

Self-Reports. Depending on the situation, students can be asked to respond anonymously. The information sought can relate to individuals or the entire population of students. There are other times when you will want to camouflage or mask the true purpose of the self-report. Thus, there are *direct* self-reports (student is able to guess what information is being sought) and *indirect* self-reports (intent is camouflaged or the desired response is not readily apparent). You should realize that indirect self-reports require that you infer from student responses that a particular belief is held. For example, a student might be asked, "Did you enjoy intramural tennis last year?" If the answer is "No," then it may be inferred that the student isn't interested in intramurals or tennis, or both.

Surveys and questionnaires are commonly used to collect informal data. Students' feelings about a sport, what they know, and their own perceptions of their abilities can be solicited. Even young learners

Sample Items for Preinstruction Inventory

Tennis Anyone?

1. How much experience have you had playing tennis?

   (a) None (c) Some

   (b) Very little (d) A great deal

2. Have you ever seen a professional tennis match on television or in person?

   ____ Yes ____ No

3. Given the opportunity, would you be interested in spending extra time outside of class to improve your tennis ability?

   ____ Yes ____ No

4. On the diagram below, draw diagonal lines to show the area that is used during a singles game in tennis. In addition, place an "X" where the server should stand to begin a game. Place an "O" where the server should stand with the score 30-15.

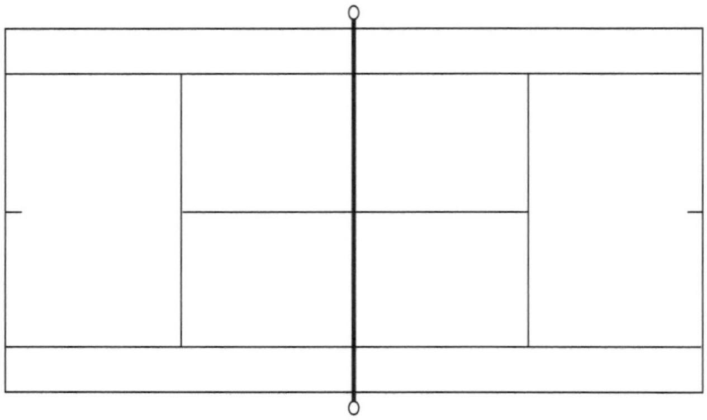

5. The correct structure of a tennis match is game-set-match.

   ____ True ____ False

6. The correct order of points in a game of tennis is:

   (a) 1-2-3 (c) Love-15-30-40

   (b) 40-30-15 (d) None of the above

7. Demonstrate the following:

   (a) Forehand drive from a self-drop

   (b) Backhand drive from a self-drop

   (c) Service

   (d) Forehand drive from a partner toss of one bounce

Criteria Checklist: A Quantitative Observation

Task: Forward roll

Start:

1. Begins from a standing or a squat position	_____	_____	_____
2. Places feet and knees together	_____	_____	_____
3. Moves to a forward position with hands on mat, shoulder-width apart	_____	_____	_____
4. Spreads fingers comfortably	_____	_____	_____

Roll:

5. Tucks head with chin to chest	_____	_____	_____
6. Shifts body weight forward until off balance	_____	_____	_____
7. Accepts body weight with arms; contacts mat in front of hands with back of the head (slightly)	_____	_____	_____

Finish:

8. Contacts mat with shoulders	_____	_____	_____
9. Grabs knees when rolling out	_____	_____	_____
10. Comes to a standing position	_____	_____	_____

can circle faces (e.g., smiling, frowning) to indicate how they feel about certain kinds of games, sports, or activities.

Another form of self-reporting is conducted through oral interviews, dialogue, or discussions with students. Although some students respond in ways they think the teacher or their peers want them to respond, individualized preassessment can be facilitated by face-to-face contact, either one-to-one or with a group. For example, through dialogue, you can determine a student's understanding of a movement task. This information would help in structuring learning objectives and experiences to develop the task. An informal, oral pretest can also be useful. Students might be asked, "How many of you have ever played speedball?" or "How many of you can walk the length of the low balance beam without losing your balance?"

▶ ***To practice relating informal assessment techniques, entry-level measures, and content goals, complete Self-Directed Activity 4.3 at the end of this chapter.***

Formal Assessment Techniques

This source of entry status yields data concerning present skill level, knowledge of activity, attitude toward activity, and potential value of activity to the student. Standardized inventories—knowledge tests, *Physical Best* (AAHPERD, 1988), skills tests, attitude scales, and social-adjustment indices—should also be considered to the degree they represent a sampling of behavior and are good predictors of overall abilities. Formal assessment techniques are generally classified as norm-referenced or criterion-referenced.

Norm-Referenced. This kind of assessment compares an individual student's performance to other students of similar age, height, weight, past experience, attitudes, or physical readiness. Normative assessment sorts students into measured groups even though results are often used to establish entry learning levels. However, it only indicates the student's relative standing above or below the defined group average.

For example, suppose that a student scored in the top fourth of all eighth graders who completed a field hockey test. Another student might have scored at the 30th percentile on the sit-and-reach test, a measure of flexibility. These assessments yield information about present achievement, but additional investigation is needed to determine how and why the student scored high or low. Thus, norm-referenced assessment is limited when it comes to identifying individual strengths and weaknesses.

Criterion-Referenced. Emphasis has been placed on mastery learning and the diagnosis of student strengths and weaknesses. Criterion-referenced assessment supports these concepts because the student's abilities are measured against a standard of performance rather than against the performance of others. It indicates what a student can and cannot do. Thus, entry-level status can be identified along a continuum of tasks leading to a given content goal.

Formal entry-level data can be collected through achievement indices that are usually teacher-made. Preassessment items should relate directly to content goals. They are designed to measure specific, individual competencies. Thus, results can be compared to the student's performance on another task

Entry appraisal is needed to establish baseline data.

and to projected criteria for successful performance. Paper-and-pencil achievement tests are associated with the cognitive domain, whereas skill tests are administered as a measure of psychomotor learning. The criterion-referenced test items on page 106 are related directly to a content goal. These items do not constitute an entire inventory; each stands alone.

▶ ***To practice distinguishing between criterion-referenced and norm-referenced assessment techniques, complete Self-Directed Activity 4.4 at the end of this chapter.***

Other Sources of Information

While behavior sampling is the primary source of entry information, other sources are worth considering. Two of the sources—cumulative record data and previous content—depend on information that already exists. Preassessment information from the two other sources—task analysis and nature of learning activity—is found within the content to be learned and the learning experience being used, respectively.

Cumulative Record Data

Analysis of students' data can influence the development of learning objectives, evaluation procedures, and learning experiences. Sample kinds of records include

- previous test scores (e.g., basketball skills tests),
- results of rating scales (e.g., analysis of gymnastics routine),
- diagnostic reviews (e.g., motor ability inventory),
- attendance records (e.g., periods of missed learning), and
- anecdotal records (e.g., notes about the development of locomotor movements).

Previous Content

This source assumes that the curriculum design reflects some degree of vertical (K–12) continuity. If so, review of previous courses, unit outlines, or materials should yield projected outcomes and, in some cases, accomplishments. Entry status could also be based on the learning objectives, evaluation procedures, and learning experiences used previously. For example, activities are often sequenced as beginning, intermediate, and advanced. In addition to maintaining program continuity, this approach establishes prerequisites that represent entry proficiencies for each level. Previous content can provide some estimation of entry status.

Task Sequence

When content goals are broken down into their component behaviors (task analysis), a sequence of learning tasks is revealed. The point at which students are able to begin the task sequence is considered a form of preassessment. Changes in behavior can be compared against this initial ability level. Students would then advance along the learning continuum (task sequence) at their own paces. For illustrative purposes, a jump rope sequence is indicated in Table 4.3. When the tasks are completed in order, the last task completed successfully becomes the learner's entry status for the next one and beyond.

Table 4.3 Illustrative Task Sequence

	Jump rope sequence
Task 1:	Hold rope so that loop is behind the ankles.
Task 2:	Swing rope over head and down under feet; raise feet enough for rope to pass under.
Task 3:	Repeat task 2 successfully, three (3) times in succession.
Task 4:	Swing rope over head and, as it reaches its full height, raise both feet lightly.
Task 5:	Repeat task 4 successfully, three (3) times in succession.
Task 6:	Jump rope eight (8) times without missing at "slow time" (one jump per turn).
Task 7:	Jump rope eight (8) times without missing at "double time" (one jump per turn).
Task 8:	Jump rope eight (8) times without missing at "fast time" (one jump per turn twice as fast).
Task 9:	Swing rope over head and under both feet, landing on the ball of the right foot with left foot extending (alternating jump).

Nature of Learning Activity

Preassessment information is available through certain kinds of learning experiences. Suppose that the student determined *present* maximums for a number of tasks. In an interval training program designed to increase speed and endurance in running, the tasks might include maximum speed for 100 yards and maximum distance run in 60 seconds. These present measurements serve as the pretest because their results indicate entry proficiency. The program is individualized because

Criterion-Referenced Test Items

Goal: Analyze the components of physical fitness

Item 1: In each pair of descriptions below, indicate which component is associated with each description.

		Muscular strength	Muscular endurance
1.	(a) One maximal contraction	______	______
	(b) Sustained contraction	______	______
2.	(a) Light weights, many repetitions	______	______
	(b) Heavy weights, few repetitions	______	______
3.	(a) Greater hypertrophy	______	______
	(b) Greater capillarization	______	______

Item 2: Identify the motor-related components of physical fitness. Indicate a physical activity (movement, sport skill) for each that depends primarily on the component for successful completion.

	Component	Activity
1.	____________________	____
2.	____________________	____
3.	____________________	____
4.	____________________	____
5.	____________________	____

Item 3: Basic principles must be applied in order to develop physical fitness successfully. Explain how each principle listed below is applied in the development of cardiorespiratory endurance.

1. Overload: ____

   ____

   ____

2. Progression: ____

   ____

   ____

3. Specificity: ____

   ____

   ____

maximums will vary among learners. The sample learning experience in Item 6 of Individualized Learning Approaches (pages 207–208) provides an example of this source.

This source can also be illustrated with a weight training circuit. Maximum and submaximum threshold performance would be determined *initially* for any number of activities (e.g., pull-ups, weighted sit-ups, vertical wall ladder, leg press curls). Performance results are the basis for any student progress following circuit training. Ideally, students will respond favorably to these data reflecting their individual accomplishments.

Previously, in Table 4.1 (page 97), the kinds of information that make up a learner analysis were categorized and listed. The sources identified in this section can be used to acquire information about these aspects. This relationship is shown in Table 4.4, where the relevant learner characteristics from Table 4.1 are matched with suggested information sources.

▶ ***Various sources should be considered when you collect entry-level information. To practice selecting useful information in different situations, complete Self-Directed Activity 4.5 at the end of this chapter.***

Table 4.4 Sources for Learner Analysis Information

Aspects of learner analysis	Sources of information
Personal characteristics	
Age, medical problems, disabling conditions	Cumulative record data
Fitness level	Cumulative record data, nature of learning activity, behavior sampling
Interest in content	Behavior sampling
Previous experience with content	Cumulative record data, previous content, behavior sampling
General abilities	
IQ level, reading level, aptitude levels	Cumulative record data
Motor development	Cumulative record data, previous content, nature of learning activity, behavior sampling
Performance in relation to goals	Cumulative record data, previous content, task sequence, nature of learning activity, behavior sampling
Learning style preferences	
Heat/Light/Sound levels, group versus individual, learning partners, receiving information, expressing information, instructional strategies	Cumulative record data, behavior sampling
Social factors	
Maturation, emotional status, socioeconomic status, response to authority, respect for authority, motivation and persistence levels, responsibility	Cumulative record data, behavior sampling

Making It Work

Have you achieved the expected outcomes (page 94)? Congratulations! You are able to conduct a learner analysis for your physical education curriculum design. Still, you may have some practical questions that need answers, such as:

- **Why conduct an analysis of the learner after goals are determined? Why not before?**

  You could analyze learners before goals are determined or even before organizing centers are created. In practice, you probably analyze learners to some degree at all of these points. It's not wrong to do that. However, by waiting until now, you have the benefit of knowing what *general* direction your curriculum is going. Content goals should help in narrowing the amount and nature of entry appraisal. You also have the advantage of content goals analysis, which offers a breakdown of tasks. If you discover that learning has already occurred, then you can eliminate, modify, or add content goals. The curriculum designing process is flexible. The main point is that you're professionally obligated to know where your students are! When or even how you do this isn't as important as the need to base your curriculum on student status. It makes little sense to do otherwise. You may end up collecting informal and formal information at different intervals, then making curriculum adjustments as necessary.

- **When students are classified into different groups, isn't this the same as labeling?**

  No! We do this all the time whether we realize it or not. For example, trying to equalize teams for competition is indirectly saying that some students belong to an advanced skill group, some are average in ability, and others are not as skilled. Teams are formed in which these groups are distributed as equally as possible. Another common practice is to put students of similar interests together in a learning group. The fact is that there are many justifiable reasons for identifying and classifying students that do not result in labeling and poor self-image.

- **Doesn't the placement of students refer only to special education?**

  The term placement has many meanings. It is not limited to students with special needs, especially those with disabling conditions. But that's how it's usually thought of. Instead, it can mean that students are "placed" at a learning station to work on skills that show the greatest need for improvement. Students won't view this negatively if they see it as a *genuine* attempt to help them improve their abilities, not to isolate or reject them. There are also times when students are placed in groups for safety reasons (e.g., swimming, gymnastic spotting). As long as there is flexibility, and student mobility from one placement to the next, then such placements should be accepted for the right reasons.

- **Is there really enough time to carry out some of the programming and intervention options?**

  Here again, you probably would use some of the suggested options, but initially on a smaller scale. For example, it is common to have students repeat some task or drill when they experience difficulty. Or you might have them try some other subtasks when they get to a task in the regular sequence and experience difficulty. The idea is ultimately to bring the student back to the regular task. While the process has been formally called a "remedial loop," it is done all the time out of common sense. You don't need task charts with arrows as long as you carry out the underlying purpose of providing remediation or enrichment. Ultimately, you might anticipate where students are going to have problems and have remedial loops ready.

- **If you carry out some preassessment strategy, won't you just be testing all the time?**

  Remember, entry appraisal should be a *sampling* of representative behaviors, not a full evaluation process. Also, it could be carried out very informally through verbal questions and answers on a one-to-one or group basis. You're not expected to carry out formal procedures for everything you do. However, some combination of informal and formal techniques is recommended so that a full range of baseline data is available. Otherwise, why bother? The other necessity is to use the information you collect. Don't simply collect it and then do what you were going to do anyway. Students will soon learn that it's meaningless and will respond lackadaisically. The information collected during entry appraisal should ultimately influence your objectives, evaluation procedures, and learning experiences.

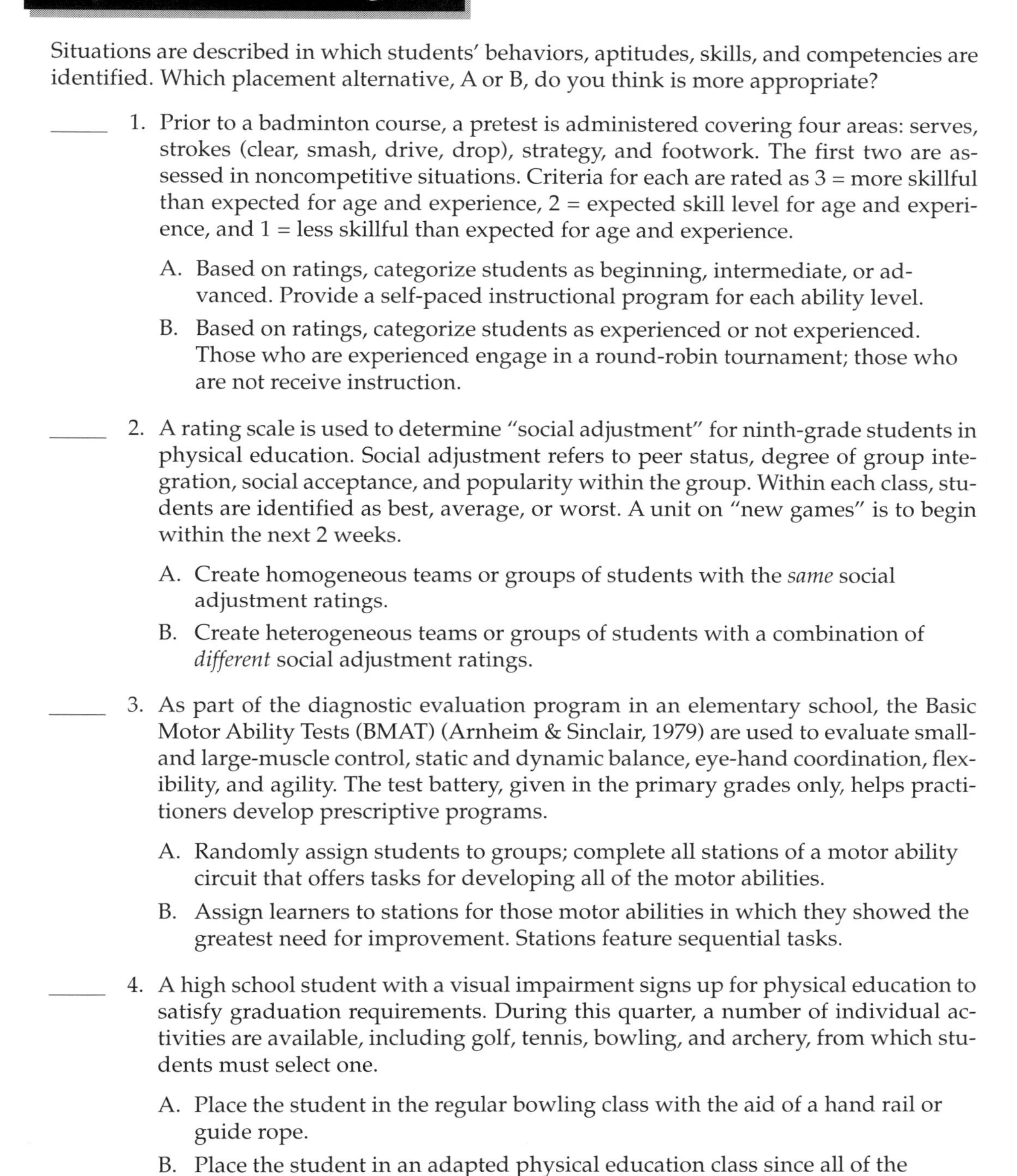

Self-Directed Activity 4.1

Situations are described in which students' behaviors, aptitudes, skills, and competencies are identified. Which placement alternative, A or B, do you think is more appropriate?

_____ 1. Prior to a badminton course, a pretest is administered covering four areas: serves, strokes (clear, smash, drive, drop), strategy, and footwork. The first two are assessed in noncompetitive situations. Criteria for each are rated as 3 = more skillful than expected for age and experience, 2 = expected skill level for age and experience, and 1 = less skillful than expected for age and experience.

A. Based on ratings, categorize students as beginning, intermediate, or advanced. Provide a self-paced instructional program for each ability level.

B. Based on ratings, categorize students as experienced or not experienced. Those who are experienced engage in a round-robin tournament; those who are not receive instruction.

_____ 2. A rating scale is used to determine "social adjustment" for ninth-grade students in physical education. Social adjustment refers to peer status, degree of group integration, social acceptance, and popularity within the group. Within each class, students are identified as best, average, or worst. A unit on "new games" is to begin within the next 2 weeks.

A. Create homogeneous teams or groups of students with the *same* social adjustment ratings.

B. Create heterogeneous teams or groups of students with a combination of *different* social adjustment ratings.

_____ 3. As part of the diagnostic evaluation program in an elementary school, the Basic Motor Ability Tests (BMAT) (Arnheim & Sinclair, 1979) are used to evaluate small- and large-muscle control, static and dynamic balance, eye-hand coordination, flexibility, and agility. The test battery, given in the primary grades only, helps practitioners develop prescriptive programs.

A. Randomly assign students to groups; complete all stations of a motor ability circuit that offers tasks for developing all of the motor abilities.

B. Assign learners to stations for those motor abilities in which they showed the greatest need for improvement. Stations feature sequential tasks.

_____ 4. A high school student with a visual impairment signs up for physical education to satisfy graduation requirements. During this quarter, a number of individual activities are available, including golf, tennis, bowling, and archery, from which students must select one.

A. Place the student in the regular bowling class with the aid of a hand rail or guide rope.

B. Place the student in an adapted physical education class since all of the available activities involve visual contact with objects, implements, and/or targets.

_____ 5. Some of the objectives in a volleyball unit are cognitive. Students' entry-level knowledge is revealed through a pretest covering rules, skills analysis, concepts of movement, offensive and defensive strategies, safety factors, and courtesies. Scores on the pretest are calculated on a percentage basis.

A. Classify students as having "achieved" the objectives (90% and above), as having "partly achieved" the objectives (70% to 89%), or as having "not achieved" the objectives (below 70%). Provide handout materials for each aspect of volleyball covered by the pretest.

B. Classify students into a single learning group that includes the full range of scores.

_____ 6. The physical fitness status of sixth-grade students is determined by a series of pretests including measures of cardiovascular endurance, muscular strength and endurance, flexibility, and body composition. From the results, local norms are developed, using percentiles, for each component.

A. Establish workout groups based on the fitness components (i.e., students engage in workouts together in an attempt to improve that fitness component).

B. Establish workout groups based on percentile rankings (i.e., students with similar fitness levels engage in the workouts together).

_____ 7. A small number of students in a middle school have cerebral palsy. At their IEP conferences, instruction in physical education is addressed with specific reference to motor performance and physical fitness.

A. Place students in an adapted physical education class due to the severity of the disabling condition.

B. Place students in an adapted physical education class with supplementary placement in regular programs when possible.

_____ 8. A coeducational, elective physical education program for seniors is available at a local high school. Following a survey, areas of interest are identified and students choose a number of "mini-courses." The number of males and females who select wrestling, touch football, basketball, and other sports involving body contact is equally distributed.

A. Group students on the basis of gender because these activities are contact sports.

B. Group students within each activity by ability as assessed by objective standards of individual performance.

Feedback

1. A

By categorizing students (i.e., beginning, intermediate, advanced), instruction can be better directed where similar abilities exist. Any loss of status among the "beginners" is offset by increased efficiency in instruction, greater attention to individual needs, and more definite and realistic goals. In addition, the upper limits of achievement are extended for the more gifted (advanced) students. Alternative B could demoralize learners. They might perceive that if "experienced," you are rewarded by playing in a tournament. If "not experienced," you are punished by receiving instruction. The chance for improvement should be available at all ability levels, and the opportunity for tournament play should be provided regardless of ability level.

2. B

   In *The New Games Book* and *More New Games* (Fluegelman, 1976, 1981), students assume various social roles through cooperative and competitive activities. If students were grouped homogeneously, as suggested in alternative A, the possibility of observing and interacting within a range of "social adjustment" levels would be limited. Heterogeneous teams made up of students with combinations of social adjustment ratings would enhance the degree of group integration, social acceptance, and popularity. Social needs rank at the top for students of adolescent age. Qualities such as tolerance, respect for others, helping others, sharing, and trust are inherent to these new games.

3. B

   From a diagnostic standpoint, intervention follows assessment. In this case, the intervention consists of sequential tasks for those motor abilities needing the greatest improvement. At each station, students begin at any point in the sequence, depending on entry proficiency. This form of individualization is more prescriptive than the random grouping in alternative A.

4. A

   Clearly, this student with a visual impairment can be integrated into regular physical education. Bowling, with the aid of a hand rail or guide rope, is an excellent modification. In fact, alternative B is not appropriate for the reasons given. Students with a visual impairment can engage in some of the other activities which normally require visual contact with objects, implements, and/or targets. For example, a ball with an audio sound device can be used in golf. In archery, a portable standard can be used so the student can determine height and direction through tactile stimulation.

5. A

   When students are classified according to achievement, time and energy are not expended in those areas where learning has previously occurred. Students who have already achieved these cognitive objectives could focus on the skills objectives. In alternative B, it would be inefficient to create groups that included a full range of scores. At some point, content would be covered that had already been learned by some and that would be too advanced for others.

6. A

   Obviously, alternative A would result in individual response to those components needing improvement. The chance for fitness gains is enhanced through workout groups based on fitness components. In addition, groups are based on pretest scores, not percentiles. Workout groups based on percentile rankings, alternative B, means that students are compared against one another (i.e., norm-referenced) instead of themselves.

7. B

   Many assume that students with cerebral palsy are limited to adapted physical education. However, some regular programming is possible. Activities depend on the nature of the cerebral palsy (e.g., spastic, athetoid) and the degree of involuntary motion (e.g., follow-through). For example, swimming activities can be completed in the regular class with the aid of a flotation device. Even archery, bowling, and golf can be performed depending on the degree of upper- and lower-body control of movement.

8. B

   Grouping on the basis of gender, alternative A, is irrational and illegal (Title IX). Students can be separated *within* physical education classes for activities involving bodily contact. Still, there is no reason why males and females cannot engage in integrated practice and skill development activities, regardless of the nature of the sport or activity. Grouping by gender may be warranted at the competitive (game) level. Alternative B is the most positive approach to grouping without regard to gender. Single standards of measuring skill or progress may be used only if the standard does not have an adverse effect on members of one sex.

Self-Directed Activity 4.2

You should be able to use entry data for programming and intervention. For each of the preassessment statements, decide which option you feel is most appropriate even though more than one may be feasible. Check (√) your selection and explain why.

Preassessment statements	Programming and intervention options			
	Conduct task analysis	Revise instruction	Repeat instructional sequence	Provide remedial loop
1. Student shows difficulty in returning tennis serves that require use of the backhand stroke.	____	____	____	____
	Why? ________________			
2. Student has not mastered the ability to perform an overhand set in volleyball after completing a series of task cards at a self-directed learning station.	____	____	____	____
	Why? ________________			
3. Student scores at the 15th percentile of the sit-and-reach test, a measure of flexibility of the back and posterior leg muscles.	____	____	____	____
	Why? ________________			
4. Analysis of the student's swimming sidestroke is diagnosed as "acceptable" for body positions, arms, coordination, and breathing, but "not acceptable" for the legs.	____	____	____	____
	Why? ________________			
5. Student's attitude toward lifetime sport activities is assessed as "unfavorable" according to results of a semantic differential scale.	____	____	____	____
	Why? ________________			
6. Student's performance on the AAHPER Archery Skill Test (AAHPER, 1967) was at the 70th percentile for accuracy, but student failed six of the eight "form" items.	____	____	____	____
	Why? ________________			
7. Student needs to improve cardiorespiratory endurance as revealed by the 1.5-mile run and 12-minute run classification tests.	____	____	____	____
	Why? ________________			
8. Student encounters a problem in completing the backward roll sequence at the point of maintaining balance when the hips go over the head.	____	____	____	____
	Why? ________________			

Feedback

1. Since proficiency in a single skill is needed, you should either *conduct a task analysis* or *repeat portions or the entirety of the instructional sequence*. The complexity of the tennis backhand warrants this degree of intervention.

2. The kind of feedback and skill analysis required to learn the overhand set would not be available through self-directed task cards. Therefore, the recommendation is to *revise instruction*. One alternative is reciprocal learning in which immediate evaluation and feedback can be built into the learning experience.

3. The remedial loop is feasible. However, since the percentile rank is so low, it would probably be most beneficial to *repeat the instructional sequence*. A more progressive flexibility task sequence could then be used.

4. The student could benefit from one or two programming options. *Repeating the portion of the instructional sequence* for the legs should improve the overall sidestroke skill. A *remedial loop* would also be effective if it involved specific leg movements. Since the student demonstrated an acceptable skill level in most aspects, the other intervention options are too extreme.

5. Preassessment involves some affective process (attitude formation). However, most of the options are content-oriented. Possibly, an unfavorable attitude toward lifetime sports is not content-related (e.g., golf, tennis, bowling, swimming). Instead, the learning approach may be the cause. As a first attempt toward changing attitude, it would be useful to *revise instruction* since it is a process-oriented option.

6. Despite a satisfactory score for accuracy, the rating for form is well below expectation. It would make sense to *conduct a task analysis* of the elements of form (e.g., bracing the bow, stance, nocking the arrow, finger placement, draw, anchor, release, follow-through). Then, the learner should *repeat the instructional sequence* with emphasis placed on these elements.

7. The development of cardiorespiratory endurance depends on the principle of progressive overload. For this reason, the most suitable intervention option would appear to be to *repeat the instructional (training) sequence*. Additional time and work may be necessary before the effects of training are achieved.

8. Since there is no problem in mastering one of the steps in the regular learning sequence (backward roll), a *remedial loop* is advised. At the point of difficulty (maintaining balance), a series of small tasks could be included such as rolling forward to original position, rolling forward to a crossed-leg standing position, and rolling backward in a hand-clasp position.

Self-Directed Activity 4.3

In this activity, you will relate entry-level measures, content goals, and informal assessment techniques. Your first task is to match each numbered goal with one of the exemplary measures by recording the appropriate letter in the "measure" column. Each of the exemplary measures may be used only once. Then, in the "type of technique" column, indicate the technique used by recording the appropriate letter from the following:

Type of technique

A = Observation (descriptive)
B = Observation (quantitative)
C = Questionnaire/Survey
D = Interview/Dialogue/Discussion

Measure	Type of technique	Goals
_____	_____	1. Perform basic manipulative movements (psychomotor)
_____	_____	2. Analyze sports skills in accordance with mechanical principles (cognitive)
_____	_____	3. Maintain a desirable level of personal fitness (affective)
_____	_____	4. Develop body awareness (psychomotor)
_____	_____	5. Accept responsibility for individual decision making (affective)
_____	_____	6. Comprehend the factors that determine the quality of movement (cognitive)
_____	_____	7. Show mutual respect and concern for others (affective)
_____	_____	8. Demonstrate complex adaptive skills (psychomotor)

Exemplary measures

(A) The students exchange ideas concerning the determination of individual performance levels as prescribed in the "learning packet" on jogging.

(B) It is noted on the student's progress chart that he or she selected a partner with a disabling condition, given the first opportunity to do so.

(C) The student satisfies 8 of the 10 criteria in performing the cartwheel.

(D) A record is made that the student fails to keep his or her eyes on the object and does not complete the follow-through when bouncing, kicking, catching, and striking an object.

(E) The student circles words such as interesting, dull, useful, worthless, etc., to indicate his or her feelings toward various kinds of activities (e.g., drills, circuit training, obstacle course, group training, and working with partners).

(F) The student is rated "above expectation" in abilities in laterality and directionality.

(G) The student matches the dimensions of space, time, force, and flow with stick-figure drawings of various movements.

(H) The student explains the concepts of velocity, acceleration, force, and power with reference to hitting a baseball, putting the shot, and throwing the javelin.

Feedback

1. D A

   This measure (D) provides a descriptive statement that could be included in the student's anecdotal record. The manipulative skills (psychomotor) are assessed through observation.

2. H D

   The ability to analyze sports skills (cognitive) is revealed by "explaining" mechanical principles. The type of technique is dialogue since the student responds orally.

3. E C

   To achieve the goal (affective), certain attitudes need to be developed toward various kinds of training activities (E). By circling words, the student is obviously responding to some kind of preassessment questionnaire or survey.

4. F B

   Laterality and directionality contribute to body awareness (psychomotor). The "above expected" rating is based on an observation rating scale (quantitative).

5. A D

   By determining individual performance levels in jogging (A), the student accepts responsibility for making decisions (affective). Prior to these decisions, the student engages in a discussion. The information derived would give some indication of the student's willingness to accept this decision-making responsibility.

6. G C

   Space, time, force, and flow are dimensions that determine quality of movement. The student completes a worksheet by matching these dimensions with stick figures (G). This pretest indicates the student's level of comprehension (cognitive).

7. B A

   The student shows mutual respect and concern for others (affective) by selecting a partner with a disabling condition (B). This behavior is observed and noted in descriptive form. It serves as baseline data since the student selected a partner for the first time.

8. C B

   By performing a cartwheel (C), the student demonstrates a complex adaptive skill (psychomotor). An observation checklist reveals that 8 of 10 entry criteria were satisfied.

Self-Directed Activity 4.4

Learning situations are described that involve entry appraisal. Indicate whether the formal assessment technique being used is criterion-referenced (C) or norm-referenced (N). Then, briefly explain the reasons for your answer.

_____ 1. Students are to select one of three cardiorespiratory training programs: running and jogging, swimming, or general aerobics. Recommended training levels and routines have been established for each of the programs. To determine initial training level, either the 1.5-mile run or 12-minute run classification test is completed. Based on results, each student begins the selected program at the appropriate training level.

Reasons: ______________________________

____

____

_____ 2. In preparing a volleyball unit for high school juniors, the teacher tests students to find out the ability level of the class. The AAHPER Volleyball Skills Test (AAHPER, 1969) is administered consisting of volleying, serving, passing, and setup. Each student is randomly assigned to two tests. An overall class percentile is determined for each test.

Reasons: ______________________________

____

____

_____ 3. Middle school students are about to engage in a combination of team sports. Common movement patterns (e.g., overhand motion, step in the direction, follow-through) and concepts (e.g., two on one, zone defense) will be learned as well as certain values of team play (e.g., cooperation, teamwork, leadership, fair play). To determine one effect of the program (changes in attitude), students complete the *Sportsmanship Attitude Scale* (Johnson, 1969) prior to instruction on football, basketball, and softball situations. The scale will be administered again at the end of instruction.

Reasons: ______________________________

____

____

_____ 4. A group of 10th graders has signed up for weight training during a supervised activity period. The primary goal of the program is to increase muscular strength and endurance. To determine a starting point, one weight training exercise is selected for each area of the body (neck, shoulders, arms, upper back, chest, lower back, abdominals, legs). Each exercise is performed at a beginning resistance equal to 8-RM for strength and 12-RM for endurance. These resistance levels are used for completing the progressive training routines.

Reasons: ______________________________

____

____

_____ 5. One goal for a gymnastics program is for students to acquire a wide range of knowledge and understanding. A comprehensive posttest is constructed that includes test items for each event. Test items cover aspects of gymnastics such as rules, spotting techniques, basic principles, terminology, concepts, skill analysis, and routine design. Students complete a pretest made up of selected items from the posttest. This sampling indicates each student's entry status and areas that need improvement.

Reasons: ____________________

____

____

_____ 6. In an elementary school, first graders are given the Basic Motor Ability Tests (BMAT) (Arnheim & Sinclair, 1979) to collect baseline data. All students complete the following subtests: bead stringing, target throwing, tapping board, back and hamstring stretch, standing long jump, face down to standing, static balance, chair push-ups, and agility run. Percentile rankings of each learner are determined and a mean percentile ranking for all subtests is calculated. These rankings will be used subsequently for comparison at the end of each grade level.

Reasons: ____________________

____

____

Feedback

1. C

   Individual achievement level is determined. The student's mastery level for the 1.5-mile run or 12-minute run is translated into a beginning training level. The student proceeds through the training routine on a self-paced basis.

2. N

   The percentile rankings indicate the student's relative standing on the test items. Since the results show differences among students, the formal assessment technique is norm-referenced.

3. C

   Although the attitude scale may appear to be "standardized," the resulting scores yield an individual behavior index. Change in sportsmanship can be determined based on this entry appraisal.

4. C

   Individual resistance levels for muscular strength and endurance training reveal what a student can do at a given time. The student's criterion levels are identified along a continuum of training RM (repetitive maximum).

5. C

   The cognitive pretest reveals students' strengths and weaknesses. This criterion-referenced assessment provides specific information concerning individual performance.

6. N

   The nature and use of this achievement index represents a form of normative assessment. Percentile rankings establish a single standard of measurement. Individual learner performance is compared to the entire group of first graders.

Self-Directed Activity 4.5

Various sources should be considered when you collect entry-level information. For each of the situations that follow, identify the *specific* kind of information from the two sources that would be useful.

1. Stability is probably the most fundamental component of "learning to move." Students in the upper elementary grades are developing specific sports skills that depend on balance.

   Previous content: ______________________________

   ____

   ____

   Task sequence: ______________________________

   ____

   ____

2. A revised secondary school curriculum in physical education is about to be implemented. In the 10th grade, the program begins with physical fitness.

   Cumulative record data: ______________________________

   ____

   ____

   Behavior sampling: ______________________________

   ____

3. Cognitive processes at the application and analysis levels are being developed by middle school students. Various individual and group physical education activities are planned for this purpose. Common elements include facts, concepts, relationships, preferences, limits, and strategies.

   Previous content: ______________________________

   ____

   ____

   Nature of learning activity: ______________________________

   ____

   ____

4. Regular sports (e.g., football, basketball, volleyball) are modified to enhance the potential for positive, gender-integrated learning. It is expected that students will respond favorably while they participate in these activities.

   Cumulative record data: ______________________________

   ____

   ____

   Behavior sampling: ______________________________

   ____

5. As part of a comprehensive, elementary school physical education curriculum, a perceptual motor program is developed for the primary grades. Through movement exploration involving space, force, time, and flow, students respond to various stimuli (e.g., visual, tactile).

   Task sequence: ____

   ____

   ____

   Nature of learning activity: ____

   ____

   ____

6. Elective mini-courses are available to high school seniors from a wide range of offerings such as beginning, intermediate, and advanced swimming. Enrollment in the intermediate swimming course is much higher than expected.

   Previous content: ____

   ____

   ____

   Behavior sampling: ____

   ____

   ____

Feedback

These responses represent *possible* answers. There are many that are equally correct, but your answers, which are more brief, should be similar to the ones offered.

1. *Previous content*: This information source might reveal whether students were to have developed confidence in going off-balance, skill in recovering balance, and ability to balance on different bases of support. If previous content included static postures (e.g., standing, inverted support) and transitional postures (e.g., rolling, dodging, landing, stopping), then students have completed the necessary prerequisites to stability.

   Task sequence: As a predictor of sports skills acquisition, students could complete a balance task sequence. One of the subtasks would be the point at which students are considered competent in stability. This preassessment would indicate those who should complete the remaining tasks and those who possess sufficient balance to develop the sports skills. The following task sequence (partial) for walking on a low balance beam could be used as a measure of stability.

   Task 1: Walk forward and backward with both arms out to the side, shoulder height; eyes open.

   Task 2: Walk forward and backward with hands clasped behind the body; eyes open.

   Task 12: Walk forward and backward with a beanbag on the head; eyes open.

   Task 13: Walk forward and backward with both arms out to the side, shoulder height; eyes closed.

2. *Cumulative record data*: Useful information includes physical fitness test scores, rating scales, diagnostic inventories, and anecdotal records. For example, end-of-year fitness scores for the junior high schools in the district could serve as preassessment data. Knowledge of general (group of 10th graders) as well as specific (individual student) areas of success and needed improvement would help in designing the final program. Learning objectives and learning experiences could then be tailored to the student based on identified needs.

   Behavior sampling: Pretest sampling of performance yields highly relevant data. For example, a customized achievement test could be administered that is based on the health-related and skill-related components of physical fitness. Possible test items are:

Fitness component	Test item
Cardiorespiratory endurance	600-yard run; 1.5-mile run; 12-minute run
Muscular strength	Hand grip; leg lifts in 20 seconds
Muscular endurance	Push-ups; bent-knee sit-ups; pull-ups
Flexibility	Sit-and-reach
Coordination	Cable jump
Agility	Figure-8 run
Speed	50-yard dash
Power	Standing long jump
Balance	Sideward leap test; lengthwise stick test

3. *Previous content*: Review of previous unit outlines and materials in a given activity would indicate whether or not certain facts, concepts, relationships, preferences, limits, and strategies were covered. It could also be determined whether learning was projected at the application and analysis levels. Using golf content, the following aspects would be useful in determining entry ability:

Aspect	Golf content
Facts	Clubs; terminology; scoring; etiquette; rules; methods
Concepts	Stance; address; body position; center of gravity; transfer of force
Relationships	Tee to green; time-space; swing; uphill and downhill lies
Limits	Wood shots; iron shots; chip shots; putting; sand shots

   Nature of learning activity: Since abilities in application and analysis are being developed, certain kinds of activities are useful indicators of entry status. Guided discovery and problem-solving approaches involve convergent and divergent thinking operations, respectively. For example, students' understanding of soccer would be revealed in their responses to questions such as: "Which body parts can be used to move the ball from point A to point B on the field?" (body-ball relationships); "What are some ways of kicking the ball and keeping it rolling?" (foot-ball-ground limits); and "How can a defender be avoided while control of the ball is maintained?" (strategies).

4. *Cumulative record data*: Given the nature of the situation, data should be sought that reveal students' attitudes toward sports, previous experiences in coeducational settings, and general interpersonal relations skills. Affective rating scales might indicate students' "adaptability" and "respect for others" regardless of gender. These results would serve as the *beginning* behaviors against which students' responses to gender-integrated learning could be compared. Anecdotal records might also be useful.

   Behavior sampling: This preassessment is not limited to cognitive and motor skill pretests. A general inventory could be used to identify entry attitudes and values toward modified, gender-integrated sports. For example, students could be observed during an initial coed volleyball game that has been modified (i.e., alternate serving by males and females; when there is more than one play on the ball, hits must be made by at least one male and one female). The teacher could tally the number of times positive and negative behaviors were exhibited, such as:

Supports, encourages opposite sex	versus	Purposely interferes with opposite sex
Passes, sets to opposite sex	versus	Ignores opposite sex
Accepts mistakes by opposite sex	versus	Reacts critically to opposite sex

5. *Task sequence*: Coordinated abilities are developed in a perceptual motor program. For example, eye-hand coordination is a combination of kinesthetic, visual, and tactile discrimination. The student's beginning task on the following partial sequence is used to determine entry-level eye-hand coordination. From this task, students advance along the learning continuum.

   Task 1: Toss a beanbag into the air with both hands; catch it with both hands.

   Task 2: Toss the beanbag into the air with one hand; catch it with the same hand; then, catch it with the opposite hand.

   Task 10: Toss the beanbag into the air with the free hand; catch it in the "scoop" held with the opposite hand.

   Task 11: Have a catch with a partner using the beanbag and the "scoop."

   Nature of learning activity: The student's response to movement questions or challenges is a good indicator of entry status, particularly perceptual motor abilities. Movement exploration, by its nature, provides useful preassessment information. For example, the student's ability to "explore general space" might serve as a *baseline*. The learner is observed carrying out the following kinds of tasks:

   - See how many places you can go without touching others.
   - Find out how many different directions you can move (backward, sideward, up, down).
   - Try to explore space at different levels (high, medium, low).
   - Change your speed when you are moving at different levels.

6. *Previous content*: It is important to review the minimum competencies for the beginning swimming mini-course. The learning objectives, learning experiences, and evaluation procedures completed in the previous beginning course are a starting point for the intermediate course. For example, content analysis would reveal the swimming strokes covered, projected goals, nature of learning activities, and performance criteria. Given this information, certain assumptions could be made about what the students are and are not able to do at the start of the course.

   Behavior sampling: The high enrollment may indicate inappropriate selection and/or placement. Therefore, it would be useful to sample students' performance through a pretest. This entry appraisal would be used as a basis for repeating parts or all of the beginning course or as the starting point for the intermediate course. For example, the following minimum standards might be established for continued enrollment:

   - Perform front crawl for 50 yards with satisfactory form.
   - Perform back crawl for 25 yards with satisfactory form.
   - Perform either the elementary backstroke or the sidestroke for 50 yards with satisfactory form.
   - Float on back for 2 minutes.
   - Perform a standing dive according to established criteria.
   - Pass written test dealing with safety and stroke analysis.

5

Deriving Learning Objectives

Key Concept

Curriculum designers transform content goals into learning objectives that specify the proposed changes in student behavior.

A state accreditation team is evaluating the school system in a town of 40,000. The physical education staff is composed of 16 teachers. Physical education is represented on the accreditation team by two teachers, one of whom teaches physical education at an elementary school and the other of whom is an adapted physical education specialist at the secondary level. They review curriculum materials, visit each of the schools, interview teachers and students, and observe classes during their 3-day visit. The recommendations of the team are discussed with the entire staff at the end of the last day. They raise three concerns. First, there is a discrepancy between program objectives and what is actually taught. Second, the evaluation instruments do not match the stated learning objectives. And third, the program objectives are far too general to be of any help in guiding learning activities and evaluation techniques. The physical education staff is strongly advised to use a more precise format for stating objectives. However, they are unsure exactly how to do that.

Expected Outcomes

This chapter helps you derive learning objectives that provide precision for your curriculum design. Upon completing it, you will be able to

- generate learning objectives that represent the cognitive, affective, and psychomotor domains;
- analyze learning objectives according to the elements of basic form;
- differentiate between individualized and nonindividualized learning objectives;
- apply the needs assessment approach for selecting learning objectives;
- identify learning objectives that are stated in explicit terms;
- evaluate the degree to which learning objectives are meaningful—crucial, clear, and worthy; and
- illustrate the arrangement of terminal and enabling objectives in a hierarchy.

General direction for the curriculum was established by converting organizing centers into content goals. Now, to guide instruction, you need to identify the *specific* changes in learning that are sought. The conversion of content goals into precise statements of intent is a difficult but essential task. The information produced through entry appraisal (chapter 4) will help you. The curriculum designing model in Figure 5.1 shows this step, *deriving learning objectives*. Thus, the question, "Where are you going?" is completely answered once learning objectives are derived.

To establish specific direction for the curriculum, a precise description of educational purpose is needed—learning objectives. They communicate intended student outcomes. Therefore, several questions arise. "What are learning objectives?" "How are learning objectives structured?" "What factors should be considered to enhance quality?" "How are learning objectives organized?" Answers to these questions are provided in the following sections. Ultimately, you should be able to derive learning objectives for your own physical education curriculum.

Framework for Precision

Transforming content goals into precise statements of intent requires a framework. One framework is presented here, beginning with a definition of learning objectives. Then, a way to structure them is proposed, showing how learning objectives may be classified within the domains and suggesting a basic form for writing them. Finally, learning objectives are analyzed according to the elements of this basic form.

Learning Objectives Defined

The learning objective communicates intent by stating the proposed changes in students. It describes *observable* and *measurable* behavior. Objectives reveal what students should be able to do, know, or feel as a result of instruction.

Deriving learning objectives is not simply selecting them. First, you should generate objectives that show high promise of supporting content goals. In turn, this will be related to an organizing center. The transformation of organizing centers to content goals to learning objectives is both logical and useful. This relationship is depicted in Figure 5.2 (page 126). The sample learning objective is stated in basic form. You will develop the ability to write learning objectives later.

Second, you should choose those learning objectives that will ultimately guide the development of evaluation procedures (chapter 6) and learning experiences (chapter 7). The quality of objectives is enhanced if you are able to consider a broad range of possible objectives.

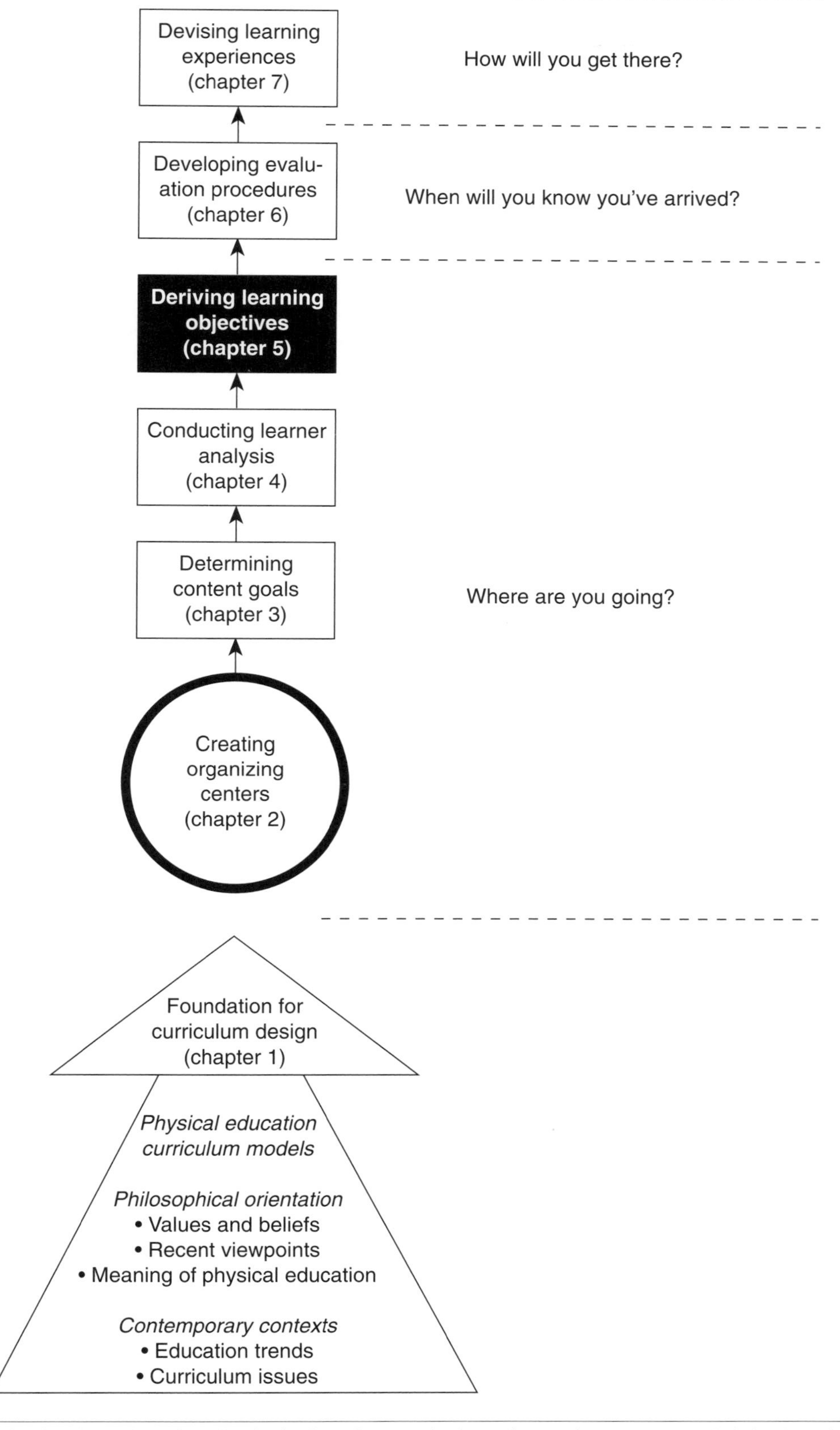

Figure 5.1 Model for designing the physical education curriculum shows the next step, *deriving learning objectives*.

Organizing center
Sensory stimulation

General outcome
Develop efficiently functioning perceptual abilities

Content goal (1st tier)
Demonstrate eye-hand coordination

Learning objective
To demonstrate eye-hand coordination, the learner will be able to catch a playground ball thrown from a distance of 10 feet, three out of five times.

Figure 5.2 Organizing center is transformed into general outcomes and content goals which in turn serve as the basis for deriving a learning objective.

Structure of Learning Objectives

Deriving learning objectives from content goals can be a demanding mental effort. Specific statements of intent foster exactness in the curriculum instead of broad "glittering" goals. To help you structure learning objectives, two processes are suggested—classifying them within a taxonomy and stating them according to basic form.

Taxonomic System

A classification scheme has been developed for categorizing learning objectives. Teachers can plan and evaluate learning and compare existing objectives with a broader spectrum of outcomes. The *Taxonomy of Educational Objectives* includes a threefold division:

- ***Cognitive domain*** (Bloom, 1956): Recall or recognition of knowledge; complex intellectual abilities and skills
- ***Affective domain*** (Krathwohl, Bloom, & Masia, 1964): Feelings and emotions; changes in interests, attitudes, and values; appreciations
- ***Psychomotor domain*** (Harrow, 1972): Reflex, basic fundamental, perceptual, and complex motor patterns

The domains should not be viewed as separate entities. The premise is that motivation (affective domain) is the foundation upon which cognitive and psychomotor tasks are built. Although they were separated so that curriculum designers can distinguish outcomes such as solving problems, forming attitudes, and performing complex motor skills, the domains are interdependent in virtually all learning situations. The major categories of the domains are described in Tables 5.1, 5.2 (page 128), and 5.3 (page 129). The illustrative objective for each category is written in partial form. The recommended form for stating learning objectives is presented in the next section.

▶ ***To practice relating learning objectives to their associated domains and corresponding domain categories, complete Self-Directed Activity 5.1 at the end of this chapter.***

Basic Form

Although objectives may be stated in a variety of ways, using a standard form will help you convert content goals into precise statements. It also makes it easier to relate learning objectives to the remaining curriculum components—evaluation procedures and learning experiences. However, some ways of stating learning objectives do *not* satisfy the recommended form. For example:

Objectives stated in terms of teacher activities

- To present the history of tennis
- To demonstrate the backstroke in swimming
- To introduce the center-back-up defense in volleyball

Objectives stated in terms of learner activities

- To learn the rules of badminton
- To participate in movement exploration activities
- To practice ball manipulation skills

Objectives stated in terms of topics, concepts, generalizations, or other elements of content

- Techniques of putting
- Sports officiating
- Progressively increasing work load is necessary to achieve functional adaptation to training

Table 5.1 Cognitive Domain Categories and Illustrative Objectives

Cognitive domain: This domain encompasses knowledge and intellectual abilities and skills ranging from simple recall tasks to synthesizing and evaluating information.

Category	Description	Objectives
1. Knowledge	Memory; recall of specifics (facts), ideas, methods, and procedures; bring to mind the appropriate material; lowest level of learning outcome	To remember rules; to label positions in soccer; to define fitness terms; to name tumbling stunts
2. Comprehension	Understand what is communicated without seeing its full implications; interpret, translate, and extrapolate verbal material; lowest level of understanding	To distinguish swimming strokes; to classify wrestling takedowns; to interpret an offensive strategy
3. Application	Use of abstractions (ideas, rules, methods, concepts, principles, theories) in new and concrete situations; higher level of understanding	To modify a running play in football; to select the rule that applies; to use a movement pattern in a new skill
4. Analysis	Break down material into its parts; organization and relationship of ideas are made explicit; selecting, relating, and inferring; higher intellectual level	To diagram a defensive alignment; to differentiate mechanical principles; to recognize checkpoints for proper execution
5. Synthesis	Parts and elements are put together to form a whole or a unified organization; arrange or create new patterns or structures	To design a gymnastics routine; to adjust the defense to a change in offense; to devise a new dance movement
6. Evaluation	Judge the value of ideas, materials, and procedures according to internal or external criteria and standards; highest learning outcome	To identify positive and negative features; to judge a dive; to compare game plans

Objectives stated in terms of generalized patterns of behavior

- To develop critical thinking
- To develop an appreciation for individual sports
- To develop favorable social attitudes

It is common to state objectives using an "outcomes approach." For example: "The student will catch a playground ball thrown from a distance of 10 feet, three out of five times." However, an educational objective is not necessarily good just because it specifies a behavioral outcome. For this reason, a different method is recommended that links content goals and learning objectives.

With the "goals approach," desired behaviors possess meaning because they contribute to some goal—students know *why* specific behaviors should be exhibited. This approach can be shown using the previous objective: "To demonstrate eye-hand coordination, the student will catch a playground ball thrown from a distance of 10 feet, three out of five times." In this example, the content goal is clearly transformed into a specific intent.

Learning objectives should reflect the purposes for developing such statements. The recommended form has four basic elements, each of which is defined. Then, the sample learning objective is analyzed accordingly.

- ***Goal component***: Identifies the intent of the learning objective; refers directly to a curriculum content goal; it is drawn from the next highest tier of goals or prerequisites in a learning hierarchy.

- ***Performance or behavioral activity (action verb)***: Describes the specific behavior or action to be elicited from the student. Action verbs specific to the educational domains are suggested in Table 5.4 (page 130).

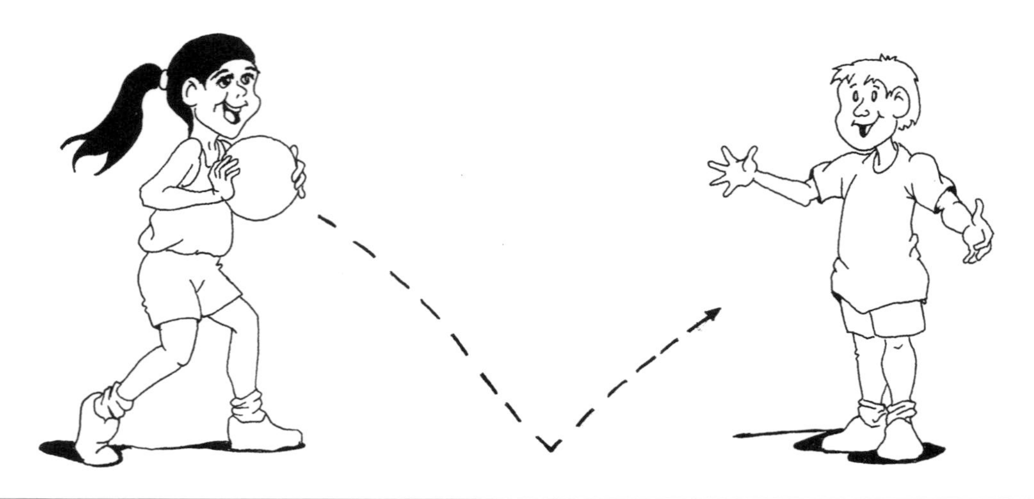

Eye-hand coordination is developed through ball catching.

Table 5.2 Affective Domain Categories and Illustrative Objectives

Affective domain: This domain encompasses likes and dislikes, attitudes, values, and beliefs ranging from a willingness to receive and respond to an established value system.

Category	Description	Objectives
1. Receiving (attending)	Willingness to be aware of or attend to a phenomenon or an event; ranges from simple awareness to selective attention; lowest level of learning outcome	To listen attentively to an analysis of a skill; to select a position to play in softball; to accept flexibility exercises as a form of warm-up
2. Responding	React to condition, phenomenon, or situation through some form of participation (overt response); "interest" to seek out and enjoy particular activities	To voluntarily assist in setting up equipment; to comply with pool regulations; to participate in a chosen team sport
3. Valuing	Worth attached to a behavior from acceptance to commitment; worth or belief in phenomenon with some degree of consistency; "attitudes" and "appreciation"	To attend optional practice sessions; to join an intramural team; to show a preference for particular sports
4. Organization	Bring different values together in an organized system; determine interrelationships of values; accept some values as dominant; compare, relate, and synthesize values; develop philosophy of life	To adhere to a physical fitness schedule; to propose alternative safety and spotting techniques; to defend an unpopular game strategy
5. Characterization by a value or value complex	Develop characteristic "lifestyle"; act in accordance with accepted values; behavior becomes part of personality; behavior is pervasive, consistent, and predictable	To maintain a personalized fitness program; to show respect for the worth and dignity of others; to serve as a volunteer coach

Table 5.3 Psychomotor Domain Categories and Illustrative Objectives

Psychomotor domain: This domain encompasses all observable voluntary human motion ranging from basic fundamental movements to modifying and creating aesthetic movement patterns.

Category	Description	Objectives
1. Reflex movements	Action elicited without conscious volition in response to some stimulus; flexing, extending, stretching, and making postural adjustments; provides base for movement behavior	Since reflex movements are not voluntary, objectives are not stated; these movements are prerequisites to the following classification levels.
2. Basic fundamental movements	Inherent movement patterns based on combination of reflex movements; patterns provide starting point for improvement of perceptual and physical abilities; basis for complex skilled movement	To be able to slide, walk, and run; to perform an overarm throw; to manipulate balls and blocks
3. Perceptual abilities	Interpretation of stimuli from various modalities so that adjustments can be made; includes auditory, visual, kinesthetic, tactile, and coordinated perceptual abilities	To maintain balance on one leg; to toss and catch a beanbag; to kick a moving playground ball
4. Physical abilities	Characteristics which, when developed to a high degree, provide the learner with a sound, efficiently functioning body; organic vigor essential to the development of highly skilled movement; includes endurance, strength, flexibility, and agility	To develop upper body strength; to improve cardiorespiratory endurance; to increase trunk-hip flexibility
5. Skilled movements	Degree of efficiency in performing a complex movement task; consists of a vertical and a horizontal continuum; based upon inherent movement patterns	To punt a football; to volley a tennis ball; to perform a series of gymnastic stunts
6. Nondiscursive communication	Movement expressions that are part of a movement repertoire; movement interpretations that include any efficiently performed skilled movement; movement patterns designed to communicate a message to the viewer; ranges from facial expressions through sophisticated choreographies	To create a movement sequence and perform it to music; to design and perform a free exercise routine; to choreograph and perform a dance routine

Table 5.4 Action Verbs for Educational Domains

Cognitive domain (hierarchical categories)			Psychomotor domain		
Knowledge	*Comprehension*	*Application*	Adjust	Flex	Pull
Define	Classify	Change	Arch	Follow	Push
Identify	Convert	Choose	Assemble	Grasp	Roll
Label	Distinguish	Discover	Bend	Grip	Run
List	Infer	Modify	Button	Hit	Skip
Match	Interpret	Relate	Catch	Hop	Slide
Name	Predict	Show	Chase	Jump	Sway
Outline	Reorder	Solve	Climb	Kick	Swim
Select	Summarize	Transfer	Construct	Lift	Swing
State	Transform	Use	Demonstrate	Manipulate	Throw
Analysis	*Synthesis*	*Evaluation*	Dodge	Operate	Toss
Categorize	Combine	Appraise	Extend	Perform	Walk
Contrast	Compose	Assess			
Derive	Construct	Compare			
Diagram	Design	Criticize			
Differentiate	Devise	Decide			
Illustrate	Formulate	Judge			
Recognize	Organize	Justify			
Select	Revise	Standardize			
Translate	Specify	Validate			

Affective domain (hierarchical categories)				
Receiving	*Responding*	*Valuing*	*Organization*	*Characterization*
Ask	Allow	Accept	Alter	Act
Choose	Answer	Agree	Arrange	Avoid
Identify	Assist	Aid	Combine	Change
Listen	Commend	Compare	Criticize	Display
Locate	Comply	Complete	Decide	Express
Name	Conform	Compliment	Defend	Maintain
Reply	Cooperate	Differentiate	Formulate	Perform
Select	Discuss	Form	Integrate	Propose
Use	Follow	Help	Modify	Resolve
	Label	Join	Order	Revise
	Participate	Justify	Persist	Solve
	Report	Prefer	Praise	Use
	Take turns	Propose	Prepare	Verify
	Tell	Share	Relate	
	Volunteer	Support	Tolerate	

• ***Criterion standard***: Specifies the minimum acceptable level of success in measurable terms; defines success in achieving the behavior. Examples of criteria for different kinds of learning outcomes appear in Table 5.5 (Hurwitz, 1993b).

• ***Conditions***: Specifies factors or criteria under which the learning must take place; this element may or may not be necessary.

	Analysis
Goal component:	To demonstrate eye-hand coordination
Behavioral activity:	Catch a playground ball (the student will)
Criterion standard:	Three out of five times
Condition:	Thrown from a distance of 10 feet

▶ ***To practice recognizing the elements of basic form that make up a learning objective, complete Self-Directed Activity 5.2 at the end of this chapter.***

Qualitative Considerations

While your learning objectives may conform to the categories of the domains and to the criteria of basic form, they may not be of sufficient *quality*. In order to add quality to your learning objectives, consideration should be given to individualization, needs assessment, explicit learning, and meaningful characteristics (cruciality, clarity, and worthiness). Although some of these aspects have overlapping features, each deserves separate treatment.

Individualization

Individualization ensures that learning is suited to students' *unique* characteristics. An individualized curriculum is student-centered and diagnostic by design. It follows that learning objectives should produce the most appropriate match with these characteristics. Unfortunately, many teachers

Table 5.5 Criterion Standards for Different Kinds of Outcomes

Outcome	What may be set	Criterion examples
Motor performance	Number of repetitions	10 times
	Characteristics	With feet together; legs bent; elbow flexed
	Accuracy, speed, distance, amount	4 out of 10; 15 seconds or less; 30 feet or more; improve by 10%; 4 errors or less; 50 pounds or more
Attitude	Tendency/Frequency of behavior	Always, most of time, usually, seldom, never; ratio of 4:1
Knowledge	Number of repetitions	3 times
	Accuracy	2 out of 3; 80% or better
Concept formation	Number of repetitions	4 times
	Accuracy	5 out of 6; 80%; all
	Quality of response	Covering at least the following points . . .
Use of rules	Number of repetitions	On 2 occasions
	Quality of product or behavior	With 3 or fewer errors; that has these characteristics . . .
Problem solving	Number of repetitions	3 times
	Quality of solution	At least 3 out of 4; that includes the following . . .

Note. Adapted from "Guidelines for Setting Mastery Criteria" by R. Hurwitz, 1993, unpublished manuscript, Cleveland State University. Adapted by permission of the author.

manipulate students to satisfy group characteristics instead of matching programming to individual student needs and interests. Individualized learning requires continuous examination of students' strengths and weaknesses and the prescription of learning tasks. Diagnostic data must be recorded and translated into precise learning objectives.

Individualization is enhanced if learning objectives incorporate the concept of "improvement" rather than absolute levels of acceptable performance. This notion was also given attention in chapter 4 (page 99). For example, improvement may be facilitated by using percentages rather than fixed numerical increases; behavior changes measured against the student's own preassessment level rather than on external norms; and steps along a continuum (range of tasks) rather than arbitrary, initial levels based on chronological age.

▶ ***To practice differentiating between individualized and nonindividualized learning objectives, complete Self-Directed Activity 5.3 at the end of this chapter.***

Needs Assessment

The cognitive, affective, and psychomotor needs of students are basic to deriving learning objectives. However, there's a problem in determining what needs and corresponding objectives *should* be sought. One of the most popular approaches for deciding on defensible objectives is needs assessment. Objectives are adjusted to match student needs and consideration is given to students' current status. The lead-up steps to the desired level could vary in terms of the beginning step, the number of steps to be sought, or the size of the steps. When conducting a needs assessment to decide the priority of learning objectives, you should follow the sequential tasks identified in Table 5.6.

▶ ***To practice prioritizing objectives, complete Self-Directed Activity 5.4 at the end of this chapter.***

Explicit Learning

Your objectives should lead to explicit learning. For example, the concept "respect for others" could be transformed into learning objectives by specifying what the student is doing (behavior) when he or she displays consideration, regard, or courtesy toward others. Specific behaviors might include

- accepts unfavorable referee decisions without overt reaction,
- makes adjustments in assisting partner that facilitate partner's performance,
- shares equipment,
- responds to feedback from another student in a reciprocal learning situation, or
- takes turns at circuit stations.

Stating objectives in explicit terms facilitates evaluation even in areas where it is difficult to identify *measurable* behaviors, such as those associated with the affective domain, which includes social, emotional, and values learning. As long as teachers identify and make judgments as to acceptable and unacceptable behaviors, explicit criteria exist. For example, teachers often make judgments about students' attitudes. Therefore, you need to specify those desirable and undesirable behaviors that indicate positive and negative attitudes, respectively. This aspect of learning objectives has implications for developing evaluation procedures (chapter 6).

▶ ***To practice recognizing objectives written in explicit terms, complete Self-Directed Activity 5.5 at the end of this chapter.***

Meaningful Characteristics

The importance of a learning objective should be apparent to the curriculum designer—*is it crucial*? The learning objective must also be understandable to others, including the student for whom it is intended—*is it stated clearly*? Finally, the learning objective may be stated clearly and in proper form, but it may be of little educational significance—*is it worthy*? Thus, meaningful learning objectives are crucial, clearly stated, and worthy.

Cruciality

Determining cruciality is another way to indicate quality. The crucial nature of a learning objective depends on the *probability* that the objective is

- *needed* in terms of students' interests, satisfaction of needs, and future learning in school and the community,
- *achievable* given time, materials, prerequisites, and developmental level required, and
- to be learned in a *school setting only*.

For example, if a particular learning objective is needed by the students, attainable by students, but available in nonschool settings, then the objective may not be considered crucial. If, however, this objective was not available in nonschool settings, then a high cruciality value would be indicated.

Table 5.6 Tasks for Conducting a Needs Assessment

Task	Description
Task 1 Identify all learning objectives from which to select the most defensible.	The number of potential learning objectives that could support a given content goal is relatively high. The factors previously identified in this chapter also influence the number of potential learning objectives. In addition, objectives may be derived from commercial and professional sources and parents, students, and other citizens.
Task 2 Establish educational preferences with respect to the relative value of each learning objective.	Subject matter experts, teachers, parents, and students can help determine the relative value of objectives through questionnaires or rating scales.
Task 3 Determine proportion of students who are expected to master the learning objectives.	Prerequisites are sorted into those that all students possess (group 1), those that some or many might not already possess (group 2), and those that most or all students probably do not possess (group 3). Objectives will ultimately reflect these prerequisites. Therefore, the desired mastery level of some objectives is expected for a certain number (proportion) of students. Other objectives would be selected for mastery by *all* students.
Task 4 Assess student status regarding preferred learning objectives.	The discrepancy between the student's present status and desired behavior may be of greater significance in determining the objectives of highest priority than those objectives that are highly preferred. Data regarding the student's status are usually collected through observations, self-reports, past records, and pretests.
Task 5 Select the most defensible learning objectives based on preferences, mastery levels, and magnitude of discrepancy in student status.	The last step is to determine objectives of highest and lowest priority. You should establish the weight given to preferences (Task 2), mastery levels (Task 3), and the differences between desired and actual status (Task 4). For example, it is necessary to determine which is more important, the rank of the objective or the gap between desired and actual mastery. Obviously, an objective that is highly preferred, where a high discrepancy exists, will receive a high priority rating.

A "cruciality formula" was devised which takes these factors into account (McNeil, 1976). The formula and steps involved in its use are indicated in Figure 5.3. Probabilities should be estimated within the context of an actual situation which includes a student or students who are familiar to the curriculum designer.

In applying the formula, the relative quality (value) of objectives can be determined and compared with other objectives. Comparisons can be made within domain classifications as well as across all objectives. It is suggested that the "behavioral activity" element of objectives be used for rating purposes. The cruciality formula is applied to several objectives in Figure 5.4.

Clarity

Learning objectives are enhanced when intended outcomes (behaviors) are clearly observable. Psychomotor behaviors may be directly observed, such as the ability to climb, jump, kick, skip, or throw. Because cognitive and affective learning can't be directly observed since they are internal processes, to comprehend, apply knowledge, value, cooperate, persevere, or show interest depends on some other observable product or activity, such as the ability to label, diagram, volunteer, jump up and down, choose a partner, or take turns. It is difficult to know for sure if cognitive and affective behaviors are genuine and representative of the outcome being sought.

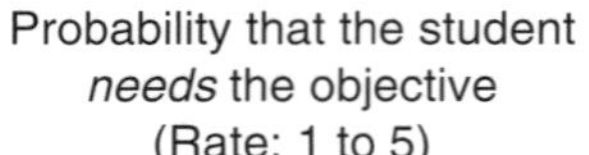

Cruciality = [Probability that the student *needs* the objective (Rate: 1 to 5) × Probability that the objective is *attainable* (Rate: 1 to 5)] / [Probability that the objective will be learned in a *nonschool setting* (Rate: 1 to 5)]

Step 1: Estimate probability of student need in terms of (1) students' interest, (2) satisfaction of cognitive, affective, and psychomotor needs, and (3) need for the objective in future learning at school and in the community. Rate the probability 1, 2, 3, 4, or 5 with 5 as the highest probability that the student needs the objective.

Step 2: Estimate the degree to which the learning objective is achievable. Consideration should be given to time, materials, prerequisites, teaching methods, and developmental level required. Rate the probability 1, 2, 3, 4, or 5 with 5 as the highest probability that the objective is attainable.

Step 3: Multiply the ratings for student need and attainability.

Step 4: Estimate probability that the learning objective will be realized in a nonschool setting. Consideration should be given to whether other educational agencies and life in the community focus on the objective and whether the objective is available to all students in nonschool settings. Rate the probability 1, 2, 3, 4, or 5 with 5 as the highest probability that the objective will be learned in a nonschool setting.

Step 5: Nonschool rating should be divided into the student need and attainability product to indicate the cruciality of the learning objective.

Figure 5.3 Cruciality formula and the steps involved in its solution are shown for determining the value of learning objectives.

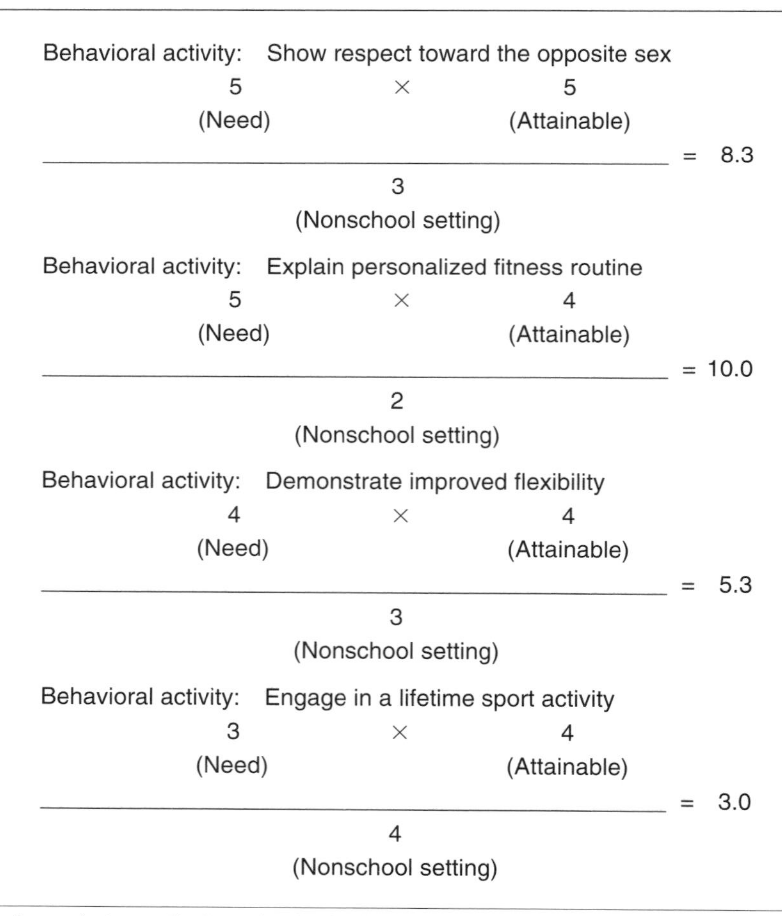

Figure 5.4 Cruciality formula is applied to physical education objectives (behavioral activity).

Clarity is facilitated if objectives are translated into the language of students. Providing students with the objectives prior to instruction appears to be beneficial to learning, and the wording, particularly the action verbs, may need to be changed to make objectives understandable to those for whom they are intended, as illustrated:

Action verbs	*Translated action verbs*
Assemble	Put together; build
Manipulate	Pick up; move; grab; put
Identify	Circle; check; underline
Select; classify	Pick out; point to
Apply	Show
Analyze	Break down
Compose	Make up
Formulate	Put together
Revise	Change

The criterion standard of a learning objective must also be stated clearly. Various standards may be established since students vary in terms of previous learning, present ability, and probable level of achievement. *Quantitative* criteria are usually communicated clearly (e.g., "perform 8 out of 10," "within 40 seconds," "improve by 10%," "with 80% accuracy," "a ratio of 4 to 1," "with no more than 2 mistakes," or "90% of all students").

Qualitative criteria can be built into learning objectives.

Qualitative criteria are more difficult to state in clear terms, particularly when students are engaged in complex problem-solving tasks or when performance tasks are to be analyzed. They indicate "how well" including proper form and technique. For example, the criteria for the overhand floater serve in volleyball can be stated clearly: (1) face net in stride position, (2) hold ball about shoulder height in line with back foot, (3) toss ball about 3 feet into the air above and in front of hitting shoulder, (4) extend hitting arm from a cocked position to contact the ball below midline with heel of hand, (5) extend arm upon contact with stiff wrist and little follow-through, and (6) hit ball over net in low trajectory.

Worthiness

An objective might be considered crucial by some in that it's needed, it's attainable, and it can be stated clearly, but it still may not have educational worth. It may actually be trivial or of fleeting importance. Consider the objective, "To understand the game of soccer, the learner will correctly identify the dimensions of a soccer field." The objective is stated clearly and you might think it's crucial, but it's of marginal worth. The objective is directed to the lowest level of the cognitive domain (knowledge of specifics). The objective's worth is improved if it is related to a higher level. For example, the objective might be stated, "To understand the game of soccer, the learner will diagram the adjustments to the "W" formation in soccer, given a variety of defensive alignments at different strategic locations on the field." This objective is directed to the analysis level. It is of greater worth simply because its mastery assumes acquisition of knowledge, comprehension, and application. If the space relationships among offensive players, defensive players, and distances on the field are part of the content, then the learner would need to *use* the knowledge of field dimensions in order to achieve the objective.

▶ ***To practice recognition of meaningful objectives, complete Self-Directed Activity 5.6 at the end of this chapter.***

Hierarchical Arrangement

Although the variety and scope of learning objectives appear infinite, a *single* learning objective is useful only to the extent that it relates to other objectives. Therefore, objectives should be systematically arranged so that learning may proceed sequentially. To arrange them, it helps to think of learning objectives as being either *terminal* or *enabling*. A combination of enabling objectives contributes to the achievement of a terminal objective.

In chapter 3 (pages 78–81), the learning hierarchy was presented as a useful planning tool to organize complex, higher level content goals and simple, lower level prerequisites. Such a hierarchy contains all of the elements of the given subject matter in a logical, simple-to-complex pattern of understandings, attitudes, and physical skills. The learning objectives derived from the goals of a learning hierarchy are called terminal and enabling since they discriminate between complex and simple learning, respectively.

Terminal Objectives

Terminal objectives are based on the general outcomes and tiers of content goals, as shown previously in Figure 3.4 (page 71). They can be derived for any or all tiers in a goal sequence. Potentially, this means that some terminal objectives would represent goals from the third tier while others would represent goals from the second tier, and so on.

The number of objectives needed to support a given goal varies. You must decide if one or more terminal objectives will be derived for a goal sequence. This decision depends on the intended time period for the goal; the generality level of the goal; the ability to adequately "cover" the outcome expressed by the goal; and the number and nature of prerequisite understandings, responses, and motor abilities. Examples of terminal objectives are indicated in Figure 5.5 for content goals from Figure 3.4. Note that in one case, more than one objective has been generated for a particular goal. Also, a terminal objective is not written for each content goal in a particular tier. Again, this will depend on the factors identified above.

Enabling Objectives

Enabling objectives are based on goal prerequisites, as shown previously in Figure 3.5 (page 75). They can be derived for the last tier of goals in a goal sequence and any of the prerequisites that support the goal. These objectives reflect the knowledge, understandings, affective behaviors, and/or motor abilities that will *enable* the student to accomplish a particular terminal objective.

The number of enabling objectives depends primarily on the need for the prerequisite. You may recall that prerequisites were sorted into three groups (page 72), two of which should be considered in terms of need. Enabling objectives should focus on those prerequisites that some or many of your students might not already possess (group 2) and those that most or all of your students probably do not possess (group 3). Examples of enabling objectives are indicated in Figure 5.6 (page 138) for selected prerequisites from Figure 3.5. Note that in some cases, more than one objective has been generated for a particular goal.

In summary, a valid learning hierarchy includes terminal objectives that reflect higher level goals and enabling objectives that are concerned with the knowledge, understandings, attitudes, values, and physical skills underlying the terminal objectives. It's a synthesis of selecting, classifying, structuring, and ordering learning objectives. The learning hierarchy provides a pathway for instruction and learning, detailing all prerequisite behaviors leading to a desired goal.

The learning hierarchy presented in Figure 5.7 (page 139) illustrates a way of arranging terminal and enabling objectives. It can be compared with the learning hierarchy presented in Figure 3.9 (pages 80–81). Note that only the behavioral activity element of the objectives is used in Figure 5.7.

▶ ***Demonstrate your ability to formulate a partial learning hierarchy by completing Self-Directed Activity 5.7 at the end of this chapter.***

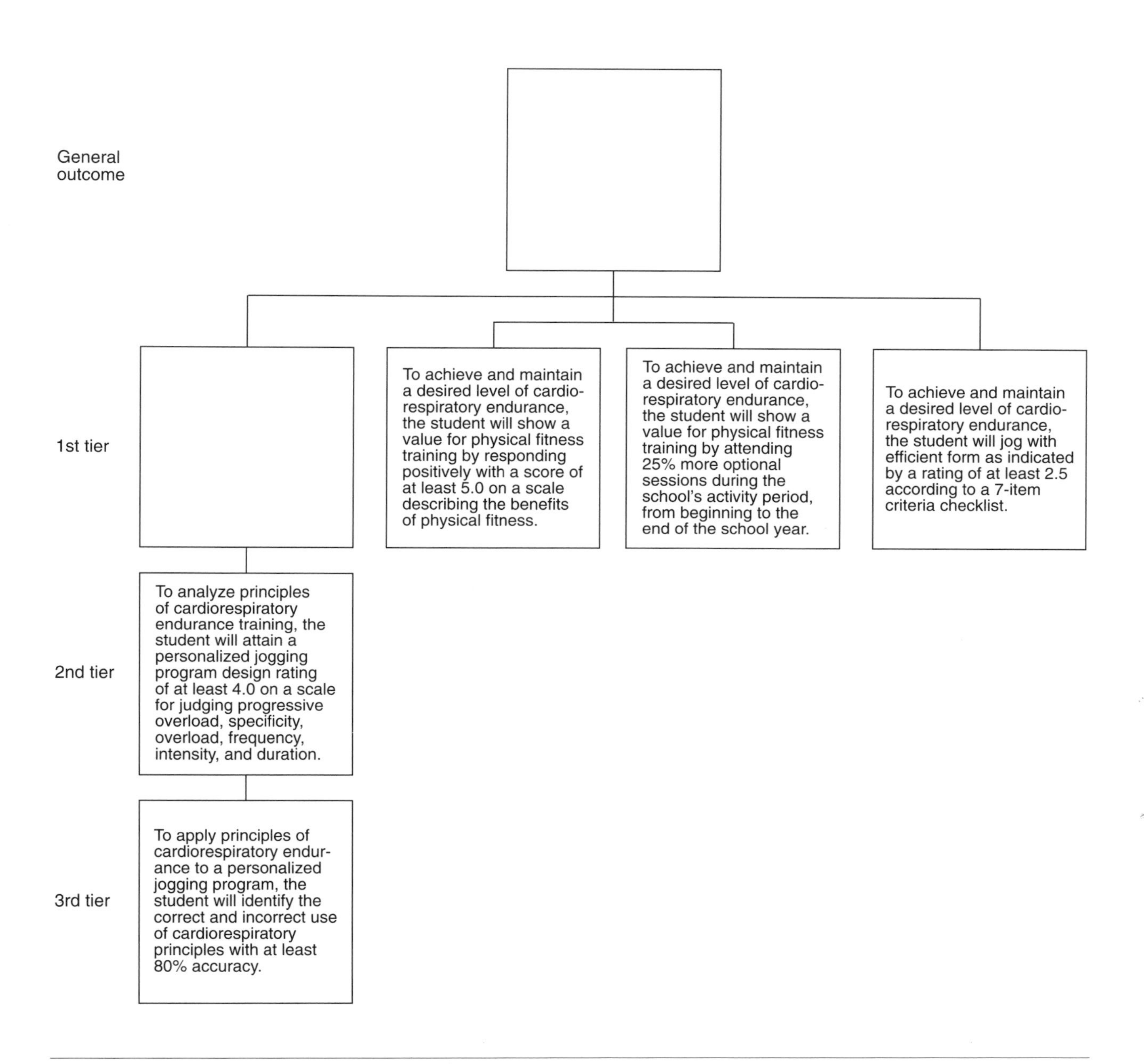

General outcome
1st tier
To achieve and maintain a desired level of cardio-respiratory endurance, the student will show a value for physical fitness training by responding positively with a score of at least 5.0 on a scale describing the benefits of physical fitness.
To achieve and maintain a desired level of cardio-respiratory endurance, the student will show a value for physical fitness training by attending 25% more optional sessions during the school's activity period, from beginning to the end of the school year.
To achieve and maintain a desired level of cardio-respiratory endurance, the student will jog with efficient form as indicated by a rating of at least 2.5 according to a 7-item criteria checklist.
2nd tier
To analyze principles of cardiorespiratory endurance training, the student will attain a personalized jogging program design rating of at least 4.0 on a scale for judging progressive overload, specificity, overload, frequency, intensity, and duration.
3rd tier
To apply principles of cardiorespiratory endurance to a personalized jogging program, the student will identify the correct and incorrect use of cardiorespiratory principles with at least 80% accuracy.

Figure 5.5 Terminal objectives are identified for selected content goals from Figure 3.4 (page 71).

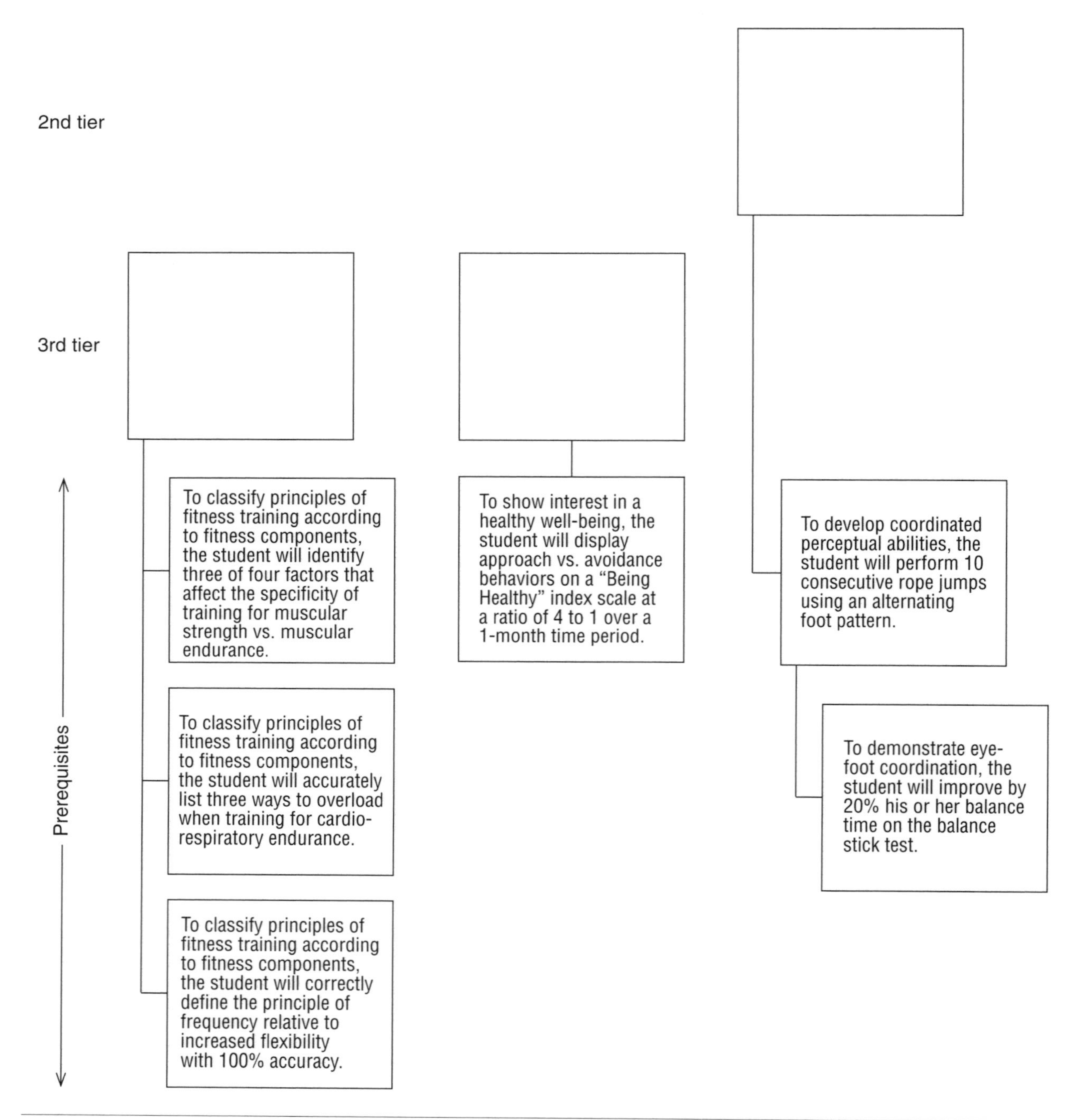

2nd tier
3rd tier
Prerequisites
To classify principles of fitness training according to fitness components, the student will identify three of four factors that affect the specificity of training for muscular strength vs. muscular endurance.
To classify principles of fitness training according to fitness components, the student will accurately list three ways to overload when training for cardio-respiratory endurance.
To classify principles of fitness training according to fitness components, the student will correctly define the principle of frequency relative to increased flexibility with 100% accuracy.
To show interest in a healthy well-being, the student will display approach vs. avoidance behaviors on a "Being Healthy" index scale at a ratio of 4 to 1 over a 1-month time period.
To develop coordinated perceptual abilities, the student will perform 10 consecutive rope jumps using an alternating foot pattern.
To demonstrate eye-foot coordination, the student will improve by 20% his or her balance time on the balance stick test.

Figure 5.6 Enabling objectives are identified for selected prerequisites from Figure 3.5 (page 75).

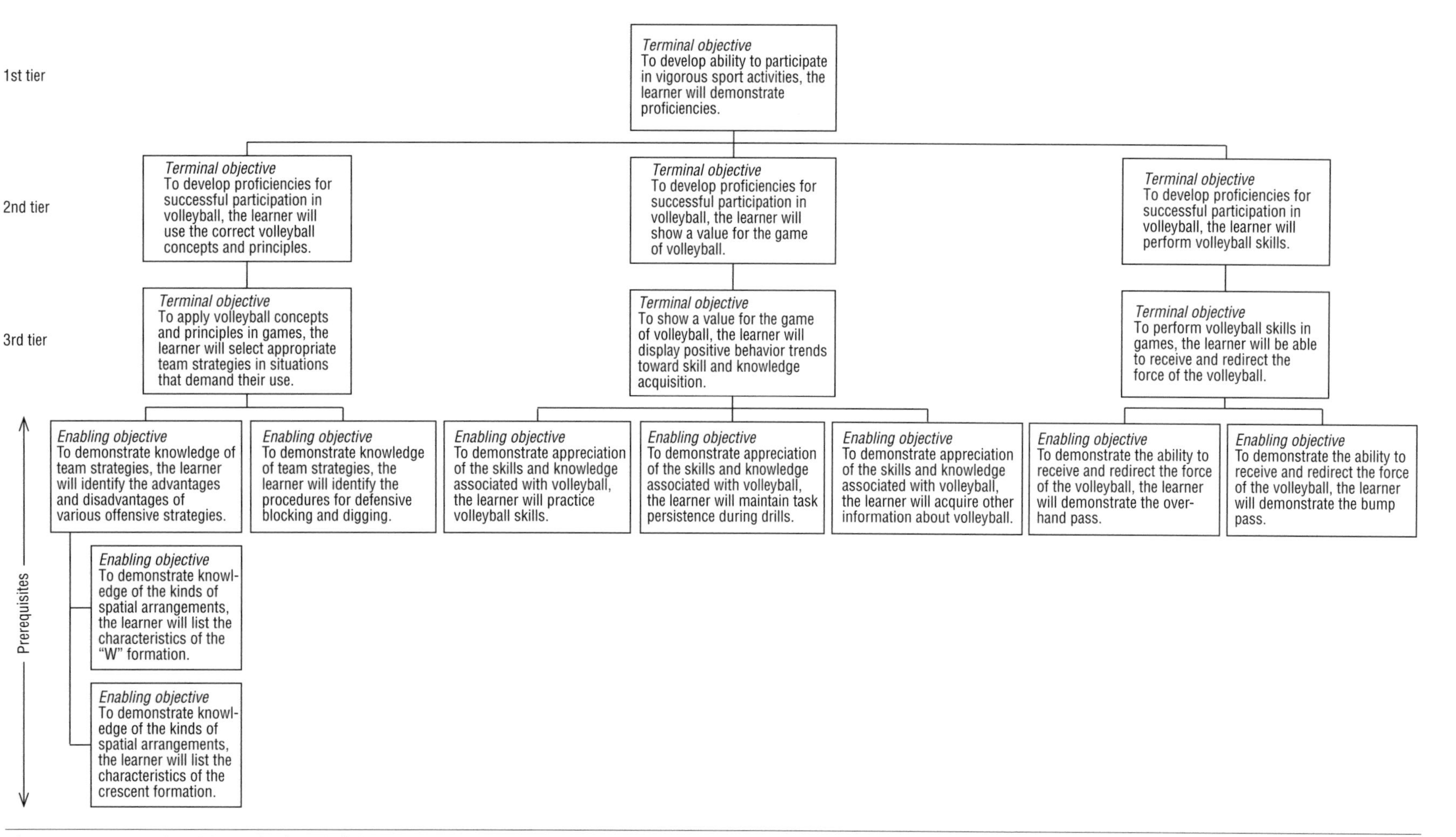

1st tier
2nd tier
3rd tier
Prerequisites
Terminal objective
To develop ability to participate in vigorous sport activities, the learner will demonstrate proficiencies.
Terminal objective
To develop proficiencies for successful participation in volleyball, the learner will use the correct volleyball concepts and principles.
Terminal objective
To develop proficiencies for successful participation in volleyball, the learner will show a value for the game of volleyball.
Terminal objective
To develop proficiencies for successful participation in volleyball, the learner will perform volleyball skills.
Terminal objective
To apply volleyball concepts and principles in games, the learner will select appropriate team strategies in situations that demand their use.
Terminal objective
To show a value for the game of volleyball, the learner will display positive behavior trends toward skill and knowledge acquisition.
Terminal objective
To perform volleyball skills in games, the learner will be able to receive and redirect the force of the volleyball.
Enabling objective
To demonstrate knowledge of team strategies, the learner will identify the advantages and disadvantages of various offensive strategies.
Enabling objective
To demonstrate knowledge of team strategies, the learner will identify the procedures for defensive blocking and digging.
Enabling objective
To demonstrate appreciation of the skills and knowledge associated with volleyball, the learner will practice volleyball skills.
Enabling objective
To demonstrate appreciation of the skills and knowledge associated with volleyball, the learner will maintain task persistence during drills.
Enabling objective
To demonstrate appreciation of the skills and knowledge associated with volleyball, the learner will acquire other information about volleyball.
Enabling objective
To demonstrate the ability to receive and redirect the force of the volleyball, the learner will demonstrate the over-hand pass.
Enabling objective
To demonstrate the ability to receive and redirect the force of the volleyball, the learner will demonstrate the bump pass.
Enabling objective
To demonstrate knowl-edge of the kinds of spatial arrangements, the learner will list the characteristics of the "W" formation.
Enabling objective
To demonstrate knowl-edge of the kinds of spatial arrangements, the learner will list the characteristics of the crescent formation.

Figure 5.7 Learning hierarchy (partial) illustrates the relationships among terminal and enabling objectives based on content goals from Figure 3.9 (pages 80–81).

MAKING IT WORK

Have you achieved the expected outcomes (page 124)? Congratulations! You are able to derive learning objectives for your physical education curriculum design. Still, you may have some practical questions that need answers, such as:

- **Do you really need to write out specific objectives if you already know what you want to achieve?**

  You may know what outcomes you are seeking, but there needs to be some way of communicating them to others. It's important for students, parents, school officials, education departments, and accreditation agencies to understand your expectations, particularly in these days of accountability. There's a tendency to ignore the developmental appropriateness of outcomes if objectives are left to intuition. As an extension of content goals, learning objectives should be the result of conscious decision making. The tough part is getting started. Once your set of objectives is written, then it becomes a matter of adding, revising, and/or eliminating objectives as your program develops. Clearly stated objectives are also needed from a liability standpoint. In physical education, negligence is often established because teachers did not have an appropriate and approved set of objectives to serve as a guide to instruction. And there are additional legal implications in the fact that short-term and long-term objectives are mandated as part of the IEP process for students with disabilities.

- **Can't objectives be written more simply than the goals approach?**

  Sure, but if you're going to write them anyway, you might as well be thorough. For example, by including some reference to goals, you offer a reason for your expected outcomes. Also, the criterion standard helps to establish your evaluation construct. A complete set of objectives will save you a lot of questions from students, parents, and other professionals in terms of what explicit kind of learning is being sought and to what degree. Students should be different as a result of your curriculum and instruction. Objectives reveal this intended learning in a way that can be understood by all. Objectives are what make organizing centers and goals realistic, and they are essential as a guide to evaluation and learning experiences. Also, with the current emphasis on outcome standards—sometimes referred to as functional competencies—linking behavior with some goal reference fits right in.

- **How do you know when you've got enough objectives?**

  There's no prescribed number. The overall number will correspond to the identified goals. They can be kept to a minimum by writing them at the highest level possible since mastery is assumed at the lower levels. This keeps the number of objectives more manageable. Also, the exact number may not be known until evaluation procedures and learning experiences are finalized. Remember that your curriculum design will and should undergo constant addition, revision, and deletion. Don't expect, or even try, to bring closure to your objectives until after these remaining components have been developed.

- **Is it necessary to determine the quality of each and every objective?**

  You should at least make sure that your objectives are clearly stated. You can informally establish priority among objectives just by keeping in mind the factors that make an objective crucial. Is it needed? Can it be attained? Is the objective best learned in the school setting? Preassessment will help in this regard. Quality is also enhanced if you determine the worth of objectives. Again, objectives should be derived that foster learning directed toward the higher, more complex learning levels. Writing objectives for the sake of writing them will be a meaningless task if no effort is made to generate *high-quality* ones.

- **Why should objectives be arranged in a hierarchy if you've already done this for goals?**

  You don't really need to repeat the process, just extend it. Since objectives should include a goal component, it's natural to fit them into the organization of goals by tiers along with supporting prerequisites. It also becomes a constant reminder that target outcomes (terminal objectives) are likely to be dependent on these prerequisites. That's why the objectives associated with these levels are called "enabling."

Self-Directed Activity 5.1

In the following table, information is organized into learning objectives, associated domains, and corresponding domain categories. Your task is to fill in the missing information. Where the objective is given, indicate its domain and category. Where the category is given, indicate the domain and then try to formulate an objective for that level.

Learning objective	Domain	Category
1. The student will improve in agility by running a 50-yard, figure-8 run in 2 seconds less time.	________	________
2. ________	________	Application
3. The student will respond to a request to play for an opposing softball team so that there is an even number of players on each team.	________	________
4. ________	________	Basic fundamental movements
5. Given a diagram of the positions in volleyball, the student will draw arrows to indicate where the players should go in defending a left-handed spiker on his or her on-hand side.	________	________
6. ________	________	Responding
7. The student will demonstrate a compound skill by correctly serving a tennis ball into the proper receiving court at designated spots 6 out of 10 times, with no ball going more than 2 feet above the net.	________	________
8. Given an unfamiliar offensive set-up in basketball, the student will be able to adjust a defensive "zone" strategy to the setup.	________	________

Feedback

1. Psychomotor; physical abilities. Agility is a component of the physical abilities category.
2. Cognitive. An application objective should represent the use of ideas, rules, methods, concepts, and principles in new situations. Your objective should be something like this: Given specific situations in softball, the student will select the decisions an umpire would make based on interpretations of the rules.
3. Affective; organization. The student who satisfies this objective is able to bring different values together such as equal competition, fair play, and respect for others.
4. Psychomotor. Basic fundamental movements include (a) locomotor movements (walking, running, jumping, sliding, hopping, rolling, climbing), (b) nonlocomotor movements (pushing, pulling, swaying, swinging, stooping, stretching, bending, twisting), and (c) manipulative movements (handling, gripping, grasping). Your objective should relate to one of these movements, for example: The student will demonstrate a locomotor movement pattern by executing a two-foot jump with both feet parallel at start, arms used for forward thrust, and feet together at landing.
5. Cognitive; analysis. The behavior calls for the breakdown of material into its parts.
6. Affective. At the responding level, the student is expected to show interest through overt behavior. An example objective is: The learner will request to work on a subject-related project such as designing a dance bulletin board.
7. Psychomotor; skilled movements. Serving a tennis ball represents a complex movement task.
8. Cognitive; synthesis. This objective requires the student to arrange or create a new pattern.

Self-Directed Activity 5.2

You should be able to recognize the elements of basic form that make up a learning objective. Analyze the following objectives by indicating these elements.

1. *Cognitive objective* (analysis)

   To analyze field hockey offensive alignments in the defensive half of the field, the student will select, with 80% accuracy, either the "W" formation, "M" formation, or diagonal formation, given situations that demand their use.

   Goal component: ______________________________

   ____

   Behavioral activity: ______________________________

   ____

   Criterion standard: ______________________________

   ____

   Conditions: ______________________________

   ____

2. *Affective objective* (valuing)

   To develop a preference for physical activity as a leisure-time activity, the student will, from the beginning to the end of the school year, attend 25% more optional sessions during the school's activity period that involve physical fitness maintenance activities.

   Goal component: ______________________________

   ____

   Behavioral activity: ______________________________

   ____

   Criterion standard: ______________________________

   ____

   Conditions: ______________________________

   ____

3. *Psychomotor objective* (physical abilities)

   To improve the physical ability of cardiovascular endurance, after a 4-week physical fitness training program the student will be able to run 1,500 meters in 10% less time than at entry.

   Goal component: ______________________________

   ____

   Behavioral activity: ______________________________

   ____

   Criterion standard: ______________________________

   ____

   Conditions: ______________________________

   ____

Feedback

1. *Goal component*: To analyze field hockey offensive alignments in the defensive half of the field

   Behavioral activity: Select either the "W" formation, "M" formation, or diagonal formation

   Criterion standard: 80% accuracy

   Conditions: Given situations that demand their use

2. *Goal component*: To develop a preference for physical activity as a leisure-time activity

   Behavioral activity: Attend optional sessions during the school's activity period that involve physical fitness maintenance activities

   Criterion standard: 25% more

   Conditions: From the beginning to the end of the school year

3. *Goal component*: To improve the physical ability of cardiovascular endurance

   Behavioral activity: Run 1,500 meters

   Criterion standard: 10% less time than at entry

   Conditions: After a 4-week physical fitness training program

Self-Directed Activity 5.3

You should be able to differentiate between individualized and nonindividualized learning objectives. For each of the following, indicate whether the objective is individualized (I) or nonindividualized (N).

_____ 1. To show the development of muscular strength, students will perform 40 bent-knee sit-ups in 60 seconds.

_____ 2. To understand a variety of defensive patterns in basketball, students will identify the advantages and disadvantages of the 2-1-2 defense in basketball.

_____ 3. To develop body awareness, students will explore "general space" while moving without touching one another.

_____ 4. To demonstrate improved cardiorespiratory endurance, students will decrease by 10% their times for running a mile.

_____ 5. To exhibit a favorable attitude toward gymnastics, students will assist in setting up equipment before the beginning of a class in gymnastics.

_____ 6. To demonstrate eye-foot coordination, students will kick a moving playground ball and hit the target 3 out of 5 times.

_____ 7. To show perseverance in skill development, students will hit short-iron golf shots by selecting and completing all elements from a task card designed to provide feedback about the quality of performance.

_____ 8. To perform complex adaptive skills in tennis, students will use the tennis forehand drive, with a self-drop technique, to hit the target area 5 out of 10 times.

Feedback

1. N

   Standard of performance is the same for all. The objective would be individualized if it were part of a self-paced learning sequence or if it represented part of an agreed-upon teacher-student "contract." An individualized objective might be: Students will improve by 20% the number of bent-knee sit-ups they can perform in 60 seconds.

2. N

   Presumably, the advantages and disadvantages of the 2-1-2 defense have been predetermined. Although the objective may be worthwhile, there is little chance for individual response. An individualized learning objective might ask each student to select a preferred defense in basketball and identify the advantages and disadvantages of that defense.

3. I

   Movement patterns in general space are unique to the individual.

4. I

   The objective is based on individual improvement (percentage) of beginning (preassessment) time for running the mile.

5. N

   As stated, the objective does not allow students to display other behaviors that would indicate cooperation or a willingness to help others. An individualized objective might be: Students will show cooperation in gymnastics by displaying behaviors such as setting up and breaking down apparatus, spotting, taking turns, and assisting others, to mention a few.

6. N

   The quantitative standard (3 out of 5) is arbitrary. An individualized objective could include steps within a range of tasks. For example: Students will progress at least three tasks from their beginning ability to kick a moving playground ball and hit the target.

7. I

   Students are able to select and complete task cards at their own pace.

8. N

   An individualized objective could be created by using a percentage gain or steps within a learning continuum as the standard of performance. The objective might be: From a self-drop technique, the student will demonstrate an improved tennis forehand drive as indicated by an overall increase of 25% in the number of times a target area is hit.

Self-Directed Activity 5.4

The behavioral activity of learning objectives has been identified representing student needs (Task 1). These objectives have been rated according to preference (Task 2) and the proportion of students expected to master the objective indicated (Task 3). The difference between student status and desired mastery is also given (Task 4). Based on this information, complete Task 5 according to your priority ranking.

Task 1	*Task 2*	*Task 3*	*Task 4*	*Task 5*
Need/Behavioral activity of learning objective	Objective preference rating	Proportion of students expected to master objective	Discrepancy between student status and desired mastery	Your priority ranking (1 = highest priority; 5 = lowest priority)
A. *Psychomotor* Demonstrate an improved level of muscular strength and endurance	1st	100%	High	______
B. *Cognitive* Identify movement skill patterns common to a variety of individual, dual, and team activities	5th	50%	Low	______
C. *Affective* (social) Exhibit a sense of trust in and respect for others in games	2nd	100%	Low	______
D. *Affective* (emotional) Display self-discipline and confidence in completing a progressive series of movement tasks	3rd	75%	None	______
E. *Affective* (value) Show a preference for tennis as an activity in which to participate outside of school	4th	100%	High	______

Feedback

Clearly, objective A should be given the highest priority since it is first in preference, all students are expected to master it, and the discrepancy is high.

Either objective C or objective E should probably be second in priority. Since all students are expected to master each objective, your priority ranking depends on the weight given to preferences and discrepancies. Although objective C is second in preference, it is low in discrepancy. Although objective E is high in discrepancy, it is fourth in preference. If you place greater emphasis on preference, then objective C should be second in priority. Greater emphasis on discrepancy would mean that objective E would be second in priority. Whichever objective is ranked second, the other objective should be ranked third.

It appears that objective D should be ranked fourth in priority since it is higher in preference and more students are expected to master it than objective B. The difference between the objectives in terms of discrepancy is not as significant as the other factors.

Even though the discrepancy is low, objective B should be given the lowest priority since it is last in preference and only half of the students are expected to master it.

Self-Directed Activity 5.5

For each of the following content goals, indicate which objective, A or B, is stated in explicit terms. Note that only the behavioral activity portion of the objectives is indicated.

_____ 1. Analyze the components of physical fitness
   A. To list the differences between muscular strength and muscular endurance
   B. To realize the contributions of cardiorespiratory endurance

_____ 2. Cooperate with others
   A. To pass the soccer ball to a team member who is in a better position to shoot
   B. To exhibit teamwork in setting up zone defenses in basketball

_____ 3. Develop complex skill movements
   A. To perform basic stunts on the uneven parallel bars
   B. To correctly serve a tennis ball into the proper receiving court

_____ 4. Assume responsibility for decision making
   A. To determine own performance levels for short and long approach shots in golf
   B. To show self-control at self-directed weight training stations

_____ 5. Comprehend mechanical principles of movement
   A. To understand the concept of "opposition" in maintaining stability
   B. To identify a movement variation of the overhand throw

_____ 6. Value personal body movement patterns
   A. To appreciate movement exploration activities
   B. To self-direct a daily calisthenic exercise routine

_____ 7. Demonstrate basic locomotor movement patterns
   A. To be able to run, jump, slide, and hop
   B. To ascend and descend a flight of stairs using an alternating foot pattern

_____ 8. Display sportsmanship

A. To accept, without any outward negative behaviors, out-of-bounds calls made by the opposing volleyball team

B. To express consideration toward an opponent during a tennis match

Feedback

1. A

   In order to list the differences, the student must be able to analyze the components. This behavior is explicit. With objective B, there is no indication as to what the student does when he or she "realizes."

2. A

   This objective explicitly illustrates cooperation. In objective B, teamwork is not related to cooperation as stated.

3. B

   In objective A, there is no way of knowing if basic stunts are complex skill movements. Objective B is stated in explicit terms.

4. A

   Decision making is required in objective A, but can only be inferred in objective B.

5. B

   It may be that both objectives could be stated in more explicit terms. However, "to identify" suggests overt action (explicit) whereas "to understand" is vague.

6. B

   Although "to appreciate" suggests that the student will value personal body movement patterns, it is unclear as to what the student does when he or she is "appreciating." A self-directed exercise routine, objective B, is an explicit transformation of the stated goal.

7. B

   The behavior desired in objective B is clearly congruent with the goal. While the locomotor movement patterns are listed in objective A, specificity is lacking.

8. A

   Objective B is not stated in explicit terms. "Expressing consideration toward an opponent" is a worthy objective, but the indicative behaviors must be inferred. The behavior stated in objective A is an explicit display of sportsmanship.

Self-Directed Activity 5.6

In this activity, you will be able to decide whether learning objectives are meaningful. Your task is to judge each of the objectives. Check (√) whether or not the objectives are crucial, clear, and worthy.

Objectives	Crucial	Clear	Worthy
1. Given the opportunity to choose a partner, the student will display acceptance by selecting a member of the opposite sex.	____	____	____
2. To develop space awareness, the student will demonstrate examples of where the body can move in terms of space, direction and pathways, and level.	____	____	____
3. Given a diagram of the positions in softball, the student will label each position correctly.	____	____	____
4. The student will listen attentively to an analysis of the volleyball spike by not talking, daydreaming, or responding to classmates' distractions.	____	____	____
5. The student will demonstrate rhythmic, creative movement by designing and performing a 30-second movement sequence that represents a rhythmic pattern, keeps time with the music, and uses at least two locomotor and one nonlocomotor movements.	____	____	____
6. To analyze synchronized swimming skills, the student will judge a synchronized swimming routine.	____	____	____

Feedback

1. Crucial √ Although the objective (acceptance) could be learned in a nonschool setting, it is needed and attainable.

   Clear √ Behavior is observable; "all-or-none" criterion is clear.

   Worthy No Domain (affective) level is low due to high inference that acceptance is genuinely displayed by "selecting."

2. Crucial √ A need is satisfied and the objective is more likely attainable in a school setting.

   Clear No Acceptable criteria are unclear. Space criteria include self-space and general space; direction criteria include forward, backward, around, over, across, etc.; and level criteria include high, medium, and low.

   Worthy √ This is an important movement education objective.

3.	Crucial	No	There is no real need for this objective since it could be easily achieved in nonschool settings.
	Clear	√	All criteria for a clearly stated objective are satisfied.
	Worthy	No	This objective represents the lowest level of the cognitive domain.
4.	Crucial	No	Since the behavioral activity is listening, the objective could hardly be judged as crucial.
	Clear	√	Observable behaviors that serve as the criterion are clearly identified.
	Worthy	No	From a classroom management standpoint, the objective is worthy, but the behavior called for is low-level (attending).
5.	Crucial	√	The objective is needed and attainable in a school setting, given that it would not likely be achieved through outside dance instruction.
	Clear	√	Behavior and qualitative criteria are identified quite clearly for an objective of this complexity.
	Worthy	√	The highest level of the psychomotor domain is sought (nondiscursive communication).
6.	Crucial	√	Making judgments is valued for future learning at school and in the community.
	Clear	No	Criteria for judging are not stated clearly, if at all.
	Worthy	√	Any behavior associated with analysis is worthy since it is associated with complex intellectual abilities.

Self-Directed Activity 5.7

If simple, lower level learning enables more complex, higher level learning, then the learning hierarchy provides a way to discriminate between terminal and enabling objectives. Demonstrate your ability to formulate a partial learning hierarchy by following these steps:

Step 1: Generate a content goal representing either the cognitive, affective, or psychomotor domain.

Step 2: Develop at least one (1) terminal objective that supports the goal.

Step 3: Identify at least two (2) enabling objectives that would lead to the achievement of the terminal objective.

Step 4: Select one of the enabling objectives and indicate at least four (4) simple abilities (behaviors) that are prerequisites to that enabling objective. These items should represent different kinds of learning (knowledge, attitudes, values, movement skills).

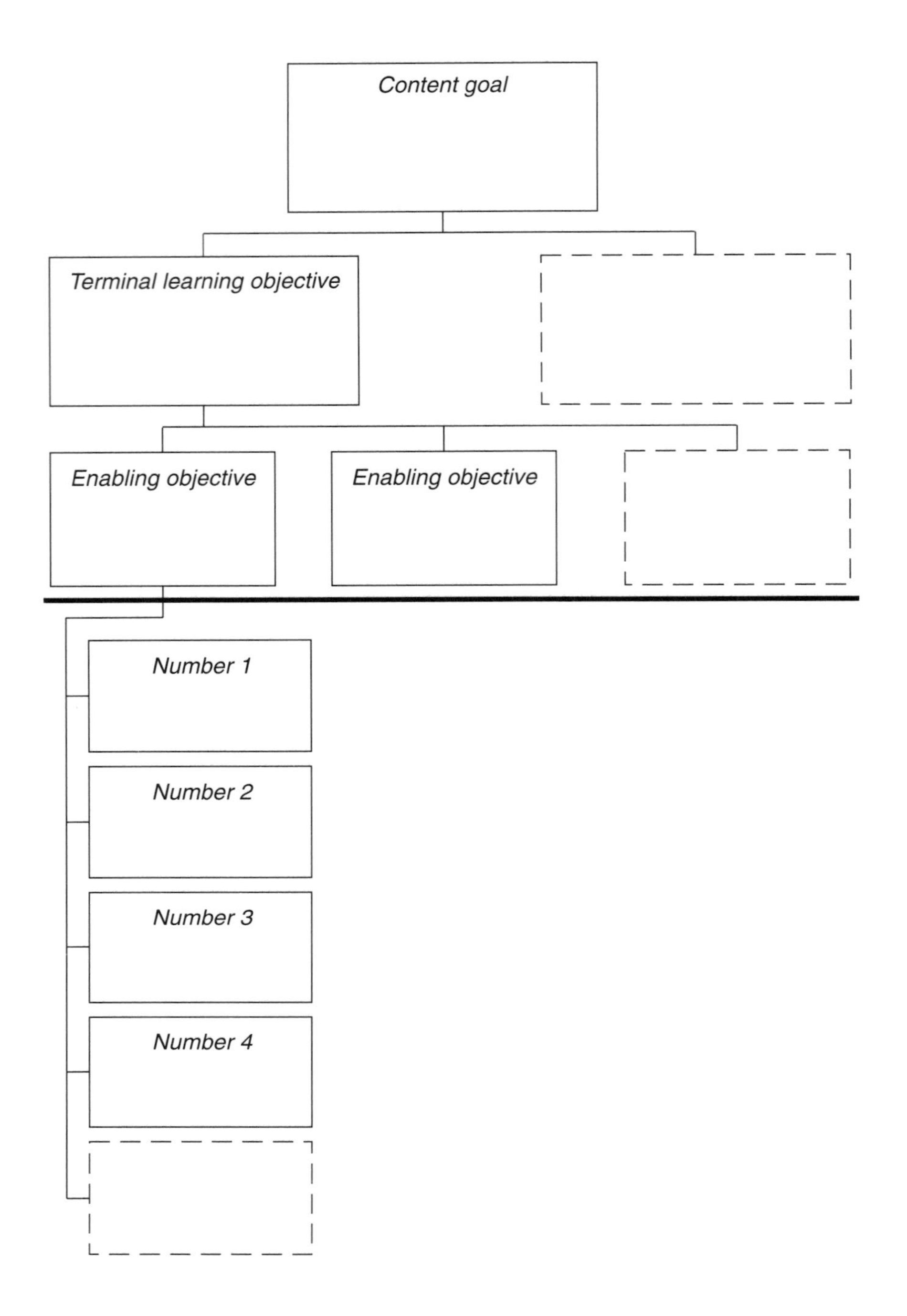

Feedback

Your content goal should clearly represent one of the domains. Terminal objectives are usually stated at a higher level of the domain. Enabling objectives could then represent the lower categories of the domain. It is possible that your terminal objective reflected learning in more than one domain. In that case, your two enabling objectives should not have been derived from the same domain. Your learning hierarchy should look like the terminal and enabling objectives identified in Figure 5.7 (page 139).

6

Developing Evaluation Procedures

Key Concept

Curriculum designers determine the degree of student change (learning) through evaluation procedures that are guided by learning objectives.

The new elementary school principal in a suburban, middle-class community announces that she will hold a conference with each teacher at the beginning of each school year. Teachers are expected to present their goals for the year. The goals of one of the physical education teachers are received favorably by the principal. However, when the discussion turns to evaluation criteria, the teacher is less confident. The principal is really committed to student outcomes and seems obsessed with student learning data. The teacher isn't able to describe his approach to measurement nor his data-collection techniques. The principal wants to know what student "gains" are being sought. Unfortunately, the physical education teacher has no response because he didn't think that evaluation would come up during the conference.

Expected Outcomes

This chapter helps you develop evaluation procedures for your curriculum design. Upon completing it, you will be able to

- identify the purposes of gathering information about student learning,
- indicate evaluation designs and measurement approaches that are applicable in various situations,
- differentiate among several general evaluation techniques,
- transform learning objectives into evaluation procedures that focus on learner needs, and
- describe the characteristics of authentic assessment and the use of portfolios in physical education.

At this point, the question "Where are you going?" has been answered. You may recall that assessment involves appraisal at the beginning (entry) and at the end (exit) of a learning sequence to determine the degree of behavioral change (learning). Therefore, the question "How will you know you've arrived?" is treated next because its answer is linked closely to the kinds of behavior and criterion standards indicated by learning objectives. The curriculum design model in Figure 6.1 shows this step, *developing evaluation procedures*. Doing this after you establish objectives ensures the *direct* measurement of intended learning.

Entry-level data were used to identify and place students and to decide on appropriate programming and intervention. Exit appraisal, often referred to as posttesting or postassessment, reveals the difference between students' previous and current abilities. This kind of ongoing assessment is consistent with *developmentally appropriate practices* in physical education (Graham, Castenada, Hopple, Manross, & Sanders, 1992). This chapter contains specific information about evaluation protocol and instrumentation.

Developing an evaluation procedure does not mean the group-administered, objectively scored, and normative interpretation of achievement tests. Rather, a comprehensive, performance-based measure of learning is recommended that documents not only understandings and skills, but other aspirations such as attitudes, motivations, social conduct, and values. Evaluation which scans this full spectrum of student learning illustrates the trend toward *authentic assessment* (Perrone, 1991). Actual samples of student work and performance data, usually in the form of portfolios, serve as the measure of learning, not the highly inferential estimates provided by group testing (Meisels, 1993). Therefore, several questions arise. "What are the purposes of evaluation?" "Should a certain evaluation design and measurement approach be used?" "What data collection schemes are available?" "How can authentic assessment be applied to physical education?" Answers to these questions are provided in the following sections. Ultimately, you should be able to develop evaluation procedures for your own physical education curriculum.

Instrumental Factors

Evaluation has been avoided by many teachers because it's complex and time-consuming, and it usually leads to the assignment of grades. However, if there is no evaluation of learning, there is no accountability for producing such learning, nor can there be hope of revising the curriculum or improving learning on a rational basis. Teachers become uneasy about evaluation when confronted with questions like: Am I a good teacher? Can I control and manage the class? Will I be helpful to the learner? Have I been fair in my judgment of each learner? Is there evidence to support my evaluations? Did I assess the learner or my own expectations? What

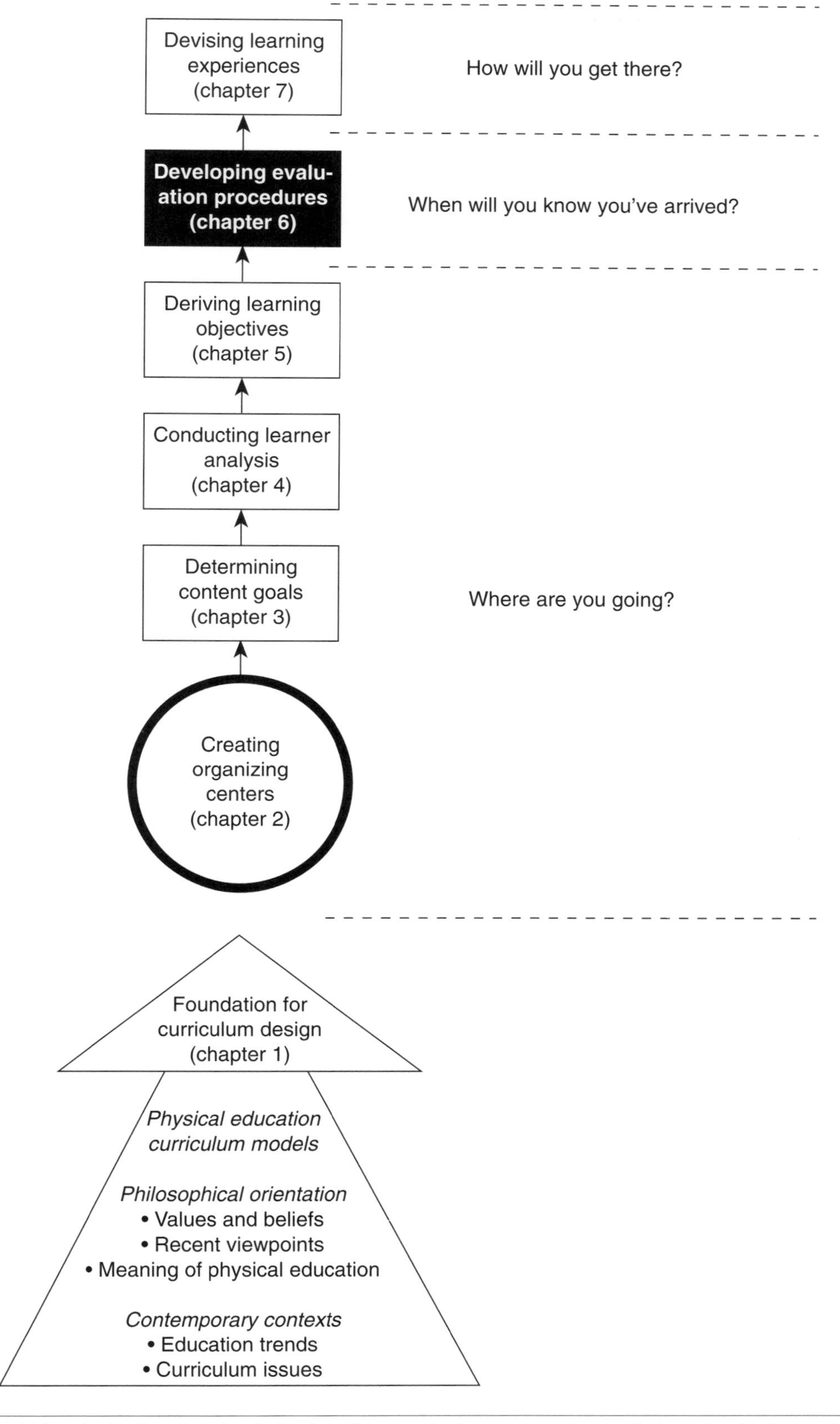

Figure 6.1 Model for designing the physical education curriculum shows the next step, *developing evaluation procedures.*

happens if parents get involved? Do learners really care about how well they've done?

Problems with evaluation have been exaggerated because of misunderstandings about the nature and function of evaluation. The results—bad feelings, lack of confidence, and failure to learn—can be prevented if evaluation is based on sound principles and if the procedure is communicated to students. Unfortunately, it's not that simple. Procedures are dependent on several instrumental factors including purposes, evaluation principles, evaluation design, and measurement approach.

Purposes of Evaluation

Evaluation should be conducted for educationally sound reasons, not because it's expected. The results are most valuable relative to students' change in behavior. Although the primary purpose of evaluation may be to determine the achievement of objectives, there are others specific to timing and the learning situation. Evaluation represents a continuous, long-range endeavor that is essential to any systematic approach to curriculum design. It's *not* the same as grading; it's much broader.

Motivation

Students can be positively motivated to improve their abilities depending on the frequency of evaluation and how the results are used. Negative motivation results if the procedure is failure-laden or frustrating. Positive motivation is more likely if there's an emphasis on self-improvement, and if learning tasks are sequenced in small enough steps so that improvement is perceptible. For example, students are involved in their own mastery evaluations when they engage in self-testing activities found in elementary programs (e.g., jump and reach, tripod, forearm headstand, shoulder stand, skin the snake, and back-to-back roll). This is illustrated at the secondary level through programmed learning activities. Examples of this form of self-evaluation are provided in chapter 7 (pages 205–211).

Learning Experience

Evaluation should not focus only on what the teacher can find out about the student. Opportunities should be afforded students to find out something about themselves. For example, when students receive feedback through peer assessment, the experience is likely to be meaningful since the "threat" of teacher evaluation is eliminated. Nonetheless, the purpose of evaluation—information about performance—is accomplished.

Feedback and Guidance

Whether feedback is provided by teacher, peer, or self, students receive assistance and information about their own abilities. In terms of guidance, students should understand the expectations of improvement and success in cognitive, affective, and psychomotor learning. Emphasis on progress from entry to exit levels reduces the problem of having to deal with unequal levels of performance among peers. This is particularly evident among students who are less competent than others. Evaluation can be a positive guiding force if the results are not used for comparison or labeling.

Diagnosis

Evaluation is used to assess the strengths and weaknesses of students. The results would establish new baseline data to determine areas of needed improvement. For example, it may be discovered that the student shows poor cardiorespiratory endurance but has excellent muscular strength and endurance. If evaluation serves the purpose of diagnosis, the needs of individual learners can be monitored continuously.

Determining Status

Evaluation is also used to identify students' *current* level of performance, usually at the end of a certain period of time (e.g., unit, semester). Comparisons can then be made among entry levels, intended mastery levels, and actual mastery levels. A negative difference between intended and actual learning specifies what remains to be learned. However, this difference may be the basis for the assignment of grades, promotion from one grade to another, or advancement to the next level of instruction.

Program Revision and Improvement

Evaluation of student learning reveals areas of needed program revision and improvement. Standards are maintained if students achieve at the desired levels indicated by learning objectives. The criterion for program effectiveness is the *overall* level of student learning for a given goal and its accompanying objectives. An evaluation of this nature reveals, for example,

- whether the instructional pace is too rapid or too slow;

- whether students find the learning sequence interesting, confusing, too difficult, or too easy; and
- whether the content is relevant, inappropriate, practical, or useless.

▶ ***To practice considering various purposes when developing an evaluation procedure, complete Self-Directed Activity 6.1 at the end of this chapter.***

Design and Measurement

An evaluation design should be selected that fits the situation and that represents what you're actually trying to evaluate. Likewise, a measurement approach is needed to obtain information that describes student behavior. The curriculum designer must determine how to measure whatever is being evaluated. Later in this section, an evaluation *design* and an approach to *measurement* are recommended. Before that, however, basic properties are reviewed that should be considered when developing evaluation procedures.

Basic Properties

Measurement and evaluation are based on certain essential qualities, without which little faith can be placed in the use of a test or measuring instrument. These basic properties are characteristic of all appropriate evaluation constructs.

Reference to Objectives. Harmony should exist between the evaluation procedure and the stated learning objectives. Confusion arises if the objective says one thing and something else is evaluated. To adequately sample learning objectives, the procedure should be sufficiently broad and a variety of techniques should be used. In addition, results offer a form of diagnosis if the evaluation procedure is designed at the same level as the objectives.

Objectivity. Results should be similar when the evaluation instrument is administered by different persons. Objectivity refers to the difference in appraisals across different administrators of the same evaluation procedure. If the appraisals vary markedly, the directions or scoring, or both, may need to be clarified, or the means by which behavior is recorded may need to be refined. Objectivity is enhanced by "low-inference" techniques such as those used to evaluate cognitive and psychomotor behaviors. "Low-inference" means that behaviors are less interpretable. "High-inference" techniques are often used to evaluate affective behaviors; they are not as objective. "High-inference" means that behaviors are more interpretable. In other words, there is greater subjectivity in the appraisal.

Validity. The evaluation procedure is valid if it actually measures what it was designed to measure. Content validity means that the procedure evaluates the subject matter that has been taught. Construct validity refers to the learning process used. For example, if learning experiences involved memory activities, then an "application" test would lack construct validity. An evaluation instrument has face validity if it directly samples the behavior specified by objectives. However, the behavior should be elicited by appropriate means only. The student should not be penalized by factors such as difficult reading matter, ambiguity, changing weather conditions, poor test construction, gender or cultural bias, or influence by other students.

Reliability. Results of evaluation should be consistent or stable. Reliability protects accuracy. The learner should respond similarly in the same situations. Since learning is measured in response to instruction, preassessment is always desirable so that what the student is able to do before instruction is known. A test-retest technique is commonly used to determine the reliability of the instrument. Reliability also refers to the adequacy of the sample behavior. Greater variability in behaviors means that a larger sample is needed to obtain a dependable response. The sample of behaviors may need to be extended or the time period increased.

Pre-Post Design

Evaluation must relate to students' progress on both short-term objectives and long-term goals. It should also relate to the instructional program that has been provided. You should constantly search for overt and covert responses that indicate either positive or negative behavior changes. The most logical way to measure learning progress is the pre-post design. It requires at least two appraisals—one during the beginning of the program and the other at a later point. Student change can therefore be attributed to the given program.

Measuring student progress means that evaluation can be conducted in relation to the student's own abilities without regard to gender, age, cultural status, or body structure. The pre-post design satisfies Title IX regulations that require objective standards of individual performance and their application without regard to gender. Similarly, it fulfills all requirements of the Individuals with

Disabilities Education Act (IDEA) and the corresponding individualized education plan (IEP).

Criterion-Referenced Measurement

The recommended approach to measurement during the exit phase is criterion-referenced. It evaluates specific competencies and performance levels on an individual basis. During entry appraisal, criterion-referenced assessment usually relates directly to content goals. In exit appraisal, criterion-referenced measurement relates directly to learning objectives. Individualized criterion standards (domain of tasks or behaviors) are directly interpretable from the established learning objectives. Measurements yield mastery levels for individuals relative to the given domain. Thus, the criterion in this sense is represented by a domain of tasks or behaviors (Safrit, 1990).

Criterion-referenced techniques are *customized* since they should evolve out of the systematic curriculum design process. Therefore, criterion-referenced "tests" are teacher-made. *A test is defined as any set of systematic observations that is used to measure human behavior*. Use of the term "test" does not imply that measurement is conducted through strict, formal "testing" procedures. In Figures 6.2, 6.3, and 6.4, measurement items are developed for learning objectives representing each domain.

In contrast, norm-referenced measurement is useful for sorting and sifting learners into groups to make instruction more manageable. But the approach is too far removed from the concept of individualization to be of much use. In the norm-referenced approach, an attempt is made to *maximize the variability* of test scores. Therefore, those test items that indicate what is best learned must be eliminated. It is extremely difficult to assess program effectiveness if the measurement technique functions like an aptitude test. Since norm-referenced tests elicit a wide range of scores, and criterion-referenced test scores relate to learning objective *standards*, it is necessary to distinguish between testing specifications and measurement for these two approaches.

A norm-referenced test *can* be used for criterion-referenced measurement, although the sampling of items may not cover a sufficient number of objectives, and a given objective may be covered by only a few items. For example, the specific items of *Physical Best* (AAHPERD, 1988) may be used for criterion-referenced measurement if test results reveal

---

Cognitive learning objective: To apply the rules of badminton, the student will identify correct scoring/serving decisions with at least 80% accuracy, given a variety of badminton situations.

Criterion-referenced item: The student refers to the badminton court diagram in answering the questions on scoring/serving.

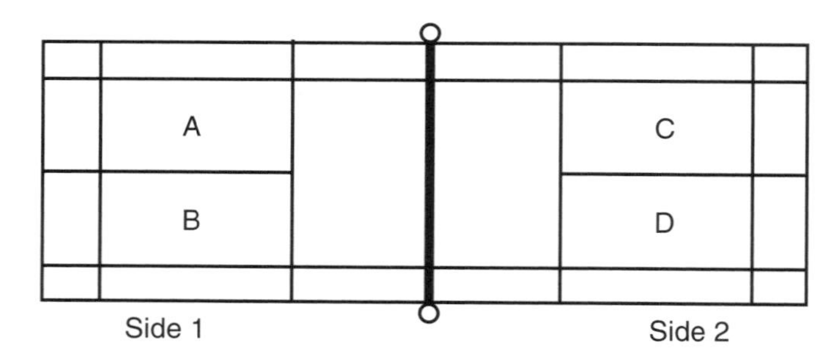

1. At the beginning of the game, Side 2 wins the toss and decides to receive. Who is the first server? _______
2. The server wins 2 points, making the score 2 (serving) to 0. The server loses the next serve. Who serves next? _______
3. From what side of the court (as server looks toward net) does the second server begin to serve? _______
4. The second server loses the serve. No points are scored. Who is the third server? _______
5. The third server scores one point and then loses the serve. Who serves next? _______
6. The fourth server wins three points and then loses the serve. What is the score at this point? _______

Figure 6.2 Criterion-referenced measurement item is shown representing the *cognitive domain*.

Affective learning objective: To develop positive values when playing volleyball, the student will exhibit desirable behaviors and undesirable behaviors at a ratio of not less than 4 to 1, respectively, during a selected application phase (game).

Criterion-referenced item: The student is observed during a 10-minute episode of team play. A record is made of the number of desirable and undesirable behaviors.

Desirable behaviors		Undesirable behaviors	
Supports, encourages opposite sex	_____	Purposely interferes with opposite sex	_____
Passes, sets when appropriate	_____	Ignores opportunity to pass, set	_____
Rolls ball under net	_____	Throws ball in disgust	_____
Observes rules	_____	Breaks rules purposely	_____
Accepts calls by other team	_____	Questions unfavorable calls	_____
Retrieves loose ball	_____	Stalls during game	_____
Others:	_____	Others:	_____
Total (A) _____		Total (B) _____	

Ratio (A/B) = ______

Figure 6.3 Criterion-referenced measurement item is shown representing the *affective domain*.

Psychomotor learning objective: To develop control of body parts (self-awareness), the student will demonstrate improved balance abilities as indicated by an overall increase of 25% from entry-level competency.

Criterion-referenced item: The student completes the balance tasks in sequence. Scores are recorded to reveal percent increase (decrease).

Task	Prelevel	Postlevel	% change
1. Stand on line; one foot; eyes open; hands on hips.	___ sec.	___ sec.	_____
2. Stand on line; one foot; eyes closed; hands on hips.	___ sec.	___ sec.	_____
3. Repeat #1; then jump and turn 180°; land on line; hold momentarily.	___ of 5	___ of 5	_____
4. Repeat #2; then jump and turn 180°; land on line; hold momentarily.	___ of 5	___ of 5	_____
5. Repeat #3; hold for 5 seconds.	___ of 5	___ of 5	_____
6. Repeat #3; land on opposite foot.	___ of 5	___ of 5	_____
7. Repeat #4; hold for 5 seconds.	___ of 5	___ of 5	_____
8. Repeat #4; land on opposite foot.	___ of 5	___ of 5	_____

Figure 6.4 Criterion-referenced measurement item is shown representing the *psychomotor domain*.

whether or not a learning objective was attained. If students are to improve cardiorespiratory endurance as revealed by a 5% reduction in the time required to complete the 1-mile run/walk, then the use of results will distinguish it as criterion-referenced.

A criterion-referenced test can also be used for norm-referenced measurements. However, since a criterion-referenced test is not constructed to maximize the variability of test scores, and relative differences among students are likely to be small, more errors in "ordering" students on a measured ability are produced with this approach. Thus, the conclusion is that norm-referenced tests can be used to make criterion-referenced measurements and vice versa, but both usages will be less than optimal.

An outcome of any evaluation procedure is to determine how student learning is reported. Although a system of marking is apparently necessary for maintaining student records and to transmit information to parents, letter grading could be eliminated in favor of a reporting system based on objectives. Since objectives include behavioral outcomes, they provide an excellent basis for marking and reporting. Given a criterion-referenced measurement approach, it is logical to develop a reporting system around the objectives underlying such tests. This means that marking will probably follow the form of pass or fail; credit or no credit; satisfactory or unsatisfactory; or achieved, needs improvement, or working to achieve. The advantages are that expected behaviors are clarified, strengths and weaknesses are diagnosed, and program continuity is enhanced.

An example of such a progress report is shown in Figure 6.5. It encompasses outcomes associated with students' needs. For practical reasons, the goal component from learning objectives serves as the criterion statement. It is intended for use in the elementary school. Different kinds of problems arise in the secondary school because of the need to use letter grades for administrative purposes such as awards, class rank, scholarships, and college admission. However, the traditional letter grade reporting system could be supplemented by a list of objectives with progress status indicated.

▶ *To practice examining evaluations from many angles, complete Self-Directed Activity 6.2 at the end of this chapter.*

Data Collection

In this section, data collection instruments are presented that reflect the full spectrum of student learning—intellectual abilities, attitudes, motivations, social conduct, values, and motor skills. They are used by the curriculum designer to make formative and summative decisions, each of which is described and illustrated. Then sample evaluation instruments are provided for the purpose of design, format, and structure. These are categorized as general techniques and learner needs.

Types of Evaluation Decisions

All evaluation procedures aim at the worth, merit, or value of "something." Assuming valid and reliable measurement, the collected information is transformed into some kind of judgment. The type of evaluation conducted depends on the decisions that follow. In this regard, a distinction is made between formative and summative evaluation.

Formative

Information is sought for help in deciding how to adjust or improve the instructional system while corrections are still possible. This suggests that evaluation must be ongoing if students are to achieve mastery. Evaluation can be a vital tool in analyzing skill development by pinpointing strengths and weaknesses, and in determining, for both teacher and student, what must still be learned. In order to ensure content validity, you should have expert knowledge of fundamental skills, since formative evaluation tends to be subjective (Strand & Wilson, 1993).

Preassessment represents a formative evaluation procedure, and the programming and intervention options identified in chapter 4 (page 99) serve this type of evaluation. Information from quizzes, self-checks, peer assessment, postsession questionnaires, and self-testing activities are also diagnostic. Formative evaluation permits changes in the learning process while changes can still affect final performance, and thus provides feedback concerning the teaching-learning process.

Summative

Evaluation of a summative nature is used to decide the extent to which a student has been successful in mastering one or more learning objectives. Formal tests (e.g., unit skills tests, knowledge tests), end-of-unit surveys, and final student products are often used for summative purposes. Many of the instruments for entry appraisal discussed in chapter 4 are also useful for assessing exit-level learning. A common practice in physical education is to evaluate

Student: ____________________ Teacher: ____________________ Date: ________________

____ 1st qtr. (Nov.) ____ 2nd qtr. (Feb.)

____ 3rd qtr. (April) ____ 4th qtr. (June)

Achieved	Needs improvement	Working to achieve	
			Intellectual
❏	❏	❏	1. Knows rules and procedures governing movement activities and games.
❏	❏	❏	2. Recognizes the effects of space, time, force, and flow on the quality of movement.
❏	❏	❏	3. Applies basic mechanical principles that affect and control human movement.
			Social
❏	❏	❏	1. Respects rights, opinions, and abilities of others.
❏	❏	❏	2. Shares, takes turns, and provides mutual assistance.
❏	❏	❏	3. Participates cooperatively in student-led activities.
			Emotional
❏	❏	❏	1. Assumes some responsibility for giving and following directions.
❏	❏	❏	2. Makes decisions individually.
❏	❏	❏	3. Responds freely and confidently through expressive bodily movement.
			Values
❏	❏	❏	1. Carries out tasks to completion.
❏	❏	❏	2. Displays preferences for various forms of movement.
❏	❏	❏	3. Engages in movement activities voluntarily.
			Physical
❏	❏	❏	1. Executes all locomotor movements in response to rhythmic accompaniments.
❏	❏	❏	2. Controls body while balancing, rolling, climbing, and hanging.
❏	❏	❏	3. Shows body control in manipulating playground balls while stationary and moving.

Figure 6.5 Progress report is illustrated including goals associated with students' cognitive (intellectual), affective (social, emotional, and values), and psychomotor (physical) needs. This example is intended for use at the elementary school level.

students only at the end of an instructional or activity unit (Strand & Wilson, 1993).

General Techniques

Individualization is a basis for effective curriculum design. Evaluation of learning should also be conducted individually; procedures should "fit" each student to the greatest extent possible. For example, in terms of cognitive evaluation, some students respond better to open-ended, written tests, while some respond better orally. Other students might perform more effectively on written projects or some kind of application exercise. In the evaluation of affective behavior, some students would rather be observed during situations in which desired behaviors may be exhibited, while others would be more responsive to a paper-and-pencil inventory as a measure of attitudes. Evaluation of motor performance also provides a range of alternatives. Some students prefer formal testing administered by the teacher. Others like the opportunity to direct their own evaluations. Still others would rather be evaluated while performing in application situations such as game play. While it's difficult to be "all things to all people," you have an obligation to provide some choice or to offer a *mix* of techniques.

In addition to individualization, multiple evaluation procedures allow the student to demonstrate learning in a variety of formal and informal testing situations. Since many objectives are reality-based, it is useful to evaluate learning in *both* controlled and natural environments. Behaviors observed in controlled testing situations should also be present when learners are in natural situations. For example, the settings for authentic assessment (pages 169, 172–179) are considered to be natural or real-life. Figure 6.6 depicts this "controlled vs. natural" environment continuum around which evaluation can be constructed. The kinds of measures that can be used are identified, examples of which are provided throughout this chapter.

To satisfy individual needs, evaluation devices should specify strengths as well as areas of needed improvement. Remember too that standardized tests or any other devices resulting in normative data cannot provide *all* the kinds of desired information. Although the teacher has traditionally assumed full responsibility for evaluation, alternative techniques should be considered that transfer partial responsibility to others. For example, peer evaluation and self-evaluation are useful techniques in judging behavior. In addition, you should consider an evaluation of the *process* of learning as well as its

Most controlled, least natural environment	⟷	Least controlled, most natural environment
Obtrusive measures in a controlled environment. Examples include (1) objective/essay cognitive exams; (2) affective (attitudes, appreciations, values) surveys/questionnaires in the form of *indirect* self-reports (intent is camouflaged or desired answer not apparent); and (3) motor performance tests.	Unobtrusive measures in a controlled environment and/or obtrusive measures in an uncontrolled environment. Examples include (1) formal question-and-answer sessions, written projects, and independent study reports; (2) affective (attitudes, appreciations, values) surveys/questionnaires in the form of *direct* self-reports (learner can guess the intent); and (3) observation of motor performance using checklists, rating scales, and peer-analysis forms.	Unobtrusive measures in an uncontrolled environment. Examples include (1) informal oral interviews, dialogue, and discussions; (2) observation of the learner's affective behavior in the community, during extracurricular activities, or while engaged in learning tasks; and (3) anecdotal record keeping of progress in motor development.

Figure 6.6 Multiple evaluation procedures are indicated along a continuum ranging from a controlled measurement environment to a natural measurement environment.

subject-related content. Each of these techniques is analyzed and illustrated here.

Teacher-Directed Evaluation

It is natural for the teacher to carry out evaluation procedures, although they vary according to personal preference, what's being evaluated, and time. Nevertheless, the teacher often directs evaluation procedures in the form of motor-related achievement tests, observational inventories, and written tests.

Motor-Related Achievement Tests. Most physical education teachers administer achievement tests as a measure of psychomotor learning. They are usually designed to measure motor ability, physical fitness, and sport skills. For example, flexibility might be determined through "twist-and-touch" and "toe-touching" tests. An evaluation item for measuring dribbling ability in soccer might be: "Determine the speed with which the student can dribble a soccer ball around six obstacles using an alternating foot-tap technique."

Other examples of motor-related achievement tests appear in Figure 6.4 for balance (page 157), Figure 6.15 for the volleyball serve (page 171), and Self-Directed Activity 6.4, Item 3, for the jump shot (page 189). Thorough analyses of tests in areas of skill-related fitness, health-related fitness, perceptual-motor skills, motor performance, and sport skills are available in numerous sources (Barrow, McGee, & Tritschler, 1989; Baumgartner & Jackson, 1982; Bosco & Gustafson, 1983; Clarke & Clarke, 1987; Johnson & Nelson, 1986; Kirkendall, Gruber, & Johnson, 1987; Miller, 1988; Safrit, 1990; Strand & Wilson, 1993).

Observational Inventories. A record of individual behavior can also be provided through systematic observational techniques. Sample checklists and rating scales for observing students' cognitive, affective, and psychomotor behavior are presented in the Criteria Checklist in chapter 4 (page 103) and in chapter 7 (pages 209 and 227).

Observation techniques are particularly useful in the affective domain (attitudes, appreciations, feelings, preferences, emotions, interests, and values). Rating scales aid in measuring behaviors associated with social, emotional, and values learning since objective testing is difficult. For example, the learner might be observed during an individualized fitness program and rated on the behavior, "Assumes responsibility for completion of tasks." This behavior could be rated according to the following scale: 5 = regularly; 4 = frequently; 3 = fairly often; 2 = seldom; and 1 = never.

Another example is to evaluate the learner's ability to move separate body parts in unison and in opposition. An item such as "While lying on back, move right arm over head and right leg to the side" could be rated according to the following scale: (+) = learner responds readily; ( ) = learner r esponds with only slight hesitation; and (–) = learner experiences difficulty in responding.

Checklists are popular since they can identify a full range of expected behavior in advance of the observation. Behaviors can be observed and recorded in large quantities. For example, you could determine whether the student exhibits the following behaviors: maintains task persistence; shows respect for equipment; cooperates with others in group decision making; contributes to group effort; and assists in setting up or putting away equipment.

Written Tests. Most teachers measure cognitive learning through written tests that provide a direct assessment of the behavior being evaluated. Usually, objective test items require short-answer responses (true-false, multiple choice, matching, fill-ins); short essay answers to general questions; problem-solving questions that may not be limited to a single answer; or all three.

When constructing such an instrument, consideration should be given to the domain level being measured. High-order abilities such as application, analysis, synthesis, and evaluation assume learning at the low-order levels of comprehension and knowledge. The most complex response possible should be used to validate the actual learning experience. For example, a knowledge item might be, "The basic offensive alignment in volleyball (4-2 pattern) employs four spikers and two setters—true or false?" An evaluation item might be, "Compare the advantages and disadvantages of using a full-court press against a fast-breaking team with a three-guard offense." Although many cognitive instruments are custom-made, a variety of tests covering a wide range of activities has been developed. Detailed descriptions and listings of these tests are presented in many of the sources identified for the motor-related achievement tests.

Peer Evaluation

In this evaluation technique, one student or group of students evaluates the ability of another student. The students develop assessment skills, concern for others, and a sense of responsibility by giving and receiving constructive or critical feedback. Peer evaluation is useful in small-group settings where one person might be an observer, another might be a recorder, and two or three might be performing a given task. Physical activities that require others (e.g., catching and throwing, kicking, spotting) offer opportunities for students to carry out these roles.

Peer evaluation is similar to the reciprocal teaching style (Mosston & Ashworth, 1986). In this style, students carry out the roles of partners, observers, or evaluators using criteria *established by the teacher.* Each student compares and contrasts another student's performance with these criteria. Results are communicated to the performer orally or through the use of a task card, rating scale, or checklist. This technique is illustrated in Figure 6.7.

Self-Evaluation

In this technique, students make critical and valid evaluations of their own abilities. They can rate their performance for comparison with individual target goals, peer standards, teacher-established criteria, or all of these. Students gain a knowledge of their own abilities and evaluate their performances realistically.

Self-evaluation is similar to the self-check and individual program teaching styles (Mosston & Ashworth, 1986). In these styles, the student is

Students can provide evaluative feedback to each other.

Task: To properly execute a cartwheel in a practice situation for later use in a routine

Directions: A partner will check your performance according to the criteria.

Perfect	Acceptable	Needs improvement	Cartwheel criteria
_____	_____	_____	1. Face mat with preferred foot forward; same-side arm is vertical.
_____	_____	_____	2. Throw weight upon preferred foot; lean forward, placing same-side hand on mat.
_____	_____	_____	3. Throw opposite leg up at the same time, placing same-side hand on the mat.
_____	_____	_____	4. Show momentary hand-balancing position with arms and legs spread wide.
_____	_____	_____	5. Bring opposite foot to the mat, raising preferred-side hand from mat.
_____	_____	_____	6. Drop preferred foot, keeping it widely separated from the other foot.
_____	_____	_____	7. Come to a stand with body erect.
_____	_____	_____	8. Maintain balance.

Figure 6.7 Peer evaluation is illustrated using a skill performance checklist.

given options in relation to the selected content. The student can choose to stay at a certain point, move on, or move back. This technique is illustrated in Figure 6.8.

Process Evaluation

In this technique the ways in which teachers and students interact are evaluated. Although objectives may not be developed for the ongoing process of learning, its evaluation can provide valuable information for improving the learning environment. Process evaluation relates directly to the achievement of objectives, which is more difficult to evaluate than content. Valid and reliable instruments are not easily designed.

Ultimately, process evaluation is best conducted through some form of direct observation of specific student behaviors. It is similar to teacher-directed evaluation, but the nature of *what* is observed is different. For example, consideration might be given to the quality and duration of student interactions, the students' independence in completing tasks, or the responses of students to the teacher.

Behaviors describing the affective domain can indicate the student's positive and negative responses to the process of learning. These behaviors indicate the student's "interest" in tennis, "appreciation" for individual sports, "favorable attitude" toward physical fitness, or "value" for physical activity. Such qualities, which are generalizations about people's behavior, are all virtuous but difficult, if not impossible, to measure. However, the attainment of these kinds of objectives can often be observed. For example, if students have a favorable attitude toward tennis, then they probably exhibit approach or "moving toward" behaviors. That is, students say positive things about tennis, place themselves in the presence of tennis, and respond voluntarily to anything relating to tennis. The process of learning can also result in negative attitudes. In this case, students elicit avoidance or "moving away from" behaviors. Students say negative things about tennis, avoid tennis, and spend as little time as possible in the presence of tennis.

The identification of approach and avoidance behaviors provides a gross assessment of positive and negative attitudes. No attempt is made at this point

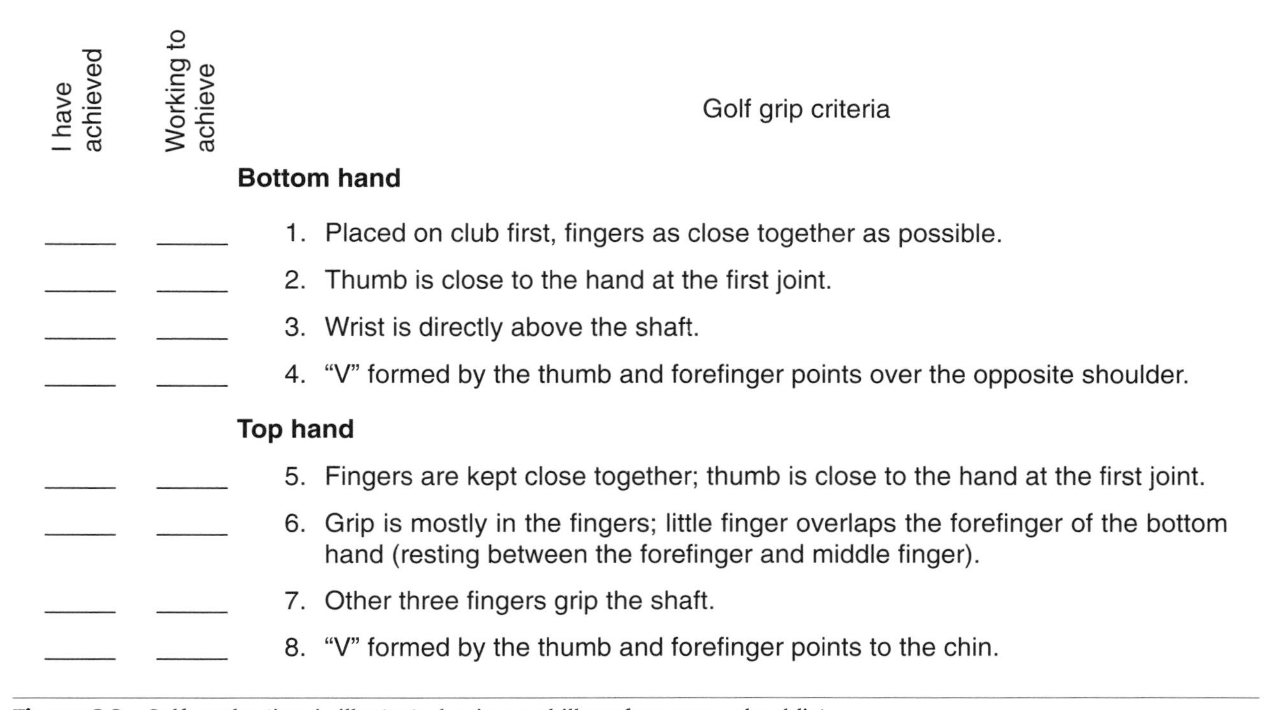

Task: To properly perform the golf grip for later use in swinging a golf club

Directions: On this worksheet, evaluate your own ability according to the criteria. You may want to request assistance from a partner, but *not* for the purpose of evaluation.

I have achieved	Working to achieve	Golf grip criteria
		Bottom hand
_____	_____	1. Placed on club first, fingers as close together as possible.
_____	_____	2. Thumb is close to the hand at the first joint.
_____	_____	3. Wrist is directly above the shaft.
_____	_____	4. "V" formed by the thumb and forefinger points over the opposite shoulder.
		Top hand
_____	_____	5. Fingers are kept close together; thumb is close to the hand at the first joint.
_____	_____	6. Grip is mostly in the fingers; little finger overlaps the forefinger of the bottom hand (resting between the forefinger and middle finger).
_____	_____	7. Other three fingers grip the shaft.
_____	_____	8. "V" formed by the thumb and forefinger points to the chin.

Figure 6.8 Self-evaluation is illustrated using a skill performance checklist.

to measure the strength of the tendency. Examples of approach behaviors are shown when learners

- remain after class for additional instruction or practice,
- attend an optional class session to practice skills that need improvement,
- request additional information,
- show a preference for physical activities rather than sedentary activities,
- desire to talk about certain physical activities, and
- attempt to involve others in a valued activity.

Although process evaluation data are usually collected via checklists and rating scales, another useful technique is *time sampling*. An observer plots the frequency or duration of a particular behavior (desirable or undesirable) along a vertical axis and plots the observation time in seconds, minutes, hours, or days on the horizontal axis. The teacher might be interested in the student's time on-task, time on productive interactions, or time off-task. Productive interactions could include assisting other students, seeking help from other students or the teacher, and asking questions. Off-task behaviors might include daydreaming, disturbing other students, practicing with less than expected intensity, and engaging in disruptive behavior (e.g., talking, fooling around, ignoring directions).

In this technique, the teacher gathers *baseline* data to determine the degree of needed intervention. For example, suppose students are given 10 minutes each class period to work independently on their personal fitness programs. On-task time would be time in which students are engaged in proper exercises, practicing skills, determining fitness level, completing a task card, or engaged in a self-testing activity. Obviously, this technique could not be applied to all students at the same time. Individual students would be targeted where problems were evident. Also, the 10-minute time period could be broken down to shorter episodes so that more than one student could be observed. In Figure 6.9, the graph on the left represents the amount of on-task time for one student during the first week.

Based on these data, it should be clear that intervention is needed. The teacher might decide to reinforce the student verbally and nonverbally for on-task behaviors and to ignore or reprimand off-task behaviors for a period of two weeks. The results of intervention during the second week are also shown in Figure 6.9. The positive gain in on-task behavior demonstrates the usefulness of process evaluation. The data show that the intervention strategy changed the student's behavior in the desired direction.

Finally, process evaluation data can also be collected through student self-reports, usually in the form of questionnaires or surveys. Items should relate to the *process* of learning rather than the content (cognitive abilities or motor skills). Results should be used to design better learning experiences and to improve the overall level of instruction. Response by students through self-reporting provides invaluable information about the process of learning. Sample items are shown in Figure 6.10.

▶ ***To practice distinguishing among teacher-directed, peer, self-, and process evaluations, complete Self-Directed Activity 6.3 at the end of this chapter.***

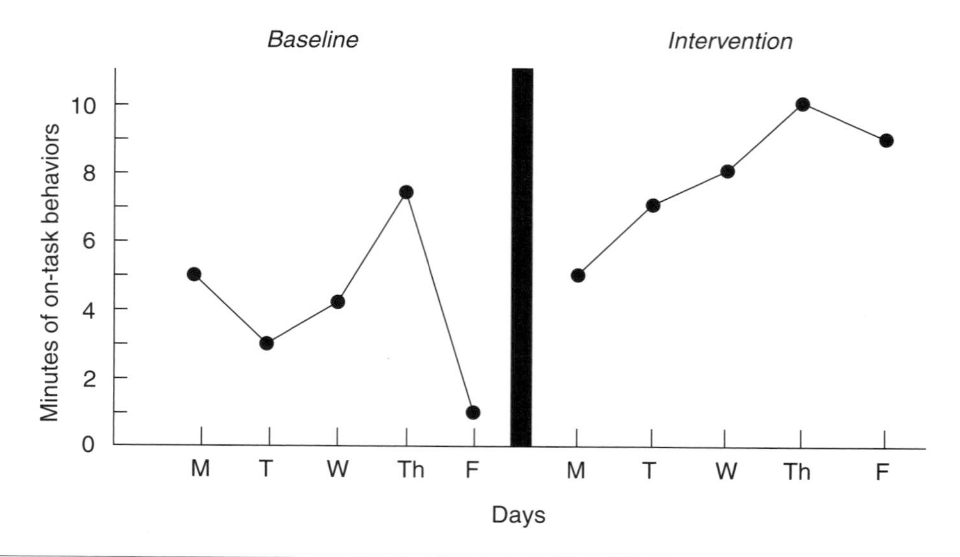

Figure 6.9 Time-sampling technique for process evaluation is illustrated. Hypothetical baseline and intervention data are shown for on-task behaviors.

1. Circle the words that tell how you feel (mostly) about gymnastics.

Interesting	Too easy	Useful	Others:
Dull	Helpful	Worthless	________
Fun	Important	Boring	________
Too hard	Super	Useless	________

2. If someone suggested that you should play intramural tennis, what would be your reply?

____

____

3. Would you like to learn more about golf?

   Yes   No   I'm not sure

4. Some of the activities that were used in the personalized fitness unit are listed below. How did you like these experiences?

	(1) Strongly dislike	(2) Dislike	(3) Unsure	(4) Like	(5) Strongly like
Drills	❑	❑	❑	❑	❑
Demonstrations	❑	❑	❑	❑	❑
Circuit training	❑	❑	❑	❑	❑
Working with partners	❑	❑	❑	❑	❑
Individual tasks	❑	❑	❑	❑	❑
Group training	❑	❑	❑	❑	❑

5. Compared to other indoor sports, floor hockey was:

   (a) Great
   (b) Good
   (c) OK
   (d) Not very good
   (e) Terrible

6. Write a brief paragraph about how you feel about speedball.

(continued)

Figure 6.10 Self-reporting technique for process evaluation is illustrated. Sample items are shown that could be used in a survey or questionnaire.

7. Check (√) the face you would wear when you look at this picture (verbal directions to younger learners).

8. Coed volleyball is:

Exciting								Dull
Boring								Fun
Worth the time								Waste of time
Stupid								Great
Uninteresting								Interesting

Scoring: Exciting — 7 6 5 4 3 2 1 — Dull
Boring — 1 2 3 4 5 6 7 — Fun

Figure 6.10 *(continued)*

Learner Needs

Evaluation procedures are suggested by the kinds of behaviors and criteria specified in learning objectives. It follows that such an evaluation represents learners' *explicit* needs. An evaluation of learning based on these behaviors is the essence of criterion-referenced measurement. Procedures are directly interpretable from the learning objectives and the corresponding criterion. To show this relationship, sample evaluation instruments are identified for cognitive, affective, and psychomotor needs.

Cognitive

In Figure 6.2 (page 156), a criterion-referenced measurement item was shown representing the cognitive domain. An evaluation instrument derived from a cognitive learning objective is illustrated in Figure 6.11.

Cognitive learning objective: To demonstrate an ability to analyze and synthesize synchronized swimming skills, the student will choreograph a synchronized swimming routine, consisting of schooled figures and original strokes, according to the established criteria.

Evaluation instrument: The student's routine is observed in terms of its choreography, *not* its performance. Criteria are applied as indicated.

How does the synchronized swimming routine meet the following criteria?	(5) Excellent	(4) Good	(3) Satisfactory	(2) Fair	(1) Poor
1. Synchronization					
a. Coincides with rhythm of music	❑	❑	❑	❑	❑
b. Uses musical measures, phrases, transitional sections, loud and soft parts, and staccato and legato	❑	❑	❑	❑	❑
2. Creativity					
a. Shows innovative surface patterns	❑	❑	❑	❑	❑
b. Includes original figures	❑	❑	❑	❑	❑
c. Contrasts speed of execution	❑	❑	❑	❑	❑
3. Fluidity					
a. Flows with rhythmical pattern	❑	❑	❑	❑	❑
b. Connects strokes to figures and vice versa	❑	❑	❑	❑	❑
c. Brings together beginning, body, and ending	❑	❑	❑	❑	❑
4. Diversity					
a. Incorporates variety of skills	❑	❑	❑	❑	❑
b. Represents three groups of schooled figures	❑	❑	❑	❑	❑
c. Offers original figures from at least four of the "variety" groupings	❑	❑	❑	❑	❑

Comments:

Figure 6.11 Criteria rating scale is shown representing a student's cognitive need.

Various types of instruments associated with cognitive evaluation are:

- Paper-and-pencil test
- Oral "test"
  - — Formal (questions and answers)
  - — Informal (discussion, dialogue)
- Criteria applied to a product (paper, report, project)
  - — Rating scale
  - — Checklist (yes/no, tally)
- Criteria applied to behavior requiring "application" of knowledge
  - — Rating scale
  - — Checklist
- Self-report

Affective

In Figure 6.3 (page 157), a criterion-referenced measurement item was shown representing the affective domain. Evaluation instruments derived from affective learning objectives are illustrated in Figures 6.12, 6.13, and 6.14 (page 170). Several examples are provided to reflect different aspects of affective needs (i.e., social, emotional, values). Various types of instruments associated with affective evaluation are the

- interest/attitude survey or questionnaire (self-report),
- frequency index (behavior trend scale),
- approach/avoidance checklist, and
- semantic differential scale.

Affective learning objective: To demonstrate positive interpersonal relations skills, the student will, following a unit involving reciprocal learning experiences, display behavior trends representing peer-group expectancy at a frequency index rating of 3.0 or better during a group physical fitness program.

Evaluation instrument: The student is observed at least two times during the group physical fitness program. Behavior trends are rated according to the criteria below. Ratings for each behavior trend are circled and averaged. The frequency index rating is calculated as indicated.

Behavior trends	1st observ.					2nd observ.					Rating average
	Never	Seldom	Fairly often	Frequently	Regularly	Never	Seldom	Fairly often	Frequently	Regularly	
1. Limits interactions to friends; excludes others	5	4	3	2	1	5	4	3	2	1	
2. Shares equipment	1	2	3	4	5	1	2	3	4	5	
3. Takes turn at circuit stations	1	2	3	4	5	1	2	3	4	5	
4. Provides mutual assistance voluntarily	1	2	3	4	5	1	2	3	4	5	
5. Seeks seclusion from fitness group	5	4	3	2	1	5	4	3	2	1	
6. Interacts consistently with both males and females	1	2	3	4	5	1	2	3	4	5	
7. Criticizes others in fitness group	5	4	3	2	1	5	4	3	2	1	
8. Shows favoritism toward highly skilled peers	5	4	3	2	1	5	4	3	2	1	
						Total:					
						Index rating: (total ÷ 8)					

Figure 6.12 Frequency index scale is shown representing a student's affective (social) need.

Affective learning objective: To demonstrate self-assurance, the student will show confidence in body movement as determined by a predominance of approach behaviors being exhibited toward participation in expressive movement sequences.

Evaluation instrument: The student is observed during movement exploration activities. The approach and/or avoidance behaviors are checked that relate to confidence in body movement.

√	Approach behaviors	Avoidance behaviors	√
	Initiates ideas for exploration	Lacks initiative; follows others	
	Shows involvement through facial expression	Is expressionless during movement	
	Carries out exploration tasks to completion	Quits on discovery-type tasks requiring perseverance	
	Seeks to become increasingly more skillful	Is slow in starting movement; deliberative	
	Responds freely to discovery activities	Reacts with moderate or deficient energy level	
	Expresses himself/herself willingly through movement sequences	Needs constant prodding	
	Makes adjustments readily; welcomes change	Prefers habits; avoids making new adjustments	
	Is self-composed; not easily embarrassed	Is self-conscious; easily embarrassed	
	Expects success	Accepts below-expected levels of performance	
	Totals		

Figure 6.13 Approach/avoidance checklist is shown representing a student's affective (emotional) need.

Psychomotor

In Figure 6.4 (page 157), a criterion-referenced measurement item was shown representing the psychomotor domain. An evaluation instrument derived from a psychomotor learning objective is illustrated in Figure 6.15 (page 171). Various types of instruments associated with psychomotor evaluation are:

- Formal skill test
- Criteria applied during performance
  - — Rating scale
  - — Checklist (yes/no, tally)
- Informal observation of performance (anecdotal record)
- Progress on a task sheet
- Self-report

▶ ***To practice devising evaluation instruments that relate to learners' needs, complete Self-Directed Activity 6.4 at the end of this chapter.***

Authentic Assessment

The school reform movement emphasizes accountability for student learning. Interest in assessment has also been prompted. Society, which has been oriented toward standardized achievement tests, is

Affective learning objective: To demonstrate improvement in attitudes toward regular and modified coeducational sports and games, the student will show a favorable change of at least 0.5 on attitudes built into a semantic differential scale.

Evaluation instrument: Students check the appropriate space according to how they feel most of the time. Each space is valued from 1 to 5 points, with 5 being most positive. In scoring results, note that some items are reversed. Thus, scores must be reversed as follows:

Dull	1	2	3	4	5	Exciting
Fun	5	4	3	2	1	Boring

Total the 14 scores and compute average for preimpact and postimpact attitudes.

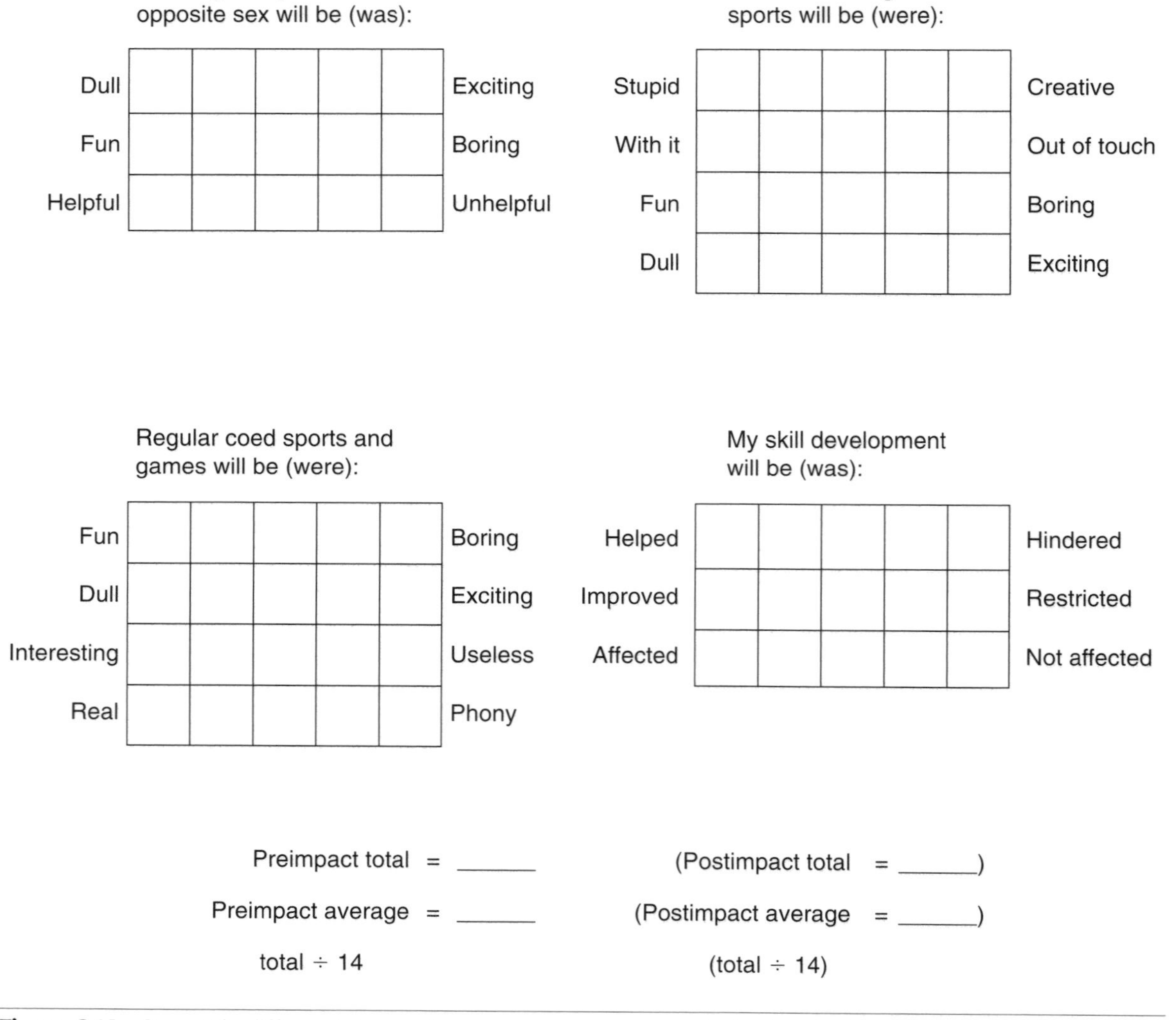

Figure 6.14 Semantic differential scale is shown representing a student's affective (values) need.

Psychomotor learning objective: To develop compound adaptive skills in volleyball, the student will demonstrate, in a noncompetitive situation, improved ability to execute the "floater" serve by attaining the *contracted* level of qualitative and quantitative performance on a serving skill test.

Evaluation instrument: Server executes 10 "floater" serves. Test administrator indicates the side of court at which server is to aim. Qualitative criteria are applied at the time of the serve and a rating is recorded. Quantitative rating is applied based on where ball lands. Total scores are calculated for each rating (qualitative and quantitative).

Qualitative criteria:

1. Shifts weight from rear foot to front foot
2. Steps in the direction ball is to be hit
3. Tosses ball 1 to 1-1/2 feet above head
4. Tosses ball out in front of body
5. Keeps tossing hand and arm extended after toss
6. Contacts ball with palm
7. Contacts center of ball
8. Eliminates follow-through (no spin)
9. Sends ball in low trajectory

Qualitative rating scale:

3 = Excellent form; all criteria met
2 = Acceptable form; more than half of criteria met
1 = Below-acceptable form; half or more of criteria need improvement
0 = No criteria met

Quantitative criteria:

1. Ball goes over net
2. Ball lands in-bounds
3. Ball lands on target side
4. Ball lands deep on target side
5. Ball lands deep and down target sideline

Quantitative rating scale:

3 = Lands on target side
2 = Lands on opposite side (deep)
1 = Lands short
0 = Hits net or lands out of bounds
-1 = High trajectory (deduct from score)

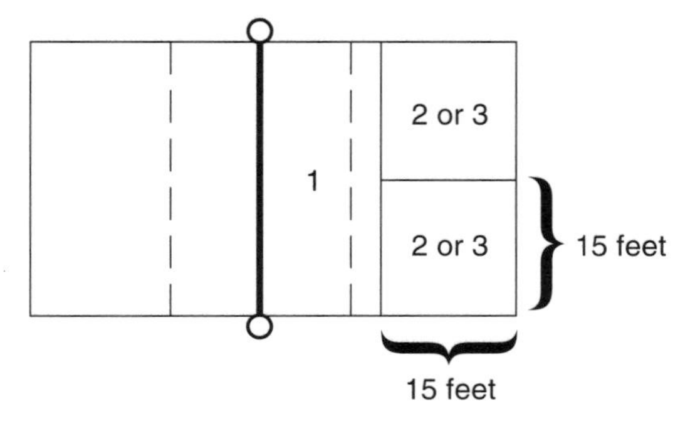

Figure 6.15 A criterion skill test is shown representing a student's psychomotor need.

apparently ready for change. Alternatives are centered on more naturalistic, performance-based approaches known as *authentic assessment*. Actual examples of student performances serve as the measure of learning instead of the highly inferential estimates provided by group testing (Meisels, 1993). In physical education, for example, students' performance in naturalistic game settings (e.g., the volleyball bump pass when returning a "real" serve) is assessed instead of students' performance on a skill test (e.g., volleyball bump pass from a partner lob).

The general characteristics of authentic assessment are identified in the first section. While there are other authentic assessment techniques, the focus has been on *portfolios* as the primary way for exhibiting student work and performance data. Portfolio assessment is designed to present a broader, more genuine picture of learning (Zessoules & Gardner, 1991). For this reason, portfolios are then described along with specific suggestions for physical education. Finally, a *system* of authentic assessment is introduced that can serve as a model for physical education.

General Characteristics

Several evaluation constructs have been advanced including entry appraisal, pre-post design, criterion-referenced measurement, alternative data collection techniques, and explicit assessment of student needs. Together, they represent an ongoing cumulative process that reflects the goals and objectives of the curriculum designer while keeping track of individual student progress. Evaluation of this nature is consistent with the meaning of *authentic assessment*, a system of documenting student learning through exhibits and work samples inherent to the school setting (Meisels, 1993).

This broadened view coincides with holistic approaches to teaching such as "whole language" and "developmentally appropriate" practice (Viechnicki, Barbour, Shaklee, Rohrer, & Ambrose, 1993). With respect to assessment, developmentally appropriate practice in physical education means that "teacher decisions are based primarily on ongoing individual assessments of children as they participate in physical education class activities (formative evaluation), and not on the basis of a single test score (summative evaluation)" (Graham, Castenada, Hopple, Manross, & Sanders, 1992, p. 7).

In general, authentic assessment provides an alternative to highly inferential estimates of learning such as those found with conventional, norm-referenced measures and standardized tests. It is non-stigmatizing, it enhances motivation, it assists teachers with decision making, and it is effective for reporting accomplishments and progress to families. This means that traditional grades may be replaced with anecdotal records, performance samples, and student profiles. For example, the progress report shown in Figure 6.5 (page 159) is based on performance indicators rather than grades.

The various forms of authentic assessment seem to have some common goals: to capitalize on the actual work of learners, to enhance teacher and student involvement in evaluation, and to satisfy the need for accountability prompted by school reform (Chittenden, 1991). Furthermore, these performance-based assessments can be longitudinal (i.e., across grade levels), multidimensional (i.e., physical, intellectual, social, and emotional), and individually modifiable (i.e., able to respond to a wide range of learner variability) (Meisels, Dichtelmiller, Dorfman, Jablon, & Marsden, 1994).

Portfolios

In physical education, as in other fields, the use of portfolios is emerging as an important technique for authentic assessment. A multifaceted approach is recommended. Ideally, all stakeholders (e.g., teacher, student, parents, community) should be involved in the process, a rationale should exist for including portfolio items, and the purposeful collection of students' work should occur over time. You can document not only school-based academic accomplishments, but the social, emotional, and physical status of students as well. As teachers and students collect portfolio data, progress should be reported at regular intervals to parents, administrators, and others, as appropriate. Various aspects of portfolio implementation are presented here (Melograno, 1994).

Teacher's Role

In the portfolio system, the teacher facilitates, guides, and offers choices. Partnerships are established among teacher, students, and parents. Traditional delivery systems, in which teachers inform, direct, and predetermine priorities, do not work. More specifically, you need to do the following:

- Deliberately plan for student involvement. Strategies are needed to ensure student input; it can't be left to chance.

- Provide time for tasks that encourage decision making and reflection; don't become overanxious because these tasks look passive.
- Demonstrate expected behaviors; actually show students what's being sought.
- Help students manage portfolios; provide assistance just as you would guide students through a difficult motor skill.
- Develop positive interactive behaviors. Students need to know where they stand; feedback and encouragement are needed because of the emphasis on self-management.
- Actually use interactions to guide instruction. Information derived from portfolios as they are developed could influence what is taught; such adjustments are formative decisions.

Some teachers look at portfolio assessment and say, "I have too many students and not enough time." However, portfolios demand a high degree of student responsibility in terms of self-management, self-assessment, self-reflection, and peer conferences and evaluation. If students are weaned toward a *system* of portfolio assessment, restrictions of time and sheer numbers are minimized. Use of partners, small groups, and self-directed tasks can reduce the seemingly high student-teacher ratios. Obviously, the system needs to be well planned and organized.

Purposes

The first consideration in any portfolio system is its purpose. There needs to be a reason for creating portfolios. Imagine the difficulty in selecting items for a portfolio with no sense of what the portfolio is to represent. Some general purposes include (Murphy & Smith, 1992)

Portfolios offer an alternative approach to traditional evaluation.

- keeping track of students' progress,
- providing students an opportunity to assess their own accomplishments,
- assisting the teacher in instructional planning,
- determining the extent to which established learning objectives have been achieved,
- helping parents understand their child's effort and progress,
- serving as a basis for program evaluation, and
- determining student placement within and outside of class.

Purposes specific to physical education might be

- helping students practice a healthy lifestyle,
- determining the degree of personal and social development in an adventure-outdoor education program, and
- communicating students' strengths and areas needing improvement in gross and fine motor skills.

Organization and Management

First, a method of construction must be decided (e.g., file folders inside an accordion file, pocket folders held together with a spiral binding, hanging files, boxes). Every item should be dated and a cumulative list of items should be maintained in the front. Second, how and where to store portfolios must be decided (e.g., milk crates, file cabinets or drawers, shelves, boxes). It is essential that portfolios be stored in locations that are visible and accessible to students. Third, the portfolios should be managed regularly to avoid a large pile of items at the end of a given collection period. And fourth, who should have access to portfolios must be decided (e.g., peers, parents, other teachers). Certain portfolio sections or items may be designated as public while others are private. Guidelines should be established from the very beginning.

Options for Selecting Items

Usually, students' first portfolio items are "baseline" samples. The information collected for entry appraisal should be contained in students' portfolios. For example, behavior sampling through informal techniques (observations and self-reports) and formal techniques (criterion-referenced measures) would yield important baseline information in order to ultimately show student change (learning). Likewise, other sources of entry information such as cumulative record data (e.g., previous test scores, diagnostic reviews, anecdotal records) and performance on a task sequence would also produce invaluable information.

Other criteria are needed for choosing portfolio items. An item might be selected that represents "something that was hard for you to do," "something that makes you feel really good," or "something that you would like to work on again." Some additional suggestions for selecting items are: a "best" or "most representative" skill (e.g., gymnastic stunt); work-in-progress with written plans for revision (e.g., dance routine); and samples organized chronologically according to a theme (e.g., personalized physical fitness program).

When students make decisions about the selection and quality of their work, they begin to establish standards by which their work can be evaluated. However, students must realize that teachers will also decide on portfolio items and that some items may be mandated by school officials (DeFina, 1992). Various sources of items are listed, many of which are illustrated throughout the book:

- Preinstruction inventory
- Task sheets
- Self-assessment checklists
- Frequency index scales
- Rating scales
- Peer reviews
- Attitude surveys
- Self-reports
- Workbook pages
- Logs
- Journals
- Student reflections
- Projects
- Independent study contracts
- Videotapes
- Teacher's anecdotal statements
- Parental observations/comments
- Skill tests
- Quizzes
- Written tests

Portfolio Evaluation

Simply collecting items in some container serves no meaningful teaching, learning, or measurement purpose. *Portfolios should be evaluated!* If nothing else, the portfolio should be linked to learning objectives, one of the stated purposes of portfolios. However, many teachers have abandoned conventional symbols—grades and scores—in favor of new ways to evaluate. Instead, they describe, analyze, moderate, discuss, annotate, and confer (Murphy & Smith, 1992). It is also important to remember that no single portfolio item should be used to evaluate students' abilities. If accurate conclusions are to be drawn, performance patterns should be analyzed over a period of time. Several aspects of portfolio evaluation are examined.

Reflection. Evaluative criteria are inherent to many of the various kinds of portfolio items listed previously. As students develop and select their work samples, they become *reflective* in the process. That is, they make value judgments about the standards being used as a guide to evaluation. Over time, high-order cognitive functions such as analysis and synthesis are promoted. To help strengthen self-reflective abilities, some structure is recommended. For example, at selected intervals, students could be expected to complete a "Self-Reflective Activity Sheet." This form of portfolio "audit" could include questions such as: What's in stock? How many items do you have? What are you working on? What problems are you having in collecting items? What are some problems you perceive in achieving your desired skill level? What are some changes you can make to deal with these problems? How do you feel about your goals? What are your goals for next month?

Reflections on individual portfolios are not limited to the student's own self-assessment. For instance, peers can offer valuable feedback. But they should not merely speculate about another student's performance; they must judge the other's work according to established criteria. Reciprocal learning approaches have built-in peer review and corresponding checklists or rating scales that could be placed in portfolios. A more general response form could be used by peers to provide an overall view of another student's portfolio. This "Peer Reflection Form" might include questions such as: What do you see as the special strength of the work? What could be improved? What suggestions would you offer based on your own experiences?

Parents should also be involved as a source of feedback and support. Portfolios offer an excellent opportunity for parents to see what their child has achieved and is trying to achieve. The more parents and children interact through portfolios, the stronger the home-school connection. Initially, the portfolio program should be introduced and explained to parents in a letter or memo or during an "open house" or "portfolio night." In terms of evaluative feedback, a "Parent Portfolio Review and Reflection Form" could be used for parents to respond to questions such as: Which items tell you most about your child's achievements? What do you see as your child's strengths? What do you see as needs to be addressed? What suggestions do you have for improving your child's performance?

Conferences. To the extent possible, a revolving schedule should be established to meet with individual students, small groups, and/or the class to analyze portfolios and evaluation measures. Because of time constraints and logistics, conferences may need to occur while the rest of the class is working independently, at stations, or in small groups. Topics to be addressed include portfolio organization, item selection, evaluation criteria, and results.

Students should be encouraged to discuss their own observations about growth and compare them to the teacher's judgments. Appropriate plans for improvement and development should be devised. Teachers should focus on accomplishments and potential growth, not problems or failures. The conference should not be perceived as an inquisition by the teacher. It is suggested that a "Conference Questions Sheet" be devised to record answers and comments in response to predetermined questions. In addition, a "Conference Evaluation Form" could be used to record both teacher and student notes. These notes, which become a form of agreement, should be placed in the portfolio.

Conferences between parents and teachers afford another opportunity to share students' portfolios and to communicate evaluative judgments. Baseline samples should be compared to present samples so parents can see their child's growth. Stated goals should also be compared to targeted areas of improvement. Guidelines for parental review should be established from the outset so that students know how their parents will be involved and how the collected information will be used (DeFina, 1992).

Progress Reports. Traditional grading systems and report cards are a reality within the educational establishment. Translating portfolio contents into report card grades can be difficult since grades typically rate students on a curve and portfolios view students on a developmental continuum. Teachers must also reconcile the fact that portfolios are normally skewed in that students' "best" works are usually presented. A full representative sample of students' actual learning should be assured. Adaptive techniques are needed if portfolios hold any promise as a complement to conventional report card grades.

By looking holistically at portfolio items, it is possible to arrange them in A, B, and C categories. Rubrics, scoring guides designed to evaluate a student's performance, can be used for this purpose (Batzle, 1992). For example, a rubric could measure the components of a dance routine (e.g., creativity, fluidity, transition, diversity). A rating scale is devised (e.g., a range of 0 to 5) with the largest number indicating "outstanding." Criteria are established for each score across each component. Report cards could be redesigned to include narrative statements or descriptive labels, or both. But it would probably be more practical to supplement report cards with *anecdotal* progress reports. The progress report shown in Figure 6.5 (page 159) is based on performance indicators rather than grades.

Collection Methods

Portfolios should not be a collection of anything and everything. Previously, various sources of portfolio items were listed. In addition, information gathering should be based on multiple methods such as observations, performance samples, and tests or testlike procedures (Chittenden, 1991).

Portfolio alternatives are outlined in Table 6.1. An attempt has been made to identify the various sources of information for each method of portfolio assessment. In addition, these sources are illustrated relative to physical education, including many of the applicable assessment instruments and procedures presented throughout the book. The range of potential "exhibits of learning" contained in an individual portfolio is unlimited.

Systematic Model

Given the pressure for school accountability, the emphasis on low-order skills (e.g., memory-level tasks, attending behaviors, simple movements) has not worked. The new authentic assessment systems offer hope, the most promising being performance assessment (Meisels, 1993). One approach is the work sampling system (Meisels, Dichtelmiller, Dorfman, Jablon, & Marsden, 1994), the purpose of which is to assess and document the full range of skills, understandings, social behaviors, and values that students display in the school environment.*

* Description of the work sampling approach is adapted from *An Overview* (3rd ed.) (pp. 7–22, 29) by S. Meisels et al., 1994, Ann Arbor, MI: Rebus Planning Associates, Inc. Adapted by permission of the author.

Table 6.1 Portfolio Alternatives

Method of assessment	Sources of information	Illustrative items
Observations	Rating scales	Synchronized swimming choreography (Figure 6.11, page 167)
	Checklists	Forward roll (Criteria Checklist, page 103)
	Frequency index scales	Interpersonal relations (Figure 6.12, page 168)
	Peer reviews	Cartwheel (Figure 6.7, page 162); tennis forehand (Figure 7.4, page 213); badminton forehand overhead clear (Figure 7.5, page 214)
	Logs	Fitness calendar showing aerobic and strength training workout schedule
	Anecdotal recordings	Descriptive statement about student's ability to change directions and levels during movement exploration
	Narrative descriptions	Summary of student's progress in developing cooperative behaviors during "new games"
Performance samples	Self-evaluations	Golf grip (Figure 6.8, page 163)
	Student reflections	Feelings about various activities (Figure 6.10, pages 165–166)
	Projects	Develop a personalized fitness program (Learning Experiences Based on Needs, affective [values], page 202); tennis contract (Individualized Learning Approaches, Item 5, page 207)
	Independent study	Badminton (Individualized Learning Approaches, Item 9, pages 209–210)
	Videotapes	Free exercise routine; swimming stroke; game play
Tests and testlike procedures	Pretests	Tennis inventory (Sample Items for Preinstruction Inventory, page 102)
	Quizzes	Rules of badminton (Figure 6.2, page 156); components of physical fitness (Criterion-Referenced Test Items, page 106)
	Self-reports	Attitude toward coed games (Figure 6.14, page 170)
	End-of-unit tasks	Balance tasks (Figure 6.4, page 157); volleyball serve (Figure 6.15, page 171)
	Commercial instruments	Bruininks-Oseretsky Test of Motor Proficiency (Bruininks, 1978); volleyball knowledge and skills (Individualized Learning Approaches, Item 10, pages 210–211)

The work sampling approach provides an ongoing evaluation process, rather than a general snapshot at a single time. Although the system was designed for use in early childhood settings (age 3 to grade 3), it can also serve as a model for authentic assessment at different educational levels and with various subject matters. The system consists of three complementary components: developmental checklists; portfolio collection; and summary reports.

Developmental Checklists

In order to keep track of what learners know and can do, developmental checklists are used for observing, recording, and evaluating behaviors. The checklists cover seven domains, each consisting of several functional components. For example, physical development includes gross and fine motor development. Personal and social development includes self-concept, self-control, approach to learning, interaction with others, group activities, and conflict resolution. Each functional component is defined by performance indicators that refer to students' specific behaviors, skills, or accomplishments. Performance indicators are identified for selected components.

Physical development

Gross motor development

- Moves with balance and control
- Coordinates movements to perform gross motor tasks

Fine motor development

- Uses strength and control to accomplish fine motor tasks
- Uses eye-hand coordination to perform fine motor tasks

Personal and social development

Self-concept

- Shows a positive sense of self
- Shows initiative and self-direction in actions

Group activities

- Participates in the group life of the class
- Plays and follows simple rules in a game of skill or chance

The performance indicators reflect common expectations structured around developmentally appropriate activities. They are not intended for comparisons among learners. After observing the learner repeatedly, performance indicators are rated according to the categories "Not Yet," "In Process," or "Proficient." This is similar to the checklists shown in Figure 6.7 (page 162), Figure 6.8 (page 163), Self-Directed Activity 6.4, Item 4 (page 192), and Self-Directed Activity 7.4, Item 10 (pages 234–235). Checklists are completed on each learner three times a year. Process notes in the form of anecdotal recordings and narrative descriptions are used during these intervals.

Portfolio Collection

The nature of portfolios in the work sampling system is basically the same as that described in the previous section. A relatively structured approach is taken that relies on core items (samples that are common to all learners in a group) and other items (samples that capture the unique characteristics of individual learners). This helps to create a manageable portfolio and allows learners to be involved in the process of selecting and judging the quality of their own work. Suggestions for portfolio items were offered in Table 6.1.

Summary Reports

This component consists of a brief summary of each learner's performance. The developmental checklists and portfolios are carefully reviewed; judgments are made in terms of "developing as expected" or "needs improvement." Progress is judged "as expected" or "not as expected." The report also includes an opportunity for general comments about strengths and learning problems in each domain. Plans for supporting learner growth can be included. A report of this nature provides an authentic way of communicating what learners have accomplished, what learners' strengths and difficulties are, and how much progress has been made. These summary reports, which replace conventional report cards, are similar to the proposed progress report shown in Figure 6.5 (page 159).

▶ ***To test your own knowledge of authentic assessment and its place in physical education, complete Self-Directed Activity 6.5 at the end of this chapter.***

Making It Work

Have you achieved the expected outcomes (page 152)? Congratulations! You are able to develop evaluation procedures for your physical education curriculum design. Still, you may have some practical questions that need answers, such as:

- **Can all the purposes of evaluation be met unless you develop several procedures, one for each?**

  Separate procedures are not needed for each purpose. Many of them overlap. For example, a single procedure (e.g., a series of self-check task cards for tennis) could easily motivate students, provide a learning experience, help guide students, serve as a diagnostic tool, and offer information about program improvement. The reverse is true as well; a single procedure may be used for only one purpose. For example, an end-of-unit skill test may be used to determine current status so that a grade can be reported. Even here, it's likely that at least one other purpose is served—motivation.

- **With such limited time, how can you perform individualized assessments in all three domains, control the students, and still teach something?**

  At this point, you may feel overwhelmed by all the possibilities and expectations for evaluation. You need to establish priorities; be selective. You shouldn't try to do it all, but you can "weight" the attention given to the separate domains. Make sure you have a basis for your decisions. Then, whatever you decide, do it well. Also, don't try to evaluate everything yourself. Use peer- and self-evaluation techniques. They really do work if students are taught the *skills* associated with each, such as observing objectively, providing feedback, cooperating, maintaining on-task behavior, and applying criteria accurately. Students should learn not to depend only on you for feedback and assistance. However, you must be prepared to establish the criteria and communicate them as simply and clearly as possible.

- **Is it worth trying to evaluate affective outcomes since it's so subjective anyway?**

  Don't bother if you're not serious about it. But then, don't make claims that students are developing positive psychosocial behaviors (e.g., fair play, cooperation, tolerance) if you can't back them up with hard data. Looking for desirable and undesirable behaviors is better than doing nothing. It reveals a general tendency which is perhaps all you can expect. Students should be taught what these behaviors look like. While you want student responses to be genuine, don't try to trick students by not showing them what is desirable. By pointing out these behaviors, you help students become more conscious of their actions. Over time, behavior changes may be significant.

- **Can you really teach anything when students' portfolio selections take you in so many directions?**

  If you're going to use portfolios, don't create a system you can't manage. Pick out those aspects that fit your situation initially and then expand as you and your students become more comfortable. For example, if you're in an elementary school, first graders might start out with only two or three parts of a portfolio. By the time they're fifth graders, they could have what you consider to be a complete portfolio. Here again, you need to establish some priorities. Otherwise, you and your students are destined to be frustrated together.

- **How can portfolios really be managed in physical education with so many students and so little time?**

  Granted, physical education is not like a single, contained classroom. However, you can certainly create a physical education *context* for portfolios. For example, maybe the physical education component of the student's portfolio can be kept with the classroom or homeroom teacher. By relying on student self-management, you can solve, or at least reduce, many of your organization and management problems. But students must be taught the skills of self-management. You can't just say, "Here, go do this on your own!" They need help and direction. Once your *system* is built, your high student-teacher ratios won't seem as great because you shouldn't have to discipline and manage as much.

Self-Directed Activity 6.1

Various purposes should be considered when developing an evaluation procedure. The following evaluation schemes are based on some of these purposes, two of which are identified. Explain how each purpose is served by the situation.

1. Students show their understanding of intermediate tennis (i.e., rules and terminology, etiquette and procedures, techniques and skills, strategy and tactics, history and equipment, safety principles). They complete an end-of-unit objective test consisting of true-false, multiple choice, matching, and completion items. Questions represent a range in cognitive levels including recall, classification, and analysis.

   Determine achievement status: ______________________________

   ____

   ____

   Indicate needed program revision or improvement: ______________________________

   ____

   ____

2. A student is observed during at least two soccer games to assess respect for the honor system of officiating, behavior toward opposing team, and cooperation with team members. A record is made of the student's response to situations such as the number of unfavorable officiating decisions reacted to negatively or positively, the number of times rules were broken or observed, and the number of negative and positive interactions with teammates (e.g., passes rather than shoots when a teammate is in a better position to shoot).

   Provide motivation: ______________________________

   ____

   ____

   Enhance feedback and guidance: ______________________________

   ____

   ____

3. Students perform basic skills that involve movement through space. A separate scale is used for evaluating each locomotor skill (walking, running, jumping, hopping, leaping, skipping, sliding, galloping). Common factors are judged, including posture, foot position, body position, leg position, transfer of weight, ankle/knee/hip flexion, and arm swing. Each factor is rated according to a three-category scoring system, indicating difficulty (–); acceptable movement response (√); or above-expected response (+).

   Facilitate learner diagnosis: ______________________________

   ____

   ____

   Indicate needed program revision or improvement: ______________________________

   ____

   ____

4. Students demonstrate their ability to execute a two-handed basketball chest pass to a classmate or against the wall 15 to 20 feet away. Three passes are performed. A partner uses a criteria checklist to evaluate one aspect for each pass (i.e., fundamental starting position, passing action, and follow-through). Afterwards, the student is asked by the partner to name at least 7 of the 10 criteria.

   Offer a learning experience: ______________________________

   ____

   ____

   Enhance feedback and guidance: ______________________________

   ____

   ____

5. Primary-aged students answer a series of alternate-response questions that measure knowledge of movement fundamentals. The teacher reads each question and waits for the students to make the appropriate mark or response on their papers. Concepts include division of space (self, general), dimensions of space (directions, levels, ranges, pathways), time (speed, rhythm), and dimensions of flow (free, bound). With the use of stick figures, sample items are: Draw a circle around the children who are exploring general space; draw a cross mark on the child who is moving forward . . . to the side . . . up . . . down; draw a circle around the child who is moving at a high level . . . low level . . . in a straight path . . . in a zigzag path.

   Provide motivation: ______________________________

   ____

   ____

   Offer a learning experience: ______________________________

   ____

   ____

6. Students determine their own physical fitness levels by completing self-directed task cards at each fitness station. The components that are tested include cardiorespiratory endurance (modified step test), muscular strength (hand grip and 10-RM knee flexion), muscular endurance (bent-knee sit-ups and flexed-arm hang), flexibility (sit-and-reach), and body composition (skinfold measurements). Students compare these exit scores with their beginning scores. A goal is established for each component for one of the following reasons: fitness gain was below expectation; no improvement was indicated; or desire to maintain a new level of fitness is present.

   Determine achievement status: ______________________________

   ____

   ____

   Facilitate learner diagnosis: ______________________________

   ____

   ____

Feedback

Possible explanations are presented. While others are equally correct, they should be similar to the ones that follow.

1. *Determine achievement status*: Students' mastery of tennis content is determined at simple and complex cognitive levels—knowledge through analysis. Students' current achievement status is indicated by the objective test.

   Indicate needed program revision or improvement: Students' response to selected test items would reveal aspects of intermediate tennis requiring more (or less) emphasis. For example, overall results might show a need to revise the learning experiences or objectives for strategy and tactics if learners' achievements were uniformly low. Results would also indicate whether students demonstrated greater competency on low-order items (recall) than on high-order items (application/analysis) or vice versa. The need for improvement in the program would be indicated where a wide discrepancy in achievement exists.

2. *Provide motivation*: Students are expected to be self-motivated to exhibit the appropriate social behaviors. This form of "values" learning places responsibility on the student to respond accordingly in the various situations created by the game.

   Enhance feedback and guidance: Through observation, the student receives direct information about affective behavior. Although the collected data are considered "high-inference," the student can be guided to more socially acceptable behavior where indicated, or reinforced for showing desirable behavior.

3. *Facilitate learner diagnosis*: Learner strengths and weaknesses are clearly revealed, and those aspects of the locomotor skill that require improvement are indicated. This new set of baseline data can then be used to determine any programming and intervention.

   Indicate needed program revision or improvement: Since each locomotor skill is evaluated separately, those that need attention are indicated. Changes in goals, objectives, and learning experiences might be suggested as they relate to each skill, including the factors within each skill.

4. *Offer a learning experience*: While students are being evaluated, they are also engaged in a meaningful learning experience. They receive one-on-one feedback during performance through peer assessment. This reciprocal learning activity also incorporates social interaction skills (e.g., acceptance, helping relationships, trust).

   Enhance feedback and guidance: Systematic assistance and information about the student's own ability is built into this form of peer evaluation. Guidance is provided by the exchange required between the student and the partner.

5. *Provide motivation*: Students should be motivated to respond by their active role in the evaluation procedure. In addition, students integrate psychomotor and cognitive learning. The use of stick figures enhances the likelihood of a positive response to the evaluation activity itself.

   Offer a learning experience: This evaluation focuses on students' opportunity to discover movement exploration concepts in an unusual way (i.e., recognition through symbols). To this extent, it serves as a learning experience. Greater emphasis is placed on the process than on the actual evaluation results.

6. *Determine achievement status*: Current fitness mastery is determined and compared with entry levels. The difference represents the degree of achievement between pre- and posttesting. Individual student goals are a natural outcome.

   Facilitate learner diagnosis: Those fitness components representing strengths and weaknesses are revealed through the self-directed process. Selected components can therefore receive programming emphasis or de-emphasis in accordance with results.

Self-Directed Activity 6.2

Evaluation descriptions are presented, followed by statements about selected factors of evaluation and measurement. As you read the statements, ask yourself the questions: Is the description related to some objective? Does the description reflect objectivity? . . . validity? . . . reliability? Is the pre-post design utilized? Does the description represent a criterion-referenced approach to measurement? Check (√) to indicate that the description satisfies the stated factor.

1. In archery, the student's shooting ability and understanding of shooting error are diagnosed. As a follow-up, the student completes a learning activity package (LAP). To measure knowledge of what causes errors, a written test is administered. The student matches "errors" (e.g., left, right, low, high) with "causes" (e.g., hips and shoulders open, anchoring high, squeezing arrow nock, moving bow hand, jerking drawing hand, dropping bow arm). In addition, the student shoots with a partner and they analyze each other's shooting form. Through the use of a performance checklist, shooting form errors are checked before shooting, causes are listed, and corrections are made after each arrow is shot.

    _____ *Reference to objective*: The evaluation instrument is congruent with the objective, "To analyze individual sport skills, the learner will match archery shooting errors and causes with 100% accuracy."

    _____ *Reliability*: A test-retest situation would yield similar results.

    _____ *Design*: Student's progress from preassessment to postassessment is indicated.

    _____ *Measurement*: The criterion-referenced standard is represented by a domain of behaviors.

2. As a measure of the student's willingness to act responsibly toward others, a record is made of whether or not desired behaviors are exhibited. The student is observed during a 15-minute practice session in gymnastics that requires spotting or assisting a partner. The behavioral criteria are: observes spotting techniques; attends to spotting role during partner's performance; makes spotting technique adjustments; spots partners of both sexes appropriately; follows directions for assisting partner; makes adjustments in assisting that help partner's performance; and assists partners of both sexes in the same way. Each criterion is rated as 5 = regularly, 4 = frequently, 3 = fairly often, 2 = seldom, or 1 = never.

    _____ *Objectivity*: Observations by two teachers would yield similar results.

    _____ *Validity*: The evaluation instrument measures whether or not the student behaves responsibly toward others.

    _____ *Design*: Student's progress from preassessment to postassessment is indicated.

    _____ *Measurement*: The criterion-referenced standard is represented by a domain of behaviors.

3. In order to measure the student's improvement in single rope jumping, a record is made of the number of consecutive jumps without error. The student jumps rope in a variety of ways to achieve the number of points and the different jumps established as the target goal. Each kind of jump is valued at 2 points. Some of the jumps are: jump on toes of both feet (60 times); jump on right foot, then left foot (15 times); rocker leap forward on left foot, leap backward on right foot (30 times); swing rope in front and side of body to form a figure 8,

alternate with 2 jumps (count of 32); move sideward right 4 steps, then left 4 steps (10 times); first person turns rope forward, second person jumps in, faces partner, and both jump (10 times); and partners stand side by side, inside hands joined, and outside hands turning rope (10 times).

_____ *Reference to objective*: The evaluation instrument is congruent with the objective, "To develop cardiorespiratory functioning, the learner will improve bench step scores by 10% following endurance-related rope jumping activities."

_____ *Objectivity*: Administration of the performance "test" by two teachers would yield similar results.

_____ *Validity*: The evaluation instrument measures whether or not the student has demonstrated improved eye-hand coordination, eye-foot coordination, rhythmic response, and spatial relationships.

_____ *Design*: Student's progress from entry to exit is revealed.

4. To measure the student's ability to apply basic principles of physical fitness, a personalized program is designed. The student selects either an individualized program, a general exercise program, or sport-leisure activities as the means of reaching fitness goals. The program design is judged in terms of fitness principles (i.e., overload, progression, specificity, activity analysis, detraining, frequency, intensity, duration). A scorecard is used to assess the degree to which the principles are reflected in the fitness program. Each principle is rated as 5 = excellent, 4 = good, 3 = satisfactory, 2 = fair, or 1 = poor.

_____ *Reference to objective*: The evaluation instrument is congruent with the objective, "To apply basic principles of physical fitness, the learner will select an alternative design and construct a personalized program that satisfactorily (4.0) reflects basic training principles."

_____ *Validity*: The evaluation instrument measures whether or not the student is interested in physical fitness maintenance.

_____ *Reliability*: Given the same set of circumstances, the student would respond similarly.

_____ *Measurement*: A norm-referenced standard is used to determine mastery levels.

5. To measure the student's skill in field hockey, a test battery of six items is administered. Separate skill tests are completed for goal shooting (straight, right, left); dribble and dodge; circular tackle and drive; fielding and drive; drive for distance; and pass. Scoring is based on either the number of successful trials or the time needed to complete a given task. In addition, a qualitative judgment is made by the teacher using a performance rating scale. The five descriptive categories range from "excellent" (e.g., superior control of stick, highly accurate timing, outstanding footwork) to "poor" (e.g., little control of stick, inaccurate timing, ineffective footwork).

_____ *Objectivity*: Administration of the test battery by two teachers would yield similar results.

_____ *Reliability*: Pretest and posttest scores would yield similar results.

_____ *Design*: Student's progress from entry to exit level is revealed.

_____ *Measurement*: A criterion-referenced standard of performance is used.

Feedback

1. Reference to objective	√	Test items are designed at the same level as the objective.
Reliability	√	Since the sample behaviors appear adequate, the test-retest results should be consistent. The student is likely to respond similarly.
Design	√	The procedure includes diagnosis and intervention (LAP) followed by an evaluation of the student's knowledge and form. This scheme illustrates the desired pre-post design.
Measurement	√	Results yield mastery levels for individual learners relative to the cognitive (knowledge and analysis) and psychomotor (shooting corrections) domains.
2. Objectivity	No	Because of the high-inference measures, observations by two teachers would probably not be similar enough to be considered *objective*. Although the procedure is clearly defined for the affective domain, the behaviors are highly interpretable.
Validity	√	The desired behaviors are directly sampled by the instrument. Thus, face validity is satisfied.
Design	No	There's no indication that the student's entry behavior was assessed. "Progress" could not be measured without such a determination.
Measurement	√	The domain of behaviors for this affective objective is specified by the instrument. In this regard, the behavioral standards are criterion-referenced.
3. Reference to objective	No	The evaluation instrument does not measure "improved cardiorespiratory functioning." Instead, a measurement procedure is described for evaluating perceptual abilities.
Objectivity	√	Since the measurement standard is quantitative, appraisals by two teachers are likely to be very similar. The number of points and different jumps makes this a low-inference measure.
Validity	√	Rope jumping is dependent on eye-hand and eye-foot coordination, rhythmic response, and spatial relationships. Therefore, the instrument possesses content validity.
Design	√	Student's improvement is measured. It may be implied that the difference is revealed between entry and exit ability.
4. Reference to objective	√	Clearly, the evaluation scorecard is directly related to the stated objective. It is designed at the same level and mastery performance is indicated.
Validity	No	A cognitive ability (application) is measured, not affective attitudes toward fitness maintenance. Willingness to design a program does not represent behavior at the interest level.
Reliability	√	This procedure would result in consistent or stable results. It is likely that the student would be able to apply the principles in the same set of circumstances. A dependable response is predicted based on the expected variability in the elicited behavior.

Measurement	No	There is no indication that the procedure shows differences among students. In fact, it provides an evaluation of individual performance. The criterion standard is directly interpretable from the established learning objective.
5. Objectivity	√	Given the combined quantitative and qualitative measures, the test battery results would be similar across different administrators. The directions and scoring are clear enough and the behaviors are refined sufficiently.
Reliability	No	Comparison of pretest and posttest scores is not an indication of reliability (similarity). Scores should actually vary markedly due to learning. A test-retest method would reveal the degree of reliability.
Design	No	Progress from entry- to exit-level ability is not included.
Measurement	No	Although mastery levels are revealed, there is no indication that a criterion-referenced standard is being used. The test battery is more norm-referenced.

Self-Directed Activity 6.3

For each of the following descriptions, indicate which evaluation technique is used by placing the appropriate letter in the space.

Evaluation techniques

A = Teacher-directed evaluation
B = Peer evaluation
C = Self-evaluation
D = Process evaluation

The first three techniques are distinguished by *who* conducts the evaluation. Where appropriate, you should select one of these techniques. However, for any description that represents an evaluation of the learning process, you should select "D" regardless of whether the evaluation is conducted by the teacher, a peer, or the student.

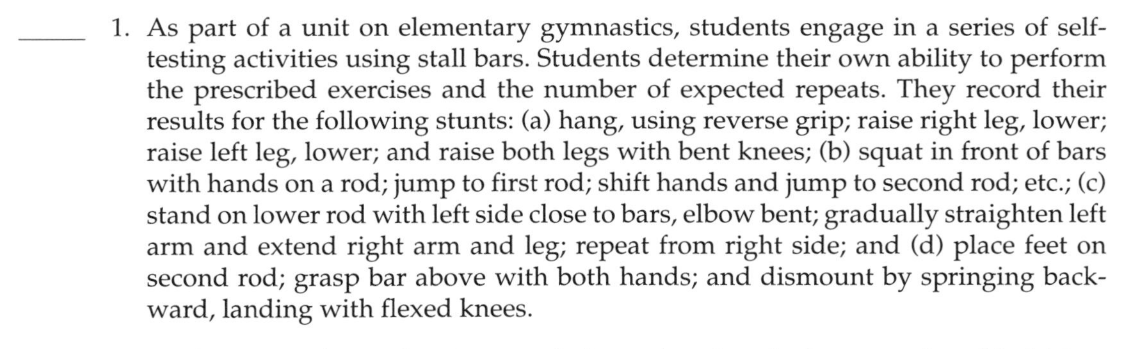

_____ 1. As part of a unit on elementary gymnastics, students engage in a series of self-testing activities using stall bars. Students determine their own ability to perform the prescribed exercises and the number of expected repeats. They record their results for the following stunts: (a) hang, using reverse grip; raise right leg, lower; raise left leg, lower; and raise both legs with bent knees; (b) squat in front of bars with hands on a rod; jump to first rod; shift hands and jump to second rod; etc.; (c) stand on lower rod with left side close to bars, elbow bent; gradually straighten left arm and extend right arm and leg; repeat from right side; and (d) place feet on second rod; grasp bar above with both hands; and dismount by springing backward, landing with flexed knees.

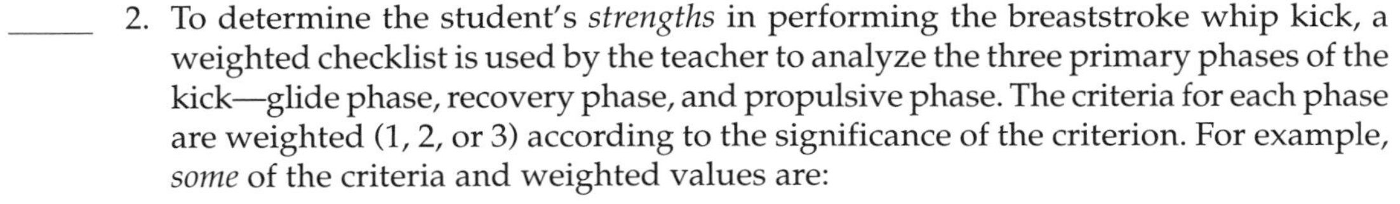

_____ 2. To determine the student's *strengths* in performing the breaststroke whip kick, a weighted checklist is used by the teacher to analyze the three primary phases of the kick—glide phase, recovery phase, and propulsive phase. The criteria for each phase are weighted (1, 2, or 3) according to the significance of the criterion. For example, *some* of the criteria and weighted values are:

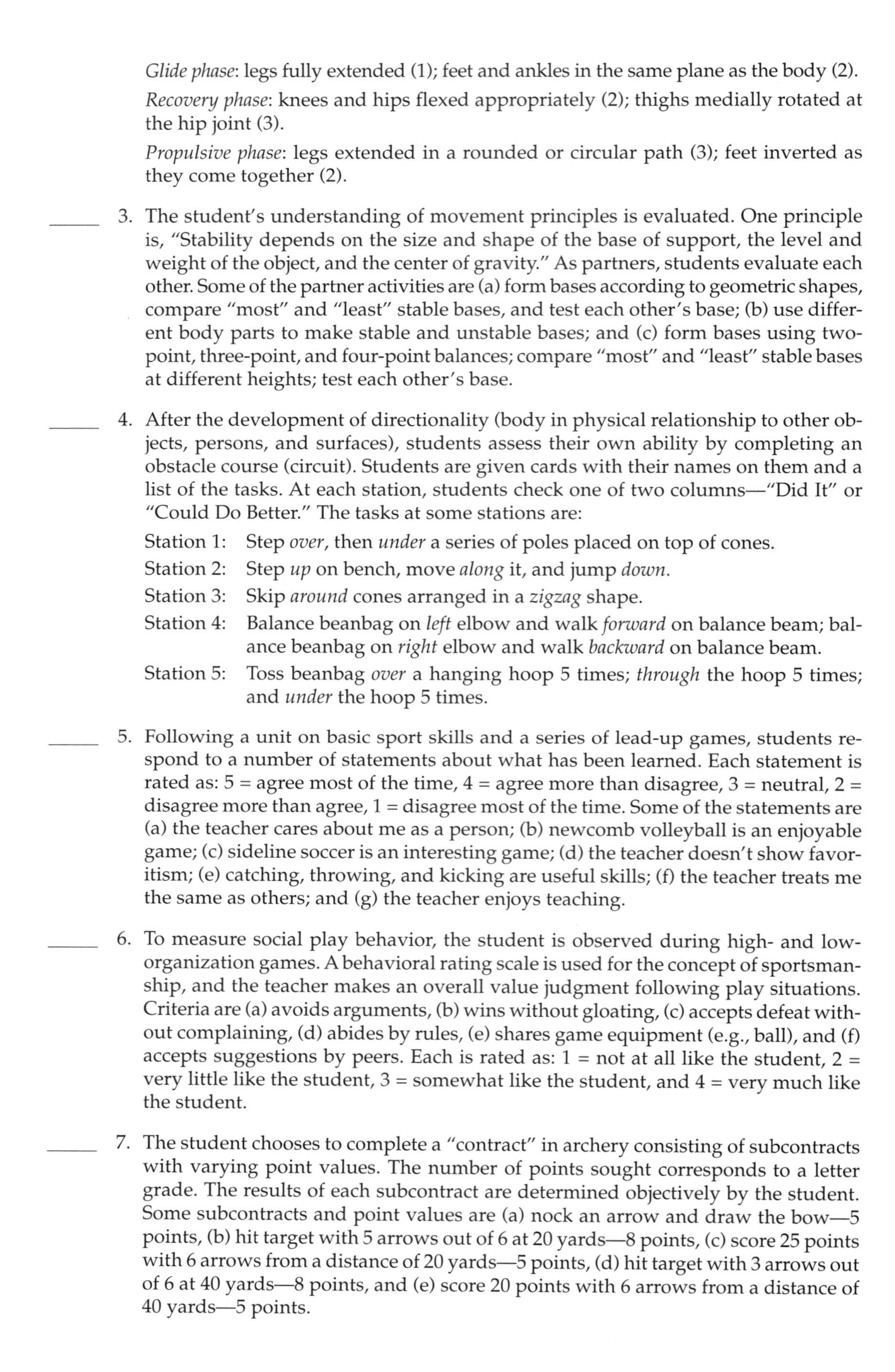

Glide phase: legs fully extended (1); feet and ankles in the same plane as the body (2).

Recovery phase: knees and hips flexed appropriately (2); thighs medially rotated at the hip joint (3).

Propulsive phase: legs extended in a rounded or circular path (3); feet inverted as they come together (2).

_____ 3. The student's understanding of movement principles is evaluated. One principle is, "Stability depends on the size and shape of the base of support, the level and weight of the object, and the center of gravity." As partners, students evaluate each other. Some of the partner activities are (a) form bases according to geometric shapes, compare "most" and "least" stable bases, and test each other's base; (b) use different body parts to make stable and unstable bases; and (c) form bases using two-point, three-point, and four-point balances; compare "most" and "least" stable bases at different heights; test each other's base.

_____ 4. After the development of directionality (body in physical relationship to other objects, persons, and surfaces), students assess their own ability by completing an obstacle course (circuit). Students are given cards with their names on them and a list of the tasks. At each station, students check one of two columns—"Did It" or "Could Do Better." The tasks at some stations are:

Station 1: Step *over*, then *under* a series of poles placed on top of cones.

Station 2: Step *up* on bench, move *along* it, and jump *down*.

Station 3: Skip *around* cones arranged in a *zigzag* shape.

Station 4: Balance beanbag on *left* elbow and walk *forward* on balance beam; balance beanbag on *right* elbow and walk *backward* on balance beam.

Station 5: Toss beanbag *over* a hanging hoop 5 times; *through* the hoop 5 times; and *under* the hoop 5 times.

_____ 5. Following a unit on basic sport skills and a series of lead-up games, students respond to a number of statements about what has been learned. Each statement is rated as: 5 = agree most of the time, 4 = agree more than disagree, 3 = neutral, 2 = disagree more than agree, 1 = disagree most of the time. Some of the statements are (a) the teacher cares about me as a person; (b) newcomb volleyball is an enjoyable game; (c) sideline soccer is an interesting game; (d) the teacher doesn't show favoritism; (e) catching, throwing, and kicking are useful skills; (f) the teacher treats me the same as others; and (g) the teacher enjoys teaching.

_____ 6. To measure social play behavior, the student is observed during high- and low-organization games. A behavioral rating scale is used for the concept of sportsmanship, and the teacher makes an overall value judgment following play situations. Criteria are (a) avoids arguments, (b) wins without gloating, (c) accepts defeat without complaining, (d) abides by rules, (e) shares game equipment (e.g., ball), and (f) accepts suggestions by peers. Each is rated as: 1 = not at all like the student, 2 = very little like the student, 3 = somewhat like the student, and 4 = very much like the student.

_____ 7. The student chooses to complete a "contract" in archery consisting of subcontracts with varying point values. The number of points sought corresponds to a letter grade. The results of each subcontract are determined objectively by the student. Some subcontracts and point values are (a) nock an arrow and draw the bow—5 points, (b) hit target with 5 arrows out of 6 at 20 yards—8 points, (c) score 25 points with 6 arrows from a distance of 20 yards—5 points, (d) hit target with 3 arrows out of 6 at 40 yards—8 points, and (e) score 20 points with 6 arrows from a distance of 40 yards—5 points.

_____ 8. The student and teacher engage in a question-answer dialogue concerning even locomotor movements (walking, running, jumping, hopping, leaping) and uneven locomotor movements (skipping, sliding, galloping). While the class is performing a series of locomotor movements to music, the student is taken aside and asked, "What's the difference between even and uneven locomotor movements?" "Why is hopping an even locomotor movement?" "Why is skipping an uneven locomotor movement?" "What is Craig doing?" "Is Mary doing an even or uneven locomotor movement?" "What movement is Bob doing?"

_____ 9. To indicate primary students' attitude toward various activities requiring manipulative skills, students complete an attitude inventory. Each item consists of a stick figure depicting the manipulation of an object. The verbal directions are, "Check the face you wear when you look at each stick figure." One face is smiling, one is frowning, and the other shows a neutral expression. The following manipulative activities are depicted: (a) ball handling, (b) rolling and catching, (c) bouncing, (d) tossing, (e) using a scoop, (f) striking, (g) kicking, (h) using a wand, (i) using a hoop, and (j) using a rope.

_____ 10. In small groups, students are hit ground balls with a softball. For each of five trials, students receive feedback from one of the group members on their fielding of the ground balls. The observer uses the following criteria: (a) knees bent when picking up ball, (b) eyes on the ball, (c) feet about shoulder-width apart, glove-side foot in front, (d) ball fielded off the glove-side foot, and (e) ball taken by the throwing hand. Each criterion is judged as: (+) = perfectly executed, (√) = satisfactorily executed, and (–) = incorrectly executed.

Feedback

1. C

   Every element refers to some form of self-evaluation (i.e., self-testing, self-determination of expected repeats, self-recording of results). Students are on their own to make critical and valid evaluations.

2. A

   Clearly, this evaluation of motor skills (breaststroke whip kick) is teacher-directed. A systematic observation technique is used for the full range of expected behavior. The criteria checklist is applied by the teacher only.

3. B

   Peer evaluation is carried out using partners. Although the criteria are applied subjectively, students are supposed to provide feedback to each other.

4. C

   The teacher-established criteria are applied by the student against his or her performance. The student makes a judgment about ability on a task continuum.

5. D

   The evaluation items and rating scale relate directly to the process of learning, including teacher qualities and specific content areas. Students' interest in and appreciation for basic sport skills and lead-up games is revealed by the questionnaire.

6. A

   The observation and recording of affective behaviors is usually conducted by the teacher because the technique is highly inferential. It's similar to maintaining an anecdotal record in the form of a rating scale. In this case, students' social play behavior is described.

7. C

   The evaluation phase of the contract is carried out by the student. Since the criteria are quantitative, results can be determined objectively by the student, who is able to realistically evaluate his or her own performance on a range of tasks.

8. A

   Through question-and-answer dialogue, the teacher can determine the student's cognitive ability (understanding of locomotor movements). This evaluation illustrates the use of verbal interaction rather than paper-and-pencil measurement.

9. D

   Results of this inventory indicate students' positive and/or negative responses to the process of learning. There is no attempt to evaluate the students' abilities. Attitude toward and value for certain manipulative skills is revealed. An avoidance response (frowning face) is likely for those activities in which the student experienced some degree of failure.

10. B

    A reciprocal teaching style is described. The teacher-established criteria are applied by the students in a small group. This form of peer evaluation goes one step further since the observer makes a value judgment regarding the *quality* of performance.

Self-Directed Activity 6.4

You should be able to devise evaluation instruments that relate to learners' needs. Identify the need represented by each stated learning objective—cognitive, affective, or psychomotor. Then, describe, illustrate, or diagram an evaluation instrument based on the content and criterion standard specified by the objective.

1. *Learning objective*: To recognize the components of expressive movements, the student will identify, with 80% accuracy, the characteristics of various dances in terms of rhythmic patterns, locomotor movements, nonlocomotor movements, dance steps, and floor patterns.

   Need: ______________________________

   Evaluation instrument:

2. *Learning objective*: To develop self-control and self-discipline, the student will maintain task persistence at self-directed physical fitness learning stations during at least 75% of practice time.

   Need: ______________________________

   Evaluation instrument:

3. *Learning objective*: To demonstrate improved complex adaptive skills in basketball, the student will perform the jump shot, while uncontested, at a level for "form" and "accuracy" that is 20% higher than the learner's preassessment level.

   Need: ______________________________

   Evaluation instrument:

4. *Learning objective*: To share in common movement goals, the student will exhibit a positive working relationship with others by displaying predominantly cooperative behaviors during group activities.

   Need: ______________________________

   Evaluation instrument:

5. *Learning objective*: To demonstrate that he or she values physical activity as a leisure activity, the student will respond favorably on an attitude scale regarding the benefits of physical activity.

   Need: ______________________________

   Evaluation instrument:

Feedback

1. *Cognitive*

   Dance movements have many characteristics that distinguish one dance from another. The student could observe demonstrations of various dances and complete a checklist including the range of characteristics. For example, the student might observe four dances. Using the following chart, the student would indicate the components of each dance by checking the characteristics that apply. The characteristics are organized as rhythmic patterns, locomotor movements, nonlocomotor movements, dance steps, and floor patterns. Accuracy percentage is based on the number of correct responses.

Name of dance:

Rhythmic patterns	Locomotor movements	Nonlocomotor movements	Dance steps	Floor patterns
___ Even	___ Walk	___ Bend/Stretch	___ Grapevine	___ ○
___ Uneven	___ Run	___ Twist/Turn	___ 3/4 run	___ □
	___ Leap	___ Swing/Sway	___ Step-hop	___ │
	___ Hop	___ Push/Pull	___ Schottische	___ 〰
	___ Jump	___ Clap/Stomp	___ Mazurka	___ ⦚
	___ Gallop		___ Polka	___ ‖
	___ Skip		___ Waltz balance	___ ◎
	___ Slide		___ Waltz	___ ×
			___ Two-step	___ △

2. *Affective (emotional)*

The student could be observed during practice episodes at the learning stations. A record could be maintained indicating time on-task versus time off-task. Exemplary on-task and off-task behaviors relating to self-control and self-discipline are listed. Beginning and ending times for on-task behavior are recorded, and time intervals are calculated. The percent of task persistence is reflected by the amount of time on-task.

On-task

Behaviors: determines beginning ability; selects achievement level; completes tasks in sequence; follows directions; seeks help; maintains diligence

Begin time	End time		Interval
________	________	=	________
________	________	=	________
________	________	=	________
________	________	=	________
________	________	=	________
	Total time:		________

Off-task

Behaviors: daydreams; bothers other learners; ignores directions; completes tasks out of sequence; shows limited intensity; is easily distracted from tasks

Begin time	End time		Interval
________	________	=	________
________	________	=	________
________	________	=	________
________	________	=	________
________	________	=	________
	Total time:		________

3. *Psychomotor*

   An evaluation instrument is suggested that includes a rating scale for form and accuracy. For example, the student is randomly assigned to four areas as shown in the following diagram, two each from areas A to E and F to J. Five trials (jump shots) are taken from each of the four areas. *Form* is evaluated on the following scale: 3 = executed perfectly, 2 = acceptable, 1 = needs improvement, and 0 = executed incorrectly. Accuracy is evaluated as: 3 = basket made, 2 = ball hits rim, 1 = ball hits backboard, and 0 = ball misses everything. Thus, the maximum score for each trial is 6; maximum score for each area is 30; and maximum test score is 120. A comparison is made between preassessment and postassessment scores to reveal percent improvement.

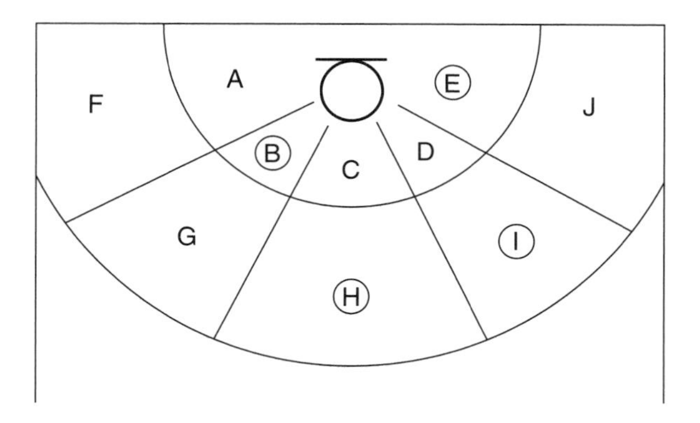

4. *Affective (social)*

   Anecdotal records could be maintained in the form of a behavioral checklist indicating the degree to which cooperative behaviors were exhibited. The checklist that follows would be completed for individual students following group activities. The *predominant* display of behaviors could be revealed by a frequency index that would indicate whether or not the desired behaviors were elicited more often than not. For example, the student is observed three times. Observed frequency is recorded for each of the behaviors. The value for each frequency level is indicated at the top. Each column total is used to determine the overall total. The frequency index is calculated as shown. An index above 1.0 would indicate a predominance of cooperative behaviors.

	Observation frequency		
Behaviors	Most of the time (2)	Fairly often/ Sometimes (1)	Seldom/ Never (0)
1. Chooses a partner who is close to him or her rather than seeking out a friend	______	______	______
2. Abides by rules and calls own infractions	______	______	______
3. Gives opponent the ball or object	______	______	______
4. Contributes to the success of others	______	______	______
5. Shares space as necessary to give equal opportunity to others	______	______	______
6. Encourages the efforts of teammates	______	______	______
7. Includes all participants in group activities	______	______	______
8. Plays his or her own areas offensively and defensively	______	______	______
9. Shows concern for the safety and well-being of others	______	______	______
10. Contributes positively to the common goals of the group	______	______	______
Column totals:	______ +	______ +	______ =

Overall total: ______ ÷ 10 = Frequency index ______

5. *Affective (values)*

   In order to assess attitude toward physical activity, the student could be asked to consider a number of concepts representing the benefits of physical activity. Attitudes are measured by the student's responses to pairs of adjectives that indicate how he or she feels most of the time about the given concept. This form of measurement—semantic differential—uses bipolar adjective pairs that represent certain dimensions such as evaluation (good/bad), potency (strong/weak), and activity (fast/slow). "Semantic spaces" are created between the pairs so the respondent can indicate the degree of feeling. For example, for each of the concepts that follow, the learner indicates how he or she feels according to particular adjective pairs. This scale provides seven (7) "spaces." The values for each space are identified and a total score can be derived. An average score above 4.0 would reveal a positive attitude.

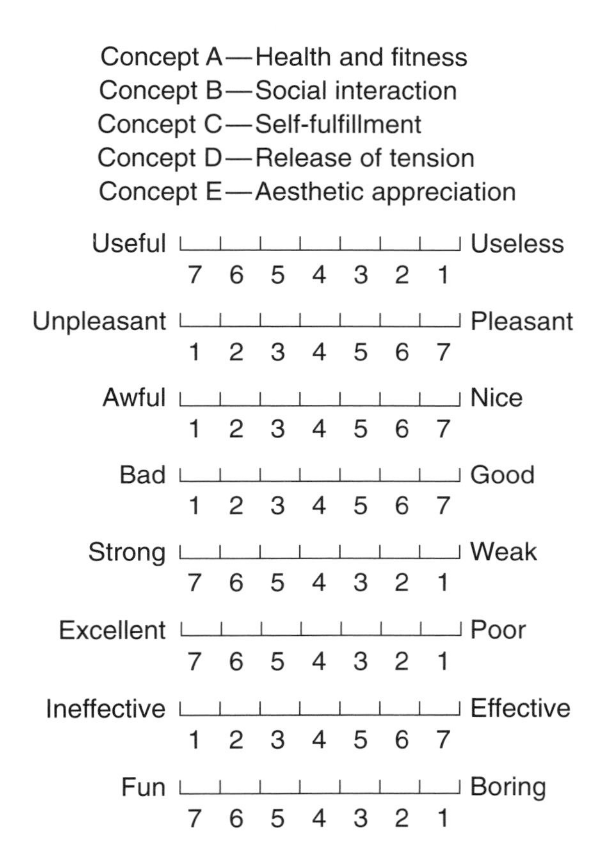

Concept A—Health and fitness
Concept B—Social interaction
Concept C—Self-fulfillment
Concept D—Release of tension
Concept E—Aesthetic appreciation
Useful 7 6 5 4 3 2 1 Useless
Unpleasant 1 2 3 4 5 6 7 Pleasant
Awful 1 2 3 4 5 6 7 Nice
Bad 1 2 3 4 5 6 7 Good
Strong 7 6 5 4 3 2 1 Weak
Excellent 7 6 5 4 3 2 1 Poor
Ineffective 1 2 3 4 5 6 7 Effective
Fun 7 6 5 4 3 2 1 Boring

Self-Directed Activity 6.5

Ideally, you now understand the nature of authentic assessment and the use of portfolios. You should also be able to see how a system of authentic assessment might operate. The questions below relate to these characteristics and to the application of authentic assessment to physical education.

1. Why is authentic assessment a more viable alternative to conventional forms of evaluation?

   ____

   ____

   ____

   ____

2. Assuming that portfolios are applicable to physical education settings, what kinds of information would you include in a portfolio, specific to physical education?

   ____

   ____

   ____

   ____

3. What features of the *work sampling system* would you find useful in developing evaluation procedures in physical education?

   ____

   ____

   ____

   ____

Feedback

1. Authentic assessment offers an alternative to highly inferential estimates of learning such as those found with conventional, norm-referenced measures and standardized tests. It is more effective for reporting actual or real-life accomplishments on an ongoing basis and presents a more genuine picture of student learning. Authentic assessment also documents student learning across a full range of social, emotional, physical, and academic performance indicators.
2. With reference to portfolio development, the range of information sources in physical education is extensive. Your response should reveal your own preferences and values. Obviously, there is no single correct answer. However, your choices of information were probably derived from three methods; i.e., observations, performance samples, and tests and testlike procedures. The specific kinds of information may be similar to the examples identified in Table 6.1 (page 176).
3. Here again, your response will reflect your own value orientation. It may be that aspects of each component—developmental checklists, portfolio collection, and summary reports—would be useful to you. Whatever features you identified, a *system* for structuring, organizing, and managing evaluation is needed.

7

Devising Learning Experiences

Key Concept

Curriculum designers achieve objectives through learning experiences that develop the intended student outcomes.

Because of budget cuts in the school district, one of the elementary physical education teachers is reassigned to the high school. He soon learns that the high school staff is somewhat laid-back. For the most part, students go through some drills and then play games. His attempt to use partners and cooperative learning groups is laughed at by some of the teachers behind his back. And some students complain, "We didn't do it this way before!" Not everyone likes his individualized approaches. He tries to use problem solving, learning activity packets, and computer-assisted instruction as much as possible. The dilemma he faces is whether to continue doing what he thinks is best or to change to the high school system—one which he feels is a "throw out the ball" approach.

Expected Outcomes

This chapter helps you devise learning experiences for your curriculum design. Upon completing it, you will be able to

- indicate the structures of learning experiences in terms of the types of model/information communication and the types of content interaction,
- formulate learning experiences that relate to learner needs (cognitive, affective, and psychomotor),
- compare various instructional options that offer the qualities of individualization,
- match descriptions with various approaches that represent the concept of individualization,
- identify the critical characteristics of interactive learning experiences,
- differentiate among learning experiences representing various approaches to interaction (reciprocal learning, role playing, simulation, cooperative learning),
- judge the degree to which learning experiences satisfy fundamental criteria for selection, and
- describe learning experiences that are effective for accommodating "special" learners (culturally diverse, at risk, gifted and talented).

Previously, you answered the question "Where are you going?" In chapter 6, you answered the question "How will you know you've arrived?" by developing evaluation procedures. The question "How will you get there?" is treated last because its answer will complete the curriculum design process and lead directly to the planning phase of instruction. The curriculum design model in Figure 7.1 shows this last step, *devising learning experiences*. Students must be given the opportunity to interact with the environment so that intended knowledge, understandings, attitudes, values, and physical skills can be acquired.

Organizing centers, content goals, and learning objectives represent the *ends* to be attained. They provide useful criteria for determining *how* these ends will be satisfied. Essentially, learning occurs when students engage in active behavior—learning experiences. *Students have learning experiences; teachers have methods*. Therefore, several questions arise. "What are learning experiences?" "How are learning experiences structured?" "How can learning experiences be individualized?" "Can learning experiences foster interaction among learners?" "On what basis are learning experiences selected?" Answers to these questions are provided in the following sections. Ultimately, you should be able to devise learning experiences for your own physical education curriculum.

Achieving Intended Outcomes

In designing the curriculum to achieve intended outcomes, you face the critical decision of what learning experiences to provide. Before doing so, however, you should know what learning experiences are and how they are structured. A definition is offered and a structure for learning experiences is suggested that includes model/information communication and content interaction. Deciding on learning experiences should also be influenced by the desire to satisfy student needs and to establish a direct relationship between learning experiences and cognitive, affective, and psychomotor needs.

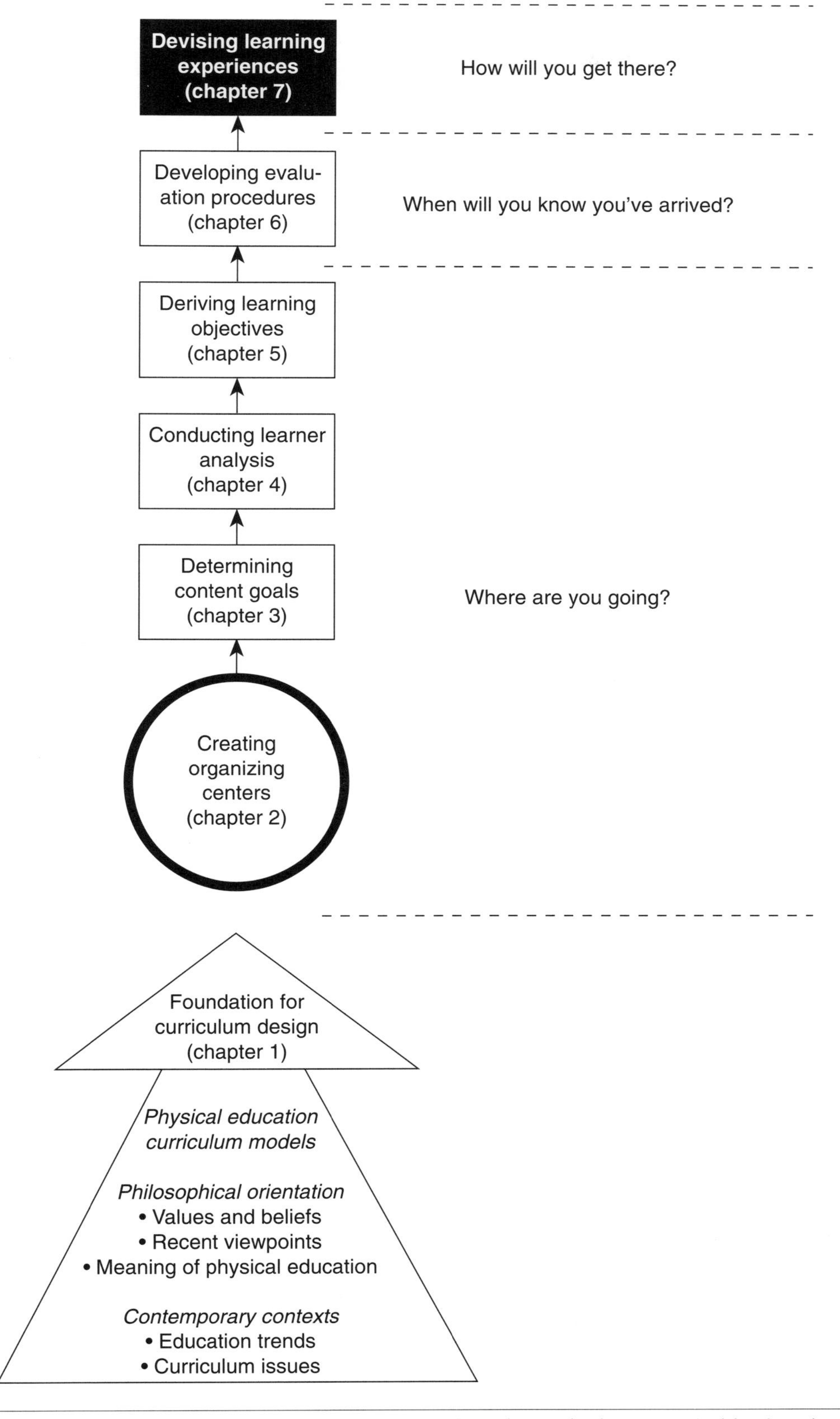

Figure 7.1 Model for designing the physical education curriculum shows the last step, *devising learning experiences*.

Learning Experiences Defined

Learning experiences are the interactions between students and the external conditions found in the environment. They should evoke the desired responses (behavioral changes) in students or exemplify some cultural or psychological value. Learning experiences are considered *valid* if they create the intended outcomes—knowledge, understandings, normative social behaviors, self-reliance, attitudes, values, and physical skills. The ultimate criterion for judging a learning experience is that this activity or instructional intervention actually creates the desired responses.

This definition is consistent with *developmentally appropriate practices* in physical education. In fact, several of these practices refer directly to the link between experience and outcome, as described here (Graham, Castenada, Hopple, Manross, & Sanders, 1992):

Cognitive Development. Experiences are provided that encourage students to question, integrate, analyze, communicate, and apply cognitive concepts, as well as to gain a multicultural view of the world.

Affective Development. Activities are intentionally designed and taught which allow students to work together for the purpose of improving their emerging social and cooperation skills, develop a positive self-concept, and experience and feel the satisfaction and joy resulting from regular participation in physical activity.

Development of Movement Concepts and Motor Skills. Frequent, meaningful, and age-appropriate practice opportunities are provided that enable students to develop a functional understanding of movement concepts (body awareness, space awareness, effort, relationships) and to build competence and confidence in their ability to perform a variety of motor skills (locomotor, nonlocomotor, and manipulative).

Concepts of Fitness. Students participate in activities designed to help them understand and value the important concepts of physical fitness and the contribution these concepts make to a healthy lifestyle.

Structure of Learning Experiences

Devising learning experiences can be a demanding task. A framework is needed to help you structure them. Consistency is fostered if a common structure is used for evoking the desired responses in students.

In order to simplify the task, a structure is suggested here that consists of *model/information communication* and *content interaction* (Hurwitz, 1985). Although various labels are given to different kinds of learning experiences (e.g., exploration, self-directed tasks, contracting), *all* learning experiences, regardless of what they are called, contain some form of model/information communication *and* content interaction.

Model/Information Communication

This component consists of either the demonstration and/or explanation of processes, skills, procedures, values, or attitudes to be learned, or the presentation and/or explanation of facts, concepts, principles, or materials that students will learn or deal with. The sources and types of model/information communication are shown in Figure 7.2. Examples in physical education are

- demonstration of the soccer dribble by a student,
- a task sheet with diagrams of flexibility exercises and explanations,
- presentation by the teacher of the characteristics of the 2-1-2 zone defense in basketball, or
- demonstration of the "observer" role in a small-group learning station for the tennis serve.

Content Interaction

This component describes how students are actually involved in dealing with skills, procedures, values, attitudes, facts, concepts, principles, or materials as they attempt to meet learning objectives. The types of content interaction and associated learning factors are shown in Figure 7.3 (page 200). Examples in physical education are

- relay drills in which the students dribble a soccer ball,
- flexibility exercises completed as described on a task sheet,
- "walk-through" 2-1-2 zone defense in basketball followed by "full-speed" practice, or
- feedback from a peer based on a criteria checklist for the tennis serve.

▶ ***To test your understanding of learning experiences and their structure, complete Self-Directed Activity 7.1 at the end of this chapter.***

Learner Needs

Learning experiences suggested by the goal, behavior, and content aspects of learning objectives should

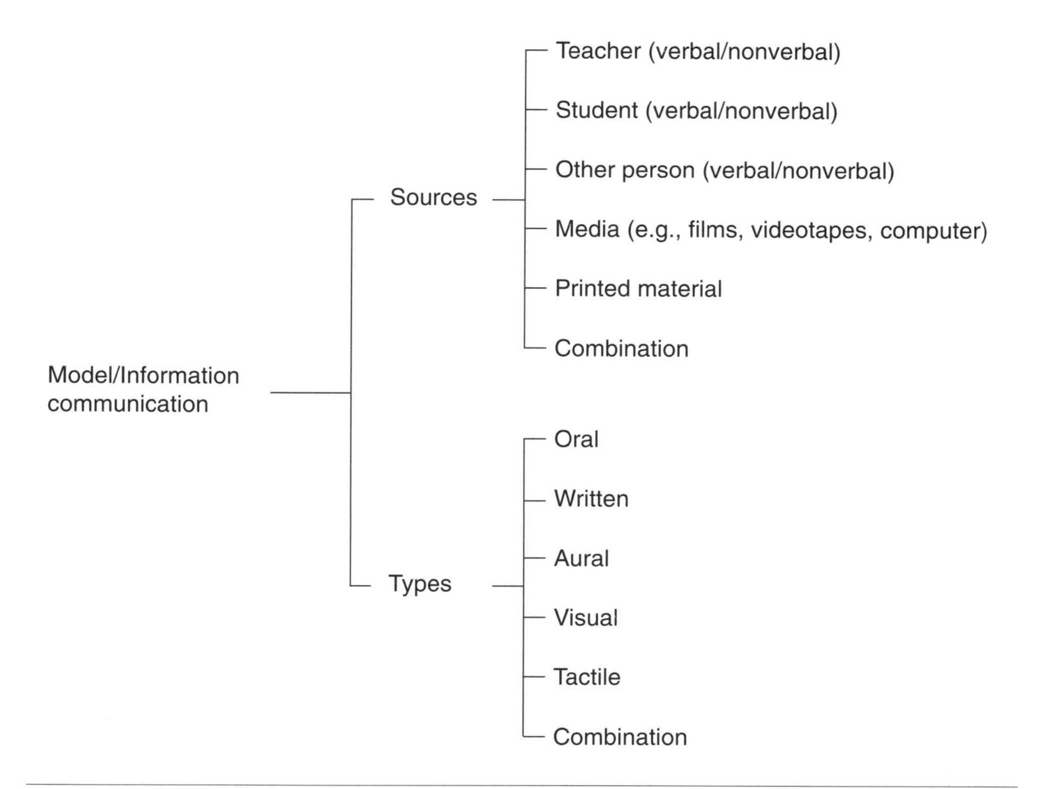

Figure 7.2 Sources and types of model/information communication are identified.
From *The Hurwitz Instructional Strategy Model (HISM)* by R. Hurwitz, 1993, unpublished manuscript, Cleveland State University. Adapted by permission of the author.

result in explicit learning. Because of the interdependent nature of learners' needs, it is difficult to isolate learning experiences for this purpose, but it is not impossible. One of the best models illustrating learning based on needs is the "spectrum of styles" (Mosston & Ashworth, 1986). Physical responses, social interaction, emotional growth, and cognitive involvement are developed through a series of learning experiences that shift decision making from the teacher to the student. Learning is facilitated in all *developmental channels* (needs) through the various styles—command, practice, reciprocal, self-check, inclusion, guided discovery, divergent, and individual program.

The physical channel involves the exploration of movement and the identification of individual physical capacities and limitations. In the cognitive channel, the student is concerned with remembering, projecting, drawing conclusions, judging information, and thinking creatively. The social channel includes interpersonal and intergroup practices. Physical self-concept and individual self-image emerge through the emotional channel. Examples of learning experiences of the various styles are presented later in this chapter.

Explicit learning experiences are formulated from the kind of behavior specified by the learning objective and the content to which the behavior is applied. To illustrate this relationship, learning experiences are described on pages 201 to 202 that correspond to cognitive, affective, and psychomotor objectives. The descriptions include model/information communication and content interaction.

▶ ***To gain experience in developing explicit learning experiences that match students' needs and corresponding objectives, including model/information communication and content interaction, complete Self-Directed Activity 7.2 at the end of this chapter.***

Individualization Pattern

Educators have long been concerned about the problem of compensating for the physiological, psychological, and sociological differences among students, and of providing experiences that meet the needs inherent in these differences. Given the stated meaning of physical education, the concept of *individualization* serves as a guiding principle.

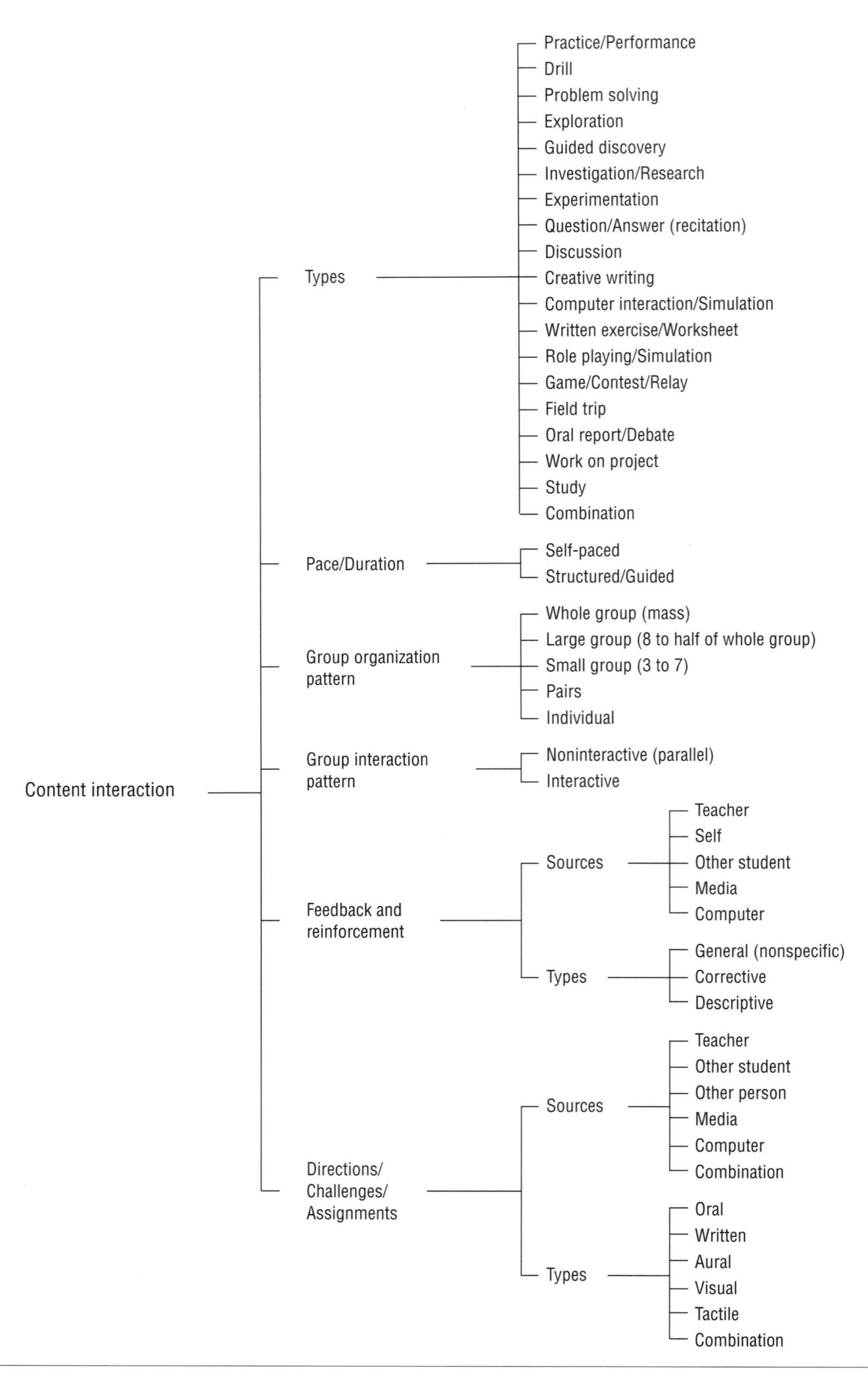

Figure 7.3 Types of content interaction and various learning factors associated with content interaction are identified.
From *The Hurwitz Instructional Strategy Model (HISM)* by R. Hurwitz, 1993, unpublished manuscript, Cleveland State University. Adapted by permission of the author.

Learning Experiences Based on Needs

Need	***Learning objective***
Cognitive	To demonstrate an understanding of basic directional movements and levels of movement, the student will use general and personal space appropriately at least 80% of the time.

Learning experience

Model/Information communication: Teacher will show the difference between general and personal space and demonstrate one direction and one level of movement.

Content interaction: Student will engage in the following activities: (1) practice running, leaping, landing, and rolling on his or her own mat; (2) show changes of direction and level by moving forward, backward, and sideways using rolls, locomotor movements, and balances; and (3) make up a sequence for traveling along the mats in different directions and levels.

Need	***Learning objective***
Affective (social)	To demonstrate an ability to function in harmony with others (teamwork), the student will exhibit approach behaviors and avoidance behaviors at a ratio of not less than 4 to 1 by sharing responsibility for reaching common movement goals while using an elastic rope.

Learning experience

Model/Information communication: Teacher will explain what it means to "share responsibility" and present one sample movement goal.

Content interaction: Student will respond to various challenges to his or her group (4–5 learners), including: (1) use different body parts to stretch the rope while forming different body shapes, geometric shapes, spatial designs, numerals, and letters; (2) use different body parts as bases of support; and (3) use two students to stretch rope into different shapes and have others leap over it; jump into it; leap into it; and jump into it, take a step, and leap out of it.

Need	***Learning objective***
Affective (emotional)	To gain self-understanding and appreciation, the student will determine his or her own ability to perform the volleyball bump pass by completing all progressive levels of an individualized worksheet.

Learning experience

Model/Information communication: Students will be used to demonstrate the bump pass; a worksheet will be discussed and clarified.

Content interaction: Student will use an individualized worksheet to evaluate his or her own performance in the following progressive levels: (1) partner drop, single bump pass; (2) self-toss, single bump pass; (3) wall rebound, single bump pass; (4) partner underhand toss, single bump pass; (5) self-toss, multiple bump passes (2–5); (6) wall rebound, multiple bump passes (2–5); (7) partner overhand throw (half force), single bump pass; and (8) partner overhand throw (half force), multiple bump passes (2–5). Criteria are (1) movement starts from ready position, (2) movement results in "creating time," and (3) ball comes down within self-space or on target.

Need	Learning objective
Affective (values)	To show a preference for maintaining physical fitness during leisure time, the student will, given a variety of choices, develop and use a personalized fitness program as indicated by an overall increase of 25% in use of leisure time from the beginning of the 6-week program.

Learning experience

Model/Information communication: Teacher will outline advantages and disadvantages of various uses of leisure time; a learning activity packet will be handed out which shows how to develop a personalized fitness program.

Content interaction: Student will engage in the following sequence: (1) plot a personal physical fitness profile summarizing his or her ratings in the various aspects of fitness; (2) generate specific physical fitness goals based on areas of concern, needed improvement, or maintenance; (3) select individualized programs, general exercise programs, and sports/leisure activities that he or she enjoys in terms of their contribution to fitness goals; and (4) design a personal fitness program based on fitness goals, selection of programs/activities, and schedule of programs/activities.

Need	Learning objective
Psychomotor	To demonstrate compound adaptive skills in basketball, the student will dribble to a one-count stop and rear pivot with at least an 80% rating for form on a criteria rating scale.

Learning experience

Model/Information communication: A videotape will be viewed that shows the stop and pivot; teacher will review the task card and procedures for getting a partner.

Content interaction: Student will complete the following tasks: (1) students select partners, (2) each partner takes two sets of 10 stops and pivots, (3) partner checks criteria on a task card for the stop (both feet hit floor at same time, wide base, knees flexed, tail dropped, on balance) and the pivot (knees flexed, ball protected, pivot foot heel raised, step with the nonpivot foot), and (4) switch roles after each set.

Individualization is the way in which students can engage in experiences suited to their unique characteristics.

Individualization should not be viewed as a method of instruction. Rather, a sufficient number of alternatives is provided so that a match can be made between the learning experience and each student's interests, abilities, achievement level, and preferred learning style. Individualization is a way of learning in which "ends" and "means" are interwoven through the respective roles of the teacher and the student. Obviously, students vary significantly in their needs and they come to school with diverse backgrounds, attitudes, motivations, behavior patterns, and experiences. In recognition of this diversity, the qualities of individualization are examined here and various approaches to individualization are illustrated.

Qualities of Individualization

The curriculum designer is obligated both ethically and educationally to devise learning experiences that can be matched with students' interests, abilities, achievement levels, and preferred learning styles. To meet this obligation, individual differences and similarities must be respected when planning learning experiences. This quality is realized through diagnostic-prescriptive learning experiences. That is, the strengths and weaknesses of each student are continuously examined and learning tasks are prescribed accordingly.

The diagnostic data generated through entry appraisal should be transferred into relevant learning experiences that will result in desired behavioral changes. This link to intended outcomes means that individualized experiences are dependent on objectives related to individual talents, needs, interests, and abilities. Individualized and nonindividualized learning objectives were differentiated in chapter 5 (page 144). It follows that the learning experiences suggested by such objectives would also be individualized.

Individualized approaches should include a wide variety of materials, individual student-teacher interaction, student selection of materials, student self-pacing, and both individual and group opportunities. The latter aspect consists of interaction between the teacher and the student (one-on-one) and between the teacher and small groups.

Finally, the individualized learning experience should incorporate a method of learning that truly permits individual pursuit of a given objective. Usually, four individualization options are available to the curriculum designer: varying the pace, providing content choices, developing alternatives on the basis of difficulty, and creating learning style choices.

Pace Options

This method permits students to decide how quickly or slowly they can learn. Student-controlled pacing often requires rigorous systems of assessment and record keeping in order to maintain

Students are engaged in self-directed learning activities.

integrity and efficiency. Self-paced programming is almost a necessity when individualizing learning experiences. Its importance is recognized, for example, as a feature of the IEP (individualized education plan) for students with disabilities.

The opportunities for self-pacing in physical education are endless. For example, students might be given a series of progressive tasks to perform, and assume responsibility for indicating the date in the "I Have Achieved" column as each task is accomplished. At certain intervals, the student indicates the status of each task in the "Working to Achieve" column. To maintain integrity, students should know that results will be randomly verified through some form of teacher assessment.

Elementary students could practice developmental skills at different assigned stations without regard for overall time or the time it takes for other students to move from station to station. Even warm-up exercise routines could be self-paced if students were permitted to complete the exercises at their own rates rather than in cadence with others.

Content Options

Students can experience different content under the same basic topic or theme. For example, the student may be expected to choose one of the distance arcs marked on the floor and complete one of three task cards for the basketball jump shot. The student obtains information from the selected task card that describes either the jump shot off a dribble, the jump shot behind a screen, or the jump shot off a pass. Content options may also be illustrated for a unit organized around a lifetime sports theme. The options might include archery, bowling, golf, racquetball, and tennis. Each student might be expected to select two of four sports.

Level-of-Difficulty Options

Establishing alternative tracks according to difficulty is particularly suited to individualization. There is no reason to develop a separate curriculum or to segregate students where different mastery levels exist. The implementation of this option depends on students' entry-level characteristics. Learning experiences that consider level of difficulty normally include a task sequence (page 105) or remedial loop (page 100), or both. In this case, provision is made for students to begin learning at different points along a learning continuum.

Learning Style Options

Another set of individualizing options emerges when consideration is given to how each student prefers to learn. Alternatives should be provided, to the degree possible, as long as students don't take advantage of them by avoiding participation in games or challenging tasks. Some of these learning style options are described.

Medium of Instruction. Some students prefer listening and responding to the teacher and other students, while others prefer interacting with printed materials such as task cards, worksheets, problems to solve, and programmed learning. Films, slides, transparencies, videotapes, and film loops provide another dimension. Adding sound to visual presentations offers still another option. As students are encouraged to select from alternative presentations—interactive, oral, visual, tactile—their motivation, attention, and perseverance in learning may be increased.

Grouping and Interaction Patterns. Some students prefer to learn as members of a large group. Others opt for interaction and activity as members of a small group. Still others prefer learning through individual study or in a tutorial setting with a peer or teacher.

Structure. Some students prefer learning in small increments with frequent feedback and reward or correction. Other students learn better when they are free to develop ideas and investigate alternatives with less supervision. These students respond well to divergent or problem-solving activities that permit them to structure tasks themselves.

▶ ***To practice differentiating among various options for individualization, complete Self-Directed Activity 7.3 at the end of this chapter.***

Approaches to Individualization

A commitment to individualization places demands of time and creative effort on the curriculum designer. This section categorizes, describes, and illustrates various approaches to individualized learning. These approaches can be as simple as giving students the chance to decide at which station to begin an obstacle course or as complex as computer-assisted learning. The approach to individualization will vary according to teacher preference and degree of application in the local setting. On pages 205 to 211, various approaches are identified and defined, and corresponding learning experiences are described that serve as a guide to individualization.

▶ ***To practice recognizing various approaches to individualized learning, complete Self-Directed Activity 7.4 at the end of this chapter.***

Individualized Learning Approaches

	Approach	Description
1.	Exploration	Movement tasks are broad in nature with no particular anticipated response. Students are encouraged to examine, investigate, and seek out a variety of responses. Experimentation is beneficial at any level of learning. A problem-solving situation is presented where the teacher poses increasingly more challenging movement problems that are solved by each student in his or her own unique way.

Sample learning experience

Student is directed to:

1. Take a beanbag to a space and hop around your beanbag.
2. Jump forward over your beanbag. "What other directions do you know?" "Show me!"
3. Make a pattern moving around your beanbag using different directions. Make up a new sequence . . . with a partner if you like.
4. Now, make a bridge with your body over the beanbag. Make a different bridge using other parts of your body. Make more than one bridge.
5. Find ways of making your beanbag travel through the arches of your bridges.

	Approach	Description
2.	Self-directed tasks	Students pursue their own learning tasks until their objectives are reached. A range of learning tasks (task continuum) can accommodate the individual student's range of capability. Tasks will vary in the amount of self-determination and independence according to the teacher/learner relationship and corresponding transactions.

Sample learning experience

Student completes the following tasks:

1. View the videotape showing the two-hand set in volleyball.
2. Take a volleyball and select one of the wall stations.
3. Stand behind the line. Throw the ball over your head.
4. Use the two-hand set technique to make the ball travel 10–15 feet in the air toward the wall. Ball should take an arch so that it just skims or touches the wall above the 8-foot line.
5. After doing part of the task, return to the videotape for additional information or insight. Then, return to the task.
6. Do the two-hand set 25 times.

	Approach	Description
3.	Guided discovery	Student is led through a carefully planned sequence of questions, clues, or tasks arranged so that the student's response is always reinforced until the correct target response is "discovered." A *convergent* thinking process is used since the discovery is directed toward a predetermined answer or movement response. The teacher's role is to guide the learner from one step to the next, thus ensuring success in learning.

Sample learning experience

Student is asked the following series of questions, each of which is followed by the student's response and the teacher's acceptance or reinforcement of that response (Mosston & Ashworth, 1986):

1. What is the main purpose of putting the shot?
2. What is needed to achieve distance?
3. What else?
4. In the total motion of putting the shot, *where* should the power and speed reach their maximum?
5. Where would be the point of minimum strength and speed?
6. In order to achieve the maximum strength and speed at the point of release, how far from this point should the starting position be?

	Approach	Description
4.	Problem solving	A task or question is designed and the student proceeds through experimentation and/or logical thinking to determine answers or solutions. The problem should allow the student to choose the best of the alternative solutions. This process of *divergent* thinking creates and promotes independence of solutions by individuals. Facts, skills, concepts, relationships, and preferences, as well as validity, limits, variations, and strategies can be learned through problem solving.

Sample learning experience

Student attempts to solve the following soccer problems pertaining to body-ball relationships in motion (Mosston & Ashworth, 1986):

1. What parts of the upper body can be used to move the ball from point A to point B?
2. Which parts of the lower body can accomplish similar results?
3. Which parts can move the ball from point A to point B, keeping the ball rolling on the ground?
4. Which parts can move the ball from point A to point B, getting the ball slightly off the ground?
5. Which parts can move the ball, getting the ball to fly above your own height?
6. Is there another part of the body that can accomplish what you did in 3, 4, and 5?
7. Which of the above parts of the body moved the ball the farthest? The shortest? The highest? Do you know why those things happened?
8. Which parts can move the ball in a straight line? Along a curved line?

	Approach	Description
5.	Contracting	Diagnosis is needed to establish an agreement between the teacher and the student regarding the expected quantity and quality of work, standard of performance, and time period required to complete the task. The student knows that the task is within his or her capability because of the diagnosis. Students are allowed to vary the time period, work at their own ability levels, select many and varied learning experiences according to interests, and work independently.

Sample learning experience

Student decides when to complete various items for a particular grade. Failure to meet the required percentage means that the grade will be based on the number achieved. A lower grade will be received if items are not completed on time. For example, a contract for a "B" might be:

1. Play three sets of tennis on different days.
2. Stroke 15 forehands and 15 backhands.
3. Serve 15 serves to both courts.
4. Interview one tennis team player. Watch the player in a practice session or match.
5. Score 75% on all quizzes (skill and written).
6. Complete a videotape analysis of your form in tennis.
7. Miss no more than two classes (serious illness excepted).

Any two items must be completed by the last class day in March, April, and May, respectively.

	Approach	Description
6.	Programmed learning	Material to be learned is divided into a large number of small steps and each step is reinforced when the presentation of an appropriate stimulus evokes a correct response. A task is offered at various levels of possible engagement. After its execution, the student determines the standard of his or her performance through self-assessment. The student makes decisions concerning starting, stopping, pacing, posture, and self-assessment (pre and post). Individually prescribed instruction and computer-assisted instruction are included.

Sample learning experience

In the following task, find out what your *maximum* (M) is today. Some of the tasks below will be repeated in different quantities. These will be in sets consisting of parts of your maximum (Mosston & Ashworth, 1986).

Tasks	Present M	X(y/M)	New M
Short sprints:			
1. Find out your maximum speed for 100 yards.	12 seconds		
2. Run the distance several times (*X*) at 3/4 speed (*y*). Rest intervals between attempts are 30 seconds.		6(3/4M)	
3. Run the distance several times (*X*) at 1/2 speed (*y*). Rest intervals are 15–20 seconds.		6(1/2M)	
4. Find your maximum speed for 50 yards.			
5. Run several 50s at 3/4 speed with 15-second intervals.			
6. Check your new maximum speed for 100 yards.			?

	Approach	Description
7.	Learning Activity Package (LAP)	Activity units are systematically designed to be virtually self-teaching. They are used by a student to supplement teacher instruction. Packets are organized to facilitate the learning of a skill, concept, generalization, or significant problem, while providing substantial opportunity for learning options. A progressive series of open and closed skill tasks and cognitive activities may require written, verbal, or movement responses.

Sample learning experience

A sample format is outlined below for an "Individualized Instructional Packet" (IIP) (Annarino, 1973):

I. Cover page (title, level, designers, school, date)

II. Table of contents (major headings, subheadings, page numbers)

III. Introduction

- A. Rationale (statement of reasons, purposes, and functions of the IIP)
- B. Learning objectives

IV. Learner IIP instructions (pretesting procedures, completing the skill, written assignments, practice procedures, use of equipment, time element, safety factors)

V. Pretest (cognitive, affective, and psychomotor)

VI. Preinstructional written assignment (origin, history, rules, terminology, and safety measures of activity)

VII. Instructional core

- A. Name of skill
- B. Student information
- C. Purpose
- D. Independent written assignment (recognition, recall, problem solving)
- E. Independent skill assignment (instructional cues, activity phase)

	Approach	Description
8.	Tutorial programs	Learning occurs on a one-to-one basis through the use of teacher assistants, paraprofessionals, or other students in tutoring. The reciprocal style of teaching is a form of tutoring. It is also accomplished through the use of audio- or videotape recordings and other visuals (films, slides, loop films).

Sample learning experience

In a reciprocal setting (small group), student performs a wrestling reversal against 50% to 75% partner resistance in a noncompetitive situation. Other observer/partner checks student's performance according to the criteria below:

Incorrect	Acceptable	Perfect	Outside switch
____	____	____	1. Sit-out at 4 o'clock by bringing inside leg under knee of outside leg. Sit on buttock, keeping back in contact with opponent. *Clear inside arm.*
____	____	____	2. Grasp opponent's hand around your waist with outside hand.
____	____	____	3. Reach over opponent's inside arm by driving elbow into near armpit and forcing hand inside to grasp inside of near leg.
____	____	____	4. Arch back onto arm being held, thus breaking down opponent to mat.
____	____	____	5. Roll outside leg over back of opponent, releasing arm. Maintain control.

	Approach	Description
9.	Independent study	With the guidance of a teacher, a student pursues an area of interest and takes responsibility for completing the task. Experiences may be organized around seminars, study periods, and outside school endeavors. Evaluation schemes include oral reports, final projects, conferences, demonstrations, and observations, in addition to traditional mastery tests.

Sample learning experience

Student arranges with teacher to complete the following badminton tasks outside of class:

1. Improve performance in six of the skills below by at least one ability rating:
   - Overhead clear
   - Forehand drive
   - Attack clear
   - Defense clear
   - Smash
   - Overhead drop
   - Long serve
   - Short serve

2. Using mechanical principles, points of contact, and possible uses of criteria, compare and contrast these skills:
   - Overhead clear versus forehand drive
   - Attack clear versus defense clear
   - Smash versus overhead drop
   - Long serve versus short serve
3. Write a brief report (4–5 pages) on the history of badminton covering facts, people, and places connected with the sport.
4. Make up a test using badminton terms, rules, and singles/doubles strategy. Give the test to three other members of class and grade it. There should be at least 25 items with three types of questions (e.g., true-false, multiple choice, matching, fill-in, short essay).

	Approach	Description
10.	Computer-assisted learning	Learning is directed through the use of a computer along with an appropriate software program. Individual goals can be set and adjusted based on performance levels. Differentiated learning activities and tasks can be prescribed. The computer can also serve as an "instructor" (e.g., drill-and-practice, tutorial) and "laboratory" (e.g., problem solving, simulation). Modeling can be used to graphically illustrate a sports skill (Donnelly, 1987).

Sample learning experience

Beginning performance levels in volleyball are determined for the student through preassessment. Target standards are set for each outcome (objective). Data are entered resulting in the following prescriptions:

Objective	Units	Current score	Current level	"C" standard	"B" standard	"A" standard	Original score
1—Underhand serve	#/10	3	<C	4	6	8	3
2—Forearm pass	#/10	4	C	3	5	8	4
3—Set	#/10	7	B	5	7	9	7
4—Positions/Rotation	Test %	86	B	70	85	95	75
5—Knowledge of rules	Test %	74	C	70	85	95	74

You are below the minimum "C" standard for these objectives. Make them your top priority and do the prescribed activities.

1. Underhand serve—To improve in this you should work with the teacher when the serve demonstration and practice is announced.

Good! You reached the minimum "C" standard for these objectives. To reach the "B" level you should do the prescribed activities.

2. Forearm pass—To improve in this you should work with a partner using task sheet VB-FP1. Do tasks 9 through 13.
5. Knowledge of rules—To improve in this you should reread and study the handout on the rules. Take turn as assistant referee in a scrimmage game during class.

Super! You surpassed the "B" standard for these objectives. To strive for the "A" level you should do the prescribed activities.

3. Set—To improve in this you should work in a group of from 2 to 4. Set to others in the group until you can set 20 in a row.
4. Positions/Rotation—To improve in this you should complete the worksheet VB-PR2 while observing a volleyball scrimmage during class.

Note. The computer-assisted approach is reprinted from Richard Hurwitz's "PERK Up Your Classes!" *Future Focus*, **13**(3), 1992, p. 22. Reprinted by permission.

Interaction Pattern

Most learning experiences involve some degree of teacher-to-student, student-to-teacher, or student-to-student interaction. For example, the student is often on the receiving end of one-way communication when the teacher tells, shows, or demonstrates subject matter followed by activities that require the student to make physical movements or to be challenged mentally. These typical forms of interaction, however, should *not* be confused with the interaction pattern of learning experiences.

The purpose of interaction in learning experiences is the *process* itself. Students seek to improve achievement while working together as partners or in small groups to discuss, question, report, and provide feedback. The interaction pattern maximizes the chance to learn social attitudes and values (e.g., respect for others, acceptance, dignity).

Given the realities of our culturally pluralistic society, it follows that positive social values such as cooperation, empathy, and caring should be learned. Because of this need, devising *interactive* learning experiences is crucial. To help you learn to devise such experiences, first, critical elements are reviewed that should be considered. Then, various approaches to interaction are identified and described; sample learning experiences are presented for each.

Critical Elements

"Interactive" learning experiences, as defined, are characteristically different from learning experiences that simply include exchanges between the teacher and students. They are structured for the purpose of *both* achievement (e.g., movement skill, cognitive ability) and social growth (e.g., responsibility, honesty, sharing). Therefore, certain critical elements are common regardless of the approach taken; namely, social skills, grouping, interdependence, and accountability. These elements, which have been adapted from the cooperative learning literature, are described here (Pasch, Sparks-Langer, Gardner, Starko, & Moody, 1991).

Social Skills

Motor skills and cognitive abilities are often learned through types of model/information communication that involve direct explanation or demonstration, or both. Similarly, social skills need to be developed explicitly. You can't assume that students know how to "help others" or "work together" in a small group. Therefore, it is necessary to explain and/or demonstrate social skills as well. For example, students need to learn how to provide feedback to others, observe and rate the performance of others, engage in a discussion, receive feedback from a partner, and assume a role in resolving a problem. Whatever approach is used, there are certain social skills inherent to the approach.

Grouping

In general, groups should be heterogeneous (mixed) in membership. The information presented in chapter 4 on identification and placement may be helpful in this regard (pages 97–98). Depending on the intended outcome, the basis for "mixing" groups could be ability (high-, middle-, low-achieving), status (popular, less popular), gender, race, ethnic and/or home background, and language proficiency. Small group sizes of 2 to 6 are recommended to ensure high participation. Even numbers are advised to allow pairs to form and to avoid "odd person out" situations.

Interdependence

Experiences should be structured, as much as possible, so that the success of the pair or small group depends on the success of each individual in the group. This creates a sense of positive interdependence. Strategies for enhancing interdependence include

- limiting materials or equipment (e.g., one copy of worksheet must be shared),
- using "experts" to teach component parts of a task,

- assigning roles (e.g., recorder, observer, encourager), and
- offering group rewards (i.e., all members must succeed for the group to receive privileges or points).

Accountability

There is an expectation that each person will learn the given skill, understanding, or value. Individuals are responsible for their own learning. For example, in a partner situation, it is not sufficient to just carry out the role of partner (e.g., observer, rater, recorder). It is expected that each partner will be able to demonstrate his or her learning. In group situations, each member is still held accountable even if the group succeeds. This means that performance tests may be used to determine individual achievement.

▶ *To test your understanding of the four critical elements to consider when devising interactive learning experiences, complete Self-Directed Activity 7.5 at the end of this chapter.*

Approaches to Interaction

Clearly, the distinguishing feature of the interaction pattern is its focus on social outcomes through the use of physical education content. You are confronted with the task of making explicit what is usually implicit—affective learning of a social nature. Some of the content interactions presented in Figure 7.3 (page 200) qualify; namely, question and answer (recitation), discussion, and oral report or debate. However, even these approaches often lack a true social element because of their emphasis on content rather than process. Therefore, several approaches to interaction are described and illustrated here which, by design, focus on the development of social skills. These approaches to interaction are reciprocal learning, role playing and simulation, and cooperative learning.

Reciprocal Learning

Intrinsic to this approach are the social relationships between peers and the conditions for immediate feedback (Mosston & Ashworth, 1986). The student's role includes observing the peer's performance, comparing and contrasting the performance against the teacher's criteria, drawing conclusions, and communicating results to the peer. The socializing process unique to this approach—to give and receive feedback with a peer—develops patience, tolerance, and dignity, and a social bond that goes beyond the task.

Reciprocal learning can be carried out in pairs, triads, or small groups. It offers the optimum one-to-one ratio for providing immediate feedback that is positively related to achievement. When students are organized as pairs, one student is designated as "doer," the other as "observer." Roles are then reversed. The teacher provides the criteria for correct performance and communicates only with the observer. Performance criteria are usually identified on a criteria checklist.

Reciprocal learning is illustrated in Figure 6.7 (page 162), Self-Directed Activity 7.2, Item 1 (page 227), Individualized Learning Approaches, Item 8 (page 209), and Self-Directed Activity 7.4, Item 10 (pages 234–235). In addition, Figure 7.4 shows a tennis forehand criteria task sheet for use with pairs. Figure 7.5 (page 214) shows a badminton forehand overhead clear criteria task sheet for use with a small group.

Role Playing and Simulation

In role playing, students pretend they are a particular person in order to solve a problem or act out a situation. Role playing may be carried out in pairs, in small groups, or in front of the entire class. With simulations, students take on lifelike roles as a simplified version of reality. Simulations usually involve a larger number of participants in a larger variety of roles than does role playing. In both role playing and simulation, the ultimate outcome rests with the students. An opportunity is afforded students to discuss the consequences of their actions (Pasch, Sparks-Langer, Gardner, Starko, & Moody, 1991).

Role playing allows students to re-create or act out issues in interpersonal relations such as social events, personal concerns, values, problem behaviors, or social skills. Students can explore and begin to understand the feelings, attitudes, and values of others in social situations, as well as the impact of their behavior on others. Procedures for role playing are as follows (Harrison & Blakemore, 1992):

1. Select and define the problem situation; clarify roles. If necessary, prepare role sheets that describe the feelings or values of the characters to be played.
2. Use a real-life situation to introduce the problem, far enough removed from the students for comfort yet close enough so that students can see parallel behavior within the class or school.
3. Select participants and observers from volunteers. Clarify setting (place, time, situation, roles) and give players time to prepare. Assign

Acc = Accomplished
n.t. = Needs more time

	Doer 1				Doer 2			
	1st set		2nd set		1st set		2nd set	
Task/Criteria*	Acc	n.t.	Acc	n.t.	Acc	n.t.	Acc	n.t.
1. Stand with left side turned to the net, with weight on the right foot. (If left-handed, do the opposite.)								
2. Swing the racket back at about hip height, after you throw the ball upward. Keep eyes on the ball.								
3. Transfer your weight onto the front foot, and swing the racket on a fairly straight line to the ball.								
4. Watch the ball until it is hit by the racket. Bend the knees slightly through the stroke.								
5. The racket contacts the ball when it is even with the front foot.								
6. Keep wrist firm and swing with the whole arm, from the shoulder.								
7. Rotate the trunk so that the shoulders and hips face the net on follow-through.								
8. Follow through with the racket, upward and forward in the direction of the hit.								

1

2

3

*In some tasks, the specific description of the "parts" constitutes the "points to look for."

Figure 7.4 Tennis forehand criteria task sheet is shown for use with pairs.

Name ______________________________
Class ______________________________
Date ______________________________
Partners ______________________________

Badminton—forehand overhead clear

To the students: This task is performed in groups of three: doer, tosser, and observer.
The tosser: Throw a high, clear service to the doer.
The doer: Practice the forehand overhead clear 10 times.
The observer: Analyze the doer's form by comparing the performance to the criteria listed below. Offer feedback about what is done well and what needs to be corrected.
Rotate roles after each inning of 10.

Task—Criteria:
1. Backswing taken with racquet, as if to throw it. __________
2. Left side of the body turned to the net as weight shifts to back leg. __________
3. Shuttle struck overhead but in front of body, with arm fully extended. __________
4. Body weight put into shot, as weight shifts onto front leg. Strong wrist action. __________
5. Follow through in direction of intended flight of bird. __________

Note: Bird should travel both high and deep to back of court; however, deep is more essential.

Figure 7.5 Badminton forehand overhead clear criteria task sheet is shown for use with a small group.

observers specific questions to answer relative to feelings of certain players or alternative endings.

4. Have players act out the roles, several times if needed. This will bring out alternative behaviors and their consequences.
5. Review the experience by discussing behaviors and feelings. Ask players to share their feelings and observers to offer their insights. Discussion should be focused on the values, attitudes, and concerns associated with the problem situation.

Role playing and simulations in physical education can range from a simple social skill (e.g., acting out effective listening with a partner by reflecting on what has been heard) to a complex social concern (e.g., acting out the formation of a volleyball team that is integrated in ability level and gender). Other interpersonal issues might include

- expressing what it feels like to be insulted or "put down" when performing a movement task,
- showing sensitivity toward students with disabling conditions who are trying to develop motor skills, and
- respecting the calls of a tennis opponent where the honor system for officiating is being used.

To further illustrate role playing, a problem situation is fully developed in Table 7.1, including an objective and descriptions of the steps to follow (Hurwitz, 1993e).

Cooperative Learning

The critical elements of interactive learning experiences presented earlier (pages 211–212) were adapted from the cooperative learning literature. Needless to say, they are integral to this approach. The characteristics of cooperative learning are (Siedentop, 1991)

- student activities require interdependence in the achievement of group goals;
- individual accountability is fostered;
- groups (teams) are heterogeneous in terms of skill level, gender, race, and/or cultural background;

Table 7.1 Role Playing as an Approach to Interaction

Objective: To develop "sharing" behaviors, the student will demonstrate a willingness to trade equipment whenever asked to do so by a peer while peers are working with a variety of equipment.

Step	Description
1. Introduction	Present idea of role playing. Tell students that they are expected to participate in good faith and that they will enjoy the experience.
2. Information communication	Describe a situation in which two students both want to use the same ball. One student gets the ball from the box and the other says, "I want to use that one." The two start to argue and a third student comes over to try to settle things.
3. Content interaction	Explain how the role playing is going to work. Pick the "actors" for the situation. Tell the rest of the class what to observe (i.e., realism, feelings brought out, how it might be played differently). Then, actors role-play the situation for 5 minutes while the teacher and rest of class observes.
4. Closure	Analyze the role playing. Discuss how real the actions were, what feelings and values were demonstrated, and how the situation might be played out differently.
5. Content interaction	With the help of the class, pick new actors. Set roles of observers again. Then repeat role playing as in Step 3.
6. Closure	Analyze the second round and summarize. Discuss conclusions as to "right" and "wrong" ways to act in the situation. Discuss the importance of sharing.
7. Assessment	The next two times that students are using a variety of equipment to practice their soccer, archery, and badminton skills, the teacher completes the "sharing behavioral checklist" as means for evaluation.
8. Closure	Discuss the results of the application and evaluation. Suggest ways to improve sharing.

Note. Adapted from "Role Playing Instructional Strategy" by R. Hurwitz, 1993, unpublished manuscript, Cleveland State University. Adapted by permission of the author.

- cooperative behaviors are treated explicitly with much feedback; and
- each group (team) is judged by its success as a group, yet the team "score" is a collection of individual scores thus maximizing the performance of each team member.

The intent of cooperative learning is to produce social outcomes along with content mastery. A review of research on cooperative learning yields support for both achievement and social growth (Glatthorn, 1993). First, achievement is improved when cooperative groups have both group goals and individual accountability. Second, relationships among different racial groups and across skill levels are improved when cooperative learning involves consistent contact over extended periods. Third, acceptance of students with disabilities in regular classes is increased. Fourth, cooperative learning seems to have a positive impact on self-esteem and motivation to learn. Finally, students display, over time, more interest in working together rather than competing with each other.

Some social skills that might be emphasized include sharing materials and equipment, being tolerant of others, praising and encouraging one another, listening to others without interruption, staying on task, ensuring equal participation, and carrying out responsibility. A variety of approaches can be used for learning these social skills including direct explanation, demonstration, guided discovery, problem solving, or role playing. Then, the work in cooperative groups provides for *practice* of the skills, in which monitoring and giving and receiving feedback are crucial (Pasch, Sparks-Langer, Gardner, Starko, & Moody, 1991). The structure of cooperative learning can vary (Siedentop, 1991); for example:

- ***Pairs-Check***: Students work in groups of four with two pairs in each group. Each pair pursues a learning task using the reciprocal approach. Then the two pairs get together to compare outcomes resulting in more feedback and follow-up practice.

- ***Jigsaw***: Students on teams become "experts" at one element or skill by working with "experts" of the same element or skill from other teams. Experts then return to their teams and teach the element or skill to their team members.

- ***Co-op Co-op***: Students work in groups leading to a group product wherein each learner makes a contribution that can be evaluated. Groups present their products to the rest of the class.

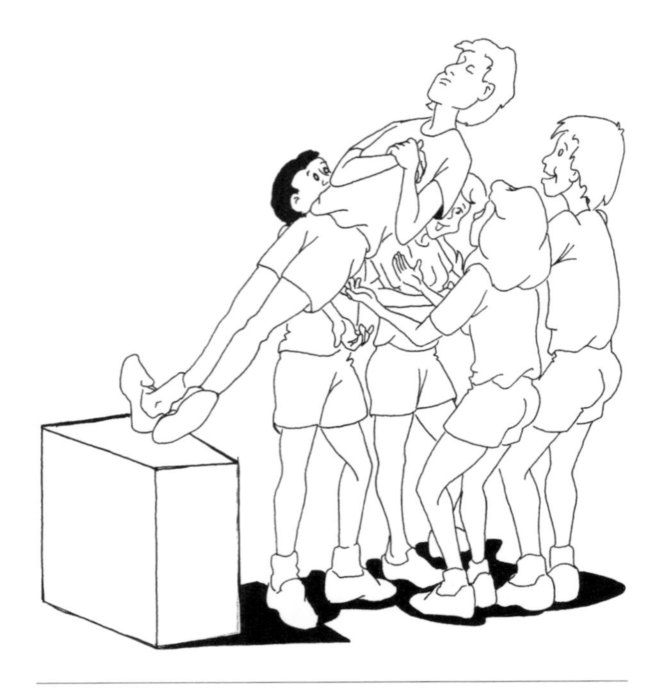

Problem solving can be developed through cooperative learning activities.

Use of cooperative learning in physical education seems unlimited for two reasons—the wide variety of content areas offers an extensive knowledge base for cooperative learning lessons, and the social values inherent to most forms of physical activity are facilitated through interactive experiences. Cooperative learning strategies have been successfully incorporated into the physical education classroom. In the example that follows, selected aspects of a cooperative learning lesson are identified, representing the psychomotor domain (Dunn & Wilson, 1991):

Volleyball Unit

Student group activities

- Develop offensive strategies based on group's strengths.
- Develop defensive strategies based on group's weaknesses.
- Practice and refine volleyball skills as a group.
- Videotape and critique group's volleyball skills.
- Participate as a group in a class volleyball tournament.

Group work activities

- As a class, complete handout to identify five key points of overhand serve.
- Briefly discuss handout; observe teacher as model.

- Assemble into groups of three; four groups are assigned to a court with two groups on a side serving across the net.
- Observer uses "five key points" handout to provide feedback.
- Groups on right side exchange with groups on left side; groups practice serving and try to hit a hula hoop on the other side; groups keep track of number of successful serves.
- Groups play modified game, rotating servers after each rally.
- Groups of three meet together and discuss which of the five key points was the most difficult.

Another popular structure is STAD, or student teams–achievement divisions (Slavin, 1990). The teacher presents information on a specific topic that could involve some discussion or guided practice. Time is provided for team study of the information. Using worksheets, and working in pairs or triads, students help each other master the material. Students are tested and earn points for their teams based on "gain scores" (improvement). Students are expected to make a genuine effort when establishing initial scores. In cases where students are clearly "faking it," their points for improvement shouldn't count.

In physical education, the sport education curriculum model (pages 20 and 22) offers potential as a cooperative learning structure. It is already characterized by many of the cooperative learning features (Siedentop, 1994b). Finally, the cooperative learning approach to interaction is completely developed in the "jigsaw" structure on pages 218 to 219 (Hurwitz, 1993a).

▶ ***To test your understanding of the various approaches to interaction, complete Self-Directed Activity 7.6 at the end of this chapter.***

Selection of Learning Experiences

The problem of selecting learning experiences is twofold. First, there is the problem of *determining* those activities likely to produce the attainment of objectives. Second, a problem exists in *arranging* situations that will provide the desired experiences. These problems are solved when the teacher controls the learning experience by manipulating the environment and setting up stimulating situations that evoke the kind of behavior desired. The underlying framework for this approach is student-centered. That is, emphasis is placed on the active role of the learner, not on the procedures and behaviors of the teacher.

Unfortunately, there are no *universal* learning experiences that relate best to a grade level, ability level, or kind of learning objective. In spite of the fact that these "perfect" learning experiences do not exist, however, fundamental criteria are suggested here that may help you. In addition, the selection of learning experiences is examined in relation to students who for one of several reasons are considered "special" (i.e., culturally diverse, at risk, or gifted and talented).

Fundamental Criteria

Because of the wealth of possibilities, organizing centers were selected on the basis of philosophical and psychological screens and learning objectives were selected on the basis of needs assessment and cruciality. Appropriate learning experiences need to be selected in the same way. Therefore, a set of fundamental criteria is offered that considers purposes served, capability and interest, satisfaction, and match with objectives.

Purposes Served

The learning experience should foster total development. Thinking, feeling, and moving are closely related. Therefore, the curriculum designer will find it useful to classify learning experiences according to the three domains.

Useful kinds of learning experiences are also associated with specific levels of learning. For example, if students are to acquire information about principles, ideas, facts, and terms, experiences such as listening to a presentation, viewing a demonstration, and reading handout materials may be helpful. If students are to develop skill in applying information, a worksheet, discussion exercise, or guided discovery activity might be desirable. When students are expected to develop social attitudes (affective), some appropriate experiences include assimilation activities, role playing, and small group exercises. In the case of psychomotor learning, some useful experiences are mental practice exercises, self-directed tasks, and problem-solving activities. It should be clear that the purpose of the learning experience serves as a criterion for its selection.

Capability and Interest

Learning experiences should be directed toward behaviors that are within the student's range of

"Jigsaw" Cooperative Learning Structure

Skills	Soccer outcomes knowledge	Attitudes/Values
Dribble	Rules	Enjoyment
Pass/Kick	Defensive strategy	Helping others
Head	Offensive strategy	Responsibility
Trap	Skill analysis	Self-improvement

	Step	Description
1.	Introduction	Orient student to the content, objectives, and process to be used. Use motivating techniques. Form five teams according to skill level with #1 being highest ranked. Use past records or pretests to rank learners. Distribute students as follows: *Team A:* 1, 10, 11, 20, 21 *Team B:* 2, 9, 12, 19, 22 *Team C:* 3, 8, 13, 18, 23 *Team D:* 4, 7, 14, 17, 24 *Team E:* 5, 6, 15, 16, 25 Check for racial and gender balance and adjust accordingly.
2.	Information communication	Establish "expert teams." Each expert team will be made up of one member from each of the teams. Since one expert team will work on dribbling, one on heading, one on the rules, and so on, the following strategy for forming the expert teams should be used: Put the most skilled student from each team on the expert team working on the hardest skill (dribbling?), the second most skilled student from each team on the expert team working on the second hardest skill, and so on. Using this strategy, the expert teams might be composed as follows: *Dribbling:* 1(A), 2(B), 3(C), 4(D), 5(E) *Heading:* 6(E), 7(D), 8(C), 9(B), 10(A) *Trapping:* 11(A), 12(B), 13(C), 14(D), 15(E) *Pass/Kick:* 16(E), 17(D), 18(C), 19(B), 20(A) *Rules:* 21(A), 22(B), 23(C), 24(D), 25(E)
3.	Content interaction	Each expert team works together at a station to become "expert" in their skill or the rules. At each station are materials to help (printed material, posters, videotapes, films, handouts prepared by teacher). The materials focus on how to teach the skill or rules. Each station shows a schedule for when the teacher will be available to cover teaching hints and skill analysis pointers. When not involved in this activity, teacher circulates to monitor expert team activity and help as needed. Students help one another develop greater expertise and devise teaching plans.

4.	Information communication	Re-form teams. Assign the following roles in each team: *Task master:* Keeps group on task; makes sure that each individual contributes *Encourager:* Gets others to share ideas, give opinions, and help others; gets group to work hard *Cheerleader:* Makes sure teammates know they are appreciated; has team celebrate when they make a gain *Gatekeeper:* Makes sure each person has a turn and that all participate about equally *Checker:* Makes sure everyone agrees with answer before group decision and that everyone understands
5.	Content interaction	Within the teams, each expert in turn teaches his or her skill or rules to the other team members. *All* of them help one another to learn and improve. The teacher circulates to monitor team progress and help as needed.
6.	Assessment	Test skills and knowledge of rules. Each student's individual performance on the tests will count toward his or her own grade. But each team can earn "team points" according to how well the team does on each test. The following chart can be used to award team points assuming skills on a 10-point scale and rules on a 50-point scale:

Average team score skill test	*Average team score rules test*	*Team points*
0–5	0–25	5
5.1–6	25.1–30	10
6.1–7	30.1–35	20
7.1–8	35.1–40	35
8.1–9	40.1–45	55
9.1–10	45.1–50	80

At the end of the unit, team point totals can be used to reward teams with certificates, ribbons, choice of activities, notice in newsletter, picture on bulletin board, or some other appropriate reward.

7.	Content interaction	Prepare for team play (of modified or lead-up game). Each team is given resources to help them devise offensive and defensive strategies. The members of each team will work together, playing the roles of task master, encourager, etc.
8.	Content interaction	Teams play in some kind of tournament. Each team accumulates additional team points for their won-lost record and for a "team play rating" as recorded by the teacher. These team points are added to the points accumulated in the testing process.
9.	Closure	Summative processing. Use discussion and processing forms within teams and as a large group to review the previous eight steps.
10.	Closure	Reward the teams according to accumulated team points.

Note. Adapted from "Cooperative Learning Sample Units: Soccer" by R. Hurwitz, 1993, unpublished manuscript, Cleveland State University. Adapted by permission of the author.

capability. There should be some indication that the student has the background necessary for successful completion of the activity. Otherwise, failure and unfulfilled objectives result. Knowledge of the student's previous and present abilities help determine whether the intended learning experience is feasible. Assessing entry behaviors (chapter 4) offers a basis for selection.

In addition, if learning experiences match the student's readiness, then curiosity and interest in learning are enhanced. For example, the degree of independence afforded in a learning activity is a factor that depends on the students. Some students may not be able to cope with much independence, while others can function very successfully.

Satisfaction

Learning experiences should be selected that will be satisfying. If they are unsatisfying or unrewarding, the student is more likely to avoid the kind of behavior implied by the learning objective and, as a result, lose motivation to learn. Students who do not experience success can't be expected to react positively to learning opportunities. For example, failure is inevitable when students are not *physically* ready to perform a particular skill movement, even though other students of similar age are mature enough to do so. However, success should not be viewed as transitory or immediate. Instead, cumulative successes in learning experiences reinforce the student's feeling of improvement.

Match With Objectives

The goal, behavioral, and content aspects of learning objectives, when taken together, serve as criteria for selecting learning experiences. The relationship between the learning objective and the learning experience must be understood by students. Learning experiences should

- match the content referred to in the objective,
- offer activities at the level of behavior called for by the objective, and
- contribute to the overall accomplishment of the goal.

The hierarchy for analyzing content goals (pages 78–81) and learning objectives (pages 135–139) is a useful framework for matching learning experiences with objectives. Depending on the level of the hierarchy, learning experiences are suggested that range from problem-solving activities to memory tasks. Affective objectives might be achieved through activities in which students acquire or transform interests, attitudes, or values. On the other hand, pencil-and-paper activities would not appear to match an objective in the area of social development. Thus, the nature of the objective becomes a criterion for selecting appropriate learning experiences.

▶ ***To practice judging a learning experience according to its stated purpose, student capability, student satisfaction, and its stated objective, complete Self-Directed Activity 7.7 at the end of this chapter.***

Accommodating Special Learners

Providing *total* equity in learning experiences is not easy. Beyond that, the thought of an "affirmative curriculum" is even more challenging to the curriculum designer (Melograno, 1981). While students may appear to be alike, this illusion of homogeneity is replaced by the reality of heterogeneity. Hellison and Templin (1991) illustrate the wide range of learner skills, interests, attitudes, and backgrounds:

> Billy wants to be there, Mary doesn't. Suzi is an exceptionally skilled athlete, Joey has difficulty with any physical activity. Danny is back in school after two suspensions, Karen has a perfect attendance record. Pam is epileptic, Larry is learning disabled, and Dave has a congenital heart defect. Tom constantly complains, and Don brings the teacher an apple every day. Andrew is a 4-foot, 5-inch ninth grader, and Jack is a 6-foot, 5-inch ninth grader. Kay's father is the CEO of one of the country's largest companies, and they live in the suburbs; Sue lives with her divorced mother in the inner city, and they are on welfare. (p. 27)

In this chapter, the importance of individualization was established. Various approaches were suggested to satisfy students' needs—preferred learning styles, interests, abilities, and achievements. Likewise, interaction was justified because of its contributions to students' dignity, responsibility, and social development. Together, these patterns would seem to offer a sufficient set of alternatives in order to recognize the full range of individual differences. However, in reality, there exist other differences that require consideration in terms of variety, adaptation, and/or treatment.

Therefore, information is offered here to help you accommodate the needs of culturally diverse, at-risk, and gifted and talented students. The characteristics of each kind of student are presented and suggestions are offered for selecting appropriate learning experiences. However, there is a great deal of overlap in two respects. First, culturally different students are often the same as those at risk. Second, learning experiences that are appropriate for these "special" learners are often useful for all students.

Culturally Diverse

As an extension of our multicultural society, multicultural education means that student differences are treated as strengths rather than as weaknesses. Regardless of cultural origin (e.g., Asian, Hispanic, African American, Native American), students deserve an equal opportunity to be physically educated. As a curriculum designer and teacher, your attitude toward culturally diverse students makes a difference. Selection of learning experiences reflects the degree to which you accept these differences. It calls for varying patterns of learning experiences as suggested by a "culturally responsive pedagogy" (pages 6–7). Equal opportunity is expected by all students. But students also have an obligation to treat others equally as they gain a multicultural perspective—a perspective intended to end prejudicial behavior and injustice (Hellison & Templin, 1991).

These students should not be thought of as "disadvantaged" or "culturally deprived," but seen as individuals experiencing *cultural discontinuity*. That is, students with a particular set of cultural values and norms find themselves in a setting with very different values and norms (Glatthorn, 1993). For example, in physical education, an individualized and competitive group structure often predominates. However, it is contrary to the more cooperative norms of some cultures. Therefore, some students may withdraw from competition. Also, cognitive style differences—preferred ways of receiving and processing information—have been associated with culture. Some students need to see the "whole" before understanding the "parts." This has implications for the learning sequence of motor skills and the nature of inductive versus deductive learning experiences.

It is one thing to understand the nature of cultural discontinuity; it is another to be able to do something about it. With this in mind, some suggestions are offered which provide a supportive and growth-enhancing environment for students from diverse cultural groups (Glatthorn, 1993).

- Empower students through learning experiences that involve decision-making and social action skills; students from victimized groups will have higher expectations of themselves.
- Challenge students to take learning risks and expand their horizons through problem-solving tasks; don't focus unduly on the minority student's everyday world.
- Systematically vary the kinds of learning experiences. Cooperative learning has positive effects on achievement, particularly for students whose cultures emphasize group activities and peer assistance. Computer-assisted approaches are particularly effective where communication skills may be lacking.
- Use alternative forms of assessment within learning experiences, such as shared responsibility (i.e., teacher and student as co-evaluators) and portfolios (e.g., samples of products, logs, self-check sheets, peer criteria task sheets). Portfolio assessment was described in chapter 6 (pages 172–175); a full range of alternatives appears in Table 6.1 (page 176).

At-Risk

The term "at risk" identifies the student who is in danger of failing to complete his or her education with an adequate level of skill or of dropping out of school before having achieved the skills needed for effective functioning in society. There are several personal, family, school, and social factors associated with this population—health problems, substance abuse, teen pregnancy, low self-esteem, low aspirations, suicidal tendencies, low socioeconomic status, single-parent homes, low parental support, neglect and abuse at home, low academic achievement, communities beset with stress and conflict, unemployment, and/or incarceration.

Physical education teachers tend to believe that students inherently enjoy physical activity. In the case of at-risk students, this is a faulty assumption (Sparks, 1993). The learning experiences devised by teachers often reinforce the socially maladjusted behaviors of at-risk students. Typically, in physical education, skills are developed progressively with complex levels dependent on *success* during early stages. At-risk students often lack this prerequisite success since they resist common learning models. Therefore, the humanistic/social development curriculum model (page 20), with an emphasis on responsibility and decision making, has been advocated for at-risk students (Hellison & Templin, 1991).

Learning deficits that are easiest to remediate are those that never occur in the first place. Although early prevention experiences are more effective than later intervention efforts (Slavin & Madden, 1989), access to effective early education programs is hardly a guarantee. And even in the absence of any primary prevention, some prescriptions can be suggested. Four approaches seem to be effective in improving the performance of at-risk students (Glatthorn, 1993).

- ***Reciprocal learning***: In this case, reciprocal learning means that students gradually assume the role of teacher. It goes beyond receiving and giving feedback by peers. The concept of "scaffolding" is advanced—a metaphor for support that is gradually removed when it is no longer needed. Emphasis is placed on the active role of the student.
- ***Cooperative learning***: As described previously, cooperative learning has been shown to be highly effective in achieving a variety of outcomes important for at-risk students. Personal responsibility (individual accountability) and decision making are inherent to this approach.
- ***Tutoring***: One-to-one tutoring by teachers or aides is effective for at-risk learners. Peer tutoring has also been established as an effective approach.
- ***Use of technology***: The use of technology such as computers, videocassette recorders, laser discs, and CD-ROM equipment seems to be effective with at-risk learners. Use of technology enhances decision making through self-directed learning. Computer-assisted learning was illustrated previously as an approach to individualization.

Gifted and Talented

Traditionally, students were thought to be especially talented or bright—usually labeled "gifted"—as revealed by a high IQ test score. However, the IQ test has been criticized because it is unreliable and invalid as a measure of intelligence, culturally biased, focused on lower mental processes, and insensitive to creativity and other types of intelligence. More recently, the concept of multiple intelligences has emerged. According to one theory (Gardner, 1983), seven independent intelligences exist including linguistic, musical, logical-mathematical, spatial, bodily-kinesthetic, interpersonal, and intrapersonal. For example, a gymnast might be gifted in bodily-kinesthetic intelligence but not gifted in linguistic or musical intelligence.

It should be clear that this discussion on gifted students is limited to accommodations in a heterogeneous (mixed) setting, not a segregated, special class for gifted students. Although unintentional, there is a tendency in physical education to discriminate in favor of highly skilled students at the expense of less-skilled students. Therefore, an atmosphere of "inclusion" should be promoted rather than an aura of "elitism." Learning experiences are advised that do not place gifted students at risk in their peer relationships.

In chapter 4, one purpose of learner analysis is to reveal individual variations. Entry appraisal provides the means for identifying gifted learners. With this information, you have an obligation to select learning experiences that will challenge gifted students in a heterogeneous setting. Two general strategies are recommended (Glatthorn, 1993).

- ***Accelerate the pace***: Enable gifted students to progress more rapidly through learning tasks. You may recall that pace options were described as a method of individualization. "Learning modules" can facilitate individual progress through self-directed tasks, contracting, programmed learning, learning activity packages, independent study, and computer-assisted learning, all of which have been covered previously.
- ***Provide for enrichment***: Select learning experiences that offer greater depth or breadth than regular experiences. Content options and level-of-difficulty options may be used for this purpose. Reciprocal learning can be effective if "cluster" groups are used. A small group of four to six gifted students could work together in a regular class on advanced topics or areas of special interest. Cooperative learning is beneficial to gifted learners when used judiciously, ensuring that excessive use does not limit growth. The "jigsaw" structure is appropriate given the use of students as experts.

▶ ***To gain experience in selecting learning experiences that accommodate "special" students, complete Self-Directed Activity 7.8 at the end of this chapter.***

Making It Work

Have you achieved the expected outcomes (page 196)? Congratulations! You are able to devise learning experiences for your physical education curriculum design. Still, you may have some practical questions that need answers, such as:

- **Why is so much attention given to the structure of learning experiences?**

  Physical education is known for its traditional teaching-learning sequence of demonstration, explanation, execution, and evaluation. In other words, you show students something, explain it, have them try it, and then test it. While these steps are not wrong, there's little opportunity for variety. Thinking in terms of alternative sources and types of model/information communication makes a more dynamic learning experience possible. Add to this the various means of content interaction, and students are more likely to show interest in physical education. If you consciously plan for how to create intended outcomes, and plan stimulating and varied opportunities, students will be more responsive.

- **How can a teacher really individualize instruction with so many different students in one class?**

  Developing individualized materials (e.g., contracts, learning packets, self-directed task cards, peer checklists, programmed learning guides, computer-assisted learning) is time-consuming and mentally challenging. Once you build this foundation, the key becomes student self-direction and self-management. After you have created student interdependence and accountability, you will realize that the excuse of having too many students to individualize is a "cop-out." Students need to be taught how to be self-directed and responsible. Once your system is in place, the high student-teacher ratios won't seem as great.

- **In physical education, will students willingly participate in some of the interaction approaches like role playing and cooperative learning?**

  Of course they will! Why not? The problem is that most students don't associate alternative patterns of interaction with physical education. They're so used to calisthenic warm-ups, followed by drills, followed by game playing that anything innovative is viewed as weird. Traditional expectations need to be broken, not just for the sake of change, but because of learners' needs. It may take time to change attitudes, so start slow, but be persistent. Physical education has been negatively stereotyped in terms of its contribution to interpersonal and social effects. You should now be able to see how progressive physical education can be with careful planning.

- **Is it possible to meet the needs of culturally diverse, at-risk, and gifted students if they're all in the same class?**

  Many of the approaches that have been found effective with these groups are good for all students. Your attitude toward these "special" students makes a difference. Varying the patterns of learning experiences while keeping in mind the particular needs of these students should improve student performance. Remember, think of student differences as strengths, not weaknesses. Capitalize on diversity, rather than view differences as an obstacle to reaching learning potential. Let students help decide how differences will be handled, both for their benefit and yours. The idea is to develop proactive experiences. You can build a sense of community right away through cooperative, noncompetitive games. However, you should be prepared to deal with racial or cultural remarks and disrespectful behavior. For example, you could talk to students one-on-one or in small conferences, use student mediators to handle disputes, and strictly enforce consequences for language, behavior, or clothing that is offensive for any reason (e.g., insulting to anyone's gender, race, socioeconomic status, cultural background, or ability level, whether limited or gifted).

Self-Directed Activity 7.1

Ideally, you now know what a learning experience is and how it is structured. In order to find out, complete the statements that describe learning experiences. Fill in the missing term in the numbered spaces. Try not to go back to the textual material!

Learning experiences are the (1)________ between the student and the (2)________ conditions found in the environment. They should evoke the desired (3)________ in the student and are considered valid if they create the intended (4)________. The two components for structuring learning experiences are (5)________ and (6)________.

With model/information communication, processes, skills, procedures, values, and attitudes to be learned are (7)________ and/or (8)________, or facts, concepts, principles, or materials to be learned are (9)________ and/or (10)________. Some sources of model/information communication are (11)________, (12)________, and (13)________. Some types of model/information communication are (14)________, (15)________, and (16)________.

Content interaction describes how students are actually involved in dealing with the skills, procedures, values, attitudes, facts, concepts, principles, and materials as they attempt to meet (17)________. Some types of content interaction are (18)________, (19)________, and (20)________. Various learning factors are associated with content interaction. Two "group organization patterns" are (21)________ and (22)________. A source and a type of "feedback and reinforcement" are (23)________ and (24)________, respectively. A type of direction, challenge, or assignment is (25)________.

Feedback

1. Interactions
2. External
3. Behaviors or responses
4. Outcomes
5. Model/information communication
6. Content interaction
7. Demonstrated
8. Explained
9. Presented
10. Explained

11./12./13. Teacher, student, other person, media, printed material, or combination

14./15./16. Oral, written, aural, visual, tactile, or combination

17. Learning objectives

18./19./20. Practice/performance, drill, problem solving, exploration, guided discovery, investigation/research, experimentation, question/answer (recitation), discussion, creative writing, computer interaction/simulation, written exercise/worksheet, role playing/simulation, game/contest/relay, field trip, oral report/debate, work on project, study, or combination

21./22. Whole group (mass), large group (8 to half of whole group), small group (3 to 7), pairs, or individual
23. Teacher, self, other student, media, or computer
24. General (nonspecific), corrective, or descriptive
25. Oral, written, aural, visual, tactile, or combination

Self-Directed Activity 7.2

In this activity, you will develop learning experiences that match students' needs and corresponding objectives. For each of the following partial learning objectives, identify the associated need—cognitive, affective, or psychomotor. Then, describe an *explicit* learning experience that fits the objective. Make sure your learning experiences include model/information communication and content interaction.

1. *Learning objective*: To show the ability to function in a helping relationship, the student will assist others in improving their abilities in tumbling.

   Need: ____________________

   Learning experience: ____________________

   ____

2. *Learning objective*: To analyze offensive strategies in individual sports, the student will be able to differentiate among the lob, volley, half-volley, and crosscourt forehand and backhand drives in appropriate tennis situations.

   Need: ____________________

   Learning experience: ____________________

   ____

3. *Learning objective*: To demonstrate that he or she values personal body movement patterns, the student will direct his or her own calisthenic routine based on circuit training principles.

   Need: ______________________________

   Learning experience: ______________________________

   ____

   ____

   ____

   ____

   ____

   ____

   ____

4. *Learning objective*: To develop functional characteristics of organic vigor (physical ability), the student will demonstrate improved upper body and hip-joint flexibility.

   Need: ______________________________

   Learning experience: ______________________________

   ____

   ____

   ____

   ____

   ____

   ____

   ____

5. *Learning objective*: To assume responsibility for making decisions, the student will determine his or her own beginning ability level, goal achievement levels, and task sequences in weight training.

   Need: ______________________________

   Learning experience: ______________________________

   ____

   ____

   ____

   ____

   ____

   ____

   ____

Feedback

1. *Affective (social)*

   Since the objective focuses on "helping relationships," the learning experience should be directed toward the behavior (assisting), *not* the content (tumbling). For example, the student could be given a task card with a list of criteria for performing various tumbling stunts. A student could demonstrate one of the stunts while the teacher *models* use of the task card. Upon reading the criteria, the student would provide feedback to a partner on his or her performance. Each level might require five trials. If the execution is not correct, the criteria that need improvement are checked. The student either tells or shows the partner what judgments have been made. A partial task card:

Level 1—Single roll across mat			**Trials**		
Starting position:	**1**	**2**	**3**	**4**	**5**
1. Parallel stance, feet closer together than shoulder width	❑	❑	❑	❑	❑
2. Arms at sides	❑	❑	❑	❑	❑
3. Eyes focused straight ahead; head up	❑	❑	❑	❑	❑
Roll action:					
4. Accepts body weight by placing hands on mat farther apart than shoulder width	❑	❑	❑	❑	❑
5. Slightly contacts back of head with mat first, then fully contacts shoulder blades with mat	❑	❑	❑	❑	❑
6. Keeps chin tucked to chest	❑	❑	❑	❑	❑
7. Grabs lower legs (shins) with completion of roll, landing on feet	❑	❑	❑	❑	❑

2. *Cognitive*

   Students could be asked to read a handout that describes offensive techniques. Then, the student should analyze various tennis situations that call for the use of a certain offensive technique. This could be provided through direct observation of tennis play or through a worksheet. For example, the student could be asked to determine the appropriate strategies, given descriptions of situations that demand their use. The student could select the desired strokes from a diagram. A sample of items is:

Select desired return of serve by the receiver

_____ 1. Serve is hard and well placed; server stays deep.
_____ 2. Second serve is soft; server stays deep.
_____ 3. Serve is hard and well placed; server comes to net.
_____ 4. Serve is sliced; server stays deep.

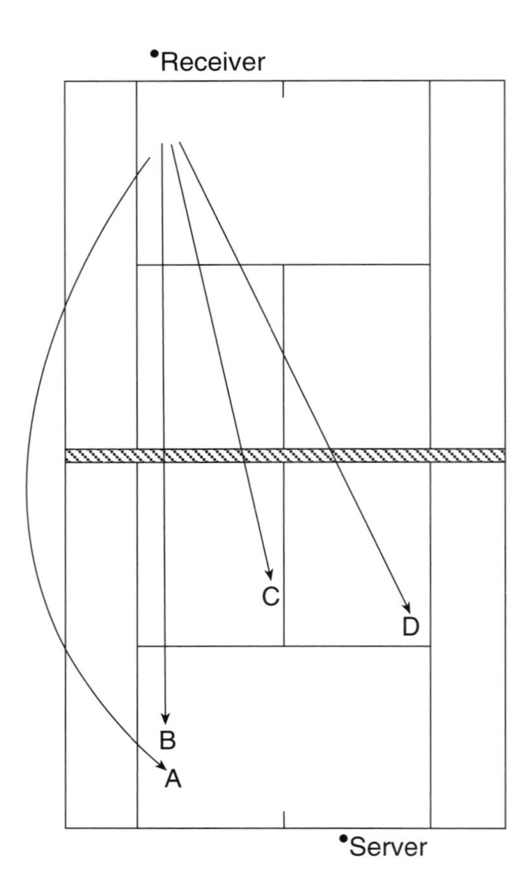

3. *Affective (values)*

   Because of the nature of the objective, an appropriate learning experience should offer some freedom of choice so that values can be displayed. A progressive calisthenic exercise program could be developed for this purpose and explained by the teacher. The routine would allow the student to progress from performance in unison with others to individualized performance that is self-directed. Each student might be given a list of task levels on which to record the date each level is achieved. A partial sequence of task levels is:

   Date achieved

   __________ *Level 1*: All exercises performed correctly in class to a command count
   __________ *Level 2*: All exercises of routine performed using the correct technique

   ----

   __________ *Level 9*: All exercises of routine performed correctly by applying circuit training principles at 2/3 maximum threshold

4. *Psychomotor*

   Flexibility is developed through progressive stretching. Therefore, the learning experience should include exercises that gradually increase the range of motion at given joints. Various flexibility exercises could be demonstrated by the teacher. Then, the student could be asked to complete an individualized task card at one of the self-directed flexibility stations. A sample task card is:

Completed sets			**Upper body and hip joint flexibility exercises**
1	2	3	
____	____	____	*Chest and shoulder stretch*: Lie on narrow bench, arms outstretched to side; hold statically, allowing arms to gradually drop toward floor.
____	____	____	*Arm pull:* Place arm behind head; gently pull elbow behind head and hold statically; repeat with other arm.
____	____	____	*Back stretch*: Lie on back and pull both knees up to shoulders tightly; hold statically.
____	____	____	*Sitting opposite toe touch*: Spread legs as far apart as possible, keeping them straight; reach with both hands toward right foot, hold statically; repeat toward left foot.
____	____	____	*Leg over*: Lie flat with feet together, arms extended to side; lift left leg straight up as high as possible over to opposite hand; return to starting position; repeat with other leg; perform 6 repetitions.

5. *Affective (emotional)*

   The behavioral and content aspects of this objective suggest a learning experience in which the student develops his or her own program. The teacher could explain how to determine beginning levels, set goals, and complete weight training tasks. Students could view a videotape that shows the proper exercise techniques. The student might select a circuit training sequence for full body development. For illustrative purposes, a sequence is:

Exercise	Repetitions	Weight	Goal
1. Bench press	10 RM	_____	_____
2. Horizontal extension	20 RM	_____	_____
3. Two-arm curl	10 RM	_____	_____
4. Two-arm press	10 RM	_____	_____
5. Lat bar pulldown	10 RM	_____	_____
6. Knee extension	10 RM	_____	_____
7. Knee flexion	10 RM	_____	_____
8. Wrist extension	20 RM	_____	_____
9. Upright rowing	10 RM	_____	_____

Self-Directed Activity 7.3

You should be able to differentiate among various options for individualization. The following chart contains descriptions of learning experiences. Which individualization option characterizes each? Even though more than one option may apply, you must decide on the primary one. Check (√) your selection. Then, briefly state why you chose it.

Individualized learning experiences	Individualization options: Pace	Content	Level of difficulty	Learning style
1. The student is challenged to perform to his or her maximum by determining how many times he or she can (a) keep a balloon in the air by batting it with open hands; (b) bat the balloon against the wall; (c) catch a sponge ball in a plastic container; (d) bounce a large ball in front and catch it with both hands; and (e) dribble ball with right hand, then left, and then alternating hands.	____ Why? ____	____	____	____
2. The student completes an individualized program in gymnastics (balance beam), progressing at his or her own rate through three sequential ability levels that involve (a) execution of a single movement (starting position, movement, and end position), (b) execution of two combined movements, (c) performance of a series of movements, and (d) performance of a sequence of movements to music.	____ Why? ____	____	____	____
3. In response to the student's preference for working with a partner or small group, the student engages in the following self-directed movement/development tasks: (a) kicks the ball to a partner, (b) runs and kicks the ball to a partner, (c) drop-kicks the ball to a partner, (d) drop-kicks the ball through the hoop held by a partner, and (e) invents a game with a partner that involves kicking a ball.	____ Why? ____	____	____	____
4. For the purpose of gaining an understanding of offensive strategy concepts common to goal-oriented sports, the student selects a problem-solving worksheet to complete on either basketball, field hockey, or soccer. Each worksheet contains problems to solve that relate to the following offensive concepts: (a) maintaining possession of the ball requires the ability to dribble, dodge, and feint;	____ Why? ____	____	____	____

(b) passing involves spatial patterns based on players' positioning; (c) spaces need to be created; (d) the ball must be placed in a strategic position in order to score; (e) goal shooting involves individual and team cooperation (e.g., screening); and (f) shots at the goal should be followed up by surrounding the goal at every angle.

5. When ready, the student completes a guided-discovery task card for maneuvers during soccer dribbling. Answers are provided on the other side of the card for feedback purposes. The task card is organized as follows. *Situation:* You are dribbling up the right side of the field (near the sideline) and encounter a defensive player about 30 meters from the goal. *Questions:* (a) What are your options? (keep dribbling); (b) If you choose to keep dribbling, what direction would you go to reduce risk? (to the left); (c) What could happen if you retreated? (offsides); (d) What could happen if you went to the right? (risk out-of-bounds); (e) What could happen if you went straight ahead? (risk ball being taken); and (f) Choosing to go left, how will you protect the ball? (keep body between defensive player and ball, switch feet).

   ____ ____ ____ ____
   Why? ____________________
   ____
   ____
   ____
   ____

6. The student chooses to contract with the teacher in a tennis unit by establishing (a) target objectives for the forehand and backhand drive, serve, volley, lob, overhead, and drop shots; (b) expected date to demonstrate understanding of rules, scoring, and strategy in doubles and singles; and (c) role to carry out in assisting others in the class.

   ____ ____ ____ ____
   Why? ____________________
   ____
   ____
   ____
   ____

7. Under the theme of manipulative skills, different options are provided, each of which may be used to develop general coordination, body awareness, spatial relationships, and eye-hand/eye-foot coordination. The student selects one of the options based on his or her preference for use of a wand, hoop, or rope. The options are as follows: *Option 1* (wand)—hold wand upright, let go, turn body around, and catch wand before it falls; balance wand horizontally on different body parts; keep wand balanced while moving body part; balance wand vertically on different levels;

   ____ ____ ____ ____
   Why? ____________________
   ____
   ____
   ____
   ____

and thread the needle. *Option 2* (hoop)—roll hoop while running beside it, ahead of it, and around it; roll hoop in a circle, while weaving around cones, and in a figure-8; crawl through hoop while it is held stationary; run through hoop while partner rolls it slowly; and roll own hoop and run through it. *Option 3* (rope)—jump turning rope forward and backward; hop over rope on right, left, and alternate feet; use a rocker step; skip over rope; jump over rope doing quarter-turns; and move through space while running, jumping, skipping, and leaping the rope.

8. In order to design a physical fitness program based on areas of needed improvement, the student determines his or her beginning status in the following fitness aspects: (a) cardiorespiratory endurance (9-minute run or mile run), (b) percent fat (skinfold measurements), (c) abdominal strength and endurance (sit-ups), (d) flexibility of the low back and posterior thigh (sit-and-reach), and (e) motor ability (battery of coordination, agility, balance, speed, and power tests).

   ____ ____ ____ ____

   Why? ______________________________

Feedback

1. Level of difficulty

   The individual maximums for these eye-hand coordination tasks will vary from student to student. The number of times each task is completed will depend on the student's level of ability and achievement.

2. Pace

   Since the student progresses at his or her own rate through the gymnastics (balance beam) program, the pace option was employed. The speed at which the three sequences are completed is determined by the individual student.

3. Learning style

   This learning experience considers the individual student's preference for a partner/small-group interactive pattern. The self-directed movement/development tasks are based primarily on learning style as the individualization option.

4. Content

   With this learning experience, students can select different content to achieve a common purpose. This content option affords an opportunity for individual learners to choose areas of interest and popularity.

5. Pace

   First, the student completes the task card when he or she is ready. Second, the guided discovery approach incorporates the notion of self-pacing since the student answers the questions and receives feedback at his or her own rate.

6. Learning style

   Contracting represents a learning style option that considers the structures of learning experiences. In this example, the student is able to choose the form of learning (contracting) and determine objectives, completion dates, and role to carry out.

7. Content

   The student is able to develop manipulative skills according to his or her content preference. The learning experience possesses the quality of individualization because of this choice.

8. Level of difficulty

   Since the student's fitness program is based on beginning status, the level-of-difficulty option was used for the purpose of individualization. The student is able to design his or her own program in areas of needed improvement.

Self-Directed Activity 7.4

In order to devise individualized learning experiences, you should be able to differentiate among various approaches. Match the learning experience descriptions with one of the following approaches.

Approaches to individualized learning

A = Exploration
B = Self-directed tasks
C = Guided discovery
D = Problem solving
E = Contracting
F = Programmed learning
G = Learning activity package (LAP)
H = Tutorial programs
I = Independent study
J = Computer-assisted learning

_____ 1. Student invents a running game for 5 to 10 people to develop endurance using a random organization and the following equipment: 2 tires, 3 jump ropes, 2 broomsticks, and 3 soccer balls.

_____ 2. Student teaches himself or herself the soccer chest trap by completing a sequence of tasks while being alert and aware of every detail described in the task. Each task is rated "fair," "good," or "excellent" based on his or her own judgment of performance. Tasks are completed as described on a self-evaluation form.

_____ 3. Student is challenged to move from one place to another without using the feet. Then, the learner tries to keep his or her body in a twisted shape while moving in a curved pathway.

_____ 4. Student engages in an outside cycling project involving the following activities:

- Collect and summarize two articles on cycling safety.
- Diagram the parts of a cycle.
- Map out and complete a cycling trip of 2 miles for a group of four people.
- Identify safety factors, how to select a cycle, proper mounting and dismounting, riding positions, pedaling techniques, and hand signals.
- Design and engage in three cycle games with two other people.
- Ride 5 miles, observing all cycle safety procedures.

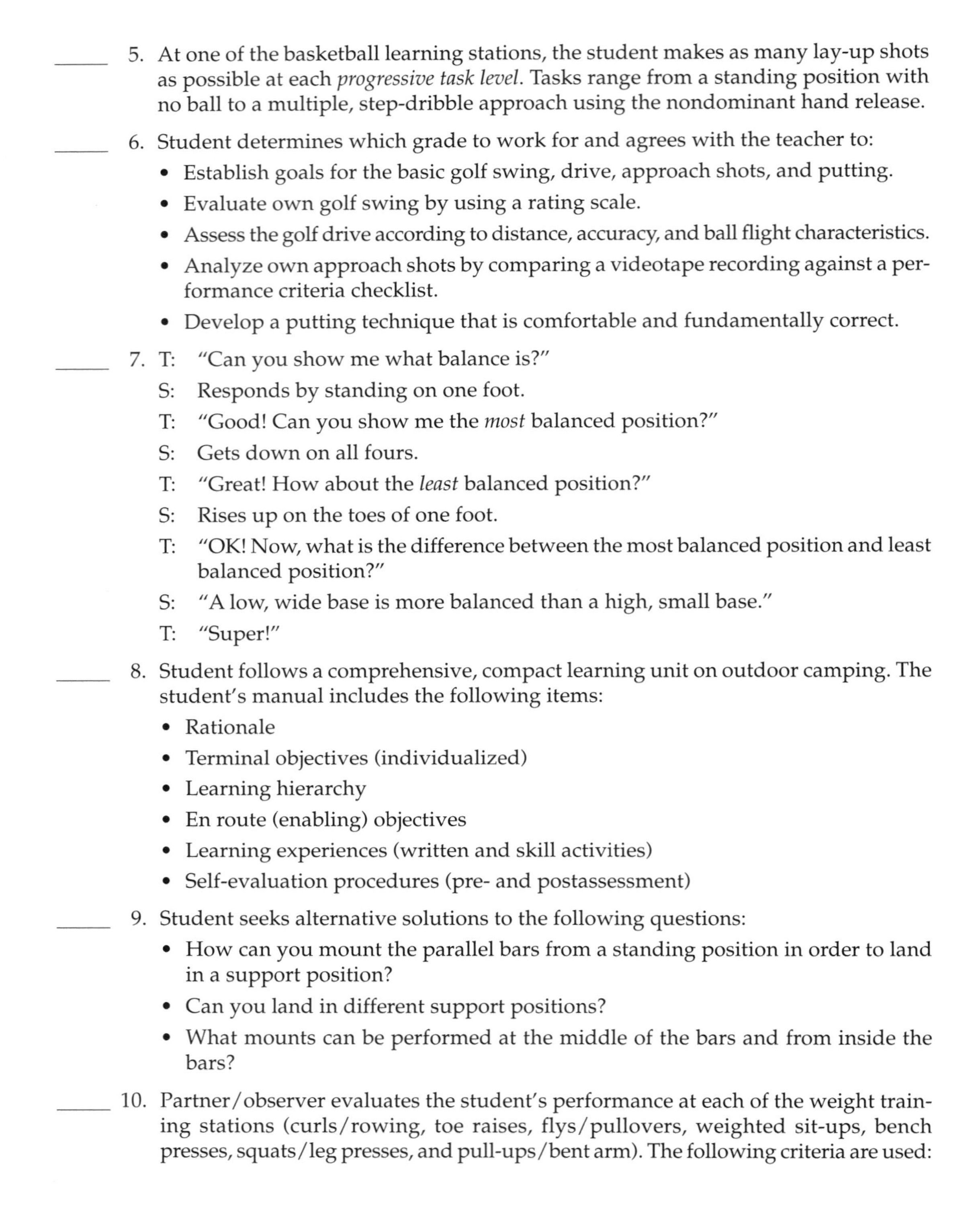

_____ 5. At one of the basketball learning stations, the student makes as many lay-up shots as possible at each *progressive task level*. Tasks range from a standing position with no ball to a multiple, step-dribble approach using the nondominant hand release.

_____ 6. Student determines which grade to work for and agrees with the teacher to:

- Establish goals for the basic golf swing, drive, approach shots, and putting.
- Evaluate own golf swing by using a rating scale.
- Assess the golf drive according to distance, accuracy, and ball flight characteristics.
- Analyze own approach shots by comparing a videotape recording against a performance criteria checklist.
- Develop a putting technique that is comfortable and fundamentally correct.

_____ 7. T: "Can you show me what balance is?"

S: Responds by standing on one foot.

T: "Good! Can you show me the *most* balanced position?"

S: Gets down on all fours.

T: "Great! How about the *least* balanced position?"

S: Rises up on the toes of one foot.

T: "OK! Now, what is the difference between the most balanced position and least balanced position?"

S: "A low, wide base is more balanced than a high, small base."

T: "Super!"

_____ 8. Student follows a comprehensive, compact learning unit on outdoor camping. The student's manual includes the following items:

- Rationale
- Terminal objectives (individualized)
- Learning hierarchy
- En route (enabling) objectives
- Learning experiences (written and skill activities)
- Self-evaluation procedures (pre- and postassessment)

_____ 9. Student seeks alternative solutions to the following questions:

- How can you mount the parallel bars from a standing position in order to land in a support position?
- Can you land in different support positions?
- What mounts can be performed at the middle of the bars and from inside the bars?

_____ 10. Partner/observer evaluates the student's performance at each of the weight training stations (curls/rowing, toe raises, flys/pullovers, weighted sit-ups, bench presses, squats/leg presses, and pull-ups/bent arm). The following criteria are used:

Achieved	Needs improvement	
		Exercise: ______________________________
❑	❑	1. Stretches muscle groups to be exercised before lifting.
❑	❑	2. Uses spotters appropriately.
❑	❑	3. Assumes correct starting position.
❑	❑	4. Carries out exercise with proper movement.
❑	❑	5. Inhales during negative or lowering phase; exhales during positive or working phase.
❑	❑	6. Completes the full range of motion during lift.

_____ 11. Student determines his or her own present performance in a series of flexibility exercises (neck/shoulders, trunk, hips/legs, and ankles/feet). Then, the student selects one of three *levels* for each exercise and practices the task accordingly. Student assesses his or her own execution of the exercise, determines *new* performance, and moves on to the next level.

_____ 12. Student practices the forehand drive in tennis against the wall using a self-drop technique. Basis for performance is a criteria checklist for the grip, self-drop technique, and swing and stroke.

_____ 13. Student enters health-related fitness data onto a computer. Software package allows student to select various target levels for each component. Upon selection, student is directed to guidelines for reaching the target level.

_____ 14. To understand the principle of propulsion in performing the front crawl, the student responds to a series of questions concerning the flutter kick (alternate, parallel, up-and-down movement), arm stroke (pull and recovery phase), and breath control (head rotated to one side on the longitudinal axis).

_____ 15. Student is asked, "Can you walk, run, climb, or jump like a dog, horse, bear, monkey, or kangaroo? Show me how!"

_____ 16. With the teacher, student chooses selected tasks that represent certain point values. Accumulated points are translated into a grade. *Some* of the tasks and point values in volleyball might be:

- Overhand serve—hit 5 of 8 cross-court into back half of court (2 points).
- Passing—wall volley for at least 1 minute with 80% of the balls hitting wall between 10 and 15 feet high (3 points).
- Setting—hit 3 out of 5 from a partner toss into a 6-foot-diameter circle from a distance of 10 feet (2 points).
- Spiking—from a partner set, hit 3 of 5 cross-court using on-hand side (1 point).

Feedback

1. D

   The type of learning is *problem solving* since the student would use divergent thinking operations to solve the problem, and several different solutions might be equally correct.

2. F

   Since this approach involves self-assessment, the student is engaged in a type of *programmed learning*. The form of evaluation distinguishes this type from the others.

3. A

   This individualized learning experience is *exploratory*. The student is challenged to experiment with no anticipated response. The experience described is too broad to be labeled problem solving.

4. I

   An *independent study* experience is described. The individual student pursues the tasks on his or her own outside of class. Teacher guidance is provided.

5. B

   The student is involved in a progressive series of *self-directed tasks*. He or she is responsible only for completing the tasks. There is no programmed learning element (self-evaluation).

6. E

   By negotiating criteria for a grade, the student is engaged in *contracting*. Agreement is reached between the teacher and student regarding the quantity and quality of work to be done.

7. C

   A convergent thinking/movement process is represented by this learning experience. This type, *guided discovery*, leads the student through a planned sequence that results in the predetermined answer or movement response.

8. G

   Although the detailed learning experience is not provided, the outline describes a *learning activity package*. This individualized approach is virtually self-teaching.

9. D

   Since the student seeks alternative solutions, a *problem-solving* approach is employed. The questions promote independence through learner experimentation and logical thinking to determine answers.

10. H

    This reciprocal learning experience is illustrative of a *tutorial program*, given the one-to-one relationship between the student and the partner/observer.

11. F

    The flexibility exercises are offered at different levels of engagement and the student determines the standard of performance through self-assessment. Thus, the approach is *programmed learning*.

12. B

    In this experience, the student is involved in a *self-directed task*. The checklist serves as a guide for reaching the objective (forehand drive).

13. J

    Fitness data are used to determine appropriate individual goals and guidelines for reaching the goals. The student accomplishes this through a *computer-assisted* approach.

14. C

    The series of questions is designed to elicit a single response. The student experiences success through this *guided discovery* approach.

15. A

    The student is encouraged to seek out a variety of responses through experimentation. This form of *exploration* allows each student to complete the movement challenge in his or her own unique way.

16. E

    In response to the individual student's capability (diagnosis), tasks can be selected in accordance with interests and ability levels. In this instance, agreement between teacher and student is an example of *contracting*.

Self-Directed Activity 7.5

You should now know the four critical elements to consider when devising interactive learning experiences. To see if you do, answer the following questions.

1. Why do social skills need to be learned? How should they be learned?

____

____

____

____

____

2. What factors should be considered when grouping students?

____

____

____

____

____

3. How can interdependence be fostered in interactive learning experiences?

____

____

____

____

____

4. What is meant by individual accountability?

Feedback

1. Students don't necessarily know how to help others set up equipment, give "pointers" to others, or rate others' performance according to a criteria checklist. Therefore, these kinds of behaviors can be learned through explanation, demonstration, and modeling.
2. Factors such as ability, status, gender, race, ethnicity, home background, and language proficiency should be considered when grouping, as well as the size of the group (usually 2 to 6 and even in number).
3. Interdependence can be fostered by limiting materials or equipment, using experts to teach components, assigning roles, and offering group rewards.
4. Individual accountability means that individual students are expected to achieve independently of partner or group success.

Self-Directed Activity 7.6

You should now be aware of the various approaches to interaction. For each of the following, describe the *content* of a learning experience which corresponds to the approach.

1. Reciprocal learning:

2. Role playing:

3. Co-op co-op (cooperative learning):

4. STAD (cooperative learning): ______________________________

____

____

____

____

Feedback

Needless to say, there are endless content possibilities in physical education that could serve as the basis for both achievement and social growth. Your responses should be similar to the examples presented before. The following comments are offered for each:

1. *Reciprocal learning*: Selected motor skills and/or cognitive abilities should lend themselves to task analyses since students provide peer feedback by applying the teacher's criteria, not their own.
2. *Role playing*: Interpersonal relations problems should parallel behavior within the class or school. Your descriptions could have ranged from a simple social skill (e.g., using names, praising, encouraging) to a complex social process (e.g., developing teamwork, showing sportsmanship).
3. *Co-op co-op*: This cooperative learning structure is useful with content that is likely to be unfamiliar to students. For example, productions of ethnic and folk dances would be an effective use of this format.
4. *STAD*: The skills and knowledge aspects of any sport can be used in this cooperative learning structure. Team play in the form of a tournament or a "team" project could be used.

Self-Directed Activity 7.7

Descriptions of learning experiences are followed by a list of criteria. Your task is to judge the learning experience according to these criteria. That is, does the learning experience relate to the stated *purpose*? Can the learning experience be completed given the stated *capability* of the student? Is the student likely to derive *satisfaction* from the learning experience? And, does the learning experience match the stated *objective*? Check (√) to indicate that the learning experience satisfies the stated criterion.

1. The student responds to the following directions: run, using all the space, without colliding with anyone; stop; find a space, lie on the floor, make yourself long and thin; get up and run again without colliding; stop; make your knees the highest part of you . . . then your elbows . . . then your nose; choose one part of your body and make it the highest.

   _____ *Purpose*: Acquire information

   _____ *Capability*: Student is already consciously aware of his or her body

   _____ *Satisfaction*: Student can experience success through the activity

   _____ *Objective*: To perform basic locomotor movement skills involving uneven rhythm (skip, slide, gallop)

2. The student answers the following series of questions: Can you name two different kinds of passes in basketball? What other kinds of passes can a player make? Why do you need a variety of passes in basketball? When would you want to use a bounce pass? Why is a lob pass used to get the ball to the center? What kind of passes should you use on a fast break?

   _____ *Purpose*: Analyze situations
   _____ *Capability*: Student has memorized the various kinds of basketball passes
   _____ *Satisfaction*: Student will enjoy question-answer exchange
   _____ *Objective*: To recognize the various kinds of basketball passes, given situations demanding their use

3. The student interacts reciprocally with a partner as follows: Watch partner perform developmental movement; provide mutual assistance in completing tasks; note the correct and incorrect aspects of partner's performance; offer observations of the correct aspects to the partner; accept comments by the observer.

   _____ *Purpose*: Value social attitudes
   _____ *Capability*: Student has displayed a sense of cooperation and trust
   _____ *Satisfaction*: Student will respond positively to reciprocal experience
   _____ *Objective*: To assist others in performing push-ups, sit-ups, pull-ups, jumping jacks, and flexibility exercises

4. The student executes the following sequence in dribbling a soccer ball: Dribble around carton obstacles; dribble toward an obstacle, circle it, and go on to the next obstacle; dribble toward an obstacle and go around it sideways; dribble toward an obstacle and go around it using a different pattern such as forward, backward, or diagonal.

   _____ *Purpose*: Develop complex movement skill
   _____ *Capability*: Student needs to improve eye-foot coordination and agility
   _____ *Satisfaction*: Student will find the experience rewarding
   _____ *Objective*: To maintain control of a soccer ball by dribbling when opposed by a defender

5. The student listens to a presentation on designing a balance beam routine that includes the following aspects: angles and ways of approaching the beam; direction of body motion on mounts; vertical and horizontal positions following mounts; effects of direction, size, speed, and intensity of stunts; flow of movements leading to dismount.

   _____ *Purpose*: Develop creativity
   _____ *Capability*: Student can identify and perform *single* mounts, movements, and dismounts
   _____ *Satisfaction*: Student will be interested in the decision-making experience
   _____ *Objective*: To design a balance beam routine according to the criteria of transition, momentum, and flow of movement

6. The student completes the following tasks in order: climb up and down a rope using both hands and feet; climb halfway up a rope using both legs and one hand only; climb halfway using two hands and one leg; repeat sequence with additional external weight (weighted vest).

   _____ *Purpose*: Improve body functions
   _____ *Capability*: Student is able to support weight using upper body parts
   _____ *Satisfaction*: Student can master tasks with practice
   _____ *Objective*: To increase muscular strength and endurance

Feedback

1.	Purpose	No	This learning experience involves the exploration of general space (psychomotor), not the acquisition of information (cognitive).
	Capability	√	Since the student has developed body awareness, he or she is *ready* to use body parts in general space and at different levels.
	Satisfaction	√	Given the student's capability, success in the learning experience is predictable, especially where there are no right or wrong responses.
	Objective	No	The learning experience does not match the stated objective. Movements with uneven rhythm are not included in the learning experience.
2.	Purpose	√	Clearly, the opportunity to analyze situations (cognitive) is incorporated in the learning experience.
	Capability	No	Other than the fact that the student *knows* various basketball passes, there is no indication that analysis skills are within the student's range of present ability.
	Satisfaction	No	Because of the level of understanding required, the student would probably find the learning experience frustrating.
	Objective	√	The objective is stated at the analysis level that matches the cognitive process used in the learning experience.
3.	Purpose	No	Basic social behaviors are elicited during the learning experience, not high-order affective responses at the *value* level.
	Capability	√	Cooperation and trust are desirable traits when participating in a reciprocal learning experience.
	Satisfaction	√	The student should enjoy the experience because of his or her sense of cooperation and trust.
	Objective	√	The learning objective and learning experience match very closely in terms of expected outcome.
4.	Purpose	√	Dribbling a soccer ball is certainly an example of a complex movement skill (psychomotor).
	Capability	No	The student is likely to *fail* in this learning experience since the activity requires a sufficient degree of eye-foot coordination and agility.
	Satisfaction	No	The high probability of failure means this would be an unrewarding experience for the student.
	Objective	√	The behavioral and content aspects of the objective are nearly identical to the nature of the learning experience.
5.	Purpose	No	There are no opportunities for creative thinking (cognitive). A good deal of low-level information processing is incorporated in the learning experience.
	Capability	No	The student shows comprehension but not cognitive ability at the level of creativity (synthesis).
	Satisfaction	No	It is doubtful that the student would find this learning experience of any great interest.
	Objective	No	The objective is stated at a much higher level than the behavioral response desired by the learning experience.

6. Purpose	√	The learning experience would definitely result in improved bodily functions (psychomotor).
Capability	√	This ability is obviously a *prerequisite* to completing the learning experience.
Satisfaction	√	It appears that this kind of learning experience would offer a positive challenge to the student.
Objective	√	The objective can be achieved by completing the learning experience tasks.

Self-Directed Activity 7.8

You should select learning experiences which accommodate "special" students. For students categorized as culturally diverse, at risk, and gifted and talented, identify two approaches that match their characteristics. Then, describe a learning experience that would be effective with that kind of student.

Culturally diverse

1. Learning experience approach: ____________________

   Description: ____________________

   ____

   ____

   ____

   ____

2. Learning experience approach: ____________________

   Description: ____________________

   ____

   ____

   ____

   ____

At risk

1. Learning experience approach: ____________________

   Description: ____________________

   ____

   ____

   ____

   ____

2. Learning experience approach: ______________________________

   Description: ______________________________

   ____

   ____

   ____

   ____

Gifted and talented

1. Learning experience approach: ______________________________

   Description: ______________________________

   ____

   ____

   ____

   ____

2. Learning experience approach: ______________________________

   Description: ______________________________

   ____

   ____

   ____

   ____

Feedback

The approaches identified were illustrated previously in this chapter. Your descriptions should be similar to those examples, appropriate to the given kind of student.

Culturally diverse: Various approaches that are effective include problem solving, cooperative learning, and computer-assisted learning. In addition, learning "portfolios" are suggested that are similar in design to learning activity packages (LAP).

At risk: Approaches that are particularly useful include reciprocal learning (scaffolding), cooperative learning (STAD), tutoring, and the use of technology.

Gifted and talented: As a general strategy, the pace of learning can be accelerated through the following approaches: self-directed tasks, contracting, programmed learning, learning activity packages, independent study, and computer-assisted learning. Acceleration works best with learning experiences that have been sequenced in a linear fashion. Providing enrichment is another effective general strategy. Reciprocal learning ("cluster" groups) and cooperative learning ("jigsaw") are particularly useful.

8

Curriculum Designing: A Case Study

Key Concept

Curriculum designers develop the ability to design physical education curricula by applying their knowledge to their own situations.

Initially, you were asked to think of curriculum designing as the answer to three questions: "Where am I going?" "How will I get there?" and "When will I know I've arrived?" You developed skills for each curriculum component in order to answer these questions. To demonstrate how you can fit together your designing skills and basic curriculum components, this final chapter presents a sample curriculum for physical education, using a case study approach. This sample design is meant to be a scaled-down version of a complete physical education curriculum. Its primary purpose is to show you the progression from organizing centers to content goals, from content goals to learner analysis, from learner analysis to learning objectives, from learning objectives to evaluation procedures, and from learning objectives to learning experiences. Although the variables may differ from school to school and year to year, the *process* you have learned is essential to your flexibility as a curriculum designer.

It's May 11 and Denise Caldwell has almost finished her first year as a physical education teacher at Sussex Middle School in the Hanover school district. When she applied for the job, she thought the community was still a white, middle-class enclave as it had been when she was growing up in the area. Ironically, she graduated from nearby Riverside High, a rival of Hanover's. According to Scott Pottieger, assistant superintendent for program and staff development, the community had changed markedly. It was now predominantly blue-collar, working class, with a large percentage of African American, Hispanic, and Asian families. About 60 percent of the families were lower-middle-class; the rest were split evenly between families at or below poverty level and upper-middle-class families.

In school, white students made up about 50% of the enrollment; African American, 25%; Hispanic, 15%; and Asian, 10%. Initially, although the environment was different than she had expected, Denise was optimistic that she could challenge them, convey high expectations, and help them learn. In fact, she admitted to herself, this diversity was exactly what was preached in her undergraduate methods courses. Professor Robinson was always saying, "Think of student differences as strengths, not weaknesses. Take advantage of them."

Well, as the only first-year physical education teacher on a staff of four (two males, two females), she did her best with the standard curriculum she inherited. In her mind, though, she wasn't that successful. It didn't matter what color they were or what their socioeconomic background was, the kids didn't seem to care about physical education. Denise blamed it on the curriculum. It was very traditional, with an emphasis on team sports.

One of the male physical education teachers, Bill Jones, was the department head, with 14 years in the system. The other male teacher, Tony Costa, was somewhat progressive in his ideas, but not very successful in changing things. At times, Denise thought of him as being "all talk and no action." The other female teacher, Sue Rodriguez, was great to work with. She was very cooperative and got along well with the kids. But teaching was just a job to her. She "moonlighted" as an aerobics instructor three nights a week and on Saturdays. Sue couldn't devote the extra time needed to change the program.

Through the grapevine, Denise heard that Hanover had received a state grant to support "venture" projects. It was part of the state's effort to encourage school reform and restructuring. Supposedly, her district matched the state funds with "curriculum improvement grants." She knew that some of the classroom teachers in her building had been working on some ideas for developing new curriculum units.

Rather than appear "out of touch" to the teachers she worked with on a daily basis, Denise was curious enough to call Scott to see what it was all about. He explained that the district was providing support for designing innovative units. The curriculum improvement grants would pay for materials, equipment, and some in-service training, if necessary. The other incentive was that during the next school year, teachers would be given an extra planning period from September through December. The special curriculum unit was to be implemented some time between January and the end of the school year. However, everyone knew that to do it right would require more time than the extra 50 minutes per week for planning.

Scott implied that Denise should have known about the project since Bill Jones had probably discussed it at one of the physical education department meetings. She really felt stupid. Angrily, she reacted with, "We don't even have meetings. I never saw anything!" Scott agreed to let her pick up the proposal guidelines, even though everything was supposed to go through the department head. If she was serious about putting a proposal together, she only had 2 more days before the due date. She went over to the administration building during her lunch break and picked up the materials.

Denise looked for Bill Jones right after school; he couldn't be found. But she did ask Betsy Murray what she thought about the project. Betsy was Denise's mentor for the year. All first-year teachers were assigned a mentor to help them during their "induction" year. Betsy told her that she should "go for it" if she was genuinely interested in writing a curriculum. "If nothing else," she said, "you'll get some exposure for physical education and yourself."

That night, after reading the proposal guidelines, Denise was really excited. She had calmed down enough to call Bill at home. She wanted to make sure he would support her, since the proposal had to be signed by the department head. She also didn't miss the chance to find out why he hadn't shared the guidelines with the physical education teachers. Bill's excuse was, "I didn't think anyone would want to do something like this. Tony's got a weekend rec job and he's taking a grad course in the fall. We all know that Sue's too busy with aerobics. And I just assumed you weren't interested since it's your first year."

Denise knew the real reasons—Bill was basically lazy and just wanted to maintain the status quo. In addition, she thought, it was administratively convenient for him to do nothing. After all, he would need to find a way to cover her extra planning period if her proposal were approved.

Denise held back her frustration and anger, and told him that she was very interested in improving the curriculum and was planning to put a proposal together. She felt good about herself . . . being assertive, that is. Bill was perceptive enough to know that he had better say yes, even though he sensed that Denise was criticizing his lack of leadership in putting together a viable curriculum.

The proposals were limited to three pages. As it turned out, of the 18 proposals submitted, Denise's was the only one in physical education. Hers focused on the fact that kids at the middle school, as "emerging adolescents," needed to develop a concept of wellness. Even then, it might be too late to break poor health habits. If they waited until high school, it would definitely be too late. It worked! Denise got word on June 3 that her proposal was one of the 10 approved. However, there was a condition. Since she was new, she had to get feedback from Bill Jones at planned stages during the curriculum project. She didn't care as long as she got the grant.

The school district established a common structure and format for the curriculum projects. The rationale for doing this was to ensure internal consistency across different subject areas and to provide a systematic approach to curriculum design. Denise was somewhat surprised to find that many of the required elements were the same as those that she had studied in a curriculum course she had taken right before student teaching. She began to feel comfortable with the project already. In fact, she decided to get started right away even though there was no expectation that teachers would devote any time to the project during the summer.

Although a step-by-step, component-by-component approach was suggested as part of the project directions, Denise knew that she could begin anywhere, as long as the *final* check of her curriculum followed the order suggested. But she decided to start with the first step, organizing centers. She also decided to develop parts of all components before the complete curriculum was designed.

Creating Organizing Centers

Denise realized that to generate potential organizing centers a broad perspective was needed, including the social context, students' needs, and physical education content. Each served as a source of organizing centers. From the standpoint of contemporary society, she reasoned that there should be an interest in personal maintenance of wellness in order to eliminate health risk factors. There should also be a concomitant concern for developing a society that has acquired the skills to engage in a variety of physical activities. Denise remembered an article in a professional journal she had read the month before. Results of national studies had revealed the poor fitness status and physical activity habits of children 10 to 18 (Ross & Pate, 1987). The authors concluded that

- children have not achieved fitness levels associated with enhanced health, and they remain sedentary over long periods of time;
- decisions about eating, drinking, smoking, coping with stress, and controlling emotions have a profound effect on health; and
- customary patterns of behavior—lifestyle—may be the most significant health risk factor; and
- children are not developing fundamental movement and basic sport skills either. Qualitative and quantitative measures of motor skill are lower than anticipated (Graham, 1987).

Denise also looked through her curriculum book from undergraduate school. The descriptions of different curriculum models caught her eye. For example, she found that the fitness curriculum model consists of the following subject matter:

- Health-related components (flexibility, cardiorespiratory endurance, muscular strength and endurance, body composition)
- Motor-related components (balance, coordination, speed, agility, power)
- Application of training and conditioning principles
- Nutrition, diet, and weight control
- Stress management
- Assessment methods for diagnosis and activity prescription
- Design and use of a personalized fitness program

In addition, she liked some others. The developmental model includes neuromuscular development relative to perceptual motor abilities (balance, kinesthesis, visual discrimination, auditory discrimination, visual motor coordination, tactile sensitivity) and fundamental movement skills (body manipulative, object manipulative, sports). The humanistic/social development model emphasizes self-awareness and choice as a basis for personal growth. She figured that the subject matter of this model would include decision making and responsibility for the consequences of one's own actions.

With all this information, Denise jotted down some of the possible organizing centers that came to mind:

- Fitness for Life
- Personal Achievement
- Self-Expression
- Challenge
- Wellness and You
- Improving Your Performance
- Personalized Fitness
- Aerobics Away
- Optimal Motor Ability
- Developmental Movement

In spite of these seemingly unlimited choices, Denise settled on two organizing centers to get started with—Responsible Lifestyles and Efficient Functioning. She was able to justify these organizing centers for two reasons. First, quality-of-life issues have resulted in the *philosophical* basis for the concept of wellness, a broad holistic view of health. Fundamental to this philosophy is the notion of lifelong involvement in fitness and sports. There are pragmatic reasons for promoting health-enhancing physical activities. A healthy society will reduce health care costs, increase work efficiency and productivity, and prolong life.

Second, students 10 to 18 years of age are physically and mentally mature enough to understand, appreciate, and carry out healthful patterns of behavior (exercise). From a *psychological* standpoint, it is developmentally appropriate for students of this age to seek a functional understanding of movement concepts and to build competence and confidence in performing various motor skills. Likewise, students are able to understand and value the contribution of physical fitness to a healthy lifestyle.

Once she had selected organizing centers, it was logical for Denise to transform them into something more useful—content goals. This would establish the general direction for her curriculum and help guide the rest of the curriculum.

Determining Content Goals

To Denise, the number of goals that could evolve from her two organizing centers seemed endless. Therefore, she decided to work with just one of the organizing centers—Responsible Lifestyles. Nine general outcomes were derived representing all three domains, although they were not meant to be exhaustive

Cognitive outcomes

- Understand the meaning of wellness
- Apply principles of training and conditioning
- Analyze alternative patterns of nutrition
- Design a personalized fitness program

Affective outcomes

- Show interest in health-enhancing leisure activities
- Appreciate the need for healthful decision making
- Value the role of physical activity in healthful living

Psychomotor outcomes

- Develop health-related fitness
- Demonstrate skill in health-enhancing activities

Because of the relationship between subject matter and goals, Denise needed to select content. She further reduced the number of general outcomes to work with during this initial phase of the project. That way she could get feedback from Scott before going too far. The three outcomes, one from each domain, which served as the basis for further development were

- understand the meaning of wellness,
- value the role of physical activity in healthful living, and
- develop health-related fitness.

Denise then needed to select content based on its contribution to the general outcomes. Therefore, content suggested by these outcomes should contain health-enhancing elements. Her attempt to satisfy this criterion resulted in

- lifestyle management,
- positive wellness,
- health-related behavior,
- lifespan fitness,
- nutrition,
- stress and relaxation,
- training methods,
- training programs,
- cycling,
- swimming,
- weight training,
- rope jumping,
- circuit training,
- soccer,
- health-related fitness, and
- skill-related fitness.

Denise knew that once a full set of content goals had been determined, the depth and breadth of subject matter would be revealed. The next step in the project directions was to *analyze* the specific elements of the subject matter and their relationships. The first thing she did was to organize her content goals according to levels of generality. Then she identified their prerequisites.

In support of the three general outcomes under the organizing center "Responsible Lifestyles," tiers of content goals were derived based on level of generality. Denise's analysis of one of the general outcomes is shown in Figure 8.1. The other two outcomes were analyzed later.

Next, the facts, responses, and motor abilities that support the higher level goals were determined. Although this was a difficult task, Denise knew that these prerequisite behaviors were needed in order to achieve the outcome expressed by the content goals. She used a combination of approaches for this purpose (i.e., outlining content, structuring of content, and conducting a task analysis). Prerequisites for *one* of the goal sequences are revealed in Figure 8.2. Prerequisites for the other two goal sequences were identified later.

One requirement under project guidelines was to present a "learning hierarchy." At first, Denise wasn't sure what this was, but then realized it was nothing more than a combination of her general outcomes, tiers of goals, and prerequisites. She could see the advantage of doing this because it showed the "pathway to learning" from the most complex goals down to the simplest knowledge, responses, and motor skills. Denise's learning hierarchy appears in Figure 8.3 (pages 252–254) for her three general outcomes.

At this point, it seemed natural for Denise to get some reaction from Scott before he went on vacation. It was now the middle of July. She had to wait anyway because the next step in the process called for the actual collection of information about her students. Although she could plan her strategy, school didn't start until the end of August.

Scott reviewed Denise's materials and got back to her in 2 days. He praised her work by saying, "You've really become quite the curriculum designer. I didn't know you had such talent, especially for physical education. Just kidding!" Denise wasn't sure if he was. Maybe he had a negative image of physical education. He ended their conversation with a bit of advice. "The next step is really important. Make sure you collect good entry data on your students so you can eventually show at the end, we hope, that they learned something."

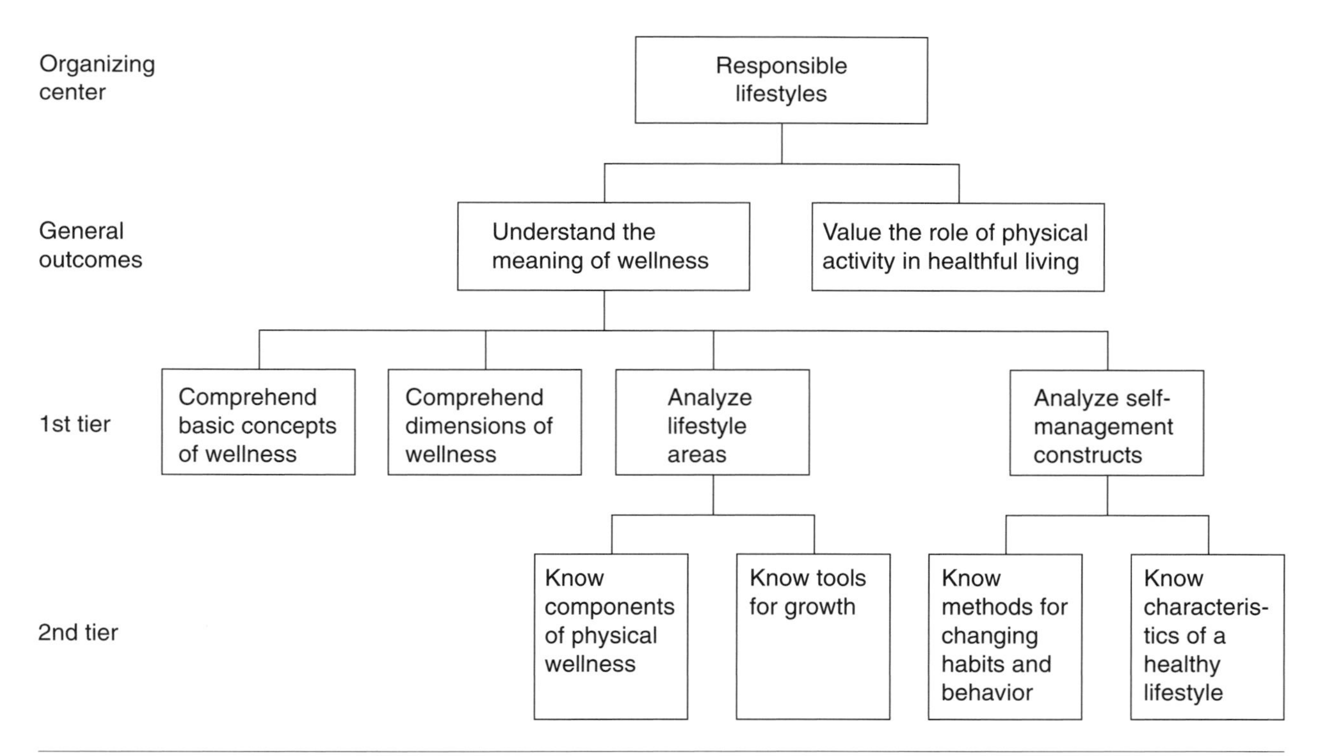

Figure 8.1 Organization of content goals is shown for one of the general outcomes.

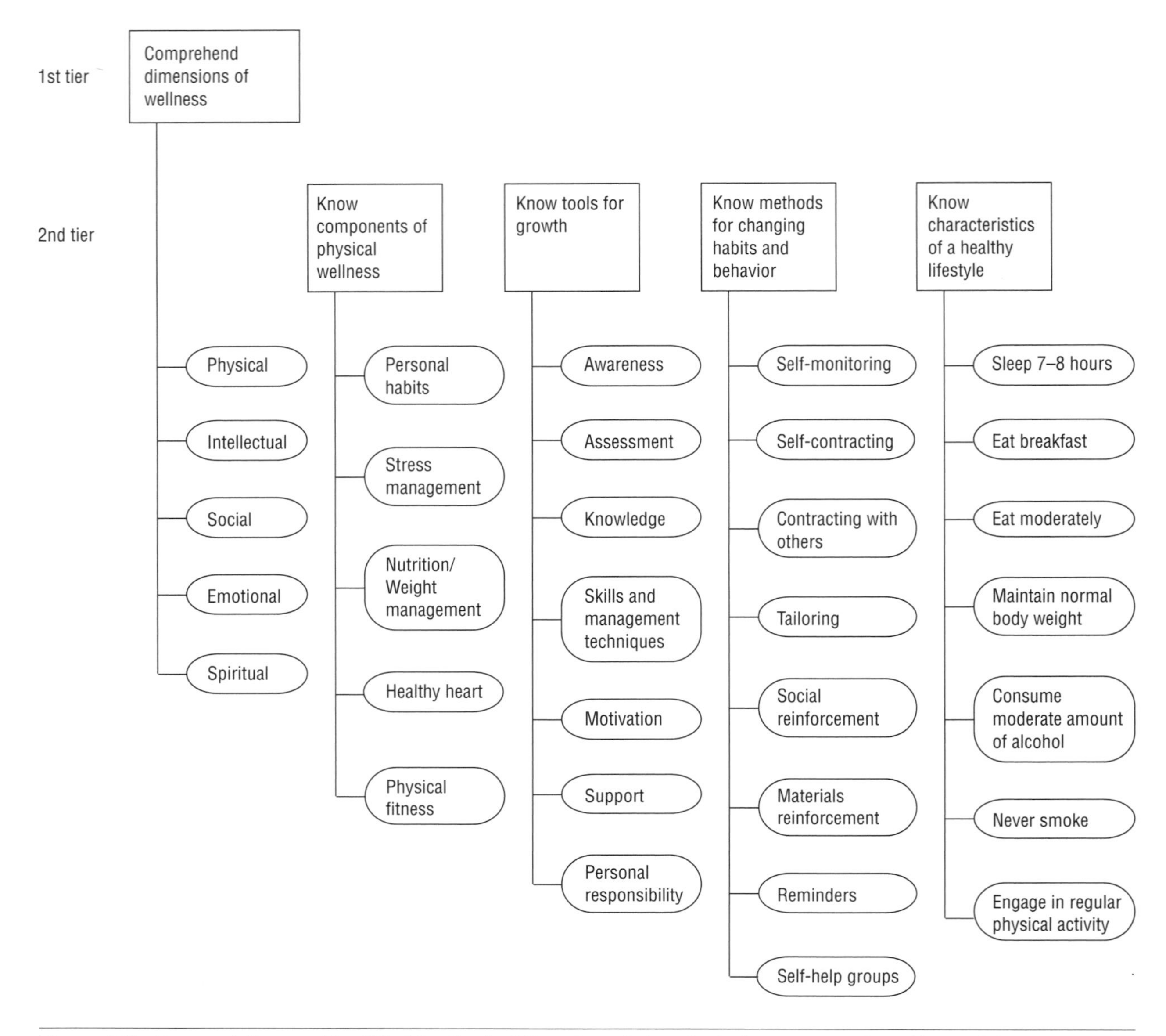

Figure 8.2 Prerequisites are identified for the last tier of goals in selected sequences from Figure 8.1.

Conducting Learner Analysis

During August, Denise devoted some time to her plans for entry appraisal even though she was going on vacation for 2 weeks just before school started. She hadn't done this before and was a little apprehensive. She started out by sorting her prerequisites into three groups:

- Those which all the students should possess and probably already do possess (group 1)
- Those which some or many of the students might not already possess (group 2)
- Those which most or all of the students probably do not possess (group 3)

Denise focused her entry appraisal on those prerequisites from group 2. She had to keep in mind that the unit was being planned for eighth graders completing a semester course that would meet 3 days a week for 1 hour each day. For student identification purposes, her preassessment would sample student behaviors across all three goals.

Although it was more time-consuming than she realized, Denise developed three techniques to determine entry-level status for the prerequisites identified from group 2. For the cognitive goal, the written questionnaire on pages 255 to 256 was designed. The self-report inventory constructed for the affective goal is shown on page 257. And the performance items and measurements selected as indicators of students' health-related fitness for the psychomotor goal are shown in Table 8.1.

Right after school started, Denise carried out the preassessment procedure. Results of data collection confirmed that the students, in general, didn't possess those prerequisites sampled through the written questionnaire and self-report inventory. Analysis of scores revealed the following:

Written questionnaire (n = 28)

Range: 15 to 29

Mean: 21

Self-report inventory (n = 28)

Range: 22 to 32

Mean: 26

While standards were available for the items selected to measure health-related fitness, entry-level results will serve as the baseline for individual student improvement. Denise felt that since fitness maintenance is an ongoing way of life, improved fitness status across all components was projected. Therefore, she wanted to make sure that learner analysis was depicted on a more individual basis. Results of data collection are shown in Table 8.2 (page 257) for a representative set of students.

Just out of curiosity, Denise also reviewed previous content in physical education and cumulative records. Her findings reinforced the conclusion that the students, in general, didn't possess those prerequisites associated with the selected content goals. She thought to herself, "This is good in a way. I can clearly show that there is a need based on tangible evidence. Now all I have to do is produce some changes." Denise then used these overall results to identify those *specific* changes in learning that were sought. This meant she needed to write objectives.

Deriving Learning Objectives

Denise knew she had her work cut out with only about 2 months to go. Given the scope of her content goals, the number of potential learning objectives in support of these goals appeared infinite. That's because objectives may be derived for all tiers of higher level content goals *and* all lower level prerequisites. Thus, her next task was to decide which objectives to pursue and which to eliminate depending on how realistic it was to achieve the objectives in the given time period.

Table 8.1 Health-Related Fitness Indicators

Component	Item	Description
Aerobic endurance	1-mile walk/run	Walk or run 1 mile at the fastest pace that can be maintained throughout the entire distance; score is in minutes and seconds.
Body composition	Sum of triceps and calf skinfolds	Measure the degree of body fatness; each site is measured three consecutive times; median score is recorded score; final score is sum of median scores for tricep *and* calf measurement.
Flexibility	Sit-and-reach	Evaluate the flexibility of the lower back and hamstring muscles; score is the most distant point reached on the fourth trial by *both* hands and *held* for 1 second; measure to the nearest centimeter.
Muscular strength/ Endurance	Modified sit-ups	Evaluate abdominal muscular strength and endurance by performing repeated sit-ups; score is the number of correctly executed sit-ups completed in 60 seconds.

Note. Adapted from *Physical Best: The American Alliance Physical Fitness Education and Assessment Program* (pp. 16–20) by the American Alliance for Health, Physical Education, Recreation and Dance, 1988, Reston, VA: Author. Copyright 1988 by AAHPERD. Adapted by permission.

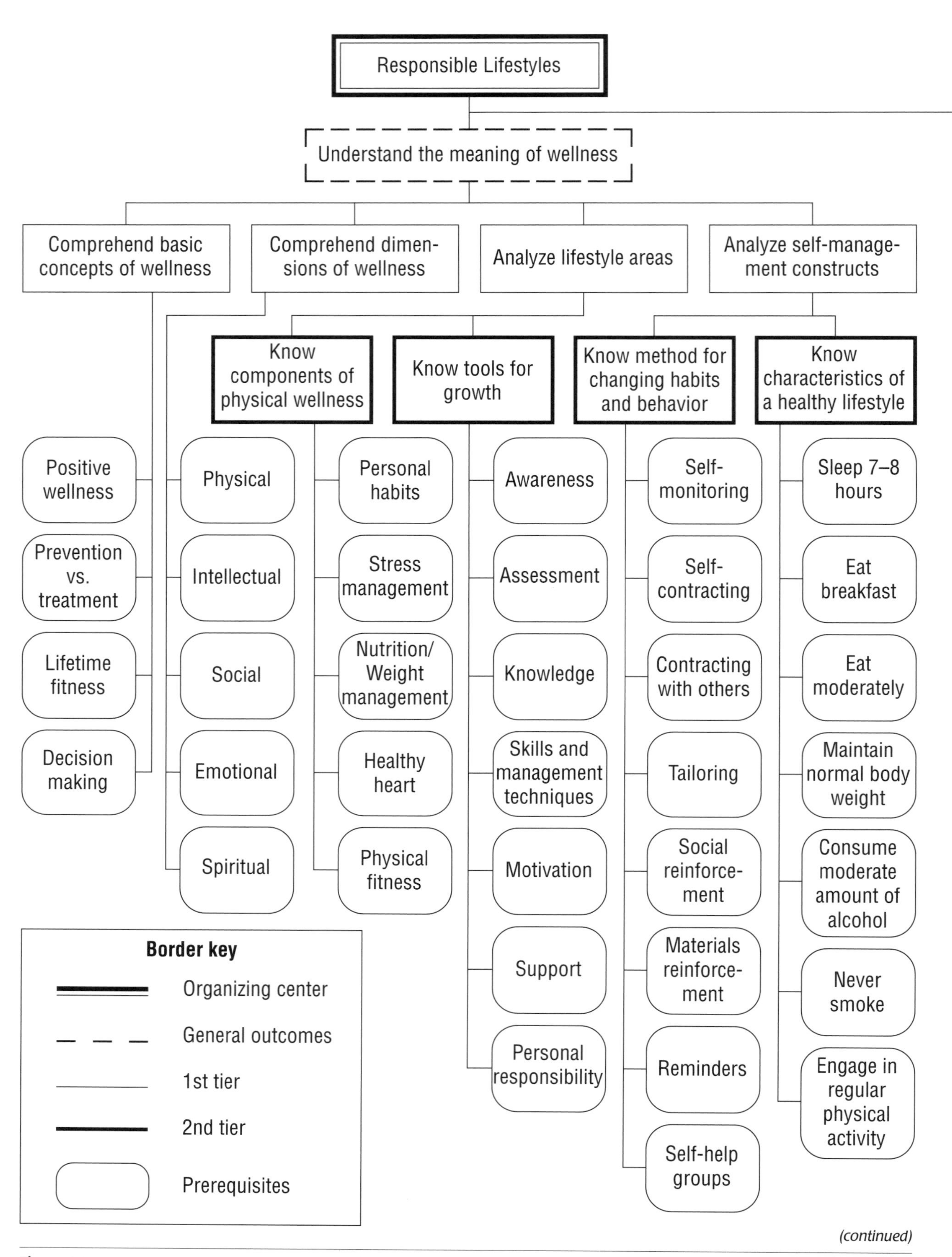

(continued)

Figure 8.3 Learning hierarchy reveals the organization of content goals and the identification of prerequisites for the organizing center "Responsible Lifestyles" (Greenberg, 1983; Melograno & Klinzing, 1992; Robbins, Powers, & Burgess, 1991).

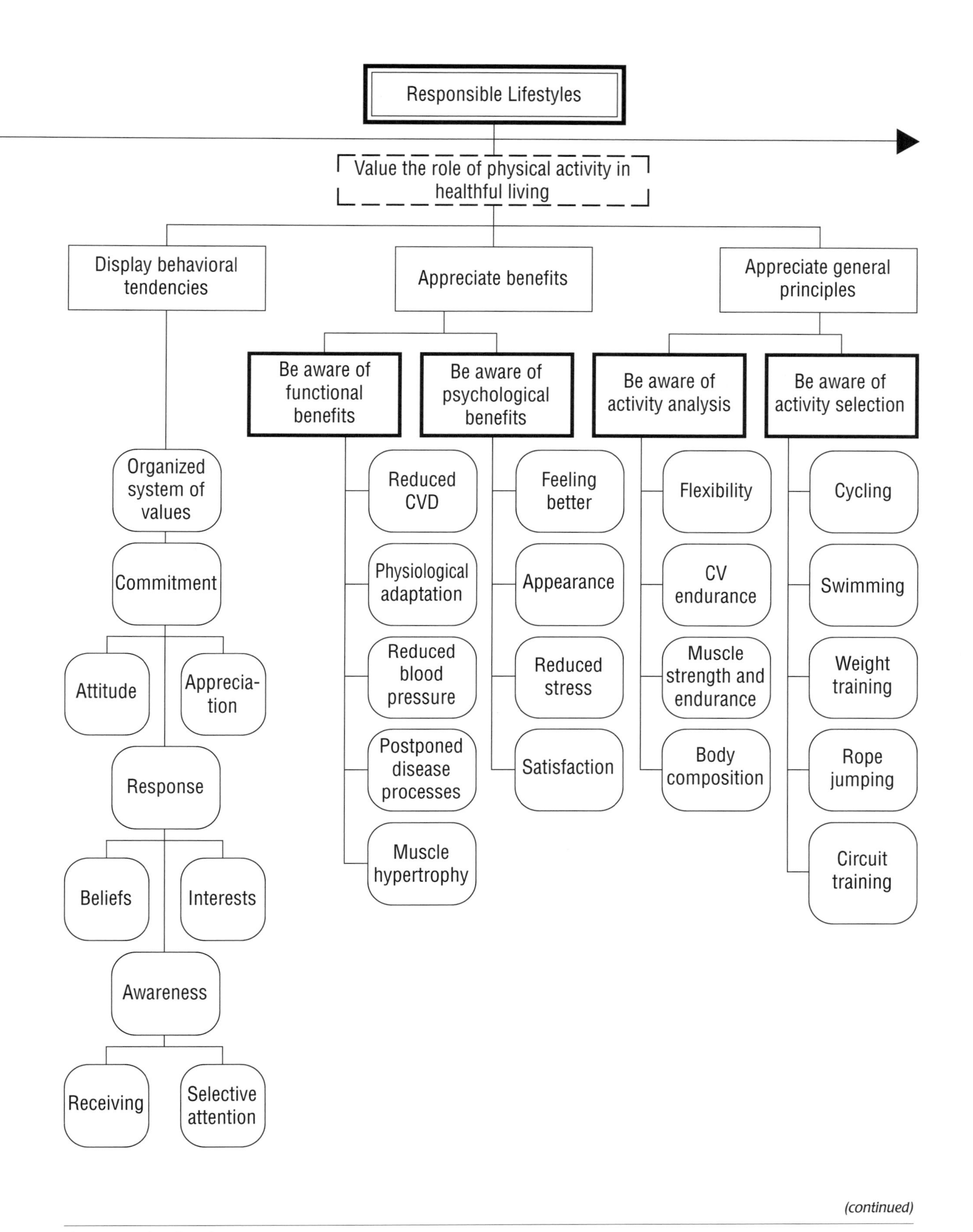

Responsible Lifestyles
Value the role of physical activity in healthful living
Display behavioral tendencies
Appreciate benefits
Appreciate general principles
Be aware of functional benefits
Be aware of psychological benefits
Be aware of activity analysis
Be aware of activity selection
Organized system of values
Commitment
Attitude
Apprecia-tion
Response
Beliefs
Interests
Awareness
Receiving
Selective attention
Reduced CVD
Physiological adaptation
Reduced blood pressure
Postponed disease processes
Muscle hypertrophy
Feeling better
Appearance
Reduced stress
Satisfaction
Flexibility
CV endurance
Muscle strength and endurance
Body composition
Cycling
Swimming
Weight training
Rope jumping
Circuit training

(continued)

Figure 8.3 *(continued)*

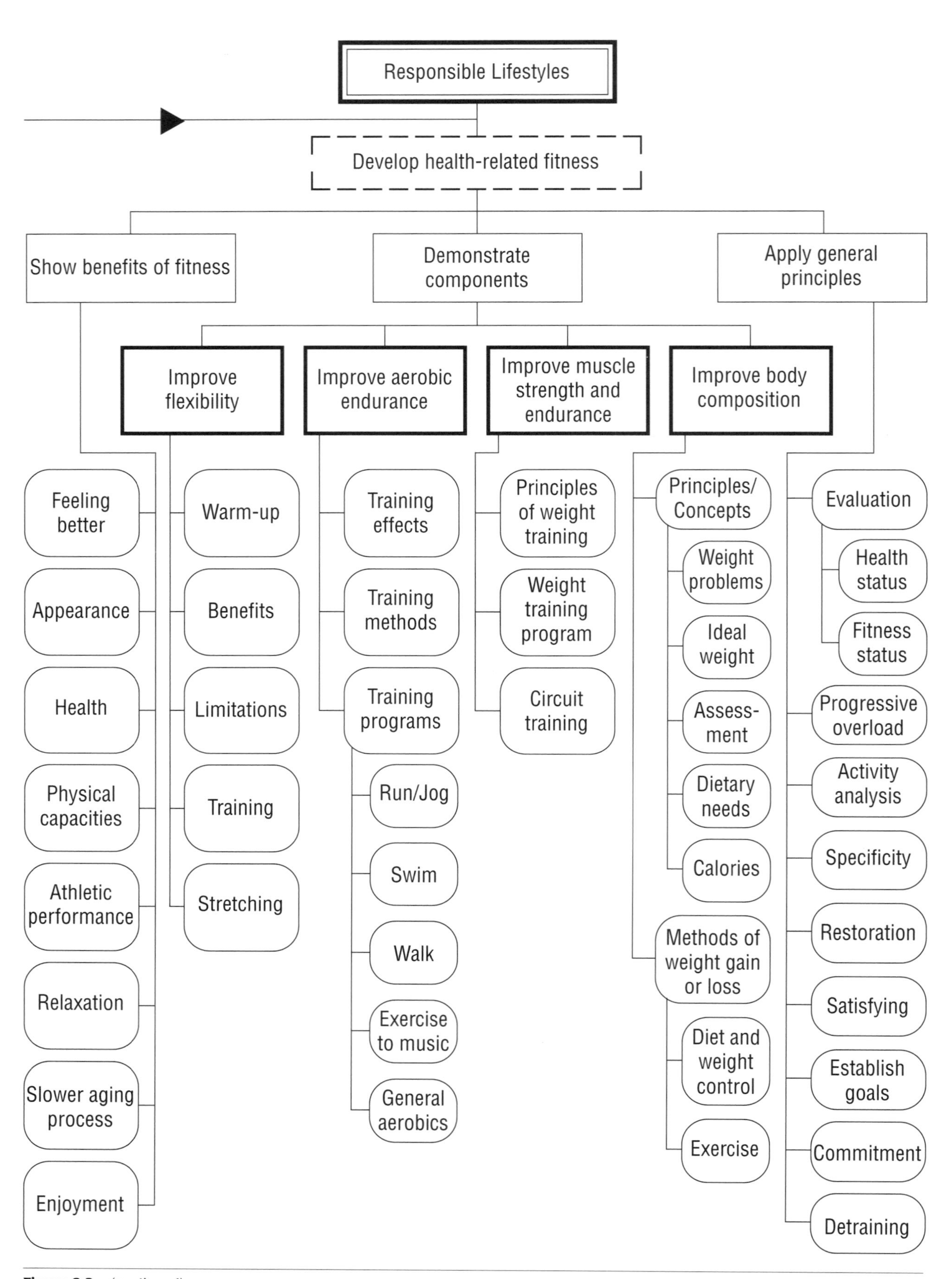

Figure 8.3 *(continued)*

Written Questionnaire

"Wellness and Me"

Directions: Answer the following questions as best you can. The results will not be used to determine a grade. Your answers will help determine what needs to be learned.

Scoring: Points for each item are indicated; total 40 points.

Rating:	36–40	Excellent
	28–35	Good
	0–27	Needs improvement

Name: ______________________________ Date: ______________

1. The wellness movement focuses on measures that will prevent disease rather than measures that treat sickness. (1 point)

   T F

2. Wellness is an enhanced dimension of health that includes a number of qualities. Identify five of these qualities. (10 points; 2 each)

   (a) ______________________________

   (b) ______________________________

   (c) ______________________________

   (d) ______________________________

   (e) ______________________________

3. Why is personal responsibility so important to wellness growth? (3 points)

   ____

   ____

   ____

   ____

4. In the United States, the emphasis on being healthy has resulted in more youths who are physically fit. (1 point)

   T F

5. A wellness lifestyle includes the five dimensions below. Identify at least one healthy behavior or habit that is associated with each. (10 points; 2 each)

   (a) Physical: ______________________________

   (b) Intellectual: ______________________________

   (c) Social: ______________________________

   (d) Emotional: ______________________________

   (e) Spiritual: ______________________________

6. Fitness is a way of life, not a state of being. The results of exercise are short-lived. Benefits diminish 48 to 72 hours following activity. (1 point)

   T F

7. What are some healthful lifestyle practices that relate to sleep, eating, drinking, smoking, and exercise? (5 points; 1 each)

   (a) ______________________________

   (b) ______________________________

   (c) ______________________________

   (d) ______________________________

   (e) ______________________________

8. Anyone under 18 years of age should not worry about coronary heart disease. (1 point)

   T F

9. Today, the leading causes of death and disability are related to our customary patterns of behavior—our lifestyles. (1 point)

   T F

10. Some ways of changing behavior are listed below. Give an example of how each could be used to change a health-related behavior (6 points; 2 each)

    Self-monitoring: ______________________________

    ____

    Contracting with others: ______________________________

    ____

    Tailoring: ______________________________

    ____

11. You can eliminate fat in your hips and waist by performing exercises that involve the hip and waist. (1 point)

    T F

Self-Report Inventory

Item	Always	Frequently	Occasionally	Seldom	Never
1. To keep my body flexible, I stretch or bend for several minutes each day.	5	4	3	2	1
2. Rather than take the elevator, I walk four or fewer flights of stairs.	5	4	3	2	1
3. In order to help maintain normal body weight, I engage in physical activities.	5	4	3	2	1
4. I engage in some form of vigorous activity for 30 minutes at least three times a week.	5	4	3	2	1
5. Whenever feasible, I walk or ride a bike instead of taking a car.	5	4	3	2	1
6. I use part of my leisure time participating in individual, family, or team activities that increase my level of fitness (e.g., cycling, swimming, circuit training).	5	4	3	2	1
7. I am aware of the calories expended when I participate in physical activities.	5	4	3	2	1
8. Things I need to do are scheduled around the time I set aside for physical activity.	5	4	3	2	1

Rating: 36–40 Excellent
28–35 Good
0–27 Needs improvement

Table 8.2 Individual Learner Analysis Results

Name	Written questionnaire score	Self-report score	Aerobic endurance	Body composition	Flexibility	Muscular strength and endurance
Marie	18	23	11:10	43	10	20
Laura	27	26	10:45	25	22	31
Craig	21	32	8:10	19	19	40
Janet	15	27	12:15	31	14	23
Tyler	17	28	9:20	30	8	30

No doubt, results of the preassessment yielded a basis for decision making. Project directions also suggested that learning objectives be selected on the basis of need and "cruciality." The needs assessment procedure was considered one of the most popular approaches for deciding on objectives. Denise applied this approach for one of her goals as shown in Table 8.3. The three potential objectives support the goal "Analyze self-management constructs" (1st tier) which in turn supports the general outcome "Understand the meaning of wellness."

To determine the cruciality of objectives, Denise established the relative value of objectives based on factors of probability. As shown in Figure 8.4, she applied the cruciality formula to the objectives from Table 8.3.

Once learning objectives were selected, Denise needed to organize them. This element was also included in the project directions. Although at first, she thought this was expecting too much, she realized later that it helped in developing evaluation procedures and devising learning experiences. She arranged the objectives in the same hierarchical pattern as the original goals and prerequisites from which they were derived. Thus, she was able to distinguish between terminal and enabling objectives.

Denise's higher level goals served as the foundation for *terminal* objectives. Some of her terminal objectives were:

1st tier

- To understand the meaning of wellness, the student will design a "Guide to a Self-Managed Lifestyle" with an average design rating of at least 7 on a 10-point scale.
- To value the role of physical activity in healthful living, the student will engage in health-related fitness activities during at least 75% of "open" activity periods at the end of each week.
- To develop health-related fitness, the student will achieve 90% of all projected goals for targeted components following a 2-month training program.

2nd tier

- To analyze lifestyle areas, the student will select, with 90% accuracy, the appropriate component of physical wellness, given situations that demand its use.
- To appreciate the benefits of physical activity, the student will show a favorable change of at least 1.0 on a values inventory regarding the functional and psychological benefits of physical activity.
- To demonstrate the development of health-related fitness components, the student will achieve 90% of all projected goals for muscular strength and endurance, following a 2-month weight training program.

Table 8.3 Needs Assessment of Learning Objectives

Potential objective	Preference	Proportion	Discrepancy	Priority
A. To analyze self-management constructs, the student will select, with 80% accuracy, the two best methods for changing habits and behaviors in situations describing "unwellness."	1st	100%	High	High
B. To analyze self-management constructs, the student will identify, in 7 of 10 cases, the presence or absence of the characteristics of a healthy lifestyle for persons with different roles in life.	3rd	100%	Low	Medium
C. To analyze self-management constructs, the student will develop a program recommending changes in health habits and behaviors with a rating of at least 3.0 on a criteria checklist for judging program effectiveness.	2nd	100%	HIgh	High

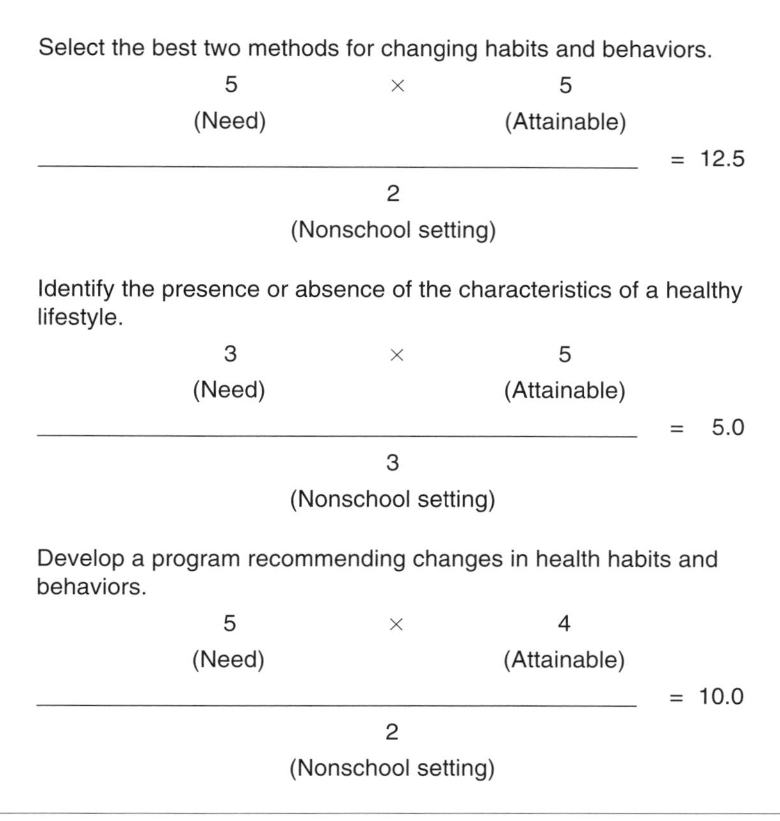
Select the best two methods for changing habits and behaviors.
5 × 5
(Need) (Attainable)
= 12.5
2
(Nonschool setting)
Identify the presence or absence of the characteristics of a healthy lifestyle.
3 × 5
(Need) (Attainable)
= 5.0
3
(Nonschool setting)
Develop a program recommending changes in health habits and behaviors.
5 × 4
(Need) (Attainable)
= 10.0
2
(Nonschool setting)

Figure 8.4 The cruciality formula is applied to the behavioral activity element of selected learning objectives.

The last tier of content goals and any level of prerequisites that supports one of these goals served as the foundation for Denise's *enabling* objectives. They reflected the knowledge, affective behaviors, and/or physical abilities that enable the student to accomplish a given terminal objective. Some of her enabling objectives were:

- To comprehend the dimensions of wellness, the student will match, with 70% accuracy, the physical, intellectual, social, emotional, and spiritual dimensions with characteristics describing the dimensions.
- To display favorable behavior tendencies toward physical activity, the student will exhibit approach versus avoidance behaviors at a ratio of 4 to 1 during participation in his or her preferred aerobic activity.
- To improve flexibility, the student will increase hip-joint flexibility by 20% and achieve satisfactory ratings on 5 of 6 full-body flexibility tasks, following a 4-week flexibility exercise program.

The entry-level status for flexibility was very low for one of her students (Dan). Therefore, the criterion standard was adjusted for the following objective: To improve flexibility, the student will increase hip-joint flexibility by 10% and achieve satisfactory ratings on 3 of 6 full-body flexibility tasks, following a 4-week flexibility exercise program.

Denise organized her objectives in the same way as she did her goals. The relationship between terminal and enabling objectives is shown in her learning hierarchy (partial) in Figure 8.5.

Now that her objectives had been finalized, Denise decided to deal with evaluation next even though it was suggested as the last step in the project directions. It made sense to her to do so because evaluation is linked so closely to the criterion standard of objectives.

Developing Evaluation Procedures

Since her objectives were stated in measurable terms, evaluation was delimited to the degree to which students achieved desired objectives. Validity would be enhanced if her evaluation instruments directly sampled the kind of behavior specified by her objectives. She was also aware that low-inference rather than high-inference techniques would increase objectivity.

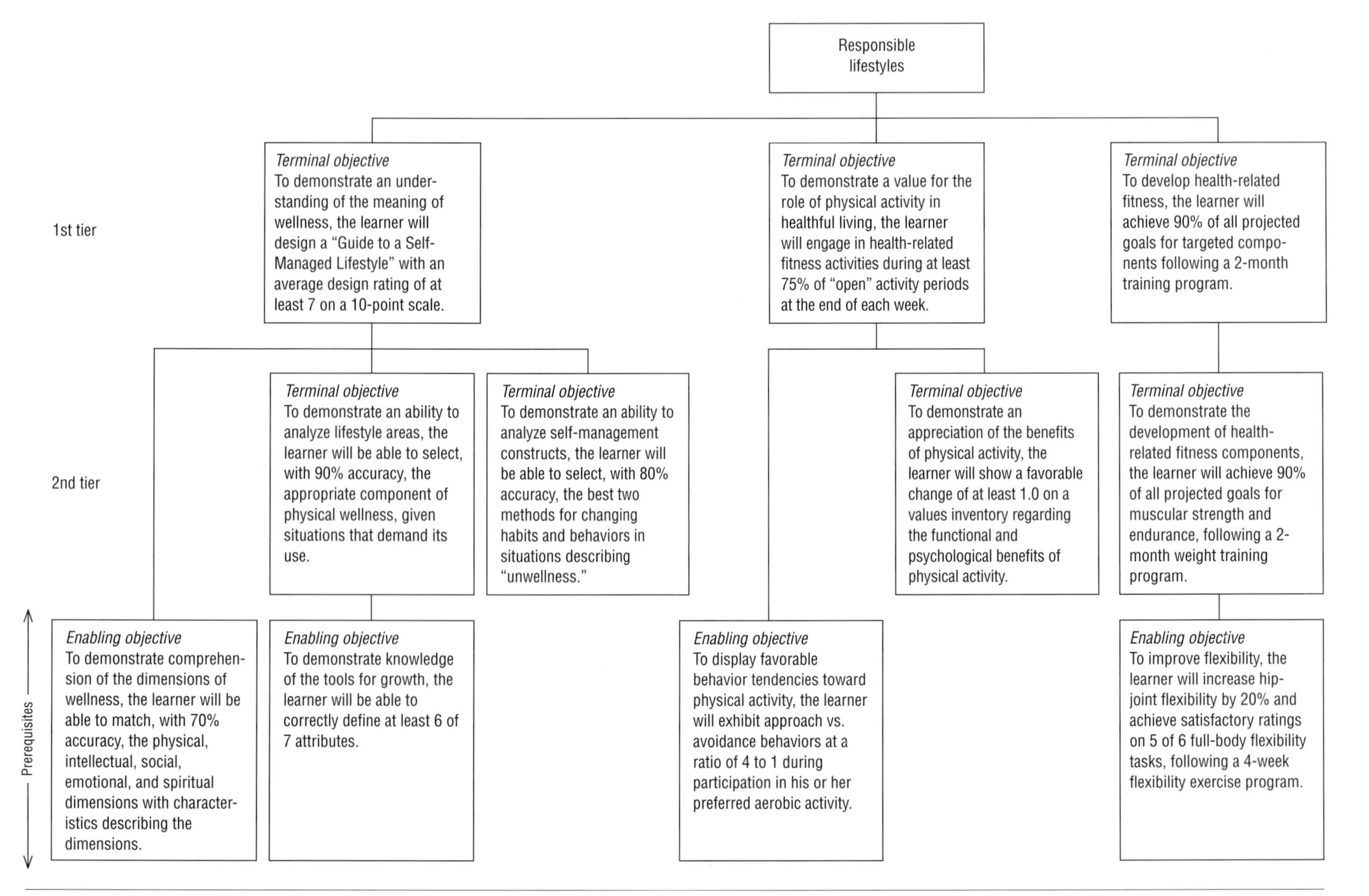

Figure 8.5 A learning hierarchy (partial) illustrates the relationships among terminal and enabling objectives based on the content goals from Figure 8.3.

Denise had already built in the "pre-post" evaluation design by having collected preassessment data. She was actually looking forward to developing the postassessment procedures because they would show changes in students that were attributed to her program. She also wanted to employ a criterion-referenced measurement approach because it would evaluate specific competencies and performance levels on an individual basis. Criterion standards were directly interpretable from her established learning objectives.

The total number of potential learning objectives for Denise's unit suggested a significant variety and quantity of evaluation instruments. She was determined to use a mixture of teacher-directed, peer-evaluation, and self-evaluation techniques. In addition to the instruments developed for entry appraisal, others were constructed. The three enabling objectives identified previously, one in each domain, were used for this purpose as shown in the Evaluation Instruments on pages 263 to 266.

Denise had an ulterior motive. Her middle school had begun a system of authentic assessment that included portfolios, and physical education was not part of the system. However, the information derived from Denise's evaluation procedures could be placed in a student's portfolio. More specifically, the items in the Evaluation Instruments for Cognitive Objective (page 263) and Psychomotor Objective (pages 265–266) represented testlike procedures while the item in the Evaluation Instrument for Affective Objective (page 264) represented an observation method in the form of a frequency index scale.

Denise finished her evaluation procedures a few days before the Thanksgiving break. She wanted to devote the upcoming off-days to the last component—learning experiences. She knew this would be a challenging task since they are the means for bringing about expected or desired behavioral changes in students.

Devising Learning Experiences

Given the way Denise had felt previously about the infinite number of potential objectives and evaluation procedures, it came as no surprise that the options for learning experiences also seemed unlimited to her. She decided to think first in terms of broad patterns, and then to think in terms of more specific approaches. Therefore, she made the distinction between the individualized and interactive patterns.

With both patterns, Denise tried to accommodate the cultural, racial, and economic diversity that described her students. During an in-service training day earlier in the year, she had learned that minority and at-risk students should be challenged to take learning risks and to pursue problem-solving tasks. It was also desirable to systematically vary learning experiences. In addition, it helped that alternative forms of assessment were planned under the evaluation component.

In terms of individualization, Denise's goal was to provide students with experiences suited to their unique characteristics. Such experiences could range from something as simple as having a student decide at which station to begin an obstacle course to something as complex as computer-assisted instruction. Examples of her individualized approaches for selected objectives are shown on pages 267 to 268. She also realized that the artifacts generated through the "Learning Activity Package" would be usable as a portfolio item.

In terms of interaction, Denise was determined to recognize *both* achievement and social growth, ranging from something as simple as recording performance results for a partner to something as complex as cooperative learning. Examples of her interactive approaches for selected objectives are shown on pages 269 to 270. In the cooperative learning approach, two learning objectives were facilitated, one representing the cognitive domain and one representing the affective domain. Denise also thought that the observational checklist under the reciprocal approach and the individual products resulting from the cooperative learning approach could be placed in students' portfolios.

After her curriculum unit was designed, Denise confided in Betsy that the project had been time-consuming and challenging. Although everything looked good on paper, she wouldn't feel fully satisfied until the curriculum was implemented. She was excited about the prospects for affecting these middle school students. In fact, Denise was actually looking forward to collecting evaluation information to help determine the effects of the new unit.

Making It Work

With this sample curriculum and the skills you've developed throughout the book, you should now be able to design your own physical education curriculum. Still, you may feel that some questions remain; perhaps you will find them answered in this section.

- **Why is so much detail needed to design a curriculum?**

  If you are starting from scratch, the detail may seem daunting. The *initial* design of a curriculum is likely to be challenging and time-consuming, even frustrating. Once a curriculum is established, however, refining it should be easier. Regardless of your experience in the designing process, you need to communicate what it is you're trying to accomplish, how you're going to do it, and how you will determine your success.

  The only true way of doing this is to write out your plan so that others (i.e., students, parents, other teachers, administrators, people in the community) can understand it. In an atmosphere where accountability is demanded, educational outcomes must be stated explicitly. For legal reasons as well it is wise to have a written curriculum that is developmentally appropriate and complete in all aspects. Curricular design and implementation by intuition is no longer acceptable. You should specify your plan of action (i.e., curriculum design) for a single lesson, series of lessons, or unit of instruction. You should be able to do this also, for example, for a semester, an academic year, an elementary school, or even a comprehensive K–12 design.

- **Do you need to follow such a linear, step-by-step approach to curricular design?**

  Not at all. Even though this system for designing implies a particular starting point and sequence, the process doesn't need to be mechanical or static. In fact, once you create organizing centers, the *initial* development of the other components may proceed in any order. Some teachers begin by outlining content or objectives, whereas others develop evaluation procedures first. Most curriculum designers take a dynamic approach, moving back and forth between components in a continuous process of refinement and adjustment. However, it is recommended that the *final* check of each component follow the sequence presented in the book to ensure that all components are "linked" properly.

- **Is it really necessary to develop so many curricular products, such as evaluation instruments (e.g., checklists, rating scales) and learning materials (e.g., criteria task sheets, learning packages)?**

  Your physical education curriculum should not be measured by the quantity of products: A high number of curricular artifacts does not guarantee a good design. From the standpoint of quality, however, a full range of evaluative instruments and learning materials is needed to implement a comprehensive design. These products can reflect most of the curricular components. For example, a reciprocal task card can show the organizing center, content goal, learning objective, and evaluation standard to which the task contributes. In this way you actually communicate the relationships among components. Here again, the most difficult step is creating the original products. No doubt, at first it hurts to think! With practice, experience, and the competencies you have developed, however, you shouldn't have many problems.

- **What are the rewards for designing such a comprehensive physical education curriculum?**

  Certainly you will feel personal satisfaction for being professionally responsible. The feedback from students, parents, and other educators should be highly favorable if your curriculum approximates the standards recommended here. You will develop a professional reputation for implementing programs of high quality, leading to peer recognition. You may receive teacher excellence awards and invitations to give presentations at professional meetings or to conduct in-service training. Over the long run, your career advancement may be enhanced because of the hard work and success in designing a curriculum. Finally, if educational expectations for the 21st century become reality, and it looks as if they will, physical educators will not get away with "throw-out-the-ball" programs. They will need to justify programs, as they can by being *curriculum designers*. You have earned that status now that you know how to be a curriculum designer. Good luck!

Evaluation Instrument for Cognitive Objective

Learning objective: To comprehend the dimensions of wellness, the student will match, with 70% accuracy, the physical, intellectual, social, emotional, and spiritual dimensions with characteristics describing the dimensions.

Evaluation instrument: The wellness lifestyle is an integrated living pattern involving five dimensions—physical, intellectual, social, emotional, and spiritual. While there is a strong interdependence among the dimensions, they function separately (Robbins, Powers, & Burgess, 1991). Characteristics of these dimensions are identified in the items that follow. Match these characteristics with the dimension using the following codes:

P = Physical
I = Intellectual
So = Social
E = Emotional
Sp = Spiritual

______ 1. Applying information
______ 2. Fairness toward others
______ 3. Ability to control or cope with personal feelings
______ 4. Components of physical fitness
______ 5. Ability to get along with others
______ 6. Acquisition of knowledge
______ 7. Development of inner self and beliefs
______ 8. Realistically assessing your own personal abilities and limitations
______ 9. Positive mental state
______ 10. Effects of dietary habits
______ 11. Curiosity
______ 12. Values clarification
______ 13. Trusting relationships
______ 14. Keeping abreast of current events
______ 15. Recognizing your own feelings
______ 16. Functional operations of the body
______ 17. Appreciating differences in people
______ 18. Ability to laugh, enjoy life, adjust to change, and manage stress
______ 19. Discovering personal meaning
______ 20. Thinking critically

Evaluation Instrument for Affective Objective

Learning objective: To display favorable behavior tendencies toward physical activity, the student will exhibit approach versus avoidance behaviors at a ratio of 4 to 1 during participation in his or her preferred aerobic activity.

Evaluation instrument: The student is observed during aerobic activities for 5-minute episodes over a 2-month training program. A record is made of the number of approach and avoidance behaviors exhibited for a series of observations.

Approach behaviors	Avoidance behaviors
_____ Shows involvement through facial expression	_____ Is expressionless during activity
_____ Carries out tasks to completion	_____ Quits on tasks that require persistence
_____ Responds willingly in group activities	_____ Needs prodding in group activities
_____ Completes tasks in proper sequence	_____ Completes tasks out of sequence
_____ Follows directions	_____ Ignores directions
_____ Remains on-task when distracted	_____ Is easily distracted from tasks
_____ Uses appropriate level of intensity	_____ Uses an intensity level below expected
_____ Others:	_____ Others:
_____ Total (A)	_____ Total (B)

Ratio (A/B) _____

Evaluation Instrument for Psychomotor Objective

Learning objective: To improve flexibility, the student will increase hip-joint flexibility by 20% and achieve satisfactory ratings on 5 of 6 full-body flexibility tasks, following a 4-week flexibility exercise program.

Evaluation instrument: A series of flexibility tasks is administered before and after the flexibility exercise program. Each task description includes the purpose, procedure, and scoring (Cooper & Fair, 1978; Melograno & Klinzing, 1992). Partners will check each other's performance according to the criteria stated.

Pre	Post	Flexibility task
______	______	**Hip-joint** Purpose: Measure flexibility of back and posterior leg muscles. Procedure: Measuring stick attached to sturdy bench is needed; remove shoes and place feet on either side of stick; keep knees locked throughout; bend forward at hips and reach slowly down over stick 3 times; on 4th time, reach fingertips as far as possible and hold position for 3 seconds; two trials are given; best score is recorded. Scoring: Score is distance reached to nearest half inch; distance short of toes is a negative (−); distance beyond toes is a positive (+).
______	______	**Gastrocnemius** Purpose: Measure flexibility of calf muscles on back of lower part of leg. Procedure: Sit with legs straight and heels against a wall; flex ankles as far as possible toward knees. Scoring: Record satisfactory (S) if a 20° angle or better is achieved between wall and plantar surface of foot.
______	______	**Low back** Purpose: Measure flexibility of low back region. Procedure: Sit on floor with knees slightly apart and bent; bend forward until shoulders touch knees; low back region should form a curved shape rather than a flat contour. Scoring: Record satisfactory (S) if shoulders touch knees and low back forms a smooth curve.
______	______	**Quadriceps** Purpose: Measure flexibility of muscles on front of thighs Procedure: Lie on floor face down with legs extended; flex right knee and bring heel as close to buttocks as possible; repeat with left leg. Scoring: Record satisfactory (S) if 130° angle or greater is formed between shin and floor with each leg.

_____ _____

Leg adductors

Purpose: Measure flexibility of muscles on inner side of thigh.

Procedure: Lie on left side with heels, buttocks, shoulder blades, and back of head against a wall; keep both knees straight; lift right leg as high as possible while keeping knee straight and heel against wall; repeat with left leg.

Scoring: Record satisfactory (S) if an angle of 45° is achieved with each leg.

_____ _____

Hamstrings

Purpose: Measure flexibility of muscle group on back of each thigh.

Procedure: Lie on back; keep feet pointing directly upward and both knees straight; lift right leg as high as possible and hold for 3 seconds without bending knee; repeat with left leg.

Scoring: Record satisfactory (S) if a vertical (90°) position or beyond is held with each leg.

_____ _____

Shoulder and shoulder girdle

Purpose: Measure flexibility of muscles of shoulder and shoulder girdle.

Procedure: Stand erect and attempt to clasp fingers of both hands with right arm behind head and left arm behind back; repeat with arm positions reversed.

Scoring: Record satisfactory (S) if fingers can be clasped in both positions.

Individualized Approaches

Approach	Learning objective
Self-directed tasks	To improve flexibility, the student will increase hip-joint flexibility by 20% and achieve satisfactory ratings on 5 of 6 full-body flexibility tasks, following a 4-week flexibility exercise program.

Learning experience

Model/Information communication: Teacher will (1) explain the benefits and phases of warm-up, (2) demonstrate a variety of warm-up exercises including stretching exercises, (3) present guidelines for cool-down, (4) explain the reasons for flexibility training and the benefits of maintaining flexibility, (5) review a handout that includes diagrams and descriptions of flexibility exercises for each area of the body, and (6) use a student to demonstrate the various flexibility exercises.

Content interaction: Student will complete the task card at one of the self-directed flexibility stations. An exemplary task card is:

Flexibility task card

Set 1	Set 2	
		Shoulder region
❑	❑	1. Arm circles: Slowly rotate arms in a large circle, stretching as far as possible; perform 10 repetitions forward and 10 backward.
❑	❑	2. Wing stretcher: With arms bent and elbows at shoulder level, slowly pull elbows back, stretching the chest muscles; hold for 5 seconds; perform 6 repetitions.
		Trunk
❑	❑	3. Hip circles: Stand with hands on hips with feet spread; slowly rotate trunk in a large circle; perform 10 repetitions clockwise and 10 counterclockwise.
❑	❑	4. Floor twist: Sit on floor with legs spread; twist far to the left; hold for 5 seconds; repeat to the right; perform 5 repetitions to each side.
		Hips
❑	❑	5. Sitting toe touch: Sit with legs straight and feet together; bend forward and reach maximally toward toes; hold for 5 seconds; perform 6 repetitions.
❑	❑	6. Rear leg raise: Standing erect, alternately lift each leg high to the rear; perform 10 repetitions with each leg.

Approach	Learning objective
Learning Activity Package (LAP)	To demonstrate that he or she values the role of physical activity in healthful living, the student will engage in health-related fitness activities during at least 75% of "open" activity periods at the end of each week.

Learning experience

Model/Information communication: Teacher will (1) outline the advantages and disadvantages of various uses of activity periods; (2) conduct an activities analysis showing the contributions of various activities to the components of health-related fitness; (3) explain the reasons for selecting cycling, swimming, weight training, rope jumping and/or circuit training as health-related activities; (4) present normative data showing the fitness status of youths; and (5) show a series of slides on how to use a Learning Activity Package (LAP) to develop a personalized fitness program.

Content interaction: Student will complete the following sequence: (1) Plot a personal health-related fitness profile based on entry appraisal data for aerobic endurance, body composition, flexibility, and muscular strength and endurance; (2) generate specific goals based on areas of concern, needed improvement, or maintenance; (3) select individualized programs, general exercise programs, and/or sports/leisure activities that he or she enjoys in terms of their contribution to his or her fitness goals; and (4) design a personal fitness program based on fitness goals, selection of programs/activities, and schedule of programs/activities. Once a personal fitness program is designed, students are asked to show how they would use their programs during "open" activity periods. The rest of the class determines whether or not the program makes maximum use of the time to move toward health-related fitness goals. Students maintain a log over several weeks and report their use of time to the entire class.

Interactive Approaches

Approach	Learning objective
Reciprocal learning	To demonstrate the development of health-related fitness components, the student will achieve 90% of all projected goals for muscular strength and endurance, following a 2-month weight training program.

Learning experience

Model/Information communication: Teacher will (1) explain the principles for weight training; (2) review the benefits, physiological changes, and training formats for muscular strength; (3) review the benefits, physiological changes, and training formats for muscular endurance; (4) highlight a handout that outlines a weight training program; (5) use a student to demonstrate the various exercises for each area of the body; (6) show a videotape that describes and demonstrates the use of circuit training; and (7) demonstrate the roles of partner and observer in carrying out the weight training program and how to use the criteria task sheet.

Content interaction: Partner/observer evaluates the student's performance at each of the weight training stations (curls/rowing, toe raises, flys/pullovers, weighted sit-ups, bench presses, squats/leg presses, pull-ups/bent arm). The following criteria are used:

Incorrect	Acceptable	Perfect	
			Cognitive/Psychomotor criteria
____	____	____	1. Selects proper weight for exercise
____	____	____	2. Breathes properly
____	____	____	3. Establishes and maintains correct foot and body position and alignment
____	____	____	4. Performs techniques of exercise
____	____	____	5. Follows all safety procedures
			Affective criteria
____	____	____	6. Demonstrates concentration while lifting
____	____	____	7. Performs at 90% or more of maximum work effort
____	____	____	8. Respects equipment used
____	____	____	9. Cooperates with others in group
____	____	____	10. Assists in setting up and putting away equipment

Approach	Learning objective
Cooperative learning	1. To analyze lifestyle areas, the student will select, with 90% accuracy, the appropriate component of physical wellness, given situations that demand its use. 2. To display favorable behavior tendencies toward physical activity, the student will exhibit approach versus avoidance behaviors at a ratio of 4 to 1 during participation in his or her preferred aerobic activity.

Learning experience

Model/Information communication: Teacher will (1) review the importance of cardiorespiratory endurance and a corresponding healthy heart as components of physical wellness, (2) orient student to the principles of cardiorespiratory conditioning, (3) explain the characteristics of an appropriate cardiorespiratory conditioning program, (4) group students randomly and heterogeneously into groups of four, and (5) facilitate the assignment of group roles (recorder, presenter, timer, and leader).

Content interaction: Individual student activities include (1) researching and reporting on the benefits of cardiorespiratory conditioning, (2) writing an individualized cardiorespiratory conditioning program, and (3) researching and reporting on exercise compliance factors. Group work activities include (1) completing worksheet with appropriate demographics including heart rate at rest and during early exercise; (2) running a specified course and monitoring heart rates of group members at rest, at 5 minutes, at 15 minutes, at 25 minutes, and at recovery; (3) plotting heart rates of each member on graph paper, discussing results and influences (e.g., weight, gender) on heart rate, and preparing report on group's graph; and (4) discussing commonalities and differences among graphs with entire class (Dunn & Wilson, 1991).

References

Albertson, L.M. (1974). Physical education or physical indoctrination? *The Physical Educator*, **31**, 90-92.

American Alliance for Health, Physical Education, Recreation and Dance. (1987). *Basic stuff: Series I and II.* Reston, VA: Author.

American Alliance for Health, Physical Education, Recreation and Dance. (1988). *Physical best: The American Alliance physical fitness education and assessment program.* Reston, VA: Author.

American Association for Health, Physical Education and Recreation. (1967). *AAHPER skills test manual for archery.* Washington, DC: Author.

American Association for Health, Physical Education and Recreation. (1969). *AAHPER skills test manual: Volleyball for boys and girls.* Washington, DC: Author.

Annarino, A.A. (1973). IIP. *Journal of Health, Physical Education and Recreation*, **44**(8), 20-23.

Annarino, A.A. (1978). Operational taxonomy for physical education objectives. *Journal of Physical Education and Recreation*, **49**(1), 54-55.

Annarino, A.A., Cowell, C.C., & Hazelton, H.W. (1980). *Curriculum theory and design in physical education* (2nd ed.). St. Louis: C.V. Mosby.

Arnheim, D.D., & Sinclair, W.A. (1979). *The clumsy child: A program of motor therapy*. St. Louis: C.V. Mosby.

Barrow, H.M., McGee, R., & Tritschler, K.A. (1989). *Practical measurement in physical education and sport*. Philadelphia: Lea & Febiger.

Batzle, J. (1992). *Portfolio assessment and evaluation: Developing and using portfolios in the classroom*. Cypress, CA: Creative Teaching Press.

Baumgartner, T.A., & Jackson, A.S. (1982). *Measurement for evaluation in physical education*. Dubuque, IA: Wm. C. Brown.

Bloom, B. (Ed.) (1956). *Taxonomy of educational objectives, handbook I: Cognitive domain*. New York: David McKay.

Bosco, J.S., & Gustafson, W.F. (1983). *Measurement and evaluation in physical education, fitness, and sports.* Englewood Cliffs, NJ: Prentice-Hall.

Bredekamp, S. (Ed.) (1987). *Developmentally appropriate practice in early childhood programs serving children from birth through age 8*. Washington, DC: National Association for the Education of Young Children.

Bruininks, R.H. (1978). *Bruininks-Oseretsky test of motor proficiency*. Circle Pines, MN: American Guidance Service.

Bucher, C.A. (1983). *Foundations of physical education & sport* (9th ed.). St. Louis: C.V. Mosby.

Burns, R., & Squires, D. (1987). *Curriculum organization in outcome-based education*. San Francisco: Far West Laboratory for Educational Research and Development. (ERIC Document Reproduction Service No. ED 294 313)

Cheffers, J., & Evaul, T. (1978). *Introduction to physical education: Concepts of human movement*. Englewood Cliffs, NJ: Prentice-Hall.

Chepyator-Thomson, J.R. (Ed.) (1994). Multicultural education: Culturally responsive teaching. *Journal of Physical Education, Recreation & Dance*, **65**(9), 31-36, 61-74.

Chittenden, E. (1991). Authentic assessment, evaluation, and documentation of student performance. In V. Perrone (Ed.), *Expanding student assessment* (pp. 22-31). Alexandria, VA: Association for Supervision and Curriculum Development.

Clarke, H.H., & Clarke, D. (1987). *Application of measurement to physical education*. Englewood Cliffs, NJ: Prentice-Hall.

Cooper, D.L., & Fair, L. (1978). Developing and testing flexibility. *Physician and Sportsmedicine*, **6**(10), 137-138.

Craft, D.H. (Ed.) (1994). Inclusion: Physical education for all. *Journal of Physical Education, Recreation & Dance*, **65**(1), 22-56.

Decker, J. (1990). Try a little cooperation! *Strategies*, **3**(5), 15-16.

DeFina, A.A. (1992). *Portfolio assessment: Getting started.* New York: Scholastic Professional Books.

Donnelly, J.E. (Ed.) (1987). *Using microcomputers in physical education and the sport sciences*. Champaign, IL: Human Kinetics.

Dunn, S.E., & Wilson, R. (1991). Cooperative learning in the physical education classroom. *Journal of Physical Education, Recreation & Dance*, **62**(6), 22-28.

Elliot, M.E. (1990). Concept learning in elementary physical education. *Strategies*, **3**(3), 8-10, 27.

Evaul, T. (1973). Where are you going? What are you going to do? In W. J. Penney (Ed.), *Proceedings of the Regional Conference on Curriculum Improvement in Secondary School Physical Education* (pp. 85-96). Washington, DC: American Association for Health, Physical Education and Recreation.

Evaul, T. (1980). Organizing centers for the 1980s. *Journal of Physical Education and Recreation*, **51**(7), 51-54.

Executive Summary: The National Education Goals Report. (1993). Washington, DC: U.S. Department of Education.

Fluegelman, A. (Ed.) (1976). *The new games book.* New York: Dolphin, Doubleday.

Fluegelman, A. (1981). *More new games.* New York: Dolphin, Doubleday.

Franck, M., Graham, G., Lawson, H., Loughrey, T., Ritson, R., Sanborn, M., & Seefeldt, V. (1992). *Outcomes of quality physical education programs.* Reston, VA: National Association for Sport and Physical Education.

Freeman, W.H. (1982). *Physical education and sport in a changing society* (2nd ed.). Minneapolis: Burgess.

Gagné, R.M., Briggs, L.J., & Wager, W.W. (1990). *Principles of instructional design* (3rd ed.). Fort Worth, TX: Holt, Rinehart and Winston.

Gardner, H. (1983). *Frames of mind: The theory of multiple intelligences.* New York: Basic Books.

Gilliom, B. (1970). *Basic movement education for children: Rationale and teaching units.* Reading, MA: Addison-Wesley.

Glatthorn, A.A. (1993). *Learning twice: An introduction to the methods of teaching.* New York: HarperCollins.

Graham, G. (1987). Motor skill acquisition: An essential goal of physical education programs. *Journal of Physical Education, Recreation & Dance,* **58**(7), 44-48.

Graham, G. (Ed.) (1992). Developmentally appropriate physical education for children. *Journal of Physical Education, Recreation & Dance,* **63**(6), 29-60.

Graham, G., Castenada, R., Hopple, C., Manross, M., & Sanders, S. (1992). *Developmentally appropriate physical education practices for children.* Reston, VA: National Association for Sport and Physical Education, Council on Physical Education for Children.

Greenberg, J.S. (1983). *Comprehensive stress management.* Dubuque, IA: Wm. C. Brown.

Hammersley, C.H. (1992). If we win, I win—Adventure education in physical education and recreation. *Journal of Physical Education, Recreation & Dance,* **63**(9), 63-67, 72.

Harrison, J.M., & Blakemore, C.L. (1992). *Instructional strategies for secondary school physical education* (3rd ed.). Dubuque, IA: Wm. C. Brown.

Harrow, A.J. (1972). *A taxonomy of the psychomotor domain.* New York: David McKay.

Hellison, D.R. (1985). *Goals and strategies for teaching physical education.* Champaign, IL: Human Kinetics.

Hellison, D.R., & Templin, T.J. (1991). *A reflective approach to teaching physical education.* Champaign, IL: Human Kinetics.

Hurwitz, R. (1985). A model for the structure of instructional strategies. *Journal of Teaching in Physical Education,* **4**(3), 190-201.

Hurwitz, R. (1992). PERK up your classes! *Future Focus,* **13**(3), 20-23.

Hurwitz, R. (1993a). *Cooperative learning sample units: Soccer.* Unpublished manuscript, Cleveland State University, HPERD Department.

Hurwitz, R. (1993b). *Guidelines for setting mastery criteria.* Unpublished manuscript, Cleveland State University, HPERD Department.

Hurwitz, R. (1993c). *The Hurwitz instructional strategy model (HISM).* Unpublished manuscript, Cleveland State University, HPERD Department.

Hurwitz, R. (1993d). *Learner analysis.* Unpublished manuscript, Cleveland State University, HPERD Department.

Hurwitz, R. (1993e). *Role playing instructional strategy.* Unpublished manuscript, Cleveland State University, HPERD Department.

Hurwitz, R. (1993f). *A suggested process for identifying prerequisites: Doing a task analysis.* Unpublished manuscript, Cleveland State University, HPERD Department.

Jewett, A.E., & Bain, L.L. (1985). *The curriculum process in physical education.* Dubuque, IA: Wm. C. Brown.

Jewett, A.E., & Mullan, M.R. (1977). *Curriculum design: Purposes and processes in physical education teaching-learning.* Washington, DC: American Alliance for Health, Physical Education, Recreation and Dance.

Johnson, B.L., & Nelson, J.K. (1986). *Practical measurement for evaluation in physical education* (4th ed.). Edina, MN: Burgess International.

Johnson, M.L. (1969). Construction of a sportsmanship attitude scale. *Research Quarterly,* **40**, 312-316.

Kirchner, G. (1992). *Physical education for elementary school children* (8th ed.). Dubuque, IA: Wm. C. Brown.

Kirkendall, E., Gruber, J., & Johnson, R. (1987). *Measurement and evaluation for physical education.* Champaign, IL: Human Kinetics.

Kohl, P.L. (1992). Sharing the power: Fact or fallacy? *Action in Teacher Education,* **14**(3), 29-36.

Krathwohl, D.R., Bloom, B.S., & Masia, B.B. (1964). *Taxonomy of educational objectives, handbook II: Affective domain.* New York: David McKay.

Lawson, H.A., & Placek, J.H. (1981). *Physical education in the secondary schools: Curricular alternatives.* Boston: Allyn and Bacon.

Lerner, J.W. (1993). *Learning disabilities: Theories, diagnosis, and teaching strategies* (6th ed.). Boston: Houghton Mifflin.

Levine, D.U., & Ornstein, A.C. (1993). School effectiveness and national reform. *Journal of Teacher Education,* **44**(5), 335-345.

Locke, L.F., & Lambdin, D. (1976). Teacher behavior. In American Alliance for Health, Physical Education and Recreation, *Personalized learning in physical education* (pp. 9-33). Reston, VA: AAHPER.

McNeil, J.D. (1976). *Designing curriculum: Self-instructional modules.* Boston: Little, Brown and Company.

Meisels, S.J. (1993). The work sampling system: An authentic performance assessment. *Principal,* **72**(5), 5-7.

Meisels, S.J., Dichtelmiller, M., Dorfman, A., Jablon, J.R., & Marsden, D.B. (1994). *An Overview* (3rd ed.). Ann Arbor, MI: Rebus Planning Associates.

Melograno, V. (1978). Status of curriculum practice—Are you a consumer or designer? *Journal of Physical Education and Recreation*, **49**(3), 27-28.

Melograno, V. (1981). Toward the design of affirmative curriculum. *Journal of Teaching in Physical Education*, Introductory Issue, 3-11.

Melograno, V. (1984). The balanced curriculum: Where is it? What is it? *Journal of Physical Education, Recreation & Dance*, **55**(6), 21-24, 52.

Melograno, V. (1994). Portfolio assessment: Documenting authentic student learning. *Journal of Physical Education, Recreation & Dance*, **65**(8), 50-55, 58-61.

Melograno, V., & Klinzing, J. (1992). *An orientation to total fitness* (5th ed.). Dubuque, IA: Kendall/Hunt.

Midgley, C., & Wood, S. (1993). Beyond site-based management: Empowering teachers to reform schools. *Phi Delta Kappan*, **75**(3), 245-252.

Miller, D.A. (1988). *Measurement by the physical educator*. Indianapolis, IN: Benchmark Press.

Mosston, M., & Ashworth, S. (1986). *Teaching physical education* (3rd ed.). New York: Macmillan.

Mosston, M., & Mueller, R. (1974). Mission, omission and submission in physical education. In G.H. McGlynn (Ed.), *Issues in physical education and sports* (pp. 97-106). Palo Alto, CA: National Press Books.

Murphy, C. (Ed.) (1984). *Outcome-based instructional systems: Primer and practice*. San Francisco: Far West Laboratory for Educational Research and Development. (ERIC Document Reproduction Service No. ED 249 265)

Murphy, S., & Smith, M. (1992). *Writing portfolios: A bridge from teaching to assessment*. Markham, ON: Pippin Publishing.

National Commission on Excellence in Education. (1983). *A nation at risk: The imperative for educational reform*. Washington, DC: GPO.

Orlick, T. (1978). *The cooperative sports and games book*. New York: Pantheon.

Orlick, T. (1982). *The second cooperative sports and games book*. New York: Pantheon.

Pasch, M., Sparks-Langer, G., Gardner, T.G., Starko, A.J., & Moody, C.D. (1991). *Teaching as decision making*. White Plains, NY: Longman.

Perrone, V. (Ed.) (1991). *Expanding student assessment*. Alexandria, VA: Association for Supervision and Curriculum Development.

Robbins, G., Powers, D., & Burgess, S. (1991). *A wellness way of life*. Dubuque, IA: Wm. C. Brown.

Rohnke, K. (1977). *Cowstails & cobras*. Hamilton, NY: Adventure Press.

Rohnke, K. (1989). *Cowstails and cobras II*. Dubuque, IA: Kendall/Hunt.

Ross, J.G., & Pate, R.R. (1987). A summary of findings. *Journal of Physical Education, Recreation & Dance*, **58**(9), 51-56.

Safrit, M.J. (1990). *Introduction to measurement in physical education and exercise science*. St. Louis: Times Mirror/Mosby.

Sanborn, M.A., & Hartman, B.G. (1983). *Issues in physical education* (3rd ed.). Philadelphia: Lea & Febiger.

Siedentop, D. (1991). *Developing teaching skills in physical education*. Mountain View, CA: Mayfield.

Siedentop, D. (1994a). *Introduction to physical education, fitness, and sport* (2nd ed.). Mountain View, CA: Mayfield.

Siedentop, D. (1994b). *Sport education*. Champaign, IL: Human Kinetics.

Siedentop, D., Mand, C., & Taggart, A. (1986). *Physical education: Teaching and curriculum strategies for grades 5-12*. Mountain View, CA: Mayfield.

Slavin, R.E. (1990). *Cooperative learning: Theory, research and practice*. Englewood Cliffs, NJ: Prentice-Hall.

Slavin, R.E., & Madden, N.A. (1989). What works for students at risk: A research synthesis. *Educational Leadership*, **46**(5), 4-13.

Sparks, W.G. (1993). Promoting self-responsibility and decision making with at-risk students. *Journal of Physical Education, Recreation & Dance*, **64**(2), 74-78.

Sterne, M.L. (1990). Cooperative learning. *Strategies*, **3**(5), 15-16.

Strand, B.N., & Wilson, R. (1993). *Assessing sport skills*. Champaign, IL: Human Kinetics.

Tyler, R.W. (1970). *Basic principles of curriculum and instruction*. Chicago: University of Chicago Press.

U.S. Department of Education. (1991). *America 2000: An education strategy*. Washington, DC: Author.

Vickers, J.N. (1990). *Instructional design for teaching physical activities: A knowledge structures approach*. Champaign, IL: Human Kinetics.

Viechnicki, K.J., Barbour, N., Shaklee, B., Rohrer, J., & Ambrose, R. (1993). The impact of portfolio assessment on teacher classroom activities. *Journal of Teacher Education*, **44**(5), 371-377.

Villa, R., & Thousand, J. (1990). Administrative supports to promote inclusive schooling. In W. Stainback & S. Stainback (Eds.), *Support networks for inclusive schooling: Integrated interdependent education* (pp. 201-218). Baltimore: Paul H. Brookes.

Villegas, A.M. (1991). *Culturally responsive pedagogy for the 1990s and beyond* (Trends and Issues Paper No. 6). Washington, DC: ERIC Clearinghouse on Teacher Education.

Will, M. (1986). Educating children with learning problems: A shared responsibility. *Exceptional Children*, **52**, 411-416.

Zessoules, R., & Gardner, H. (1991). Authentic assessment: Beyond the buzzword and into the classroom. In V. Perrone (Ed.), *Expanding student assessment* (pp. 47-71). Alexandria, VA: Association for Supervision and Curriculum Development.

Index

Related books from Human Kinetics

Christine J. Hopple, MS

1995 • Spiral • 232 pp • Item BHOP0712
ISBN 0-87322-712-3 • $28.00 ($38.95 Canadian)

"Bridges the gap between NASPE's outcomes and the real world. I have never seen such a comprehensive book directed toward physical education, outcomes-based education, or assessment."
Larry Satchwell
Elementary Physical Education Specialist
Shiloh Elementary School, GA

This is the first book to provide elementary physical education specialists and district supervisors with practical guidelines for the planning, instruction, and assessment of an outcomes-related curriculum. But this book does much more than present cutting-edge information on curriculum planning and new methods of assessment; it also helps educators put this information into practice in the gym and the classroom.

A REFLECTIVE APPROACH TO TEACHING PHYSICAL EDUCATION
Donald R. Hellison
Thomas J. Templin

Donald R. Hellison, PhD, and Thomas J. Templin, PhD

1991 • Cloth • 208 pp • Item BHEL0311
ISBN 0-87322-311-X • $30.00 ($41.95 Canadian)

"One of the most concise and practical books I have read concerning the reality of teaching physical education. Theory transforms so smoothly that a teacher could use this book as a handbook or guide to teaching physical education."
Illinois Journal for HPERD

This book helps undergraduate students develop a more self-aware teaching approach based on their own values and style. It encourages reflection—a way of thinking that can clarify values, create a personal teaching experience, and encourage a satisfying learning environment. By having future teachers answer the questions "What's worth doing?" and "Is what I'm doing working?," the book helps them plan a curriculum and deal with everyday concerns.

To place an order: U.S. customers call TOLL-FREE 1-800-747-4457; customers outside of U.S. use the appropriate telephone number/address shown in the front of this book.

Prices subject to change.

Human Kinetics
The Information Leader in Physical Activity

2335